European Community Trade Mark

European Community Trade Mark

Commentary to the European Community Regulations

Coordinator

Mario Franzosi

Authors

M.A. Baz
F. Calvetti
A. Ebert-Weidenfeller
M. Edenborough
A. de Elzaburu
J. Feldges
M. Franzosi
I. Frost
Ch. Gielen
H. Goddar
W.A. Hoyng
M.J.M. van Kaam
G.F. Kunze
F. López de Rego
W. von Meibom
T. Mollet-Viéville
C. Morcom QC
F. Rödiger
S. Sandri
V. Scordamaglia
R.M. Winkler

KLUWER LAW INTERNATIONAL
THE HAGUE / LONDON / BOSTON

A C.I.P. Cataloque record for this book is available from the Library of Congress

ISBN 90-411-0453-4

Published by Kluwer Law International,
P.O. Box 85889, 2508 CN The Hague, The Netherlands.

Sold and distributed in the U.S.A. and Canada
by Kluwer Law International,
675 Massachusetts Avenue, Cambridge, MA 02139, U.S.A.

In all other countries, sold and distributed
by Kluwer Law International,
P.O. Box 85889, 2508 CN The Hague, The Netherlands.

Printed on acid-free paper

Printed in the Netherlands

Table of Contents

Comments:

Preface

The Council of the European Union constantly tends towards the creation of legal conditions to enable undertakings to adapt their activities to the scale of the Community, whether in manufacturing and distributing goods or in providing services.

For this purpose, after having issued the First Council Directive 89/104/EEC of 21 December 1988 to approximate the laws of the Member States relating to trade marks, a Regulation has been adopted which contains common rules (hereinafter Community Trade Mark Regulation).

On the basis of this Regulation, European and non European undertakings can, by means of one procedural system, obtain Community Trade Marks to which uniform protection is given and which produce their effects throughout the entire area of the Community.

The registration system instituted by the Community Trade Mark Regulation was put into operation on 1 April 1996 and at a distance of one year there are about 40.000 applications for Community Trade Marks, where 57% are from the European Union countries and 42% from countries not member of the EU of all over the world. This huge figure reflects the importance of the Regulation not only in Europe but also in the whole world.

This book explains and analyses the features and effects of the Regulation.

The format is similar to that adopted for the Commentary to Directive and Regulation Proposals on Design Protection by the same editor (Franzosi et al., European Design Protection, Kluwer 1996).

The issues concerning the new discipline introduced by the Council Regulation are examined by jurists who are both professionally and accademically active in the field.

Unlike the book on European Design Protection, which gives an Article by Article analysis of the Proposals, this commentary is carried out by subject (it was felt that an Article by Article analysis could be repetitive).

The first part contains the basic texts:

the First Council Directive 89/104/EEC of 21 December 1988 to approximate the laws of the Member States relating to trade marks;

the Council Regulation 40/94 of 20 December 1993 on the Community Trade Mark;

the Commission Regulation 2868/95 of 13 December 1995 implementing the Council Regulation on the Community trade mark;

the Commission Regulation 2869/95 of 13 December 1995 on the fees payable to the Office for Harmonization in the Internal Market (Trade Marks and Design);

the Commission Regulation 216/96 of 5 February 1996 laying down the rules of procedure of the Boards of Appeal of the Office for Harmonization in the Internal Market (Trade Marks and Designs);

the Statements for entry in the minutes of the Council meeting at which the Regulation was adopted;

the Proposal for a Council Decision approving the accession of the European Community to the Protocol Relating to the Madrid Agreement Concerning the International Registration of Marks, adopted at Madrid on 27 June 1989; and

the Proposal for a Council Regulation modifying the Council Regulation (EC) N 40/94 of 20 December 1993 on the Community trade mark to give effect to the accession of the European Community to the Protocol Relating to the Madrid Agreement Concerning the International Registration of Marks, adopted at Madrid on 27 June 1989.

All these texts have been reproduced in their official English version.

The second part consists of commentaries written by:

- Matthieu van Kaam, head of Trade Marks Department, Philips International BV, Eindhoven;
- Thierry Mollet-Viéville, attorney-at-law in Paris with Duclos, Thorne, Mollet-Viéville et Associés;
- Christopher Q.C. Morcom and M. Edenborough, barristers in London;
- Wolfgang von Meibom and Felix Rödiger, attorneys-at-law with Wessing Berenberg-Gossler Zimmermann Lange, Düsseldorf;
- Heinz Goddar and Andreas Ebert-Weidenfeller, attorneys-at-law with Boehmert & Boehmert, Bremen (Mr. H. Goddar is visiting Professor, Universities of Washington and Bremen);
- Rolf M. Winkler, attorney-at-law with Haver & Mailänder, Stuttgard;
- Dr. Gerard F. Kunze, Of Counsel, Walder Wyss & Partners in Zürich, and adjunct Professor, Franklin Pierce Law Center, Concord N.H. and John Marshall Law School Chicago;
- Willem A. Hoyng, attorney-at-law with De Brauw Blakstone Westbroek, Eindhoven, the Netherlands, and Professor of Industrial Property at the University of Brabant;
- Fernando López de Rego, Head of the Legal Affairs and Litigation Service of the OHIM;
- Mario Franzosi, attorney-at-law with Franzosi Dal Negro & Associati, Milan – Rome – Washington and Professor of Industrial Property in Italy and European Patent Law, University of Washington;

- Joachim Feldges, attorney-at-law with Pünder Volhard Weber & Axster, Münich, and Ina Frost;
- Charles Gielen PhD, attorney-at-law with Nauta Dutilh, Amsterdam and Professor of Intellectual Property, University of Groningen;
- Alberto de Elzaburu and Miguel A. Baz, attorneys-at-law with Elzaburu firm, Madrid;
- Vincenzo Scordamaglia, Hon. Director-General of the Council of the European Union, Consultant with the EU Commission and Visiting Professor of Intellectual Property at the Universities of Grenoble and Alicante;
- Stefano Sandri, attorney-at-law with Simmons & Simmons, Rome and Milan, visiting Professor of Intellectual Property at Alicante;
- Frederick Calvetti, attorney-at-law in Washington, Professor at the George Washington University.

General contributions have been made, assistance and co-ordination provided by Marie-Hélène Polo, Yee Mun Loh and Jimena López-Menchero, at Franzosi Dal Negro & Associati firm.

The work is not written in a uniform style due to the many contributors, the style of which has intentionally been left unchanged in order not to forgo the individual characteristics of each author's section.

First Council Directive

of 21 December 1988
to approximate the laws of the Member States relating to trade marks
(89/104/EEC)

THE COUNCIL OF THE EUROPEAN COMMUNITIES

Having regard to the Treaty establishing the European Economic Community, and in particular Article 100a thereof,

Having regard to the proposal from the Commission,[1]

In co-operation with the European Parliament,[2]

Having regard to the opinion of the Economic and Social Committee,[3]

Whereas the trade mark laws at present applicable in the Member States contain disparities which may impede the free movement of goods and freedom to provide services and may distort competition within the common market; whereas it is therefore necessary, in view of the establishment and functioning of the internal market, to approximate the laws of Member States;

Whereas it is important not to disregard the solutions and advantages which the Community trade mark system may afford to undertakings wishing to acquire trade marks;

Whereas it does not appear to be necessary at present to undertake full scale approximation of the trade mark laws of the Member States and it will be sufficient if approximation is limited to those national provisions of law which most directly affect the functioning of the internal market;

Whereas the Directive does not deprive the Member States of the right to continue to protect trade marks acquired through use but takes them into account only in regard to the relationship between them and trade marks acquired by registration;

Whereas Member States also remain free to fix the provisions of procedure concerning the registration, the revocation and the invalidity of trade marks acquired by registration; whereas they can, for example, determine the form of

[1] OJ No. C 351, 31.12.1980, p. 1 and OJ No. C 351, 31.12.1985, p. 4.
[2] OJ No. C 307, 14.11.1983, p. 66 and OJ No. C 309, 5.12.1988.
[3] OJ No. C 310, 30.11.1981, p. 22.

trade mark registration and invalidity procedures, decide whether earlier rights should be invoked either in the registration procedure or in the invalidity procedure or in both and, if they allow earlier rights to be invoked in the registration procedure, have an opposition procedure or an ex officio examination procedure or both; whereas Member States remain free to determine the effects of revocation or invalidity of trade marks;

Whereas this Directive does not exclude the application to trade marks of provisions of law of the Member States other than trade mark law, such as the provisions relating to unfair competition, civil liability or consumer protection;

Whereas attainment of the objectives at which this approximation of laws is aiming requires that the conditions for obtaining and continuing to hold a registered trade mark are, in general, identical in all Member States; whereas, to this end, it is necessary to list examples of signs which may constitute a trade mark, provided that such signs are capable of distinguishing the goods or services of one undertaking from those of other undertakings; whereas the grounds for refusal or invalidity concerning the trade mark itself, for example, the absence of any distinctive character, or concerning conflicts between the trade mark and earlier rights, are to be listed in an exhaustive manner, even if some of these grounds are listed as an option for the Member States which will therefore be able to maintain or introduce those grounds in their legislation; whereas Member States will be able to maintain or introduce into their legislation grounds of refusal or invalidity linked to conditions for obtaining and continuing to hold a trade mark for which there is no provision of approximation, concerning, for example, the eligibility for the grant of a trade mark the renewal of the trade mark or rules on fees, or related to the non-compliance with procedural rules;

Whereas in order to reduce the total number of trade marks registered and protected in the Community and, consequently, the number of conflicts which arise between them, it is essential to require that registered trade marks must actually be used or, if not used, be subject to revocation; whereas it is necessary to provide that a trade mark cannot be invalidated on the basis of the existence of a non-used earlier trade mark, while the Member States remain free to apply the same principle in respect of the registration of a trade mark or to provide that a trade mark may not be successfully invoked in infringement proceedings if it is established as a result of a plea that the trade mark could be revoked; whereas in all these cases it is up to the Member States to establish the applicable rules of procedure;

Whereas it is fundamental, in order to facilitate the free circulation of goods and services, to ensure that henceforth registered trade marks enjoy the same protection under the legal systems of all the Member States; whereas this should however not prevent the Member States from granting at their option extensive protection to those trade marks which have a reputation;

Whereas the protection afforded by the registered trade mark, the function of which is in particular to guarantee the trade mark as an indication of origin, is absolute in the case of identity between the mark and the sign and goods or services; whereas the protection applies also in case of similarity between the mark and the sign and the goods or services; whereas it is indispensable to give an interpretation of the concept of similarity in relation to the likelihood of confusion; whereas the likelihood of confusion, the appreciation of which depends on numerous elements and, in particular, on the recognition of the trade mark on the market, of the association which can be made with the used or registered sign, of the degree of similarity between the trade mark and the sign and between the goods or services identified, constitutes the specific condition for such protection; whereas the ways in which likelihood of confusion may be established, and in particular the onus of proof, are a matter for national procedural rules which are not prejudiced by the Directive;

Whereas it is important, for reasons of legal certainty and without inequitably prejudicing the interests of a proprietor of an earlier trade mark, to provide that the latter may no longer request a declaration of invalidity nor may he oppose the use of a trade mark subsequent to his own of which he has knowingly tolerated the use for a substantial length of time, unless the application for the subsequent trade mark was made in bad faith;

Whereas all Member States of the Community are bound by the Paris Convention for the Protection of Industrial Property; whereas it is necessary that the provisions of this Directive are entirely consistent with those of the Paris Convention; whereas the obligations of the Member States resulting from this Convention are not affected by this Directive; whereas, where appropriate, the second subparagraph of Article 234 of the Treaty is applicable,

HAS ADOPTED THIS DIRECTIVE:

Article 1
Scope
This Directive shall apply to every trade mark in respect of goods or services which is the subject of registration or of an application in a Member State for registration as an individual trade mark, a collective mark or a guarantee or certification mark, or which is the subject of a registration or an application for registration in the Benelux Trade Mark Office or of an international registration having effect in a Member State.

Article 2
Signs of which a trade mark may consist
A trade mark may consist of any sign capable of being represented graphically, particularly words, including personal names, designs, letters, numerals, the shape of goods or of their packaging, provided that such signs are capable of distinguishing the goods or services of one undertaking from those of other undertakings.

Article 3

Grounds for refusal or invalidity

1. The following shall not be registered or if registered shall be liable to be declared invalid:

(a) signs which cannot constitute a trade mark;

(b) trade marks which are devoid of any distinctive character;

(c) trade marks which consist exclusively of signs or indications which may serve, in trade, to designate the kind, quality, quantity, intended purpose, value, geographical origin, or the time of production of the goods or of rendering of the service, or other characteristics of the goods or service;

(d) trade marks which consist exclusively of signs or indications which have become customary in the current language or in the bona fide and established practices of the trade;

(e) signs which consist exclusively of:

- the shape which results from the nature of the goods themselves, or
- other shape of goods which is necessary to obtain a technical result, or
- the shape which gives substantial value to the goods;

(f) trade marks which are contrary to public policy or to accepted principles of morality;

(g) trade marks which are of such a nature as to deceive the public, for instance as to the nature, quality or geographical origin of the goods or service;

(h) trade marks which have not been authorized by the competent authorities and are to be refused or invalidated pursuant to Article 6 *ter* of the Paris Convention for the Protection of Industrial Property, hereinafter referred to as the "Paris Convention".

2. Any Member State may provide that a trade mark shall not be registered or, if registered, shall be liable to be declared invalid where and to the extent that:

(a) the use of that trade mark may be prohibited pursuant to provisions of law other than trade mark law of the Member State concerned or of the Community;

(b) the trade mark covers a sign of high symbolic value, in particular a religious symbol;

(c) the trade mark includes badges, emblems and escutcheons other than those covered by Article 6 *ter* of the Paris Convention and which are of public interest, unless the consent of the appropriate authorities to its registration has been given in conformity with the legislation of the Member State;

(d) the application for registration of the trade mark was made in bad faith by the applicant.

3. A trade mark shall not be refused registration or be declared invalid in accordance with paragraph 1 (b), (c) or (d) if, before the date of application for registration and following the use which has been made of it, it has acquired a distinctive character. Any Member State may in addition provide that this provision

shall also apply where the distinctive character was acquired after the date of application for registration or after the date of registration.

4. Any Member State may provide that, by derogation from the preceding paragraphs, the grounds of refusal of registration or invalidity in force in that State prior to the date on which the provisions necessary to comply with this Directive enter into force, shall apply to trade marks for which application has been made prior to that date.

Article 4

Further grounds for refusal or invalidity concerning conflicts with earlier rights

1. A trade mark shall not be registered or, if registered, shall be liable to be declared invalid:

(a) if it is identical with an earlier trade mark, and the goods or services for which the trade mark is applied for or is registered are identical with the goods or services for which the earlier trade mark is protected;

(b) if because of its identity with, or similarity to, the earlier trade mark and the identity or similarity of the goods or services covered by the trade marks, there exists a likelihood of confusion on the part of the public which includes the likelihood of association with the earlier trade mark.

2. "Earlier trade marks" within the meaning of paragraph 1 means:

(a) trade marks of the following kinds with a date of application for registration which is earlier than the date of application for registration of the trade mark, taking. account, where appropriate, of the priorities claimed in respect of those trade marks:

(i) Community trade marks;

(ii) trade marks registered in the Member State or, in the case of Belgium, Luxembourg or the Netherlands, at the Benelux Trade Mark Office;

(iii) trade marks registered under international arrangements which have effect in the Member State;

(b) Community trade marks which validly claim seniority, in accordance with the Regulation on the Community trade mark, from a trade mark referred to in (a) (ii) and (iii), even when the latter trade mark has been surrendered or allowed to lapse;

(c) applications for the trade marks referred to in (a) and (b), subject to their registration;

(d) trade marks which, on the date of application for registration of the trade mark, or, where appropriate, of the priority claimed in respect of the application for registration of the trade mark, are well known in a Member State, in the sense in which the words "well known" are used in Article 6 *bis* of the Paris Convention.

3. A trade mark shall furthermore not be registered or, if registered, shall be liable to be declared invalid if it is identical with, or similar to, an earlier Community trade mark within the meaning of paragraph 2 and is to be, or has been, registered for goods or services which are not similar to those for which the earlier Community trade mark is registered, where the earlier Community trade mark has a reputation in the Community and where the use of the later trade mark without due cause would take unfair advantage of, or be detrimental to, the distinctive character or the repute of the earlier Community trade mark.

4. Any Member State may furthermore provide that a trade mark shall not be registered or, if registered, shall be liable to be declared invalid where, and to the extent that:

(a) the trade mark is identical with, or similar to, an earlier national trade mark within the meaning of paragraph 2 and is to be, or has been registered for goods or services which are not similar to those for which the earlier trade mark is registered, where the earlier trade mark has a reputation in the Member State concerned and where the use of the later trade mark without due cause would take unfair advantage of, or be detrimental to, the distinctive character or the repute of the earlier trade mark;

(b) rights to a non-registered trade mark or to another sign used in the course of trade were acquired prior to the date of application for registration of the subsequent trade mark, or the date of the priority claimed for the application for registration of the subsequent trade mark and that non registered trade mark or other sign confers on its proprietor the right to prohibit the use of a subsequent trade mark;

(c) the use of the trade mark may be prohibited by virtue of an earlier right other than the rights referred to in paragraphs 2 and 4 (b) and in particular:
(i) a right to a name;
(ii) a right of personal portrayal;
(iii) a copyright;
(iv) an industrial property right;

(d) the trade mark is identical with, or similar to, an earlier collective trade mark conferring a right which expired within a period of a maximum of three years preceding application;

(e) the trade mark is identical with, or similar to, an earlier guarantee or certification mark conferring a right which expired within a period preceding application the length of which is fixed by the Member State;

(f) the trade mark is identical with, or-similar to, an earlier trade mark which was registered for identical or similar goods or services and conferred on them a right which has expired for failure to renew within a period of a maximum of two years preceding application, unless the proprietor of the earlier trade mark gave his agreement for the registration of the later mark or did not use his trade mark;

(g) the trade mark is liable to be confused with a mark which was in use abroad on the filing date of the application and which is still in use there, provided that at the date of the application the applicant was acting in bad faith.

5. The Member States may permit that in appropriate circumstances registration need not be refused or the trade mark need not be declared invalid where the proprietor of the earlier trade mark or other earlier right consents to the registration of the later trade mark.

6. Any Member State may provide that, by derogation from paragraphs 1 to 5, the grounds for refusal of registration or invalidity in force in that State prior to the date on which the provisions necessary to comply with this Directive enter into force, shall apply to trade marks for which application has been made prior to that date.

Article 5

Rights conferred by a trade mark

1. The registered trade mark shall confer on the proprietor exclusive rights therein. The proprietor shall be entitled to prevent all third parties not having his consent from using in the course of trade:

(a) any sign which is identical with the trade mark in relation to goods or services which are identical with those for which the trade mark is registered;

(b) any sign where, because of its identity with, or similarity to, the trade mark and the identity or similarity of the goods or services covered by the trade mark and the sign, there exists a likelihood of confusion on the part of the public, which includes the likelihood of association between the sign and the trade mark.

2. Any Member State may also provide that the proprietor shall be entitled to prevent all third parties not having his consent from using in the course of trade any sign which is identical with, or similar to, the trade mark in relation to goods or services which are not similar to those for which the trade mark is registered, where the latter has a reputation in the Member State and where use of that sign without due cause takes unfair advantage of, or is detrimental to, the distinctive character or the repute of the trade mark.

3. The following, *inter alia*, may be prohibited under paragraphs 1 and 2:

(a) affixing the sign to the goods or to the packaging thereof;

(b) offering the goods, or putting them on the market or stocking them for these purposes under that sign, or offering or supplying services there under;

(c) importing or exporting the goods under the sign;

(d) using the sign on business papers and in advertising.

4. Where, under the law of the Member State, the use of a sign under the conditions referred to in 1 (b) or 2 could not be prohibited before the date on which the provisions necessary to comply with this Directive entered into force in the

Member State concerned, the rights conferred by the trade mark may not be relied on to prevent the continued use of the sign.

5. Paragraphs 1 to 4 shall not affect provisions in any Member States relating to the protection against the use of a sign other than for the purposes of distinguishing goods or services, where use of that sign without due cause takes unfair advantage of, or is detrimental to, the distinctive character or the repute of the trade mark.

Article 6
Limitation of the effects of a trade mark
The trade mark shall not entitle the proprietor to prohibit: a third party from using, in the course of trade,

(a) his own name or address;

(b) indications concerning the kind, quality, quantity, intended purpose, value, geographical origin, the time of production of goods or of rendering of the service, or other characteristics of goods or services;

(c) the trade mark where it is necessary to indicate the intended purpose of a product or service, in particular as accessories or spare parts;

provided he uses them in accordance with honest practices in industrial or commercial matters.

2. The trade mark shall not entitle the proprietor to prohibit a third party from using, in the course of trade, an earlier right which only applies in a particular locality if that right is recognized by the laws of the Member State in question and within the limits of the territory in which it is recognized.

Article 7
Exhaustion of the rights conferred by a trade mark
1. The trade mark shall not entitle the proprietor to prohibit its use in relation to goods which have been put on the market in the Community under that trade mark by the proprietor or with his consent.

2. Paragraph 1 shall not apply where there exist legitimate reasons for the proprietor to oppose further commercialization of the goods, especially where the condition of the goods is changed or impaired after they have been put on the market.

Article 8
Licensing
1. A trade mark may be licensed for some or all of the goods or services for which it is registered and for the whole or part of the Member State concerned. A license may be exclusive or non-exclusive.

2. The proprietor of a trade mark may invoke the rights conferred by that trade mark against a licensee who contravenes any provision in his licensing contract with regard to its duration, the form covered by the registration in which the trade mark may be used, the scope of the goods or services for which the licence is granted, the territory in which the trade mark may be affixed, or the quality of the goods manufactured or of the services provided by the licensee.

Article 9
Limitation in consequence of acquiescence
Where, in a Member State, the proprietor of an earlier trade mark as referred to in Article 4 (2) has acquiesced, for a period of five successive years, in the use of a later trade mark registered in that Member State while being aware of such use, he shall no longer be entitled on the basis of the earlier trade mark either to apply for a declaration that the later trade mark is invalid or to oppose the use of the later trade mark in respect of the goods or services for which the later trade mark has been used, unless registration of the later trade mark was applied for in bad faith.

2. Any Member State may provide that paragraph 1 shall apply *mutatis mutandis* to the proprietor of an earlier trade mark referred to in Article 4 (4)(a) or an other earlier right referred to in Article 4 (4) (b) or (c).

3. In the cases referred to in paragraphs 1 and 2, the proprietor of a later registered trade mark shall not be entitled to oppose the use of the earlier right, even though that right may no longer be invoked against the later trade mark.

Article 10
Use of trade marks
1. If, within a period of five years following the date of the completion of the registration procedure, the proprietor has not put the trade mark to genuine use in the Member State in connection with the goods or services in respect of which it is registered, or if such use has been suspended during an uninterrupted period of five years, the trade mark shall be subject to the sanctions provided for in this Directive, unless there are proper reasons for non-use.

2. The following shall also constitute use within the meaning of paragraph 1:
(a) use of the trade mark in a form differing in elements which do not alter the distinctive character of the mark in the form in which is was registered;
(b) affixing of the trade mark to goods or to the packaging thereof in the Member State concerned solely for export purposes.

3. Use of the trade mark with the consent of the proprietor or by any person who has authority to use a collective mark or a guarantee or certification mark shall be deemed to constitute use by the proprietor.

4. In relation to trade marks registered before the date on which the provisions necessary to comply with this Directive enter into force in the Member State concerned:

(a) where a provision in force prior to that date attaches sanctions to non use of a trade mark during an uninterrupted period, the relevant period of five years mentioned in paragraph 1 shall be deemed to have begun is to run at the same time as any period of non-use which is already running at that date;

(b) where there is no use provision in force prior to that date, the periods of five years mentioned in paragraph 1 shall be deemed to run from that is date at the earliest.

Article 11

Sanctions for non use of a trade mark in legal or administrative proceedings

1. A trade mark may not be declared invalid on the ground that there is an earlier conflicting trade mark if the latter does not fulfil the requirements of use set out in Article 10 (1), (2) and (3) or in Article 10 (4), as the case may be.

2. Any Member State may provide that registration of a trade mark may not be refused on the ground that there is an earlier conflicting trade mark if the latter does not fulfil the requirements of use set out in Article 10 (1), (2) and (3) or in Article 10 (4), as the case may be.

3. Without prejudice to the application of Article 12, where a counter-claim for revocation is made, any Member State may provide that: a trade mark may not be successfully invoked in infringement proceedings if it is established as a result of a plea that the trade mark could be revoked pursuant to Article 12 (1).

4. If the earlier trade mark has been used in relation to part only of the goods or services for which it is registered, it shall, for purposes of applying paragraphs 1, 2 and 3, be deemed to be registered in respect only of that part of the goods or services.

Article 12

Grounds for revocation

1. A trade mark shall be liable to revocation if, within a continuous period of five years, it has not been put to genuine use in the Member State in connection with the goods or services in respect of which it is registered, and there are no proper reasons for non-use; however, no person may claim that the proprietor's rights in a trade mark should be revoked where, during the interval between expiry of the five-year period and filing of the application for revocation, genuine use of the trade mark has been started or resumed; the commencement or resumption of use within a period of there months preceding the filing of the application for revocation which began at the earliest on expiry of the continuous period of five years of non-use, shall, however, be disregarded where prep-

arations for the commencement or resumption occur only after the proprietor becomes aware that the application for revocation may be filed.

2. A trade mark shall also be liable to revocation if, after the date on which it was registered,

(a) in consequence of acts or inactivity of the proprietor, it has become the common name in the trade for a product or service in respect of which it is registered;

(b) in consequence of the use made of it by the proprietor of the trade mark or with his consent in respect of the goods or services for which it is registered, it is liable to mislead the public, particularly as to the nature, quality or geographical origin of those goods or services.

Article 13

Grounds for refusal or revocation or invalidity relating to only some of the goods or services

Where grounds for refusal or registration or for revocation or invalidity of and trade mark exist in respect of only some of the goods or services for which to that trade mark has been applied for or registered, refusal of registration or revocation or invalidity shall cover those goods or services only.

Article 14

Establishment a posteriori of invalidity or revocation of a trade mark

Where the seniority of an earlier trade mark which has been surrendered or allowed to lapse, is claimed for a Community trade mark, the invalidity or revocation of the earlier trade mark may be established a posteriori.

Article 15

Special provisions in respect of collective marks, guarantee marks and certification marks

1. Without prejudice to Article 4, Member States whose laws authorize the registration of collective marks or of guarantee or certification marks may provide that such marks shall not be registered, or shall be revoked or declared invalid, on grounds additional to those specified in Articles 3 and 12 where the function of those marks so requires.

2. By way of derogation from Article 3 (1) (c), Member States may provide, that signs or indications which may serve, in trade, to designate the geographical origin of the goods or services may constitute collective, guarantee or certification marks. Such a mark does not entitle the proprietor to prohibit a third party from using in the course of trade such signs or indications, provided he uses them in accordance with honest practices in industrial or commercial matters; in particular, such a mark may not be invoked against a third party who is entitled to use a geographical name.

Article 16

National provisions to be adopted pursuant to this Directive

1. The Member States shall bring into force the laws, regulations and is administrative provisions necessary to comply with this Directive not later than 28 December 1991. They shall immediately inform the Commission thereof .

2. Acting on a proposal from the Commission, the Council, acting by qualified majority, may defer the date referred to in paragraph 1 until 31 December 1992 at the latest.

3. Member States shall communicate to the Commission the next of the main provisions of national law which they adopt in the field governed by this Directive.

Article 17

Addressees

This Directive is addressed to the Member States.

Done at Brussels, 21 December 1988.

For the Council
The President.
V. PAPANDREOU

Council Regulation (EC) No. 40/94

of 20 December 1993
on the Community Trade Mark

THE COUNCIL OF THE EUROPEAN UNION,

Having regard to the Treaty establishing the European Community, and in particular Article 235 thereof,

Having regard to the proposal from the Commission,[1]

Having regard to the opinion of the European Parliament,[2]

Having regard to the opinion of the Economic and Social Committee,[3]

Whereas it is desirable to promote throughout the Community a harmonious development of economic activities and a continuous and balanced expansion by completing an internal market which functions properly and offers conditions which are similar to those obtaining in a national market;

Whereas in order to create a market of this kind and make it increasingly a single market, not only must be barriers to free movement of goods and services be removed and arrangements be instituted which ensure that competition is not distorted, but, in addition, legal conditions must be created which enable undertakings to adapt their activities to the scale of the Community, whether in manufacturing and distributing goods or in providing services;

Whereas for those purposes, trade marks enabling the products and services of undertakings to be distinguished by identical means throughout the entire Community, regardless of frontiers, should feature amongst the legal instruments which undertakings have at their disposal;

Whereas action by the Community would appear to be necessary for the purpose of attaining the Community's said objectives;

Whereas such action involves the creation of Community arrangements for trade marks whereby undertakings can by means of one procedural system obtain Community trade marks to which uniform protection is given and which produce their effects throughout the entire area of the Community;

[1] OJ No. C 351, 31.12.1980, p. 1 and OJ No. C 230, 31.8.1984, p. 1.
[2] OJ No. C 307, 14.11.1983, p. 46 and OJ No. C 280, 28.10.1991, p. 153.
[3] OJ No. C 310, 30.11.1981, p. 22.

Whereas the principle of the unitary character of the Community trade mark thus stated will apply unless otherwise provided for in this Regulation;

Whereas the barrier of territoriality of the rights conferred on proprietors of trade marks by the laws of the Member States cannot be removed by approximation of laws;

Whereas in order to open up unrestricted economic activity in the whole of the common market for the benefit of undertakings, trade marks need to be created which are governed by a uniform Community law directly applicable in all Member States;

Whereas since the Treaty has not provided the specific powers to establish such a legal instrument, Article 235 of the Treaty should be applied;

Whereas the Community law relating to trade marks nevertheless does not replace the laws of the Member States on trade marks;

Whereas it would not in fact appear to be justified to require undertakings to apply for registration of their trade marks as Community trade marks;

Whereas national trade marks continue to be necessary for those undertakings which do not want protection of their trade marks at Community level;

Whereas the rights in a Community trade mark may not be obtained otherwise than by registration, and registration is to be refused in particular if the trade mark is not distinctive, if it is unlawful or if it conflicts with earlier rights.

Whereas the protection afforded by a Community trade mark, the function of which is in particular to guarantee the trade mark as an indication of origin, is absolute in the case of identity between the mark and the sign and the goods or services;

Whereas the protection applies also in cases of similarity between the mark and the sign and the goods or services;

Whereas an interpretation should be given of the concept of similarity in relation to the likelihood of confusion;

Whereas the likelihood of confusion, the appreciation of which depends on numerous elements and, in particular, on the recognition of the trade mark on the market, the association which can be made with the used or registered sign, the degree of similarity between the trade mark and the sign and between the goods or services identified, constitutes the specific condition for such protection;

Whereas it follows from the principle of free flow of goods that the proprietor of a Community trade mark must not be entitled to prohibit its use by a third party in relation to goods which have been put into circulation in the Community, under the trade mark, by him or with his consent, save where there exist legitimate reasons for the proprietor to oppose further commercialization of the goods;

Whereas there is no justification for protecting Community trade marks or, as against them, any trade mark which has been registered before them, except where the trade marks are actually used;

Whereas a Community trade mark is to be regarded as an object of property which exists separately from the undertakings whose goods or services are designated by it;

Whereas accordingly, it must be capable of being transferred, subject to the overriding need to prevent the public being misled as a result of the transfer. It must also be capable of being charged as security in favour of a third party and of being the subject matter of licences;

Whereas administrative measures are necessary at Community level for implementing in relation to every trade mark the trade mark law created by this Regulation;

Whereas it is therefore essential, while retaining the Community's existing institutional structure and balance of powers, to establish an Office for Harmonization in the Internal Market (trade marks and designs) which is independent in relation to technical matters and has legal, administrative and financial autonomy;

Whereas to this end it is necessary and appropriate that it should be a body of the Community having legal personality and exercising the implementing powers which are conferred on it by this Regulation, and that it should operate within the framework of Community law without detracting from the competencies exercised by the Community institutions;

Whereas it is necessary to ensure that parties who are affected by decisions made by the Office are protected by the law in a manner which is suited to the special character of trade mark law;

Whereas to that end provision is made for an appeal to lie from decisions of the examiners and of the various divisions of the Office;

Whereas if the department whose decision is contested does not rectify its decision it is to remit the appeal to a Board of Appeal of the Office, which is to decide on it;

Whereas decisions of the Boards of Appeal are, in turn, amenable to actions before the Court of Justice of the European Communities, which has jurisdiction to annul or to alter the contested decision.

Whereas under Council Decision 88/591/ECSC, EEC, Euratom of 24 October 1988 establishing a Court of First Instance of the European Communities,[4] as amended by Decision 93/350/Euratom, ECSC, EEC of 8 June 1993,[5] that Court shall exercise at the first instance the jurisdiction conferred on the Court of Justice by the Treaties establishing the Communities – with particular regard to appeals lodged under the second subparagraph of Article 173 of the EC Treaty – and by the acts adopted in implementation thereof, save as otherwise provided in an act setting up a body governed by Community law;

Whereas the jurisdiction which this Regulation confers on the Court of Justice to cancel and reform decisions of the appeal courts shall accordingly be exercised at the first instance by the Court in accordance with the above Decision;

Whereas in order to strengthen the protection of Community trade marks the Member States should designate, having regard to their own national system, as

[4] OJ No. L 319, 25.11.1988, p. 1 and corrigendum in OJ No. L 241, 17.8.1989, p. 4.
[5] OJ No. L 144, 16.6.1993, p. 21.

limited a number as possible of national courts of first and second instance having jurisdiction in matters of infringement and validity of Community trade marks;

Whereas decisions regarding the validity and infringement of Community trade marks must have effect and cover the entire area of the Community, as this is the only way of preventing inconsistent decisions on the part of the courts and the Office and of ensuring that the unitary character of Community trade marks is not undermined;

Whereas the rules contained in the Brussels Convention of Jurisdiction and the Enforcement of Judgments in Civil and Commercial Matters will apply to all actions at law relating to Community trade marks, save where this Regulation derogates from those rules;

Whereas contradictory judgments should be avoided in actions which involve the same acts and the same parties and which are brought on the basis of a Community trade mark and parallel national trade marks;

Whereas for this purpose, when the actions are brought in the same Member State, the way in which this is to be achieved is a matter for national procedural rules, which are not prejudiced by this Regulation, whilst when the actions are brought in different Member States, provisions modelled on the rules on *lis pendens* and related actions of the abovementioned Brussels Convention appear appropriate;

Whereas in order to guarantee the full autonomy and independence of the Office, it is considered necessary to grant it an autonomous budget whose revenue comes principally from fees paid by the users of the system;

Whereas however, the Community budgetary procedure remains applicable as far as any subsidies chargeable to general budget of the European Communities are concerned;

Whereas moreover, the auditing of accounts should be undertaken by the Court of Auditors;

Whereas implementing measures are required for the Regulation's application, particularly as regards the adoption and amendment of fees regulations and an Implementing Regulation;

Whereas such measures should be adopted by the Commission, assisted by a Committee composed of representatives of the Member States, in accordance with the procedural rules laid down in Article 2, procedure III(b), of Council Decisions 87/373/EEC of 13 July 1987 laying down the procedures for the exercise of implementing powers conferred on the Commission,[6]

[6] OJ No. L 197, 18.7.1987, p. 33.

HAS ADOPTED THIS REGULATION:

TITLE I

General Provisions

Article 1

Community trade mark

1. A trade mark for goods or services which is registered in accordance with the conditions contained in this Regulation and in the manner herein provided is hereinafter referred to as a "Community trade mark".

2. A Community trade mark shall have a unitary character. It shall have equal effect throughout the Community: it shall not be registered, transferred or surrendered or be the subject of a decision revoking the rights of the proprietor or declaring it invalid, nor shall its use be prohibited, save in respect of the whole Community. This principle shall apply unless otherwise provided in this Regulation.

Article 2

Office

An Office for Harmonization in the Internal Market (trade marks and designs), hereinafter referred to as "the Office", is hereby established.

Article 3

Capacity to act

For the purpose of implementing this Regulation, companies or firms and other legal bodies shall be regarded as legal persons if, under the terms of the law governing them, they have the capacity in their own name to have rights and obligations of all kinds, to make contracts or accomplish other legal acts and to sue and be sued.

TITLE II

The Law relating to Trade Marks

SECTION 1

Definition of a Community Trade Mark obtaining a Community Trade Mark

Article 4

Signs of which a Community trade mark may consist

A Community trade mark may consist of any signs capable of being represented graphically, particularly words, including personal names, designs, letters, numerals, the shape of goods or of their packaging, provided that such signs are capable of distinguishing the goods or services of one undertaking from those of other undertakings.

Article 5

Persons who can be proprietors of Community trade marks

1. The following natural or legal persons, including authorities established under public law, may be proprietors of Community trade marks:

(a) nationals of the Member States; or

(b) nationals of other States which are parties to the Paris Convention for the protection of industrial property, hereinafter referred to as "the Paris Convention"; or

(c) nationals of States which are not parties to the Paris Convention who are domiciled or have their seat or who have real and effective industrial or commercial establishments within the territory of the Community or of a State which is party to the Paris Convention; or

(d) nationals, other than those referred to under subparagraph (c), of any State which is not party to the Paris Convention and which, according to published findings, accords to nationals of all the Member States the same protection for trade marks as it accords to its own nationals and, if nationals of the Member States are required to prove registration in the country of origin, recognizes the registration of Community trade marks as such proof.

2. With respect to the application of paragraph 1, stateless persons as defined by Article 1 of the Convention relating to the Status of Stateless Persons signed at New York on 28 September 1954, and refugees as defined by Article 1 of the Convention relating to the Status of Refugees signed at Geneva on 28 July 1951 and modified by the Protocol relating to the Status of Refugees signed at New York on 31 January 1967, shall be regarded as nationals of the country in which they have their habitual residence.

3. Persons who are nationals of a State covered by paragraph 1 (d) must prove that the trade mark for which an application for a Community trade mark has been submitted is registered in the State of origin, unless, according to published findings, the trade marks of nationals of the Member States are registered in the State of origin in question without proof of prior registration as a Community trade mark or as a national trade mark in a Member State. Article 6 Means whereby a Community trade mark is obtained A Community trade mark shall be obtained by registration.

Article 7

Absolute grounds for refusal

1. The following shall not be registered:

(a) signs which do not conform to the requirements of Article 4;

(b) trade marks which are devoid of any distinctive character;

(c) trade marks which consist exclusively of signs or indications which may serve, in trade, to designate the kind, quality, quantity, intended purpose, value, geographical origin or the time of production of the goods or of rendering of the service, or other characteristics of the goods or service. 5 OF 22.

(d) trade marks which consist exclusively of signs or indications which have become customary in the current language or in the bona fide and established practices of the trade;

(e) signs which consist exclusively of:

(i) the shape which results from the nature of the goods themselves; or

(ii) the shape of goods which is necessary to obtain a technical result; or

(iii) the shape which gives substantial value to the goods;

(f) trade marks which are contrary to public policy or to accepted principles of morality;

(g) trade marks which are of such a nature as to deceive the public, for instance as to the nature, quality or geographical origin of the goods or service;

(h) trade marks which have not been authorized by the competent authorities and are to be refused pursuant to Article 6 *ter* of the Paris Convention;

(i) trade marks which include badges, emblems or escutcheons other than those covered by Article 6 *ter* of the Paris Convention and which are of particular public interest, unless the consent of the appropriate authorities to their registration has been given.

2. Paragraph 1 shall apply notwithstanding that the grounds of non-registrability obtain in only part of the Community.

3. Paragraph 1 (b), (c) and (d) shall not apply if the trade mark has become distinctive in relation to the goods or services for which registration is requested in consequence of the use which has been made of it.

Article 8

Relative grounds for refusal

1. Upon opposition by the proprietor of an earlier trade mark, the trade mark applied for shall not be registered:

(a) if it is identical with the earlier trade mark and the goods or services for which registration is applied for are identical with the goods or services for which the earlier trade mark is protected;

(b) if because of its identity with or similarity to the earlier trade mark and the identity or similarity of the goods or services covered by the trade marks there exists a likelihood of confusion on the part of the public in the territory in which the earlier trade mark is protected; the likelihood of confusion includes the likelihood of association with the earlier trade mark.

2. for the purposes of paragraph 1, "Earlier trade marks" means:

(a) trade marks of the following kinds with a date of application for registration which is earlier than the date of application for registration of the Community

trade mark, taking account, where appropriate, of the priorities claimed in respect of those trade marks:
(i) Community trade marks;
(ii) trade marks registered in a Member State, or, in the case of Belgium, the Netherlands or Luxembourg, at the Benelux Trade Mark Office;
(iii) trade marks registered under international arrangements which have effect in a Member State;

(b) applications for the trade marks referred to in subparagraph (a), subject to their registration;

(c) trade marks which, on the date of application for registration of the Community trade mark, or, where appropriate, of the priority claimed in respect of the application for registration of the Community trade mark, are well known in a Member State, in the sense in which the words "well known" are used in Article 6 *bis* of the Paris Convention.

3. Upon opposition by the proprietor of the trade mark, a trade mark shall not be registered where an agent or representative of the proprietor of the trade mark applies for registration thereof in his own name without the proprietor's consent, unless the agent or representative justifies his action.

4. Upon opposition by the proprietor of a non-registered trade mark or of another sign used in the course of trade of more than mere local significance, the trade mark applied for shall not be registered where and to the extent that, pursuant to the law of the Member State governing that sign,

(a) rights to that sign were acquired prior to the date of application for registration of the Community trade mark, or the date of the priority claimed for the application for registration of the Community trade mark.

(b) that sign confers on its proprietor the right to prohibit the use of a subsequent trade mark.

5. Furthermore, upon opposition by the proprietor of an earlier trade mark within the meaning of paragraph 2, the trade mark applied for shall not be registered where it is identical with or similar to the earlier trade mark and is to be registered for goods or services which are not similar to those for which the earlier trade mark is registered, where in the case of an earlier Community trade mark the trade mark has a reputation in the Community and, in the case of an earlier national trade mark, the trade mark has a reputation in the Member State concerned and where the use without due cause of the trade mark applied for would take unfair advantage of, or be detrimental to, the distinctive character or the repute of the earlier trade mark.

SECTION 2

Effects of Community Trade Marks

Article 9

Rights conferred by a Community trade mark

1. A Community trade mark shall confer on the proprietor exclusive rights therein. The proprietor shall be entitled to prevent all third parties not having his consent from using in the course of trade:

(a) any sign which is identical with the Community trade mark in relation to goods or services which are identical with those for which the Community trade mark is registered;

(b) any sign where, because of its identity with or similarity to the Community trade mark and the identity or similarity of the goods or services covered by the Community trade mark and the sign, there exists a likelihood of confusion on the part of the public; the likelihood of confusion includes the likelihood of association between the sign and the trade mark;

(c) any sign which is identical with or similar to the Community trade mark in relation to goods or services which are not similar to those for which the Community trade mark is registered, where the latter has a reputation in the Community and where use of that sign without due cause takes unfair advantage of, or is detrimental to, the distinctive character or the repute of the Community trade mark.

2. The following, *inter alia*, may be prohibited under paragraph 1:

(a) affixing the sign to the goods or to the packaging thereof;

(b) offering the goods, putting them on the market or stocking them for these purposes under that sign, or offering or supplying services thereunder;

(c) importing or exporting the goods under that sign;

(d) using the sign on business papers and in advertising.

3. The rights conferred by a Community trade mark shall prevail against third parties from the date of publication of registration of the trade mark. Reasonable compensation may, however, be claimed in respect of matters arising after the date of publication of a Community trade mark application, which matters would, after publication of the registration of the trade mark, be prohibited by virtue of that publication. The court seized of the case may not decide upon the merits of the case until the registration has been published.

Article 10

Reproduction of Community trade marks in dictionaries

If the reproduction of a Community trade mark in a dictionary, encyclopaedia or similar reference work gives the impression that it constitutes the generic name of the goods or services for which the trade mark is registered, the publisher of the work shall, at the request of the proprietor of the Community trade mark, ensure that the reproduction of the trade mark at the latest in the next edition of the publication is accompanied by an indication that it is a registered trade mark.

Article 11

Prohibition on the use of a Community trade mark registered in the name of an agent or representative

Where a Community trade mark is registered in the name of the agent or representative of a person who is the proprietor of that trade mark, without the proprietor's authorization, the latter shall be entitled to oppose the use of his mark by his agent or representative if he has not authorized such use, unless the agent or representative justifies his action.

Article 12

Limitation of the effects of a Community trade mark

A Community trade mark shall not entitle the proprietor to prohibit a third party from using in the course of trade:

(a) his own name or address;

(b) indications concerning the kind, quality, quantity, intended purpose, value, geographical origin, the time of production of the goods or of rendering of the service, or other characteristics of the goods or service;

(c) the trade mark where it is necessary to indicate the intended purpose of a product or service, in particular as accessories or spare parts, provided he uses them in accordance with honest practices in industrial or commercial matters.

Article 13

Exhaustion of the rights conferred by a Community trade mark

1. A Community trade mark shall not entitle the proprietor to prohibit its use in relation to goods which have been put on the market in the Community under that trade mark by the proprietor or with his consent.

2. Paragraph 1 shall not apply where there exist legitimate reasons for the proprietor to oppose further commercialization of the goods, especially where the condition of the goods is changed or impaired after they have been put on the market.

Article 14

Complementary application of national law relating to infringement

1. The effects of Community trade marks shall be governed solely by the provisions of this Regulation. In other respects, infringement of a Community trade mark shall be governed by the national law relating to infringement of a national trade mark in accordance with the provisions of Title X.

2. This Regulation shall not prevent actions concerning a Community trade mark being brought under the law of Member States relating in particular to civil liability and unfair competition. 3. The rules of procedure to be applied shall be determined in accordance with the provisions of Title X.

Section 3

Use of Community Trade Marks

Article 15

Use of Community trade marks

1. If, within a period of five years following registration, the proprietor has not put the Community trade mark to genuine use in the Community in connection with the goods or services in respect of which it is registered, or if such use has been suspended during an uninterrupted period of five years, the Community trade mark shall be subject to the sanctions provided for in this Regulation, unless there are proper reasons for non-use.

2. The following shall also constitute use within the meaning of paragraph 1:

(a) use of the Community trade mark in a form differing in elements which do not alter the distinctive character of the mark in the form in which it was registered;

(b) affixing of the Community trade mark to goods or to the packaging thereof in the Community solely for export purposes.

3. Use of the Community trade mark with the consent of the proprietor shall be deemed to constitute use by the proprietor.

Section 4

Community Trade Marks as Objects of Property

Article 16

Dealing with Community trade marks as national trade marks

1. Unless Articles 17 to 24 provide otherwise, a Community trade mark as an object of property shall be dealt with in its entirety, and for the whole area of the Community, as a national trade mark registered in the Member State in which, according to the Register of Community trade marks,

(a) the proprietor has his seat or his domicile on the relevant date; or

(b) where subparagraph (a) does not apply, the proprietor has an establishment on the relevant date.

2. In cases which are not provided for by paragraph 1, the Member State referred to in that paragraph shall be the Member State in which the seat of the Office is situated.

3. If two or more persons are mentioned in the Register of Community trade marks as joint proprietors, paragraph 1 shall apply to the joint proprietor first mentioned; failing this, it shall apply to the subsequent joint proprietors in the

order in which they are mentioned. Where paragraph 1 does not apply to any of the joint proprietors, paragraph 2 shall apply.

Article 17
Transfer
1. A Community trade mark may be transferred, separately from any transfer of the undertaking, in respect of some or all of the goods or services for which it is registered.

2. A transfer of the whole of the undertaking shall include the transfer of the Community trade mark except where, in accordance with the law governing the transfer, there is agreement to the contrary or circumstances clearly dictate otherwise. This provision shall apply to the contractual obligation to transfer the undertaking.

3. Without prejudice to paragraph 2, an assignment of the Community trade mark shall be made in writing and shall require the signature of the parties to the contract, except when it is a result of a judgment; otherwise it shall be void.

4. Where it is clear from the transfer documents that because of the transfer the Community trade mark is likely to mislead the public concerning the nature, quality or geographical origin of the goods or services in respect of which it is registered, the Office shall not register the transfer unless the successor agrees to limit registration of the Community trade mark to goods or services in respect of which it is not likely to mislead.

5. On request of one of the parties a transfer shall be entered in the Register and published.

6. As long as the transfer has not been entered in the Register, the successor in title may not invoke the rights arising from the registration of the Community trade mark.

7. Where there are time limits to be observed *vis-à-vis* the Office, the successor in title may make the corresponding statements to the Office once the request for registration of the transfer has been received by the Office.

8. All documents which require notification to the proprietor of the Community trade mark in accordance with Article 77 shall be addressed to the person registered as proprietor.

Article 18
Transfer of a trade mark registered in the name of an agent
Where a Community trade mark is registered in the name of the agent or representative of a person who is the proprietor of that trade mark, without the

proprietor's authorization, the latter shall be entitled to demand the assignment in his favour of the said registration, unless such agent or representative justifies his action.

Article 19
Rights *in rem*
1. A Community trade mark may, independently of the undertaking, be given as security or be the subject of rights *in rem*.

2. On request of one of the parties, rights mentioned in paragraph 1 shall be entered in the Register and published.

Article 20
Levy of execution
1. A Community trade mark may be levied in execution.

2. As regards the procedure for levy of execution in respect of a Community trade mark, the courts and authorities of the Member States determined in accordance with Article 16 shall have exclusive jurisdiction.

3. On request of one the parties, levy of execution shall be entered in the Register and published.

Article 21
Bankruptcy or like proceedings
1. Until such time as common rules for the Member States in this field enter into force, the only Member State in which a Community trade mark may be involved in bankruptcy or like proceedings shall be that in which such proceedings are first brought within the meaning of national law or of conventions applicable in this field.

2. Where a Community trade mark is involved in bankruptcy or like proceedings, on request of the competent national authority an entry to this effect shall be made in the Register and published.

Article 22
Licensing
1. A Community trade mark may be licensed for some or all of the goods or services for which it is registered and for the whole or part of the Community. A licence may be exclusive or non-exclusive.

2. The proprietor of a Community trade mark may invoke the rights conferred by that trade mark against a licensee who contravenes any provision in his licensing contract with regard to its duration, the form covered by the registration in which the trade mark may be used, the scope of the goods or services for which

the licence is granted, the territory in which the trade mark may be affixed, or the quality of the goods manufactured or of the services provided by the licensee.

3. Without prejudice to the provisions of the licensing contract, the licensee may bring proceedings for infringement of a Community trade mark only if its proprietor consents thereto. However, the holder of an exclusive licence may bring such proceedings if the proprietor of the trade mark, after formal notice, does not himself bring infringement proceedings within an appropriate period.

4. A licensee shall, for the purpose of obtaining compensation for damage suffered by him, be entitled to intervene in infringement proceedings brought by the proprietor of the Community trade mark. 5. On request of one of the parties the grant or transfer of a licence in respect of a Community trade mark shall be entered in the Register and published.

Article 23

Effects *vis-à-vis* third parties

1. Legal acts referred to in Article 17, 19 and 22 concerning a Community trade mark shall only have effects *vis-à-vis* third parties in all the Member States after entry in the Register. Nevertheless, such an act, before it is so entered, shall have effect *vis-à-vis* third parties who have acquired rights in the trade mark after the date of that act but who knew of the act at the date on which the rights were acquired.

2. Paragraph 1 shall not apply in the case of a person who acquires the Community trade mark or a right concerning the Community trade mark by way of transfer of the whole of the undertaking or by any other universal succession.

3. The effects *vis-à-vis* third parties of the legal acts referred to in Article 20 shall be governed by the law of the Member State determined in accordance with Article 16.

4. Until such time as common rules for the Member States in the field of bankruptcy enter into force, the effects *vis-à-vis* third parties of bankruptcy or like proceedings shall be governed by the law of the Member State in which such proceedings are first brought within the meaning of national law or of conventions applicable in this field.

Article 24

The application for a Community trade mark as an object of property

Articles 16 to 23 shall apply to applications for Community trade marks.

Title III

Application for Community Trade Marks

Section 1

Filing of Applications and the Conditions which govern them

Article 25
Filing of applications
1. An application for a Community trade mark shall be filed, at the choice of the applicant,
(a) at the Office; or
(b) at the central industrial property office of a Member State or at the Benelux Trade Mark Office. An application filed in this way shall have the same effect as if it had been filed on the same date at the Office.

2. Where the application is filed at the central industrial property office of a Member State or at the Benelux Trade Mark Office, that office shall take all steps to forward the application to the Office within two weeks after filing. It may charge the applicant a fee which shall not exceed the administrative costs of receiving and forwarding the application.

3. Applications referred to in paragraph 2 which reach the Office more than one month after filing shall be deemed withdrawn.

4. Ten years after the entry into force of this Regulation, the Commission shall draw up a report on the operation of the system of filing applications for Community trade marks, together with any proposals for modifying this system.

Article 26.
Conditions with which applications must comply
1. An application for a Community trade mark shall contain:
(a) a request for the registration of a Community trade mark;
(b) information identifying the applicant;
(c) a list of the goods or services in respect of which the registration is requested;
(d) a representation of the trade mark.

2. The application for a Community trade mark shall be subject to the payment of the application fee and, when appropriate, of one or more class fees.

3. An application for a Community trade mark must comply with the conditions laid down in the implementing Regulation referred to in Article 140.

Article 27
Date of filing
The date of filing of a Community trade mark application shall be the date on which documents containing the information specified in Article 26 (1) are filed with the Office by the applicant or, if the application has been filed with the central office of a Member State or with the Benelux Trade Mark Office, with that office, subject to payment of the application fee within a period of one month of filing the above-mentioned documents.

Article 28
Classification
Goods and services in respect of which Community trade marks are applied for shall be classified in conformity with the system of classification specified in the Implementing Regulation.

Section 2

Priority

Article 29
Right of priority
1. A person who has duly filed an application for a trade mark in or for any State party to the Paris Convention, or his successors in title, shall enjoy, for the purpose of filing a Community trade mark application for the same trade mark in respect of goods or services which are identical with or contained within those for which the application has been filed, a right of priority during a period of six months from the date of filing of the first application.

2. Every filing that is equivalent to a regular national filing under the national law of the State where it was made or under bilateral or multilateral agreements shall be recognized as giving rise to a right of priority.

3. By a regular national filing is meant any filing that is sufficient to establish the date on which the application was filed, whatever may be the outcome of the application.

4. A subsequent application for a trade mark which was the subject of a previous first application in respect of the same goods or services, and which is filed in or in respect of the same State shall be considered as the first application for the purposes of determining priority, provided that, at the date of filing of the subsequent application, the previous application has been withdrawn, abandoned or refused, without being open to public inspection and without leaving any rights outstanding, and has not served as a basis for claiming a right of priority. The previous application may not thereafter serve as a basis for claiming a right of priority.

5. If the first filing has been made in a State which is not a party to the Paris Convention, paragraphs 1 to 4 shall apply only in so far as that State, according to published findings, grants, on the basis of a first filing made at the Office and subject to conditions equivalent to those laid down in this Regulation, a right of priority having equivalent effect.

Article 30
Claiming priority
An applicant desiring to take advantage of the priority of a previous application shall file a declaration of priority and a copy of the previous application. If the language of the latter is not one of the languages of the Office, the applicant shall file a translation of the previous application in one of those languages.

Article 31
Effect of priority right
The right of priority shall have the effect that the date of priority shall count as the date of filing of the Community trade mark application for the purposes of establishing which rights take precedence.

Article 32
Equivalence of Community filing with national filing
A Community trade mark application which has been accorded a date of filing shall, in the Member States, be equivalent to a regular national filing, where appropriate with the priority claimed for the Community trade mark application.

SECTION 3

Exhibition Priority

Article 33
Exhibition priority
1. If an applicant for a Community trade mark has displayed goods or services under the mark applied for, at an official or officially recognized international exhibition falling within the terms of the Convention on International Exhibitions signed at Paris on 22 November 1928 and last revised on 30 November 1972, he may, if he files the application within a period of six months from the date of the first display of the goods or services under the mark applied for, claim a right of priority from that date within the meaning of Article 31.

2. An applicant who wishes to claim priority pursuant to paragraph 1 must file evidence of the display of goods or services under the mark applied for under the conditions laid down in the Implementing Regulation.

3. An exhibition priority granted in a Member State or in a third country does not extend the period of priority laid down in Article 29.

Section 4

Claiming the Seniority of a National Trade Mark

Article 34
Claiming the seniority of a national trade mark
1. The proprietor of an earlier trade mark registered in a Member State, including a trade mark registered in the Benelux countries, or registered under international arrangements having effect in a Member State, who applies for an identical trade mark for registration as a Community trade mark for goods or services which are identical with or contained within those for which the earlier trade mark has been registered, may claim for the Community trade mark the seniority of the earlier trade mark in respect of the Member State in or for which it is registered.

2. Seniority shall have the sole effect under this Regulation that, where the proprietor of the Community trade mark surrenders the earlier trade mark or allows it to lapse, he shall be deemed to continue to have the same rights as he would have had if the earlier trade mark had continued to be registered.

3. The seniority claimed for the Community trade mark shall lapse if the earlier trade mark the seniority of which is claimed is declared to have been revoked or to be invalid or if it is surrendered prior to the registration of the Community trade mark.

Article 35
Claiming seniority after registration of the Community trade mark
1. The proprietor of a Community trade mark who is the proprietor of an earlier identical trade mark registered in a Member State, including a trade mark registered in the Benelux countries, or of a trade mark registered under international arrangements having effect in a Member State, for identical goods or services, may claim the seniority of the earlier trade mark in respect of the Member State in or for which it is registered.

2. Article 34 (2) and (3) shall apply.

Title IV

Registration Procedure Section 1 Examination of Applications

Article 36
Examination of the conditions of filing
1. The Office shall examine whether:
(a) the Community trade mark application satisfies the requirements for the accordance of a date of filing in accordance with Article 27;

(b) the Community trade mark application complies with the conditions laid down in the Implementing Regulation;

(c) where appropriate, the class fees have been paid within the prescribed period.

2. Where the Community trade mark application does not satisfy the requirements referred to in paragraph 1, the Office shall request the applicant to remedy the deficiencies or the default on payment within the prescribed period.

3. If the deficiencies or the default on payment established pursuant to paragraph 1 (a) are not remedied within this period, the application shall not be dealt with as a Community trade mark application. 12 OF 22. If the applicant complies with the Office's request, the Office shall accord as the date of filing of the application the date on which the deficiencies or the default on payment established are remedied.

4. If the deficiencies established pursuant to paragraph 1 (b) are not remedied within the prescribed period, the Office shall refuse the application.

5. If the default on payment established pursuant to paragraph 1 (c) is not remedied within the prescribed period, the application shall be deemed to be withdrawn unless it is clear which categories of goods or services the amount paid is intended to cover.

6. Failure to satisfy the requirements concerning the claim to priority shall result in loss of the right of priority for the application.

7. Failure to satisfy the requirements concerning the claiming of seniority of a national trade mark shall result in loss of that right for the application.

Article 37

Examination of the conditions relating to the entitlement of the proprietor

1. Where, pursuant to Article 5, the applicant may not be the proprietor of a Community trade mark, the application shall be refused.

2. The application may not be refused before the applicant has been given the opportunity to withdraw his application or submit his observations.

Article 38

Examination as to absolute grounds for refusal

1. Where, under Article 7, a trade mark is ineligible for registration in respect of some or all of the goods or services covered by the Community trade mark application, the application shall be refused as regards those goods or services.

2. Where the trade mark contains an element which is not distinctive, and where the inclusion of said element in the trade mark could give rise to doubts as to the scope of protection of the trade mark, the Office may request, as a condition for registration of said trade mark, that the applicant state that he disclaims any exclusive right to such element. Any disclaimer shall be published together with the application or the registration of the Community trade mark, as the case may be.

3. The application shall not be refused before the applicant has been allowed the opportunity of withdrawing or amending the application or of submitting his observations.

Section 2

Search

Article 39

Search

1. Once the Office has accorded a date of filing to a Community trade mark application and has established that the applicant satisfies the conditions referred to in Article 5, it shall draw up a Community search report citing those earlier Community trade marks or Community trade mark applications discovered which may be invoked under Article 8 against the registration of the Community trade mark applied for.

2. As soon as a Community trade mark application has been accorded a date of filing, the Office shall transmit a copy thereof to the central industrial property office of each Member State which has informed the Office of its decision to operate a search in its own register of trade marks in respect of Community trade mark applications.

3. Each of the central industrial property offices referred to in paragraph 2 shall communicate to the Office within three months as from the date on which it received the Community trade mark application a search report which shall either cite those earlier national trade marks or trade mark applications discovered which may be invoked under Article 8 against the registration of the Community trade mark applied for, or state that the search has revealed no such rights.

4. An amount shall be paid by the Office to each central industrial property office for each search report provided by that office in accordance with paragraph 3. The amount, which shall be the same for each office, shall be fixed by the Budget Committee by means of a decision adopted by a majority of three-quarters of the representatives of the Member States.

5. The Office shall transmit without delay to the applicant for the Community trade mark the Community search report and the national search reports received within the time limit laid down in paragraph 3.

6. Upon publication of the Community trade mark application, which may not take place before the expiry of a period of one month as from the date on which the Office transmits the search reports to the applicant, the Office shall inform the proprietors of any earlier Community trade marks or Community trade mark applications cited in the Community search report of the publication of the Community trade mark application.

7. The Commission shall, five years after the opening of the Office for the filing of applications, submit to the Council a report on the operation of the system of searching resulting from this Article, including the payments made to Member States under paragraph 4, and, if necessary, appropriate proposals for amending this Regulation with a view to adapting the system of searching on the basis of the experience gained and bearing in mind developments in searching techniques.

Section 3

Publication of the Application

Article 40
Publication of the application
1. If the conditions which the application for a Community trade mark must satisfy have been fulfilled and if the period referred to in Article 39 (6) has expired, the application shall be published to the extent that it has not been refused pursuant to Articles 37 and 38.

2. Where, after publication, the application is refused under Articles 37 and 38, the decision that it has been refused shall be published upon becoming final.

Section 4

Observations by Third Parties and Opposition

Article 41
Observations by third parties
1. Following the publication of the Community trade mark application, any natural or legal person and any group or body representing manufacturers, producers, suppliers of services, traders or consumers may submit to the Office written observations, explaining on which grounds under Article 7, in particular, the

trade mark shall not be registered ex officio. They shall not be parties to the proceedings before the Office.

2. The observations referred to in paragraph 1 shall be communicated to the applicant who may comment on them.

Article 42
Opposition
1. Within a period of three months following the publication of a Community trade mark application, notice of opposition to registration of the trade mark may be given on the grounds that it may not be registered under Article 8:

(a) by the proprietors of earlier trade marks referred to in Article 8 (2) as well as licensees authorized by the proprietors of those trade marks, in respect of Article 8 (1) and (5);

(b) by the proprietors of trade marks referred to in Article 8 (3);

(c) by the proprietors of earlier marks or signs referred to in Article 8 (4) and by persons authorized under the relevant national law to exercise these rights.

2. Notice of opposition to registration of the trade mark may also be given, subject to the conditions laid down in paragraph 1, in the event of the publication of an amended application in accordance with the second sentence of Article 44 (2).

3. Opposition must be expressed in writing and must specify the grounds on which it is made. It shall not be treated as duly entered until the opposition fee has been paid. Within a period fixed by the Office, the opponent may submit in support of his case facts, evidence and arguments.

Article 43
Examination of opposition
1. In the examination of the opposition the Office shall invite the parties, as often as necessary, to file observations, within a period set them by the Office, on communications from the other parties or issued by itself.

2. If the applicant so requests, the proprietor of an earlier Community trade mark who has given notice of opposition shall furnish proof that, during the period of five years preceding the date of publication of the Community trade mark application, the earlier Community trade mark has been put to genuine use in the Community in connection with the goods or services in respect of which it is registered and which he cites as justification for his opposition, or that there are proper reasons for non-use, provided the earlier Community trade mark has at that date been registered for not less than five years. In the absence of proof to this effect, the opposition shall be rejected. If the earlier Community trade mark has been used in relation to part only of the goods or services for which it is registered it shall, for the purposes of the examination of the opposition, be deemed to be registered in respect only of that part of the goods or services.

3. Paragraph 2 shall apply to earlier national trade marks referred to in Article 8 (2) (a), by substituting use in the Member State in which the earlier national trade mark is protected for use in the Community.

4. The Office may, if it thinks fit, invite the parties to make a friendly settlement.

5. If examination of the opposition reveals that the trade mark may not be registered in respect of some or all of the goods or services for which the Community trade mark application has been made, the application shall be refused in respect of those goods or services. Otherwise the opposition shall be rejected. 6. The decision refusing the application shall be published upon becoming final.

Section 5

Withdrawal, Restriction and Amendment of the Application

Article 44
Withdrawal, restriction and amendment of the application
1. The applicant may at any time withdraw his Community trade mark application or restrict the list of goods or services contained therein. Where the application has already been published, the withdrawal or restriction shall also be published.

2. In other respects, a Community trade mark application may be amended, upon request of the applicant, only by correcting the name and address of the applicant, errors of wording or of copying, or obvious mistakes, provided that such correction does not substantially change the trade mark or extend the list of goods or services. Where the amendments affect the representation of the trade mark or the list of goods or services and are made after publication of the application, the trade mark application shall be published as amended.

Section 6

Registration

Article 45
Registration
Where an application meets the requirements of this Regulation and where no notice of opposition has been given within the period referred to in Article 42 (1) or where opposition has been rejected by a definitive decision, the trade mark shall be registered as a Community trade mark, provided that the registration fee has been paid within the period prescribed. If the fee is not paid within this period the application shall be deemed to be withdrawn.

Title V

Duration, Renewal and Alteration of Community Trade Marks

Article 46
Duration of registration
Community trade marks shall be registered for a period of ten years from the date of filing of the application. Registration may be renewed in accordance with Article 47 for further periods of ten years.

Article 47
Renewal
1. Registration of the Community trade mark shall be renewed at the request of the proprietor of the trade mark or any person expressly authorized by him, provided that the fees have been paid.

2. The Office shall inform the proprietor of the Community trade mark, and any person having a registered right in respect of the Community trade mark, of the expiry of the registration in good time before the said expiry. Failure to give such information shall not involve the responsibility of the Office.

3. The request for renewal shall be submitted within a period of six months ending on the last day of the month in which protection ends. The fees shall also be paid within this period. Failing this, the request may be submitted and the fees paid within a further period of six months following the day referred to in the first sentence, provided that an additional fee is paid within this further period.

4. Where the request is submitted or the fees paid in respect of only some of the goods or services for which the Community trade mark is registered, registration shall be renewed for those goods or services only.

5. Renewal shall take effect from the day following the date on which the existing registration expires. The renewal shall be registered.

Article 48
Alteration
1. The Community trade mark shall not be altered in the register during the period of registration or on renewal thereof.

2. Nevertheless, where the Community trade mark includes the name and address of the proprietor, any alteration thereof not substantially affecting the identity of the trade mark as originally registered may be registered at the request of the proprietor.

3. The publication of the registration of the alteration shall contain a representation of the Community trade mark as altered. Third parties whose rights may be affected by the alteration may challenge the registration thereof within a period of three months following publication.

TITLE VI

Surrender, Revocation and Invalidity

SECTION 1

Surrender

Article 49
Surrender
1. A Community trade mark may be surrendered in respect of some or all of the goods or services for which it is registered.

2. The surrender shall be declared to the Office in writing by the proprietor of the trade mark. It shall not have effect until it has been entered in the Register.

3. Surrender shall be entered only with the agreement of the proprietor of a right entered in the Register. If a licence has been registered, surrender shall only be entered in the Register if the proprietor of the trade mark proves that he has informed the licensee of his intention to surrender; this entry shall be made on expiry of the period prescribed by the Implementing Regulation.

SECTION 2

Grounds for Revocation

Article 50
Grounds for revocation
1. The rights of the proprietor of the Community trade mark shall be declared to be revoked on application to the Office or on the basis of a counterclaim in infringement proceedings:

(a) if, within a continuous period of five years, the trade mark has not been put to genuine use in the Community in connection with the goods or services in respect of which it is registered, and there are no proper reasons for non-use; however, no person may claim that the proprietor's rights in a Community trade mark should be revoked where, during the interval between expiry of the five-year period and filing of the application or counterclaim, genuine use of the trade mark has been started or resumed; the commencement or resumption of use within a period of three months preceding the filing of the application or counterclaim which began at the earliest on expiry of the continuous period of five years of non-use shall, however, be disregarded where preparations for the commencement or resumption occur only after the proprietor becomes aware that the application or counterclaim may be filed;

(b) if, in consequence of acts or inactivity of the proprietor, the trade mark has become the common name in the trade for a product or service in respect of which it is registered;

(c) if, in consequence of the use made of it by the proprietor of the trade mark or with his consent in respect of the goods or services for which it is registered, the trade mark is liable to mislead the public, particularly as to the nature, quality or geographical origin of those goods or services;

(d) if the proprietor of the trade mark no longer satisfies the conditions laid down by Article 5.

2. Where the grounds for revocation of rights exist in respect of only some of the goods or services for which the Community trade mark is registered, the rights of the proprietor shall be declared to be revoked in respect of those goods or services only.

Section 3

Grounds for Invalidity

Article 51

Absolute grounds for invalidity

1. A Community trade mark shall be declared invalid on application to the Office or on the basis of a counterclaim in infringement proceedings,

(a) where the Community trade mark has been registered in breach of the provisions of Article 5 or of Article 7;

(b) where the applicant was acting in bad faith when he filed the application for the trade mark.

2. Where the Community trade mark has been registered in breach of the provisions of Article 7 (1) (b), (c) or (d), it may nevertheless not be declared invalid if, in consequence of the use which has been made of it, it has after registration acquired a distinctive character in relation to the goods or services for which it is registered.

3. Where the ground for invalidity exists in respect of only some of the goods or services for which the Community trade mark is registered, the trade mark shall be declared invalid as regards those goods or services only.

Article 52

Relative grounds for invalidity

1. A Community trade mark shall be declared invalid on application to the Office or on the basis of a counterclaim in infringement proceedings:

(a) where there is an earlier trade mark as referred to in Article 8 (2) and the conditions set out in paragraph 1 or paragraph 5 of that Article are fulfilled;

(b) where there is a trade mark as referred to in Article 8 (3) and the conditions set out in that paragraph are fulfilled;

(c) where there is an earlier right as referred to in Article 8 (4) and the conditions set out in that paragraph are fulfilled.

2. A Community trade mark shall also be declared invalid on application to the Office or on the basis of a conterclaim in infringement proceedings where the use of such trade mark may be prohibited pursuant to the national law governing the protection of any other earlier right an in particular:

(a) a right to a name;

(b) a right of personal portrayal;

(c) a copyright;

(d) an industrial property right.

3. A Community trade mark may not be declared invalid where the proprietor of a right referred to in paragraphs 1 or 2 consents expressly to the registration of the Community trade mark before submission of the application for a declaration of invalidity or the counterclaim.

4. Where the proprietor of one of the rights referred to in paragraphs 1 or 2 has previously applied for a declaration that a Community trade mark is invalid or made a counterclaim in infringement proceedings, he may not submit a new application for a declaration of invalidity or lodge a counterclaim on the basis of another of the said rights which he could have invoked in support of his first application or counterclaim.

5. Article 51 (3) shall apply.

Article 53

Limitation in consequence of acquiescence

1. Where the proprietor of a Community trade mark has acquiesced, for a period of five successive years, in the use of a later Community trade mark in the Community while being aware of such use, he shall no longer be entitled on the basis of the earlier trade mark either to apply for a declaration that the later trade mark is invalid or to oppose the use of the later trade mark in respect of the goods or services for which the later trade mark has been used, unless registration of the later Community trade mark was applied for in bad faith.

2. Where the proprietor of an earlier national trade mark as referred to in Article 8 (2) or of another earlier sign referred to in Article 8 (4) has acquiesced, for a period of five successive years, in the use of a later Community trade mark in the Member State in which the earlier trade mark or the other earlier sign is protected while being aware of such use, he shall no longer be entitled on the basis of the earlier trade mark or of the other earlier sign either to apply for a declaration that the later trade mark is invalid or to oppose the use of the later trade mark in respect of the goods or services for which the later trade mark has been used, unless registration of the later Community trade mark was applied for in bad faith.

3. In the cases referred to in paragraphs 1 and 2, the proprietor of a later Community trade mark shall not be entitled to oppose the use of the earlier right, even though that right may no longer be invoked against the later Community trade mark.

Section 4

Consequences of Revocation and Invalidity

Article 54

Consequences of revocation and invalidity

1. The Community trade mark shall be deemed not to have had, as from the date of the application for revocation or of the counterclaim, the effects specified in this Regulation, to the extent that the rights of the proprietor have been revoked. An earlier date, on which one of the grounds for revocation occurred, may be fixed in the decision at the request of one of the parties.

2. The Community trade mark shall be deemed not to have had, as from the outset, the effects specified in this Regulation, to the extent that the trade mark has been declared invalid.

3. Subject to the national provisions relating either to claims for compensation for damage caused by negligence or lack of good faith on the part of the proprietor of the trade mark, or to unjust enrichment, the retroactive effect of revocation or invalidity of the trade mark shall not affect:

(a) any decision on infringement which has acquired the authority of a final decision and been enforced prior to the revocation or invalidity decision;

(b) any contract concluded prior to the revocation or invalidity decision, in so far as it has been performed before that decision; however, repayment, to an extent justified by the circumstances, of sums paid under the relevant contract, may be claimed on grounds of equity.

SECTION 5

Proceedings in the Office in Relation to Revocation or Invalidity

Article 55
Application for revocation or for a declaration of invalidity
1. An application for revocation of the rights of the proprietor of a Community trade mark or for a declaration that the trade mark is invalid may be submitted to the Office:

(a) where Articles 50 and 51 apply, by any natural or legal person and any group or body set up for the purpose of representing the interests of manufacturers, producers, suppliers of services, traders or consumers, which under the terms of the law governing it has the capacity in its own name to sue and be sued;

(b) where Article 52 (1) applies, by the persons referred to in Article 42 (1);

(c) where Article 52 (2) applies, by the owners of the earlier rights referred to in that provision or by the persons who are entitled under the law of the Member State concerned to exercise the rights in question.

2. The application shall be filed in a written reasoned statement. It shall not be deemed to have been filed until the fee has been paid.

3. An application for revocation or for a declaration of invalidity shall be inadmissible if an application relating to the same subject matter and cause of action, and involving the same parties, has been adjudicated on by a court in a Member State and has acquired the authority of a final decision.

Article 56
Examination of the application
1. In the examination of the application for revocation of rights or for a declaration of invalidity, the Office shall invite the parties, as often as necessary, to file observations, within a period to be fixed by the Office, on communications from the other parties or issued by itself.

2. If the proprietor of the Community trade mark so requests, the proprietor of an earlier Community trade mark, being a party to the invalidity proceedings, shall furnish proof that, during the period of five years preceding the date of the application for a declaration of invalidity, the earlier Community trade mark has been put to genuine use in the Community in connection with the goods or services in respect of which it is registered and which he cites as justification for his application, or that there are proper reasons for non-use, provided the earlier Community trade mark has at that date been registered for non-use, provided the earlier Community trade mark has at that date been registered for not less than five years. If, at the date on which the Community trade mark application was published, the earlier Community trade mark had been registered for not less than five years, the proprietor of the earlier Community trade mark shall

furnish proof that, in addition, the conditions contained in Article 43 (2) were satisfied at that date. In the absence of proof to this effect the application for a declaration of invalidity shall be rejected. If the earlier Community trade mark has been used in relation to part only of the goods or services for which it is registered it shall, for the purpose of the examination of the application for a declaration of invalidity, be deemed to be registered in respect only of that part of the goods or services.

3. Paragraph 2 shall apply to earlier national trade marks referred to in Article 8 (2) (a), by substituting use in the Member State in which the earlier national trade mark is protected for use in the Community.

4. The Office may, if it thinks fit, invite the parties to make a friendly settlement.

5. If the examination of the application for revocation of rights or for a declaration of invalidity reveals that the trade mark should not have been registered in respect of some or all of the goods or services for which it is registered, the rights of the proprietor of the Community trade mark shall be revoked or it shall be declared invalid in respect of those goods or services. Otherwise the application for revocation of rights or for a declaration of invalidity shall be rejected.

6. The decision revoking the rights of the proprietor of the Community trade mark or declaring it invalid shall be entered in the Register upon becoming final.

Title VII

Appeals

Article 57
Decisions subject to appeal
1. An appeal shall lie from decisions of the examiners, Opposition Divisions, Administration of Trade Marks and Legal Devision and Cancellation Divisions. It shall have suspensive effect.

2. A decision which does not terminate proceedings as regards one of the parties can only be appealed together with the final decision, unless the decision allows separate appeal.

Article 58
Persons entitled to appeal and to be parties to appeal proceedings
Any party to proceedings adversely affected by a decision may appeal. Any other parties to the proceedings shall be parties to the appeal proceedings as of right.

Article 59

Time limit and form of appeal

Notice of appeal must be filed in writing at the Office within two months after the date of notification of the decision appealed from. The notice shall be deemed to have been filed only when the fee for appeal has been paid. Within four months after the date of notification of the decision, a written statement setting out the grounds of appeal must be filed.

Article 60

Interlocutory revision

1. If the department whose decision is contested considers the appeal to be admissible and well founded, it shall rectify its decision. This shall not apply where the appellant is opposed by another party to the proceedings.

2. If the decision is not rectified within one month after receipt of the statement of grounds, the appeal shall be remitted to the Board of Appeal without delay, and without comment as to its merit.

Article 61

Examination of appeals

1. If the appeal is admissible, the Board of Appeal shall examine whether the appeal is allowable.

2. In the examination of the appeal, the Board of Appeal shall invite the parties, as often as necessary, to file observations, within a period to be fixed by the Board of Appeal, on communications from the other parties or issued by itself.

Article 62

Decisions in respect of appeals

1. Following the examination as to the allowability of the appeal, the Board of Appeal shall decide on the appeal. The Board of Appeal may either exercise any power within the competence of the department which was responsible for the decision appealed or remit the case to that department for further prosecution.

2. If the Board of Appeal remits the case for further prosecution to the department whose decision was appealed, that department shall be bound by the ratio decidendi of the Board of Appeal, in so far as the facts are the same.

3. The decisions of the Boards of Appeal shall take effect only as from the date of expiration of the period referred to in Article 63 (5) or, if an action has been brought before the Court of Justice within that period, as from the date of rejection of such action.

Article 63

Actions before the Court of Justice

1. Actions may be brought before the Court of Justice against decisions of the Boards of Appeal on appeals.

2. The action may be brought on grounds of lack of competence, infringement of an essential procedural requirement, infringement of the Treaty, of this Regulation or of any rule of law relating to their application or misuse of power.

3. The Court of Justice has jurisdiction to annul or to alter the contested decision.

4. The action shall be opened to any party to proceedings before the Board of Appeal adversely affected by its decision.

5. The action shall be brought before the Court of Justice within two months of the date of notification of the decision of the Board of Appeal.

6. The Office shall be required to take the necessary measures to comply with the judgement of the Court of Justice.

TITLE VIII

Community Collective Marks

Article 64

Community collective marks

1. A Community collective mark shall be a Community trade mark which is described as such when the mark is applied for and is capable of distinguishing the goods or services of the members of the association which is the proprietor of the mark from those of other undertakings. Associations of manufacturers, producers, suppliers of services, or traders which, under the terms of the law governing them, have the capacity in their own name to have rights and obligations of all kinds, to make contracts or accomplish other legal acts and to sue and be sued, as well as legal persons governed by public law, may apply for Community collective marks.

2. In derogation from Article 7 (1) (c), signs or indications which may serve, in trade, to designate the geographical origin of the goods or services may constitute Community collective marks within the meaning of paragraph 1. A collective mark shall not entitle the proprietor to prohibit a third party from using in the course of trade such signs or indications, provided he uses them in accordance with honest practices in industrial or commercial matters; in particular, such a mark may not be invoked against a third party who is entitled to use a geographical name.

3. The provisions of this Regulation shall apply to Community collective marks, unless Articles 65 to 72 provide otherwise.

Article 65
Regulations governing use of the mark
1. An applicant for a Community collective mark must submit regulations governing its use within the period prescribed.

2. The regulations governing use shall specify the persons authorized to use the mark, the conditions of membership of the association and, where they exist, the conditions of use of the mark including sanctions. The regulations governing use of a mark referred to in Article 64 (2) must authorize any person whose goods or services originate in the geographical area concerned to become a member of the association which is the proprietor of the mark.

Article 66
Refusal of the application
1. In addition to the grounds for refusal of a Community trade mark application provided for in Articles 36 and 38, an application for a Community collective mark shall be refused where the provisions of Article 64 or 65 are not satisfied, or where the regulations governing use are contrary to public policy or to accepted principles of morality.

2. An application for a Community collective mark shall also be refused if the public is liable to be misled as regards the character or the significance of the mark, in particular if it is likely to be taken to be something other than a collective mark.

3. An application shall not be refused if the applicant, as a result of amendment of the regulations governing use, meets the requirements of paragraphs 1 and 2.

Article 67
Observations by third parties
Apart from the cases mentioned in Article 41, any person, group or body referred to in that Article may submit to the Office written observations based on the particular grounds on which the application for a Community collective mark should be refused under the terms of Article 66.

Article 68
Use of marks
Use of a Community collective mark by any person who has authority to use it shall satisfy the requirements of this Regulation, provided that the other conditions which this Regulation imposes with regard to the use of Community trade marks are fulfilled.

Article 69
Amendment of the regulations governing use of the mark
1. The proprietor of a Community collective mark must submit to the Office any amended regulations governing use.

2. The amendment shall not be mentioned in the Register if the amended regulations do not satisfy the requirements of Article 65 or involve one of the grounds for refusal referred to in Article 66.

3. Article 67 shall apply to amended regulations governing use.

4. For the purposes of applying this Regulation, amendments to the regulations governing use shall take effect only from the date of entry of the mention of the amendment in the Register.

Article 70
Persons who are entitled to bring an action for infringement
1. The provisions of Article 22 (3) and (4) concerning the rights of licensees shall apply to every person who has authority to use a Community collective mark.

2. The proprietor of a Community collective mark shall be entitled to claim compensation on behalf of persons who have authority to use the mark where they have sustained damage in consequence of unauthorized use of the mark.

Article 71
Grounds for revocation
Apart from the grounds for revocation provided for in Article 50, the rights of the proprietor of a Community collective mark shall be revoked on application to the Office or on the basis of a counterclaim in infringement proceedings, if:

(a) the proprietor does not take reasonable steps to prevent the mark being used in a manner incompatible with the conditions of use, where these exist, laid down in the regulations governing use, amendments to which have, where appropriate, been mentioned in the Register;

(b) the manner in which the mark has been used by the proprietor has caused it to become liable to mislead the public in the manner referred to in Article 66 (2);

(c) an amendment to the regulations governing use of the mark has been mentioned in the Register in breach of the provisions of Article 69 (2), unless the proprietor of the mark, by further amending the regulations governing use, complies with the requirements of those provisions.

Article 72
Grounds for invalidity
Apart from the grounds for invalidity provided for in Articles 51 and 52, a Community collective mark which is registered in breach of the provisions of Article 66 shall be declared invalid on application to the Office or on the basis

of a counterclaim in infringement proceedings, unless the proprietor of the mark, by amending the regulations governing use, complies with the requirements of those provisions.

TITLE IX

Procedure

SECTION 1

General Provisions

Article 73
Statement of reasons on which decisions are based
Decisions of the Office shall state the reasons on which they are based. They shall be based only on reasons or evidence on which the parties concerned have had on opportunity to present their comments.

Article 74
Examination of the facts by the Office of its own motion
1. In proceedings before it the Office shall examine the facts of its own motion; however, in proceedings relating to relative grounds for refusal of registration, the Office shall be restricted in this examination to the facts, evidence and arguments provided by the parties and the relief sought.

2. The Office may disregard facts or evidence which are not submitted in due time by the parties concerned.

Article 75
Oral proceedings
1. If the Office considers that oral proceedings would be expedient they shall be held either at the instance of the Office or at the request of any party to the proceedings.

2. Oral proceedings before the examiners, the Opposition Division and the Administration of Trade Marks and Legal Division shall not be public.

3. Oral proceedings, including delivery of the decision, shall be public before the Cancellation Division and the Boards of Appeal, in so far as the department before which the proceedings are taking place does not decide otherwise in cases where admission of the public could have serious and unjustified disadvantages, in particular for a party to the proceedings.

Article 76
Taking of evidence
1. In any proceedings before the Office, the means of giving or obtaining evidence shall include the following:

(a) hearing the parties;
(b) requests for information;
(c) the production of documents and items of evidence;
(d) hearing witnesses;
(e) opinions by experts;
(f) statements in writing sworn or affirmed or having a similar effect under the law of the State in which the statement is drawn up.

2. The relevant department may commission one of its members to examine the evidence adduced.

3. If the Office considers it necessary for a party, witness or expert to give evidence orally, it shall issue a summons to the person concerned to appear before it.

4. The parties shall be informed of the hearing of a witness or expert before the Office. They shall have the right to be present and to put questions to the witness or expert.

Article 77
Notification
The Office shall, as a matter of course, notify those concerned of decisions and summonses and of any notice or other communication from which a time limit is reckoned, or of which those concerned must be notified under other provisions of this Regulation or of the Implementing Regulation, or of which notification has been ordered by the President of the Office.

Article 78
Restitutio in integrum
1. The applicant for or proprietor of a Community trade mark or any other party to proceedings before the Office who, in spite of all due care required by the circumstances having been taken, was unable to observe a time limit *vis-à-vis* the Office shall, upon application, have his rights re-established if the non-observance in question has the direct consequence, by virtue of the provisions of this Regulation, of causing the loss of any right or means of redress.

2. The application must be filed in writing within two months from the removal of the cause of non-compliance with the time limit. The omitted act must be completed within this period. The application shall only be admissible within the year immediately following the expiry of the unobserved time limit. In the case of non-submission of the request for renewal of registration or of non-pay-

ment of a renewal fee, the further period of six months provided in Article 47 (3), third sentence, shall be deducted from the period of one year.

3. The application must state the grounds on which it is based and must set out the facts on which it relies. It shall not be deemed to be filed until the fee for re-establishment of rights has been paid.

4. The department competent to decide on the omitted act shall decide upon the application.

5. The provisions of this Article shall not be applicable to the time limits referred to in paragraph 2 of this Article, Articles 29 (1) and 42 (1).

6. Where the applicant for or proprietor of a Community trade mark has his rights re-established, he may not invoke his rights *vis-à-vis* a third party who, in good faith, has put goods on the market or supplied services under a sign which is identical with or similar to the Community trade mark in the course of the period between the loss of rights in the application or in the Community trade mark and publication of the mention of re-establishment of those rights.

7. A third party who may avail himself of the provisions of paragraph 6 may bring third party proceedings against the decision re-establishing the rights of the applicant for or proprietor of a Community trade mark within a period of two months as from the date of publication of the mention of re-establishment of those rights.

8. Nothing in this Article shall limit the right of a Member State to grant restitutio in integrum in respect of time limits provided for in this Regulation and to be observed *vis-à-vis* the authorities of such State.

Article 79
Reference to general principles
In the absence of procedural provisions in this Regulation, the Implementing Regulation, the fees regulations or the rules of procedure of the Boards of Appeal, the Office shall take into account the principles of procedural law generally recognized in the Member States.

Article 80
Termination of financial obligations
1. Rights of the Office to the payment of a fee shall be extinguished after four years from the end of the calendar year in which the fee fell due.

2. Rights against the Office for the refunding of fees or sums of money paid in excess of a fee shall be extinguished after four years from the end of the calendar year in which the right arose.

3. The period laid down in paragraphs 1 and 2 shall be interrupted in the case covered by paragraph 1 by a request for payment of the fee and in the case covered by paragraph 2 by a reasoned claim in writing. On interruption it shall begin again immediately and shall end at the latest six years after the end of the year in which it originally began, unless, in the meantime, judicial proceedings to enforce the right have begun; in this case the period shall end at the earliest one year after the judgement has acquired the authority of a final decision.

Section 2

Costs

Article 81
Costs
1. The losing party in opposition proceedings, proceedings for revocation, proceedings for a declaration of invalidity or appeal proceedings shall bear the fees incurred by the other party as well as all costs, without prejudice to Article 115 (6), incurred by him essential to the proceedings, including travel and subsistence and the remuneration of an agent, adviser or advocate, within the limits of the scales set for each category of costs under the conditions laid down in the Implementing Regulation.

2. However, where each party succeeds on some and fails on other heads, or if reasons of equity so dictate, the Opposition Division, Cancellation Division or Board of Appeal shall decide a different apportionment of costs.

3. The party who terminates the proceedings by withdrawing the Community trade mark application, the opposition, the application for revocation of rights, the application for a declaration of invalidity or the appeal, or by not renewing registration of the Community trade mark or by surrendering the Community trade mark, shall bear the fees and the costs incurred by the other party as stipulated in paragraphs 1 and 2.

4. Where a case does not proceed to judgment the costs shall be at the discretion of the Opposition Division, Cancellation Division or Board of Appeal.

5. Where the parties conclude before the Opposition Division, Cancellation Division or Board of Appeal a settlement of costs differing from that provided for in the preceding paragraphs, the department concerned shall take note of that agreement.

6. On request the registry of the Opposition Division or Cancellation Division or Board of Appeal shall fix the amount of the costs to be paid pursuant to the preceding paragraphs. The amount so determined may be reviewed by a decision

of the Opposition Division or Cancellation Division or Board of Appeal on a request filed within the prescribed period.

Article 82
Enforcement of decisions fixing the amount of costs
1. Any final decision of the Office fixing the amount of costs shall be enforceable.

2. Enforcement shall be governed by the rules of civil procedure in force in the State in the territory of which it is carried out. The order for its enforcement shall be appended to the decision, without other formality than verification of the authenticity of the decision, by the national authority which the Government of each Member State shall designate for this purpose and shall make known to the Office and to the Court of Justice.

3. When these formalities have been completed on application by the party concerned, the latter may proceed to enforcement in accordance with the national law, by bringing the matter directly before the competent authority.

4. Enforcement may be suspended only by a decision of the Court of Justice. However, the courts of the country concerned shall have jurisdiction over complaints that enforcement is being carried out in an irregular manner.

SECTION 3

Information of the Public and of the Official Authorities of the Member States

Article 83
Register of Community trade marks
The Office shall keep a register to the known as the Register of Community trade marks, which shall contain those particulars the registration or inclusion of which is provided for by this Regulation or by the Implementing Regulation. The Register shall be open to public inspection.

Article 84
Inspection of files
1. The files relating to Community trade mark applications which have not yet been published shall not be made available for inspection without the consent of the applicant.

2. Any person who can prove that the applicant for a Community trade mark has stated that after the trade mark has been registered he will invoke the rights under it against him may obtain inspection of the files prior to the publication of that application and without the consent of the applicant.

3. Subsequent to the publication of the Community trade mark application, the files relating to such application and the resulting trade mark may be inspected on request.

4. However, where the files are inspected pursuant to paragraphs 2 or 3, certain documents in the file may be withheld from inspection in accordance with the provisions of the Implementing Regulation.

Article 85
Periodical publications
The Office shall periodically publish:

(a) a Community Trade Marks Bulletin containing entries made in the Register of Community trade marks as well as other particulars the publication of which is prescribed by this Regulation or by the Implementing Regulation;

(b) an Official Journal containing notices and information of a general character issued by the President of the Office, as well as any other information relevant to this Regulation or its implementation.

Article 86
Administrative cooperation
Unless otherwise provided in this Regulation or in national laws, the Office and the courts or authorities of the Member States shall on request give assistance to each other by communicating information or opening files for inspection. Where the Office lays files open to inspection by courts, Public Prosecutors' Offices or central industrial property offices, the inspection shall not be subject to the restrictions laid down in Article 84.

Article 87
Exchange of publications
1. The Office and the central industrial property offices of the Member States shall despatch to each other on request and for their own use one or more copies of their respective publications free of charge.

2. The Office may conclude agreements relating to the exchange or supply of publications.

Section 4

Representation

Article 88
General principles of representation
1. Subject to the provisions of paragraph 2, no person shall be compelled to be represented before the Office.

2. Without prejudice to paragraph 3, second sentence, natural or legal persons not having either their domicile or their principal place of business or a real and effective industrial or commercial establishment in the Community must be represented before the Office in accordance with Article 89 (1) in all proceedings established by this Regulation, other than in filing an application for a Community trade mark; the Implementing Regulation may permit other exceptions.

3. Natural or legal persons having their domicile or principal place of business or a real and effective industrial or commercial establishment in the Community may be represented before the Office by an employee, who must file with it a signed authorization for insertion on the files, the details of which are set out in the Implementing Regulation. An employee of a legal person to which this paragraph applies may also represent other legal persons which have economic connections with the first legal person, even if those other legal persons have neither their domicile nor their principal place of business nor a real and effective industrial or commercial establishment within the Community.

Article 89
Professional representatives
1. Representation of natural or legal persons before the Office may only be undertaken by;

(a) any legal practitioner qualified in one of the Member States and having his place of business within the Community, to the extent that he is entitled, within the said State, to act as a representative in trade mark matters; or

(b) professional representatives whose names appear on the list maintained for this purpose by the Office. Representatives acting before the Office must file with it a signed authorization for insertion on the files, the details of which are set out in the Implementing Regulation.

2. Any natural person who fulfils the following conditions may be entered on the list of professional representatives:

(a) he must be a national of one of the Member States;

(b) he must have his place of business or employment in the Community;

(c) he must be entitled to represent natural or legal persons in trade mark matters before the central industrial property office of the Member State in which he has his place of business or employment. Where, in that State, the entitlement is not conditional upon the requirement of special professional qualifications, persons applying to be entered on the list who act in trade mark matters before the central industrial property office of the said State must have habitually so acted for at least five years. However, persons whose professional qualification to represent natural or legal persons in trade mark matters before the central industrial property office of one of the Member States is officially recognized in accordance with the regulations laid down by such State shall not be subject to the condition of having exercised the profession.

3. Entry shall be effected upon request, accompanied by a certificate furnished by the central industrial property office of the Member State concerned, which must indicate that the conditions laid down in paragraph 2 are fulfilled.

4. The President of the Office may grant exemption from:

(a) the requirement of paragraph 2 (c), second sentence, if the applicant furnishes proof that he has acquired the requisite qualification in another way;

(b) the requirement of paragraph 2 (a) in special circumstances.

5. The conditions under which a person may be removed from the list of professional representatives shall be laid down in the Implementing Regulation.

TITLE X

Jurisdiction and Procedure in Legal Actions relating to Community Trade Marks

SECTION 1

Application of the Convention on Jurisdiction and Enforcement

Article 90

Application of the Convention on Jurisdiction and Enforcement

1. Unless otherwise specified in this Regulation, the Convention on Jurisdiction and the Enforcement of Judgments in Civil and Commercial Matters, signed in Brussels on 27 September 1968, as amended by the Conventions on the Accession to that Convention of the States acceding to the European Communities, the whole of which Convention and of which Conventions of Accession are hereinafter referred to as the "Convention on Jurisdiction and Enforcement", shall apply to proceedings relating to Community trade marks and applications for Community trade marks, as well as to proceedings relating to simultaneous and successive actions on the basis of Community trade marks and national trade marks.

2. In the case of proceedings in respect of the actions and claims referred to in Article 92:

(a) Articles 2, 4, 5 (1), (3), (4) and (5) and Article 24 of the Convention on Jurisdiction and Enforcement shall not apply;

(b) Articles 17 and 18 of that Convention shall apply subject to the limitations in Article 93 (4) of this Regulation.

(c) the provisions of Title II of that Convention which are applicable to persons domiciled in a Member State shall also be applicable to persons who do not have a domicile in any Member State but have an establishment therein.

SECTION 2

Disputes concerning the Infringement and Validity of Community Trade Marks

Article 91
Community trade mark courts
1. The Member States shall designate in their territories as limited a number as possible of national courts and tribunals of first and second instance, hereinafter referred to as "Community trade mark courts", which shall perform the functions assigned to them by this Regulation.

2. Each Member State shall communicate to the Commission within three years of the entry into force of this Regulation a list of Community trade mark courts indicating their names and their territorial jurisdiction.

3. Any change made after communication of the list referred to in paragraph 2 in the number, names or territorial jurisdiction of the courts shall be notified without delay by the Member State concerned to the Commission.

4. The information referred to in paragraphs 2 and 3 shall be notified by the Commission to the Member States and published in the Official Journal of the European Communities.

5. As long as a Member State has not communicated the list as stipulated in paragraph 2, jurisdiction for any proceedings resulting from an action or application covered by Article 92, and for which the courts of that State have jurisdiction under Article 93, shall lie with that court of the State in question which would have jurisdiction *ratione loci* and *ratione materiae* in the case of proceedings relating to a national trade mark registered in that State.

Article 92
Jurisdiction over infringement and validity
The Community trade mark courts shall have exclusive jurisdiction:
(a) for all infringement actions and – if they are permitted under national law – actions in respect of threatened infringement relating to Community trade marks;
(b) for actions for declaration of non-infringement, if they are permitted under national law;
(c) for all actions brought as a result of acts referred to in Article 9 (3), second sentence;
(d) for counterclaims for revocation or for a declaration of invalidity of the Community trade mark pursuant to Article 96.

Article 93
International jurisdiction
1. Subject to the provisions of this Regulation as well as to any provisions of the Convention on Jurisdiction and Enforcement applicable by virtue of Article 90,

proceedings in respect of the actions and claims referred to in Article 92 shall be brought in the courts of the Member State in which the defendant is domiciled or, if he is not domiciled in any of the Member States, in which he has an establishment.

2. If the defendant is neither domiciled nor has an establishment in any of the Member States, such proceedings shall be brought in the courts of the Member State in which the plaintiff is domiciled or, if he is not domiciled in any of the Member States, in which he has an establishment.

3. If neither the defendant nor the plaintiff is so domiciled or has such an establishment, such proceedings shall be brought in the courts of the Member State where the Office has its seat.

4. Notwithstanding the provisions of paragraphs 1, 2 and 3:
(a) Article 17 of the Convention on Jurisdiction and Enforcement shall apply if the parties agree that a different Community trade mark court shall have jurisdiction;
(b) Article 18 of that Convention shall apply if the defendant enters an appearance before a different Community trade mark court.

5. Proceedings in respect of the actions and claims referred to in Article 92, with the exception of actions for a declaration of non-infringement of a Community trade mark, may also be brought in the courts of the Member State in which the act of infringement has been committed or threatened, or in which an act within the meaning of Article 9 (3), second sentence, has been committed.

Article 94
Extent of jurisdiction
1. A Community trade mark court whose jurisdiction is based on Article 93 (1) to (4) shall have jurisdiction in respect of: – acts of infringement committed or threatened within the territory of any of the Member States, – acts within the meaning of Article 9 (3), second sentence, committed within the territory of any of the Member States.

2. A Community trade mark court whose jurisdiction is based on Article 93 (5) shall have jurisdiction only in respect of acts committed or threatened within the territory of the Member State in which that court is situated.

Article 95
Presumption of validity – Defence as to the merits
1. The Community trade mark courts shall treat the Community trade mark as valid unless its validity is put in issue by the defendant with a counterclaim for revocation or for a declaration of invalidity.

2. The validity of a Community trade mark may not be put in issue in an action for a declaration of non-infringement.

3. In the actions referred to in Article 92 (a) and (c) a plea relating to revocation or invalidity of the Community trade mark submitted otherwise than by way of a counterclaim shall be admissible in so far as the defendant claims that the rights of the proprietor of the Community trade mark could be revoked for lack of use or that Community trade mark could be declared invalid on account of an earlier right of the defendant.

Article 96
Counterclaims
1. A counterclaim for revocation or for a declaration of invalidity may only be based on the grounds for revocation or invalidity mentioned in this Regulation.

2. A Community trade mark court shall reject a counterclaim for revocation or for a declaration of invalidity if a decision taken by the Office relating to the same subject matter and cause of action and involving the same parties has already become final.

3. If the counterclaim is brought in a legal action to which the proprietor of the trade mark is not already a party, he shall be informed thereof and may be joined as a party to the action in accordance with the conditions set out in national law.

4. The Community trade mark court with which a counterclaim for revocation or for a declaration of invalidity of the Community trade mark has been filed shall inform the Office of the date on which the counterclaim was filed. The latter shall record this fact in the Register of Community trade marks.

5. Article 56 (3), (4), (5) and (6) shall apply.

6. Where a Community trade mark court has given a judgment which has become final on a counterclaim for revocation or for invalidity of a Community trade mark, a copy of the judgment shall be sent to the Office. Any party may request information about such transmission. The Office shall mention the judgment in the Register of Community trade marks in accordance with the provisions of the Implementing Regulation.

7. The Community trade mark court hearing a counterclaim for revocation or for a declaration of invalidity may stay the proceedings on application by the proprietor of the Community trade mark and after hearing the other parties and may request the defendant to submit an application for revocation or for a declaration of invalidity to the Office within a time limit which it shall determine. If the application is not made within the time limit, the proceedings shall continue; the counterclaim shall be deemed withdrawn. Article 100 (3) shall apply.

Article 97
Applicable law
1. The Community trade mark courts shall apply the provisions of this Regulation.

2. On all matters not covered by this Regulation a Community trade mark court shall apply its national law, including its private international law.

3. Unless otherwise provided in this Regulation, a Community trade mark court shall apply the rules of procedure governing the same type of action relating to a national trade mark in the Member State where it has its seat.

Article 98
Sanctions
1. Where a Community trade mark court finds that the defendant has infringed or threatened to infringe a Community trade mark, it shall, unless there are special reasons for not doing so, issue an order prohibiting the defendant from proceeding with the acts which infringed or would infringe the Community trade mark. It shall also take such measures in accordance with its national law as are aimed at ensuring that this prohibition is complied with.

2. In all other respects the Community trade mark court shall apply the law of the Member State to which the acts of infringement or threatened infringement were committed, including the private international law.

Article 99
Provisional and protective measures
1. Application may be made to the courts of a Member State, including Community trade mark courts, for such provisional, including protective, measures in respect of a Community trade mark or Community trade mark application as may be available under the law of that State in respect of a national trade mark, even if, under this Regulation, a Community trade mark court of another Member State has jurisdiction as to the substance of the matter.

2. A Community trade mark court whose jurisdiction is based on Article 93 (1), (2), (3) or (4) shall have jurisdiction to grant provisional and protective measures which, subject to any necessary procedure for recognition and enforcement pursuant to Title III of the Convention on Jurisdiction and Enforcement, are applicable in the territory of any Member State. No other court shall have such jurisdiction.

Article 100
Specific rules on related actions
1. A Community trade mark court hearing an action referred to in Article 92, other than an action for a declaration of non-infringement shall, unless there are special grounds for continuing the hearing, of its own motion after hearing the

parties or at the request of one of the parties and after hearing the other parties, stay the proceedings where the validity of the Community trade mark is already in issue before another Community trade mark court on account of a counterclaim or where an application for revocation or for a declaration of invalidity has already been filed at the Office.

2. The Office, when hearing an application for revocation or for a declaration of invalidity shall, unless there are special grounds for continuing the hearing, of its own motion after hearing the parties or at the request of one of the parties and after hearing the other parties, stay the proceedings where the validity of the Community trade mark is already in issue on account of a counterclaim before a Community trade mark court. However, if one of the parties to the proceedings before the Community trade mark court so requests, the court may, after hearing the other parties to these proceedings, stay the proceedings. The Office shall in this instance continue the proceedings pending before it.

3. Where the Community trade mark court stays the proceedings it may order provisional and protective measures for the duration of the stay.

Article 101

Jurisdiction of Community trade mark courts of second instance – Further appeal

1. An appeal to the Community trade mark courts of second instance shall lie from judgments of the Community trade mark courts of first instance in respect of proceedings arising from the actions and claims referred to in Article 92.

2. The conditions under which an appeal may be lodged with a Community trade mark court of second instance shall be determined by the national law of the Member State in which that court is located.

3. The national rules concerning further appeal shall be applicable in respect of judgments of Community trade mark courts of second instance.

SECTION 3

Other Disputes Concerning Community Trade Marks

Article 102

Supplementary provisions on the jurisdiction of national courts other than Community trade mark courts

1. Within the Member State whose courts have jurisdiction under Article 90 (1). Those courts shall have jurisdiction for actions other than those referred to in Article 92, which would have jurisdiction *ratione loci* and *ratione materiae* in the case of actions relating to a national trade mark registered in that State.

2. Actions relating to a Community trade mark, other than those referred to in Article 92, for which no court has jurisdiction under Article 90 (1) and paragraph 1 of this Article may be heard before the courts of the Member State in which the Office has its seat.

Article 103
Obligation of the national court
A national court which is dealing with an action relating to a Community trade mark, other than the action referred to in Article 92, shall treat the trade mark as valid.

Section 4

Transitional Provision

Article 104
Transitional provision relating to the application of the Convention on Jurisdiction and Enforcement
The provisions of the Convention on Jurisdiction and Enforcement which are rendered applicable by the preceding Articles shall have effect in respect of any Member State solely in the text of the Convention which is in force in respect of that State at any given time.

Title XI

Effects on the Laws of the Member States

Section 1

Civil Actions on the Basis of more than one Trade Mark

Article 105
Simultaneous and successive civil actions on the basis of Community trade marks and national trade marks
1. Where actions for infringement involving the same cause of action and between the same parties are brought in the courts of different Member States, one seized on the basis of a Community trade mark and the other seized on the basis of a national trade mark:

(a) the court other than the court first seized shall of its own motion decline jurisdiction in favour of that court where the trade marks concerned are identical and valid for identical goods or services. The court which would be required to decline jurisdiction may stay its proceedings if the jurisdiction of the other court is contested;

(b) the court other than the court first seized may stay its proceedings where the trade marks concerned are identical and valid for similar goods or services and where the trade marks concerned are similar and valid for identical or similar goods or services.

2. The court hearing an action for infringement on the basis of a Community trade mark shall reject the action if a final judgment on the merits has been given on the same cause of action and between the same parties on the basis of an identical national trade mark valid for identical goods or services.

3. The court hearing an action for infringement on the basis of a national trade mark shall reject the action if a final judgment on the merits has been given on the same cause of action and between the same parties on the basis of an identical Community trade mark valid for identical goods or services.

4. Paragraphs 1, 2 and 3 shall not apply in respect of provisonal, including protective, measures.

Section 2

Application of National Laws for the Purpose of Prohibiting the Use of Community Trade Marks

Article 106
Prohibition of use of Community trade marks
1. This Regulation shall, unless otherwise provided for, not affect the right existing under the laws of the Member States to invoke claims for infringement of earlier rights within the meaning of Article 8 or Article 52 (2) in relation to the use of a later Community trade mark. Claims for infringement of earlier rights within the meaning of Article 8 (2) and (4) may, however, no longer be invoked if the proprietor of the earlier right may no longer apply for a declaration that the Community trade mark is invalid in accordance with Article 53 (2).

2. This Regulation shall, unless otherwise provided for, not affect the right to bring proceedings under the civil, administrative or criminal law of a Member Sate or under provisions of Community law for the purpose of prohibiting the use of a Community trade mark to the extent that the use of a national trade mark may be prohibited under the law of that Member State or under Community law.

Article 107
Prior rights applicable to particular localities
1. The proprietor of an earlier right which only applies to a particular locality may oppose the use of the Community trade mark in the territory where his right is protected in so far as the law of the Member State concerned so permits.

2. Paragraph 1 shall cease to apply if the proprietor of the earlier right has acquiesced in the use of the Community trade mark in the territory where his right is protected for a period of five successive years, being aware of such use, unless the Community trade mark was applied for in bad faith.

3. The proprietor of the Community trade mark shall not be entitled to oppose use of the right referred to in paragraph 1 even though that right may no longer be invoked against the Community trade mark.

Section 3

Conversion into a National Trade Mark Application

Article 108

Request for the application of national procedure

1. The applicant for or proprietor of a Community trade mark may request the conversion of his Community trade mark application or Community trade mark into a national trade mark application

(a) to the extent that the Community trade mark application is refused, withdrawn, or deemed to be withdrawn;

(b) to the extent that the Community trade mark ceases to have effect.

2. Conversion shall not take place:

(a) where the rights of the proprietor of the Community trade mark have been revoked on the grounds of non-use, unless in the Member State for which conversion is requested the Community trade mark has been put to use which would be considered to be genuine use under the laws of that Member State;

(b) for the purpose of protection in a Member State in which, in accordance with the decision of the Office or of the national court, grounds for refusal of registration or grounds for revocation or invalidity apply to the Community trade mark application or Community trade mark.

3. The national trade mark application resulting from the conversion of a Community trade mark application or a Community trade mark shall enjoy in respect of the Member State concerned the date of filing or the date of priority of that application or trade mark and, where appropriate, the seniority of a trade mark of that State claimed under Article 34 or 35.

4. Where:

- the Community trade mark application is deemed to be withdrawn or is refused by a decision of the Office which has become final,
- the Community trade mark ceases to have effect as a result of a decision of the Office which has become final or as a result of registration of surrender of the Community trade mark,

- the Office shall notify to the applicant or proprietor a communication fixing a period of three months from the date of that communication in which a request for conversion may be filed.

5. Where the Community trade mark application is withdrawn or the Community trade mark ceases to have effect as a result of failure to renew the registration, the request for conversion shall be filed within three months after the date on which the Community trade mark application is withdrawn or on which the registration of the Community trade mark expires.

6. Where the Community trade mark ceases to have effect as a result of a decision of a national court, the request for conversion shall be filed within three months after the date on which that decision acquired the authority of a final decision.

7. The effect referred to in Article 32 shall lapse if the request is not filed in due time.

Article 109
Submission, publication and transmission of the request for conversion
1. A request for conversion shall be filed with the Office and shall specify the Member States in which application of the procedure for registration of a national trade mark is desired. The request shall not be deemed to be filed until the conversion fee has been paid.

2. If the Community trade mark application has been published, receipt of any such request shall be recorded in the Register of Community trade marks and the request for conversion shall be published.

3. The Office shall check whether conversion may be requested in accordance with Article 108 (1), whether the request has been filed within the period laid down in Article 108 (4), (5) or (6), as the case may be, and whether the conversion fee has been paid. If these conditions are fulfilled, the Office shall transmit the request to the central industrial property offices of the States specified therein. At the request of the central industrial property office of a State concerned, the Office shall give it any information enabling that office to decide as to the admissibility of the request.

Article 110
Formal requirements for conversion
1. Any central industrial property office to which the request is transmitted shall decide as to its admissibility,

2. A Community trade mark application or a Community trade mark transmitted in accordance with Article 109 shall not be subjected to formal requirements

of national law which are different from or additional to those provided for in this Regulation or in the Implementing Regulation.

3. Any central industrial property office to which the request is transmitted may require that the applicant shall, within not less than two months:

(a) pay the national application fee;

(b) file a translation in one of the official languages of the State in question of the request and of the documents accompanying it;

(c) indicate an address for service in the State in question;

(d) supply a representation of the trade mark in the number of copies specified by the State in question.

Title XII

The Office

Section 1

General Provisions

Article 111
Legal status
1. The Office shall be a body of the Community. It shall have legal personality.

2. In each of the Member States the Office shall enjoy the most extensive legal capacity accorded to legal persons under their laws; it may, in particular, acquire or dispose of movable and immovable property and may be a party to legal proceedings.

3. The Office shall be represented by its President.

Article 112
Staff
1. The Staff Regulations of officials of the European Communities, the Conditions of Employment of other servants of the European Communities, and the rules adopted by agreement between the Institutions of the European Communities for giving effect to those Staff Regulations and Conditions of Employment shall apply to the staff of the Office, without prejudice to the application of Article 131 to the members of the Boards of Appeal.

2. Without prejudice to Article 120, the powers conferred on each Institution by the Staff Regulations and by the Conditions of Employment of other servants shall be exercised by the Office in respect of its staff.

Article 113
Privileges and immunities
The Protocol on the Privileges and Immunities of the European Communities shall apply to the Office.

Article 114
Liability
1. The contractual liability of the Office shall be governed by the law applicable to the contract in question.

2. The Court of Justice shall be competent to give judgment pursuant to any arbitration clause contained in a contract concluded by the Office.

3. In the case of non-contractual liability, the Office shall, in accordance with the general principles common to the laws of the Member States, make good any damage caused by its departments or by its servants in the performance of their duties.

4. The Court of Justice shall have jurisdiction in disputes relating to compensation for the damage referred to in paragraph 3.

5. The personal liability of its servants towards the Office shall be governed by the provisions laid down in their Staff Regulations or in the Conditions of Employment applicable to them.

Article 115
Languages
1. The application for a Community trade mark shall be filed in one of the official languages of the European Community.

2. The languages of the Office shall be English, French, German, Italian and Spanish.

3. The applicant must indicate a second language which shall be a language of the Office the use of which he accepts as a possible language of proceedings for opposition, revocation or invalidity proceedings. If the application was filed in a language which is not one of the languages of the Office, the Office shall arrange to have the application, as described in Article 26 (1), translated into the language indicated by the applicant.

4. Where the applicant for a Community trade mark is the sole party to proceedings before the Office, the language of proceedings shall be the language used for filing the application for a Community trade mark. If the application was made in a language other than the languages of the Office, the Office may send written communications to the applicant in the second language indicated by the applicant in his application.

5. The notice of opposition and an application for revocation or invalidity shall be filed in one of the languages of the Office.

6. If the language chosen, in accordance with paragraph 5, for the notice of opposition or the application for revocation or invalidity is the language of the application for a trade mark or the second language indicated when the application was filed, that language shall be the language of the proceedings. If the language chosen, in accordance with paragraph 5, for the notice of opposition or the application for revocation or invalidity is neither the language of the application for a trade mark nor the second language indicated when the application was filed, the opposing party or the party seeking revocation or invalidity shall be required to produce, at his own expense, a translation of his application either into the language of the application for a trade mark, provided that it is a language of the Office, or into the second language indicated when the application was filed. The translation shall be produced within the period prescribed in the implementing regulation. The language into which the application has been translated shall then become the language of the proceedings.

7. Parties to opposition, revocation, invalidity or appeal proceedings may agree that a different official language of the European Community is to be the language of the proceedings.

Article 116
Publication; entries in the Register
1. An application for a Community trade mark, as described in Article 26 (1), and all other information the publication of which is prescribed by this Regulation or the implementing regulation, shall be published in all the official languages of the European Community.

2. All entries in the Register of Community trade marks shall be made in all the official languages of the European Community.

3. In cases of doubt, the text in the language of the Office in which the application for the Community trade mark was filed shall be authentic. If the application was filed in an official language of the European Community other than one of the languages of the Office, the text in the second language indicated by the applicant shall be authentic.

Article 117
The translation services required for the functioning of the Office shall be provided by the Translation Centre of the Bodies of the Union once this begins operation.

Article 118
Control of legality
1. The Commission shall check the legality of those acts of the President of the Office in respect of which Community law does not provide for any check on legality by another body and of acts of the Budget Committee attached to the Office pursuant to Article 133.

2. It shall require that any unlawful acts as referred to in paragraph 1 be altered or annulled.

3. Member States and any person directly and personally involved may refer to the Commission any act as referred to in paragraph 1, whether express or implied, for the Commission to examine the legality of that act. Referral shall be made to the Commission within 15 days of the day on which the party concerned first became aware of the act in question. The Commission shall take a decision within one month. If no decision has been taken within this period, the case shall be deemed to have been dismissed.

Section 2

Management of the Office

Article 119
Powers of the President
1. The Office shall be managed by the President.

2. To this end the President shall have in particular the following functions and powers:

(a) he shall take all necessary steps, including the adoption of internal administrative instructions and the publication of notices, to ensure the functioning of the Office;

(b) he may place before the Commission any proposal to amend this Regulation, the Implementing Regulation, the rules of procedure of the Boards of Appeal, the fees regulations and any other rules applying to Community trade marks after consulting the Administrative Board and, in the case of the fees regulations and the budgetary provisions of this Regulation, the Budget Committee;

(c) he shall draw up the estimates of the revenue and expenditure of the Office and shall implement the budget;

(d) he shall submit a management report to the Commission, the European Parliament and the Administrative Board each year;

(e) he shall exercise in respect of the staff the powers laid down in Article 112 (2);

(f) he may delegate his powers.

3. The President shall be assisted by one or more Vice-Presidents. If the President is absent or indisposed, the Vice-President or one of the Vice-Presidents shall take his place in accordance with the procedure laid down by the Administrative Board.

Article 120

Appointment of senior officials

1. The President of the Office shall be appointed by the Council from a list of at most three candidates, which shall be prepared by the Administrative Board. Power to dismiss the President shall lie with the Council, acting on a proposal from the Administrative Board.

2. The term of office of the President shall not exceed five years. This term of office shall be renewable.

3. The Vice-President or Vice-Presidents of the Office shall be appointed or dismissed as in paragraph 1, after consultation of the President.

4. The Council shall exercise disciplinary authority over the officials referred to in paragraphs 1 and 3 of this Article.

SECTION 3

Administrative Board

Article 121

Creation and powers

1. An Administrative Board is hereby set up, attached to the Office. Without prejudice to the powers attributed to the Budget Committee in Section 5 – budget and financial control – the Administrative Board shall have the powers defined below.

2. The Administrative Board shall draw up the lists of candidates provided for in Article 120.

3. It shall fix the date for the first filing of Community trade mark applications, pursuant to Article 143 (3).

4. It shall advise the President on matters for which the Office is responsible.

5. It shall be consulted before adoption of the guidelines for examination in the Office and in the other cases provided for in this Regulation.

6. It may deliver opinions and requests for information to the President and to the Commission where it considers that this is necessary.

Article 122
Composition
1. The Administrative Board shall be composed of one representative of each Member State and one representative of the Commission and their alternates.

2. The members of the Administrative Board may, subject to the provisions of its rules of procedure, be assisted by advisers or experts.

Article 123
Chairmanship
1. The Administrative Board shall elect a chairman and a deputy chairman from among its members. The deputy chairman shall ex officio replace the chairman in the event of his being prevented from attending to his duties.

2. The duration of the terms of office of the chairman and the deputy chairman shall be three years. The terms of office shall be renewable.

Article 124
Meetings
1. Meetings of the Administrative Board shall be convened by its chairman.

2. The President of the Office shall take part in the deliberations, unless the Administrative Board decides otherwise.

3. The Administrative Board shall hold an ordinary meeting once a year; in addition, it shall meet on the initiative of its chairman or at the request of the Commission or of one-third of the Member States.

4. The Administrative Board shall adopt rules of procedure.

5. The Administrative Board shall take its decisions by a simple majority of the representatives of the Member States. However, a majority of three-quarters of the representatives of the Member States shall be required for the decisions which the Administrative Board is empowered to take under Article 120 (1) and (3). In both cases each Member State shall have one vote.

6. The Administrative Board may invite observers to attend its meetings.

7. The Secretariat for the Administrative Board shall be provided by the Office.

Section 4

Implementation of Procedures

Article 125
Competence
For taking decisions in connection with the procedures laid down in this Regulation, the following shall be competent:

(a) Examiners;
(b) Opposition Divisions;
(c) an Administration of Trade Marks and Legal Division;
(d) Cancellation Divisions;
(e) Boards of Appeal.

Article 126
Examiners
An examiner shall be responsible for taking decisions on behalf of the Office in relation to an application for registration of a Community trade mark, including the matters referred to in Articles 36, 37, 38 and 66, except in so far as an Opposition Division is responsible.

Article 127
Opposition Divisions
1. An Opposition Division shall be responsible for taking decisions on an opposition to an application to register a Community trade mark.

2. An Opposition Division shall consist of three members. At least one of the members must be legally qualified.

Article 128
Administration of Trade Marks and Legal Division
1. The Administration of Trade Marks and Legal Division shall be responsible for those decisions required by this Regulation which do not fall within the competence of an examiner, an Opposition Division or a Cancellation Division. It shall in particular be responsible for decisions in respect of entries in the Register of Community trade marks.

2. It shall also be responsible for keeping the list of professional representatives which is referred to in Article 89.

3. A decision of the Division shall be taken by one member.

Article 129
Cancellation Divisions
1. A Cancellation Division shall be responsible for taking decisions in relation to an application for the revocation or declaration of invalidity of a Community trade mark.

2. A Cancellation Division shall consist of three members. At least one of the members must be legally qualified.

Article 130
Boards of Appeal
1. The Boards of Appeal shall be responsible for deciding on appeals from decisions of the examiners, Opposition Divisions, Administration of Trade Marks and Legal Division and Cancellation Divisions.

2. A Board of Appeal shall consist of three members. At least two of the members must be legally qualified.

Article 131
Independence of the members of the Boards of Appeal
1. The members, including the chairmen, of the Boards of Appeal shall be appointed, in accordance with the procedure laid down in Article 120, for the appointment of the President of the Office, for a term of five years. They may not be removed from office during this term, unless there are serious grounds for such removal and the Court of Justice, on application by the body which appointed them, takes a decision to this effect. Their term of office shall be renewable.

2. The members of the Boards of Appeal shall be independent. In their decisions they shall not be bound by any instructions.

3. The members of the Boards of Appeal may not be examiners or members of the Opposition Divisions, Administration of Trade Marks and Legal Division or Cancellation Divisions.

Article 132
Exclusion and objection
1. Examiners and members of the Divisions set up within the Office or of the Boards of Appeal may not take part in any proceedings if they have any personal interest therein, or if they have previously been involved as representatives of one of the parties. Two of the three members of an Opposition Division shall not have taken part in examining the application. Members of the Cancellation Divisions may not take part in any proceedings if they have participated in the final decision on the case in the proceedings for registration or opposition proceedings. Members of the Boards of Appeal may not take part in appeal proceedings if they participated in the decision under appeal.

2. If, for one of the reasons mentioned in paragraph 1 or for any other reason, a member of a Division or of a Board of Appeal considers that he should not take part in any proceedings, he shall inform the Division or Board accordingly.

3. Examiners and members of the Divisions or of a Board of Appeal may be objected to by any party for one of the reasons mentioned in paragraph 1, or if suspected of partiality. An objection shall not be admissible if, while being aware of a reason for objection, the party has taken a procedural step. No objection may be based upon the nationality of examiners or members.

4. The Divisions and the Boards of Appeal shall decide as to the action to be taken in the cases specified in paragraphs 2 and 3 without the participation of the member concerned. For the purposes of taking this decision the member who withdraws or has been objected to shall be replaced in the Division or Board of Appeal by his alternate.

Section 5

Budget and Financial Control

Article 133
Budget Committee
1. A Budget Committee is hereby set up, attached to the Office. The Budget Committee shall have the powers assigned to it in this Section and in Article 39 (4).

2. Articles 121 (6), 122, 123 and 124 (1) to (4), (6) and (7) shall apply to the Budget Committee *mutatis mutandis*.

3. The Budget Committee shall take its decisions by a simple majority of the representatives of the Member States. However, a majority of three-quarters of the representatives of the Member States shall be required for the decisions which the Budget Committee is empowered to take under Articles 39 (4), 135 (3) and 138. In both cases each Member State shall have one vote.

Article 134
Budget
1. Estimates of all the Office's revenue and expenditure shall be prepared for each financial year and shall be shown in the Office's budget, and each financial year shall correspond with the calendar year.

2. The revenue and expenditure shown in the budget shall be in balance.

3. Revenue shall comprise, without prejudice to other types of income, total fees payable under the fees regulations, and, to the extent necessary, a subsidy entered against a specific heading of the general budget of the European Communities, Commission Section.

Article 135
Preparation of the budget
1. The President shall draw up each year an estimate of the Office's revenue and expenditure for the following year and shall send it to the Budget Committee not later than 31 March in each year, together with a list of posts.

2. Should the budget estimates provide for a Community subsidy, the Budget Committee shall immediately forward the estimate to the Commission, which shall forward it to the budget authority of the Communities. The Commission may attach an opinion on the estimate along with an alternative estimate.

3. The Budget Committee shall adopt the budget, which shall include the Office's list of posts. Should the budget estimates contain a subsidy from the general budget of the Communities, the Office's budget shall, if necessary, be adjusted.

Article 136
Financial control
Control of commitment and payment of all expenditure and control of the existence and recovery of all revenue of the Office shall be carried out by the Financial Controller appointed by the Budget Committee.

Article 137
Auditing of accounts
1. Not later than 31 March in each year the President shall transmit to the Commission, the European Parliament, the Budget Committee and the Court of Auditors accounts of the Office's total revenue and expenditure for the preceding financial year. The Court of Auditors shall examine them in accordance with Article 188c of the Treaty.

2. The Budget Committee shall give a discharge to the President of the Office in respect of the implementation of the budget.

Article 138
Financial provisions
The Budget Committee shall, after consulting the Court of Auditors of the European Communities and the Commission, adopt internal financial provisions specifying, in particular, the procedure for establishing and implementing the Office's budget. As far as is compatible with the particular nature of the Office, the financial provisions shall be based on the financial regulations adopted for other bodies set up by the Community.

Article 139
Fees regulations
1. The fees regulations shall determine in particular the amounts of the fees and the ways in which they are to be paid.

2. The amounts of the fees shall be fixed at such a level as to ensure that the revenue in respect thereof is in principle sufficient for the budget of the Office to be balanced.

3. The fees regulations shall be adopted and amended in accordance with the procedure laid down in Article 141.

Title XIII

Final Provisions

Article 140
Community implementing provisions
1. The rules implementing this Regulation shall be adopted in an Implementing Regulation.

2. In addition to the fees provided for in the preceding Articles, fees shall be charged, in accordance with the detailed rules of application laid down in the Implementing Regulation, in the cases listed below:

1. alteration of the representation of a Community trade mark;
2. late payment of the registration fee;
3. issue of a copy of the certificate of registration;
4. registration of the transfer of a Community trade mark;
5. registration of a licence or another right in respect of a Community trade mark;
6. registration of a licence or another right in respect of an application for a Community trade mark;
7. cancellation of the registration of a licence or another right;
8. alteration of a registered Community trade mark;
9. issue of an extract from the Register;
10. inspection of the files;
11. issue of copies of file documents;
12. issue of certified copies of the application;
13. communication of information in a file;
14. review of the determination of the procedural costs to be refunded.

3. The Implementing Regulation and the rules of procedure of the Boards of Appeal shall be adopted and amended in accordance with the procedure laid down in Article 141.

Article 141

Establishment of a committee and procedure for the adoption of implementing regulations

1. The Commission shall be assisted by a Committee on Fees, Implementation Rules and the Procedure of the Boards of Appeal of the Office for Harmonization in the Internal Market (trade marks and designs), which shall be composed of representatives of the Member States and chaired by a representative of the Commission.

2. The representative of the Commission shall submit to the Committee a draft of the measures to be taken. The Committee shall deliver its opinion on the draft within a time limit which the chairman may lay down according to the urgency of the matter. The opinion shall be delivered by the majority laid down in Article 148 (2) of the Treaty in the case of decisions which the Council is required to adopt on a proposal from the Commission. The votes of the representatives of the Member States within the Committee shall be weighted in the manner set out in that Article. The chairman shall not vote. The Commission shall adopt the measures envisaged if they are in accordance with the opinion of the Committee. If the measures envisaged are not in accordance with the opinion of the Committee, or if no opinion is delivered, the Commission shall, without delay, submit to the Council a proposal relating to the measures to be taken. The Council shall act by a qualified majority. If, on the expiry of a period of three months from the date of referral to the Council, the Council has not acted, the proposed measures shall be adopted by the Commission, save where the Council has decided against the measures by a simple majority.

Article 142

Compatibility with other Community legal provisions This Regulation shall not affect Council Regulation (EEC) No. 2081/92 on the protection of geographical indications and designations of origin for agricultural products and foodstuffs[7] of 14 July 1992, and in particular Article 14 thereof.

Article 143

Entry into force

1. This Regulation shall enter into force on the 60th day following that of its publication in the Official Journal of the European Communities.

2. The Member States shall within three years following entry into force of this Regulation take the necessary measures for the purpose of implementing Articles 91 and 110 hereof and shall forthwith inform the Commission of those measures.

[7] OJ No. L 208, 24.7.1992, p. 1.

3. Applications for Community trade marks may be filed at the Office from the date fixed by the Administrative Board on the recommendation of the president of the Office.

4. Applications for the Community trade marks filed within three months before the date referred to in paragraph 3 shall be deemed to have been filed on that date.

This Regulation shall be binding in its entirety and directly applicable in all Member States.

Done at Brussels, 20 December 1993.

For the Council
The President
A. BOURGEOIS

Statement by the council and the Commission on the seat of the Office for Harmonization in the Internal Market (trade marks and designs)

'In adopting the Regulation on the Community Trade Mark, the Council and the Commission note:

– that the representatives of the Governments of the Member States, meeting at Head of State and Government level on 29 October 1993, decided that the Office for Harmonization in the Internal Market (trade marks and designs) should have its seat in Spain, in a town to be determined by the Spanish Government;
– that the Spanish Government has designated Alicante as the seat of the Office.'

Commission Regulation (EC) No. 2868/95

of 13 December 1995
implementing Council Regulation (EC) No. 40/94 on the Community trade mark

THE COMMISSION OF THE EUROPEAN COMMUNITIES,

Having regard to the Treaty establishing the European Community,

Having regard to Council Regulation (EC) No. 40/94 of 20 December 1993 on the Community trade mark[1] as amended by Regulation (EC) No. 3288/94,[2] and in particular Article 140 thereof,

Whereas Regulation (EC) No. 40/94 (hereinafter "the Regulation") creates a new trade mark system allowing a trade mark having effect throughout the Community to be obtained on the basis of an application to the Office for Harmonization in the Internal Market (trade marks and designs) ("the Office");

Whereas for this purpose, the Regulation contains the necessary provisions for a procedure leading to the registration of a Community trade mark, as well as for the administration of Community trade marks, for appeals against decisions of the Office and for proceedings for the revocation or invalidation of a Community trade mark;

Whereas Article 140 of the Regulation provides that the rules implementing the Regulation shall be adopted in an implementing regulation;

Whereas the implementing regulation is to be adopted in accordance with the procedure laid down in Article 141 of the Regulation;

Whereas this implementing regulation therefore lays down the rules necessary for implementing the provisions of the Regulation on the Community trade mark;

Whereas these rules should ensure the smooth and efficient operating of trade mark proceedings before the Office;

Whereas in accordance with Article 116 (1) of the Regulation, all the elements of the application for a Community trade mark specified in its Article 26 (1) as well as any other information the publication of which is prescribed by this implementing regulation should be published in all the official languages of the Community;

[1] OJ No. L 11, 14.1.1994, p. 1.
[2] OJ No. L 349, 31.12.1994, p. 83.

Whereas, however, it is not appropriate for the trade mark itself, names, addresses, dates and any other similar data to be translated and published in all the official languages of the Community;

Whereas the Office should make available standard forms for proceedings before the Office in all official languages of the Community;

Whereas the measures envisaged in this Regulation are in accordance with the opinion of the Committee established under Article 141 of the Regulation,

HAS ADOPTED THIS REGULATION:

Article 1

The rules implementing the Regulation shall be as follows:

TITLE I

Application Procedure

Rule 1

Content of the application

1. The application for a Community trade mark shall contain:

(a) a request for registration of the mark as a Community trade mark;

(b) the name, address and nationality of the applicant and the State in which he is domiciled or has his seat or an establishment. Names of natural persons shall be indicated by the person's family name and given name(s). Names of legal entities, as well as bodies falling under Article 3 of the Regulation, shall be indicated by their official designation, which may be abbreviated in a customary manner; furthermore, the law of the State governing them shall be indicated. The telegraphic and teletype address, telephone as well as fax numbers and details of other data communications links may be given. Only one address shall, in principle, be indicated for each applicant; where several addresses are indicated, only the address mentioned first shall be taken into account, except where the applicant designates one of the addresses as an address for service;

(c) a list of the goods and services for which the trade mark is to be registered, in accordance with Rule 2;

(d) a representation of the mark in accordance with Rule 3;

(e) if the applicant has appointed a representative, his name and the address of his place of business in accordance with point (b); if the representative has more than one business address or if there are two or more representatives with different business addresses, the application shall indicate which address shall be used as an address for service; where such an indication is not made, only the first- mentioned address shall be taken into account as an address for service;

(f) where the priority of a previous application is claimed pursuant to Article 30 of the Regulation, a declaration to that effect, stating the date on which and the country in or for which the previous application was filed;

(g) where exhibition priority is claimed pursuant to Article 33 of the Regulation, a declaration to that effect, stating the name of the exhibition and the date of the first display of the goods or services;

(h) where the seniority of one or more earlier trade marks, registered in a Member State, including a trade mark registered in the Benelux countries or registered under international arrangements having effect in a Member State (hereinafter referred to as "earlier registered trade marks, as referred to in Article 34 of the Regulation") is claimed pursuant to Article 34 of the Regulation, a declaration to that effect, stating the Member State or Member States in or for which the earlier mark is registered, the date from which the relevant registration was effective, the number of the relevant registration, and the goods and services for which the mark is registered;

(i) where applicable, a statement that the application is for registration of a Community collective mark pursuant to Article 64 of the Regulation;

(j) specification of the language in which the application has been filed, and of the second language pursuant to Article 115 (3) of the Regulation;

(k) the signature of the applicant or his representative.

2. The application for a Community collective mark may include the regulations governing its use.

3. The application may include a statement by the applicant that he disclaims any exclusive right to an element of the trade mark which is not distinctive, to be specified by the applicant.

4. If there is more than one applicant, the application may contain the appointment of one applicant or representative as common representative.

Rule 2

List of goods and services

1. The common classification referred to in Article 1 of the Nice Agreement Concerning the International Classification of Goods and Services for the Purposes of the Registration of Marks of 15 June 1957, as revised and amended, shall be applied to the classification of the goods and services.

2. The list of goods and services shall be worded in such a way as to indicate clearly the nature of the goods and services and to allow each item to be classified in only one class of the Nice Classification.

3. The goods and services shall, in principle, be grouped according to the classes of the Nice classification, each group being preceded by the number of the

class of that Classification to which that group of goods or services belongs and presented in the order of the classes under that Classification.

4. The classification of goods and services shall serve exclusively administrative purposes. Therefore, goods and services may not be regarded as being similar to each other on the ground that they appear in the same class under the Nice Classification, and goods and services may not be regarded as being dissimilar from each other on the ground that they appear in different classes under the Nice Classification.

Rule 3

Representation of the mark

1. If the applicant does not wish to claim any special graphic feature or colour, the mark shall be reproduced in normal script, as for example, by typing the letters, numerals and signs in the application. The use of small letters and capital letters shall be permitted and shall be followed accordingly in publications of the mark and in the registration by the Office.

2. In cases other than those referred to in paragraph 1, the mark shall be reproduced on a sheet of paper separate from the sheet on which the text of the application appears. The sheet on which the mark is reproduced shall not exceed DIN A4 size (29,7 cm high, 21 cm wide) and the space used for the reproduction (type-area) shall not be larger than 26,2 cm x 17 cm. A margin of at least 2,5 cm shall be left on the left-hand side. Where it is not obvious, the correct position of the mark shall be indicated by adding the word "top" to each reproduction. The reproduction of the mark shall be of such quality as to enable it to be reduced or enlarged to a size not more than 8 cm wide by 16 cm high for publication in the Community Trade Mark Bulletin. The separate sheet shall also indicate the name and address of the applicant. Four copies of the separate sheet carrying the reproduction shall be filed.

3. In cases to which paragraph 2 applies, the application shall contain an indication to that effect. The application may contain a description of the mark.

4. Where registration of a three-dimensional mark is applied for, the application shall contain an indication to that effect. The representation shall consist of a photographic reproduction or a graphic representation of the mark. The representation may contain up to six different perspectives of the mark.

5. Where registration in colour is applied for, the application shall contain an indication to that effect. The colours making up the mark shall also be indicated. The reproduction under paragraph 2 shall consist of the colour reproduction of the mark.

6. The President of the Office may determine that, as far as the requirements of paragraph 2 are concerned, the mark may be reproduced in the text of the application itself and not on a separate sheet of paper and that the the number of copies of the reproduction of the mark may be less than four.

Rule 4
Fees for the application
The fees payable for the application shall be:
(a) the basic fee; and
(b) a class fee for each class exceeding three to which the goods or services belong according to Rule 2.

Rule 5
Filing of the application
1. The Office shall mark the documents making up the application with the date of its receipt and the file number of the application. The Office shall issue to the applicant without delay a receipt which shall include at least the file number, a representation, description or other identification of the mark, the nature and the number of the documents and the date of their receipt.

2. If the application is filed with the central industrial property office of a Member Sate or at the Benelux Trade Mark Office in accordance with Article 25 of the Regulation, the office of filing shall number all the pages of the application with arabic numerals. Before forwarding, the office of filing shall mark the documents making up the application with the date of receipt and the number of pages. The office of filing shall issue to the applicant without delay a receipt which shall include at least the nature and the number of the documents and the date of their receipt.

3. If the Office receives an application forwarded by the central industrial property office of a Member State or the Benelux Trade Mark Office, it shall mark the application with the date of receipt and the file number and shall issue to the applicant without delay a receipt in accordance with the second sentence of paragraph 1, indicating the date of receipt at the Office.

Rule 6
Claiming priority
1. Where the priority of one or more previous applications pursuant to Article 30 of the Regulation is claimed in the application, the applicant shall indicate the file number of the previous application and file a copy of it within three months from the filing date. The copy shall be certified to be an exact copy of the previous application by the authority which received the previous application, and shall be accompanied by a certificate issued by that authority stating the date of filing of the previous application.

2. Where the applicant wishes to claim the priority of one or more previous applications pursuant to Article 30 of the Regulation subsequent to the filing of the application, the declaration of priority, stating the date on which and the country in or for which the previous application was made, shall be submitted within a period of two months from the filing date. The indications and evidence required under paragraph 1 shall be submitted to the Office within a period of three months from receipt of the declaration of priority.

3. If the language of the previous application is not one of the languages of the Office, the Office shall require the applicant to file, within a period specified by the Office, which shall be not less than three months, a translation of the previous application into one of these languages.

4. The President of the Office may determine that the evidence to be provided by the applicant may consist of less than is required under paragraph 1, provided that the information required is available to the Office from other sources.

Rule 7
Exhibition priority
1. Where the exhibition priority pursuant to Article 33 of the Regulation has been claimed in the application, the applicant shall, within three months from the filing date, file a certificate issued at the exhibition by the authority responsible for the protection of industrial property at the exhibition. This certificate shall declare that the mark was in fact used for the goods or services, and shall state the opening date of the exhibition and, where the first public use did not coincide with the opening date of the exhibition, the date of such first public use. The certificate must be accompanied by an identification of the actual use of the mark, duly certified by the abovementioned authority.

2. Where the applicant wishes to claim an exhibition priority subsequently to the filing of the application, the declaration of priority, indicating the name of the exhibition and the date of the first display of the goods or services, shall be submitted within a period of two months from the filing date. The indications and evidence required under paragraph 1 shall be submitted to the Office within a period of three months from receipt of the declaration of priority.

Rule 8
Claiming the seniority of a national trade mark
1. Where the seniority of one or more earlier registered trade marks, as referred to in Article 34 of the Regulation, has been claimed in the application, the applicant shall, within three months from the filing date, submit a copy of the relevant registration. The copy must be certified by the competent authority to be an exact copy of the relevant registration.

2. Where the applicant wishes to claim the seniority of one or more earlier registered trade marks as referred to in Article 34 of the Regulation, subsequent to the filing of the application, the declaration of seniority, indicating the Member State or Member States in or for which the mark is registered, the date from which the relevant registration was effective, the number of the relevant registration, and the goods and services for which the mark is registered, shall be submitted within a period of two months from the filing date. The evidence required under paragraph 1 shall be submitted to the Office within a period of three months from receipt of the declaration of seniority.

3. The Office shall inform the Benelux Trade Mark Office or the central industrial property office of the Member State concerned of the effective claiming of seniority.

4. The President of the Office may determine that the evidence to be provided by the applicant may consist of less than is required under paragraph 1, provided that the information required is available to the Office from other sources

Rule 9

Examination of requirements for a filing date and of formal requirements

1. If the application fails to meet the requirements for according a filing date because:

(a) the application does not contain:

(i) a request for registration of the mark as a Community trade mark;

(ii) information identifying the applicant;

(iii) a list of the goods and services for which the mark is to be registered;

(iv) a representation of the trade mark; or

(b) the basic fee for the application has not been paid within one month of the filing of the application with the Office or, if the application has been filed with the central industrial property office of a Member State or with the Benelux Trade Mark Office, with that office,

the Office shall notify the applicant that a date of filing cannot be accorded in view of those deficiencies.

2. If the deficiencies referred to under paragraph 1 are remedied within two months of receipt of the notification, the date on which all the deficiencies are remedied shall determine the date of filing. If the deficiencies are not remedied before the time limit expires, the application shall not be dealt with as a Community trade mark application. Any fees paid shall be refunded.

3. Where, although a date of filing has been accorded, the examination reveals that

(a) the requirements of Rules 1, 2 and 3 or the other formal requirements governing applications laid down in the Regulation or in these Rules are not complied with;

(b) the full amount of the class fees payable under Rule 4 (b), read in conjunction with Commission Regulation (EC) No. 2869/95[3] (hereinafter "the Fees Regulation") has not been received by the Office;

(c) where priority has been claimed pursuant to Rules 6 and 7, either in the application itself or within two months after the date of filing, the other requirements of the said Rules are not complied with; or

(d) where seniority has been claimed pursuant to Rule 8, either in the application itself or within two months after the date of filing, the other requirements of Rule 8 are not complied with,

the Office shall invite the applicant to remedy the deficiencies noted within such period as it may specify.

4. If the deficiencies referred to in paragraph 3 (a) are not remedied before the time limit expires, the Office shall reject the application.

5. If the outstanding class fees are not paid before the time limit expires, the application shall be deemed to have been withdrawn, unless it is clear which class or classes the amount paid is intended to cover. In the absence of other criteria to determine which classes are intended to be covered, the Office shall take the classes in the order of the classification. The application shall be deemed to have been withdrawn with regard to those classes for which the class fees have not been paid or have not been paid in full.

6. If the deficiencies referred to in paragraph 3 concern the claim to priority, the right of priority for the application shall be lost.

7. If the deficiencies referred to in paragraph 3 concern the claim to seniority, the right of seniority in respect of that application shall be lost.

8. If the deficiencies referred to in paragraph 3 concern only some of the goods and services, the Office shall refuse the application, or the right of priority or the right of seniority shall be lost, only in so far as those goods and services are concerned.

Rule 10

Examination of the conditions relating to the entitlement to be proprietor

Where, pursuant to Article 5 of the Regulation, the applicant is not entitled to be the proprietor of a Community trade mark, the Office shall notify the applicant thereof. The Office shall specify a period within which the applicant may withdraw the application or submit his observations. Where the applicant fails to overcome the objections to registration, the Office shall refuse the application.

[3] See p. 33 of this Official Journal.

Rule 11

Examination as to absolute grounds for refusal

1. Where, pursuant to Article 7 of the Regulation, the trade mark may not be registered for all or any part of the goods or services applied for, the office shall notify the applicant of the grounds for refusing registration. The Office shall specify a period within which the applicant may withdraw or amend the application or submit his observations.

2. Where, pursuant to Article 38 (2) of the Regulation, registration of the Community trade mark is subject to the applicant's stating that he disclaims any exclusive right in the non-distinctive elements in the mark, the Office shall notify the applicant thereof, stating the reasons, and shall invite him to submit the relevant statement within such period as it may specify.

3. Where the applicant fails to overcome the ground for refusing registration or to comply with the condition laid down in paragraph 2 within the time limit, the Office shall refuse the application in whole or in part.

Rule 12

Publication of the application

The publication of the application shall contain:

(a) the applicant's name and address;

(b) where applicable, the name and business address of the representative appointed by the applicant other than a representative falling within the first sentence of Article 88 (3) of the Regulation; if there is more than one representative with the same business address, only the name and business address of the first-named representative shall be published and it shall be followed by the words "and others"; if there are two or more representatives with different business addresses, only the address for service determined pursuant to Rule 1 1 (e) shall be published; where an association of representatives is appointed under Rule 76 9, only the name and business address of the association shall be published;

(c) the reproduction of the mark, together with the indications and descriptions pursuant to Rule 3; where registration in colour is applied for, the publication shall contain the indication "in colour" and indicate the colour or colours making up the mark;

(d) the list of goods and services, grouped according to the classes of the Nice classification, each group being preceded by the number of the class of that classification to which that group of goods or services belongs, and presented in the order of the classes of that classification;

(e) the date of filing and the number;

(f) where applicable, particulars of the claim of priority pursuant to Article 30 of the Regulation;

(g) where applicable, particulars of the claim of exhibition priority pursuant to Article 33 of the Regulation;

(h) where applicable, particulars of the class of seniority pursuant to Article 34 of the Regulation;

(i) where applicable, a statement that the mark has become distinctive in consequence of the use which has been made of it, pursuant to Article 7 (3) of the Regulation;

(j) where applicable, a statement by the applicant desclaiming any exclusive right to an element of the mark pursuant to Rule 1 3 or Rule 11 2;

(l) the language in which the application was filed and the second language which the applicant has indicated pursuant to Article 115 (3) of the Regulation.

Rule 13

Amendment of the application

1. An applicant for amendment of the application under Article 44 of the Regulation shall contain:

(a) the file number of the application;

(b) the name and the address of the applicant in accordance with Rule 1 1 (b);

(c) where the applicant has appointed a representative, the name and the business address of the representative in accordance with Rule 1 1 (e);

(d) the indication of the element of the application to be corrected or amended, and that amendment in its corrected or amended version;

(e) where the amendment relates to the representation of the mark, a representation of the mark as amended, in accordance with Rule 3.

2. Where the application for amendment is subject to the payment of a fee, the application shall not be deemed to have been filed until the required fee has been paid. If the fee has not been paid in full, the Office shall inform the applicant accordingly.

3. If the requirements governing the amendment of the application are not fulfilled, the Office shall communicate the deficiency to the applicant. If the deficiency is not remedied within a period to be specified by the Office, the Office shall reject the application for amendment.

4. Where the amendment is published pursuant to Article 44 (2) of the Regulation, Rules 15 to 22 shall apply *mutatis mutandis*.

5. A single application for amendment may be made for the amendment of the same element in two or more applications of the same applicant. Where the application for amendment is subject to the payment of a fee, the required fee shall be paid in respect of each application to be amended.

6. Paragraphs 1 to 5 shall apply *mutatis mutandis* for applications to correct the name or the business address of a representative appointed by the applicant. Such applications shall not be subject to the payment of a fee.

Rule 14

Correction of mistakes and errors in publications

1. Where the publication of the application contains a mistake or error attributable to the Office, the Office shall correct the mistake or error acting of its own motion or at the request of the applicant.

2. Where a request as referred to in paragraph 1 is made by the applicant, Rule 13 shall apply *mutatis mutandis*. The request shall not be subject to the payment of a fee.

3. The corrections effected under this Rule shall be published.

4. Article 42 (2) of the Regulation and Rules 15 to 22 shall apply *mutatis mutandis* where the correction concerns the list of goods or services or the representation of the mark.

TITLE II

Procedure for Opposition and Proof of Use

Rule 15

Contents of the notice of opposition

1. Opposition may be entered on the basis of one or more earlier marks within the meaning of Article 8 (2) of the Regulation ("earlier marks") or of one or more other earlier rights within the meaning of Article 8 (4) of the Regulation ("earlier rights")

2. The notice of opposition shall contain:

(a) as concerns the application against which opposition is entered:

(i) the file number of the application against which opposition is entered;

(ii) an indication of the goods and services listed in the Community trade mark application against which opposition is entered;

(iii) the name of the applicant for the Community trade mark;

(b) as concerns the earlier mark or the earlier right on which the opposition is based:

(i) where the opposition is based on an earlier mark, a statement to that effect and an indication that the earlier mark is a Community mark or an indication of the Member State or Member States including, where applicable, the Benelux, where the earlier mark has been registered or applied for, or, where the earlier mark is an internationally registered mark, an indication of the Member State or Member States including, where applicable, the Benelux, to which protection of that earlier mark has been extended;

(ii) where available, the file number or the registration number and the filing date, including the priority date of the earlier mark;

(iii) where the opposition is based on an earlier mark which is a well-known mark within the meaning of Article 8 (2) (c) of the Regulation, an indication to that effect and an indication of the Member State or Member States in which the earlier mark is well-known;
(iv) where the opposition is based on an earlier mark having a reputation within the meaning of Article 8 (5) of the Regulation, an indication to that effect, and an indication of where that earlier mark is registered or applied for in accordance with subparagraph (i).
(v) where the opposition is based on an earlier right, an indication to that effect, and an indication of the Member State or Member States where that earlier right exists;
(vi) a representation and, where appropriate, a description of the earlier mark or earlier right;
(vii) the goods and services in respect of which the earlier mark has been registered or applied for or in respect of which the earlier mark is well-known within the meaning of Article 8 (2) (c) of the Regulation or has a reputation within the meaning of Article 8 (5) of the Regulation; the opposing party shall, when indicating all the goods and services for which the earlier mark is protected, also indicate those goods and services on which the opposition is based;

(c) as concerns the opposing party:

(i) where the opposition is entered by the proprietor of the earlier mark or of the earlier right, his name and address in accordance with Rule 1 1 (b) and an indication that he is the proprietor of such mark or right;
(ii) where opposition is entered by a licensee. the name of the licensee and his address in accordance with Rule 1 1 (b) and an indication that he has been authorized to enter the opposition;
(iii) where the opposition is entered by the successor in title to the registered proprietor of a Community trade mark who has not yet been registered as new proprietor, an indication to that effect, the name and address of the opposing party in accordance with Rule 1 1 (b), and an indication of the date on which the application for registration of the new proprietor was received by the Office or, where this information is not available, was sent to the Office;
(iv) where opposition is entered on the basis of an earlier right by a person who is not the proprietor of that right, the name of the person and his address in accordance with Rule 1 1 (b) and an indication that the is entitled under the relevant national law to exercise that right;
(v) where the opposing party has appointed a representative, the name of the representative and his business in accordance with Rule 1 1 (e);

(d) a specification of the grounds on which the opposition is based.

3. Paragraphs 1 and 2 shall apply *mutatis mutandis* to an opposition entered pursuant to Article 8 (3) of the Regulation.

Rule 16

Facts, evidence and arguments presented in support of the opposition

1. Every notice of opposition may contain particulars of the facts, evidence and arguments presented in support of the opposition, accompanied by the relevant supporting documents.

2. If the opposition is based on an earlier mark which is not a Community trade mark, the notice of opposition shall preferably be accompanied by evidence of the registration or filing of that earlier mark, such as a certificate of registration. If the opposition is based on a well-known mark as referred to in Article 8 (2) (c) of the Regulation or on a mark having a reputation as referred to in Article 8 (5) of the Regulation, the notice of opposition shall in principle be accompanied by evidence attesting that it is well-known or that it has a reputation. If the opposition is entered on the basis of any other earlier right, the notice of opposition shall in principle be accompanied by appropriate evidence on the acquisition and scope of protection of that right.

3. The particulars of the facts, evidence and arguments and other supporting documents as referred to in paragraphs 1, and the evidence referred to in paragraph 2 may, if they are not submitted together with the notice of opposition or subsequent thereto, be submitted within such period after commencement of the opposition proceedings as the Office may specify pursuant to Rule 20 2.

Rule 17

Use of languages in opposition proceedings

1. Where the notice of opposition is not filed in the language of the application for registration of the Community trade mark, if that language is one of the languages of the Office, or in the second language indicated when the application was filed, the opposing party shall file a translation of the notice of opposition in one of those languages within a period of one month from the expiry of the opposition period.

2. Where the evidence in support of the opposition as provided for in Rule 16 1 and 2 is not filed in the language of the opposition proceedings, the opposing party shall file a translation of that evidence into that language within a period of one month from the expiry of the opposition period or, where applicable, within the period specified by the Office pursuant to Rule 16 3.

3. Where the opposing party or the applicant informs the Office, before the date on which the opposition proceedings shall be deemed to commence pursuant to Rule 19 1, that the applicant and the opposing party have agreed on a different language for the opposition proceeding pursuant to Article 115 (7) of the Regulation, the opposing party shall, where the notice of opposition has not been filed in that language, file a translation of the notice of opposition in that language within a period of one month from the said date.

Rule 18
Rejection of notice of opposition as inadmissible
1. If the Office finds that the notice of opposition does not comply with the provisions of Article 42 of the Regulation, or where the notice of opposition does not clearly identify the application against which opposition is entered or the earlier mark or the earlier right on the basis of which the opposition is being entered, the Office shall reject the notice of opposition as inadmissible unless those deficiencies have been remedied before expiry of the opposition period. If the opposition fee has not been paid within the opposition period, the notice of opposition shall be deemed not to have been entered. If the opposition fee has been paid after the expiry of the opposition period, it shall be refunded to the opposing party.

2. If the Office finds that the notice of opposition does not comply with other provisions of the Regulation or of these Rules, it shall inform the opposing party accordingly and shall call upon him to remedy the deficiencies noted within a period of two months. If the deficiencies are not remedied before the time limit expires, the Office shall reject the notice of opposition as inadmissible.

3. Any decision to reject a notice of opposition as inadmissible under paragraphs 1 or 2 shall be communicated to the applicant.

Rule 19
Commencement of opposition proceedings
1. If the Office does not reject the notice of opposition in accordance with Rule 18, it shall communicate the opposition to the applicant and shall invite him to file his observations within such period as it may specify. The Office shall draw the applicant's attention to the fact that the opposition proceedings shall be deemed to commence two months after receipt of the communication, unless the applicant informs the Office, before the expiry of this period, that he withdraws his application or restricts the application to goods and services against which the opposition is not directed.

2. The Office may, pursuant to Rule 71, grant an extension of the period referred to in the second sentence of paragraph 1 where such request is presented jointly by the applicant and the opposing party.

3. There the application is withdrawn or restricted within the period specified in the second sentence of paragraph 1 or within any extension of that period granted under paragraph 2, the Office shall inform the opposing party accordingly and shall refund the opposition fee.

Rule 20

Examination of opposition

1. If the application is not withdrawn or restricted pursuant to Rule 19, the applicant shall file his observations within the period specified by the Office in its communication referred to in the first sentence of Rule 19 1.

2. Where the notice of opposition does not contain particulars of the facts, evidence and arguments as referred to in Rule 16 1 and 2, the Office shall call upon the opposing party to submit such particulars within a period specified by the Office. Any submission by the opposing party shall be communicated to the applicant who shall be given an opportunity to reply within a period specified by the Office.

3. If the applicant files no observations, the Office may give a ruling on the opposition on the basis of the evidence before it.

4. The observations filed by the applicant shall be communicated to the opposing party who shall be called upon by the Office, if it considers it necessary to do so, to reply within a period specified by the Office.

5. If, pursuant to Article 44 (1) of the Regulation, the applicant restricts the list of goods and services, the Office shall communicate this to the opposing party and call upon him, within such period as it may specify, to submit observations stating whether he maintains the opposition and, if so, against which of the remaining goods and services.

6. The Office may suspend any opposition proceeding where the opposition is based on an application for registration pursuant to Article 8 (2) (b) of the Regulation until a final decision is taken in that proceeding, or where other circumstances are such that such suspension is appropriate.

Rule 21

Multiple oppositions

1. Where a number of oppositions have been entered in respect of the same application for a Community trade mark, the Office may deal with them in one set of proceedings. The Office may subsequently decide to no longer deal with them in this way.

2. If a preliminary examination of one or more oppositions reveals that the Community trade mark for which an application for registration has been filed is possibly not eligible for registration in respect of some or all of the goods or services for which registration is sought, the Office may suspend the other opposition proceedings. The Office shall inform the remaining opposing parties of any relevant decisions taken during those proceedings which are continued.

3. Once a decision rejecting the application has become final, the oppositions on which a decision was deferred in accordance with paragraph 2 shall be deemed to have been disposed of and the opposing parties concerned shall be informed accordingly. Such disposition shall be considered to constitute a case which has not proceeded to judgment within the meaning of Article 81 (4) of the Regulation.

4. The Office shall refund 50% of the opposition fee paid by each opposing party whose opposition is deemed to have been disposed of in accordance with paragraphs 1, 2 and 3.

Rule 22
Proof of use
1. Where, pursuant to Article 43 (2) or (3) of the Regulation, the opposing party has to furnish proof of use or show that there are proper reasons for non-use, the Office shall invite him to provide the proof required within such period as it shall specify. If the opposing party does not provide such proof before the time limit expires, the Office shall reject the opposition.

2. The indications and evidence for the furnishing of proof of use shall consist of indications concerning the place, time, extent and nature of use of the opposing trade mark for the goods and services in respect of which it is registered and on which the opposition is based, and evidence in support of these indications in accordance with paragraph 3.

3. The evidence shall, in principle, be confined to the submission of supporting documents and items such as packages, labels, price lists, catalogues, invoices, photographs, newspaper advertisements, and statements in writing as referred to in Article 76 (1) (f) of the Regulation. (4) Where the evidence supplied pursuant to paragraphs 1, 2 and 3 is not in the language of the opposition proceedings, the Office may require the opposing party to submit a translation of that evidence in that language, within a period specified by the Office.

Title III

Registration Procedure

Rule 23
Registration of the trade mark
1. The registration fee provided for in Article 45 of the Regulation shall consist of

(a) a basic fee;

and

(b) a class fee for each class exceeding three in respect of which the mark is to be registered.

2. Where no opposition has been entered or where any opposition entered has been finally disposed of by withdrawal, rejection or other disposition, the Office shall request the applicant to pay the registration fee within two months of receipt of the request.

3. If the registration fee is not paid within due time, it may still be validly paid within two months of notification of a communication pointing out the failure to observe the time limit, provided that within this period the additional fee specified in the Fees Regulations is paid.

4. On receipt of the registration fee the mark applied for and the particulars referred to in Rule 84 2 shall be recorded in the Register of Community trade marks.

5. The registration shall be published in the *Community Trade Marks Bulletin*.

6. The registration fee shall be refunded if the trade mark applied for is not registered.

Rule 24
Certificate of registration
1. The Office shall issue to the proprietor of the trade mark a certificate of registration which shall contain the entries in the Register provided for in Rule 84 2 and a statement to the effect that those entries have been recorded in the Register.

2. The proprietor of the trade mark may request that certified or uncertified copies of the certificate of registration be supplied to him upon payment of a fee.

Rule 25
Alteration of the registration
1. An application for alteration of the registration pursuant to Article 48 (2) of the Regulation shall contain:

(a) the registration number,

(b) the name and the address of the proprietor of the mark in accordance with Rule 1 1 (b);

(c) where the proprietor has appointed a representative, the name and the business address of the representative in accordance with Rule 1 1 (e);

(d) the indication of the element in the representation of the mark to be altered and that element in its altered version;

(e) a representation of the mark as altered, in accordance with Rule 3.

2. The application shall be deemed not to have been filed until the required fee has been paid. If the fee has not been paid or has not been paid in full, the Office shall inform the applicant accordingly.

3. If the requirements governing the alteration of the registration are not fulfilled, the Office shall communicate the deficiency to the applicant. If the deficiency is not remedied within a period to be specified by the Office, the Office shall reject the application.

4. Where the registration of the alteration is challenged pursuant to Article 48 (3) of the Regulation, the provisions on opposition contained in the Regulation and in these Rules shall apply *mutatis mutandis*.

5. A single application may be made for the alteration of the same element in two or more registrations of the same proprietor. The required fee shall be paid in respect of each registration to be altered.

Rule 26

Change of the name or address of the proprietor of the Community trade mark or of his registered representative

1. A change of the name or address of the proprietor of the Community trade mark which is not an alteration of the Community trade mark pursuant to Article 48 (2) of the Regulation and which is not the consequence of a whole or partial transfer of the registered mark shall, at the request of the proprietor, be recorded in the register.

2. An application for the change of the name or address of the proprietor of the registered mark shall contain:

(a) the registration number of the mark;

(b) the name and the address of the proprietor of the mark as recorded in the register;

(c) the indication of the name and address of the proprietor of the mark, as amended, in accordance with Rule 1 1 (e).

(d) where the proprietor has appointed a representative, the name and the business address of the representative, in accordance with Rule 1 1 (e).

3. The application shall not be subject to payment of a fee.

4. A single application may be made for the change of the name or address in respect of two or more registrations of the same proprietor.

5. If the requirements governing the recording of a change are not fulfilled, the Office shall communicate the deficiency to the applicant. If the deficiency is not remedied within a period to be specified by the Office, the Office shall reject the application.

6. Paragraphs 1 to 5 shall apply *mutatis mutandis* to a change of the name or address of the registered representative.

7. Paragraphs 1 to 6 shall apply *mutatis mutandis* to applications for Community trade marks. The change shall be recorded in the files kept by the Office on the Community trade mark application.

Rule 27

Correction of mistakes and errors in the register and in the publication of the registration

1. Where the registration of the mark or the publication of the registration contains a mistake or error attributable to the Office, the Office shall correct the error or mistake of its own motion or at the request of the proprietor.

2. Where such a request is made by the proprietor, Rule 26 shall apply *mutatis mutandis*. The request shall not be subject to payment of a fee.

3. The Office shall publish the corrections made under this Rule.

Rule 28

Claiming seniority after registration of the Community trade mark

1. An application pursuant to Article 35 of the Regulation to obtain the seniority of one or more earlier registered trade marks as referred to in Article 34 of the Regulation, shall contain:

(a) the registration number of the Community trade mark;

(b) the name and address of the proprietor of the Community trade mark in accordance with Rule 1 1 (b);

(c) where the proprietor has appointed a representative, the name and the business address of the representative in accordance with Rule 1 1 (e);

(d) an indication of the Member State or Member States in or for which the earlier mark is registered, the date from which the relevant registration was effective, the number of the relevant registration, and the goods and services for which the earlier mark is registered;

(e) an indication of the goods and services in respect of which seniority is claimed;

(f) a copy of the relevant registration; the copy must be certified as an exact copy of the relevant registration by the competent authority.

2. If the requirements governing the claiming of seniority are not fulfilled, the Office shall communicate the deficiency to the applicant. If the deficiency is not remedied within a period specified by the Office, the Office shall reject the application.

3. The Office shall inform the Benelux Trade Mark Office or the central industrial property office of the Member State concerned of the effective claiming of seniority.

4. The President of the Office may determine that the material to be provided by the applicant may consist of less than is required under paragraph 1 (f), provided that the information required is available to the Office from other sources.

Title IV

Renewal

Rule 29

Notification of expiry

At least six months before expiry of the registration the Office shall inform the proprietor of the Community trade mark, and any person having a registered right, including a licence, in respect of the Community trade mark, that the registration is approaching expiry. Failure to give such notification shall not affect the expiry of the registration.

Rule 30

Renewal of registration

1. An application for renewal shall contain.

(a) where the application is filed by the proprietor of the trade mark, his name and address in accordance with Rule 1 1 (b);

(b) where the application is filed by a person expressly authorized to do so by the proprietor of the mark, the name and address of that person and evidence that he is authorized to file the application;

(c) where the applicant has appointed a representative, the name and business address of the representative in accordance with Rule 1 1 (e);

(d) the registration number;

(e) an indication that renewal is requested for all the goods and services covered by the registration or, if the renewal is not requested for all the goods and services for which the mark is registered, an indication of those classes or those goods and services for which renewal is requested or those classes or those goods and services for which renewal is not requested, grouped according to the classes of the Nice classification, each group being preceded by the number of the class of that classification to which that group of goods or services belongs and presented in the order of the classes of that classification.

2. The fees payable under Article 47 of the Regulation for the renewal of a Community trade mark shall consist of:

(a) a basic fee;

(b) a class fee for each class exceeding three in the list of classes in respect of which renewal is applied for as shown in paragraph 1 (e); and

(c) where applicable, the additional fee for late payment of the renewal fee or late submission of the request for renewal, pursuant to Article 47 (3) of the Regulation, as specified in the Fees Regulation.

3. Where the application for renewal is filed within the time periods provided for in Article 47 (3) of the Regulation, but the other conditions governing renewal provided for in Article 47 of the Regulation and these Rules are not satisfied, the Office shall inform the applicant of the deficiencies found. If the application is filed by a person whom the proprietor of the trade mark has expressly authorized to do so, the proprietor of the trade mark shall receive a copy of the notification.

4. Where an application for renewal is not submitted or is submitted after expiry of the period provided for in the third sentence of Article 47 (3) of the Regulation, or if the fees are not paid or are paid only after the period in question has expired, or if the deficiencies are not remedied within that period, the Office shall determine that the registration has expired and shall so notify the proprietor of the Community trade mark and, where appropriate, the applicant and the person recorded in the Register as having rights in the mark. Where the fees paid are insufficient to cover all the classes of goods and services for which renewal is requested, such a determination shall not be made if it is clear which class or classes are to be covered. In the absence of other criteria, the Office shall take the classes into account in the order of classification.

5. Where the determination made pursuant to paragraph 4 has become final, the Office shall cancel the mark from the register. The cancellation shall take effect from the day following the day on which the existing registration expired.

6. Where the renewal fees provided for in paragraph 2 have been paid but the registration is not renewed, those fees shall be refunded.

TITLE V

Transfer, Licenses and other Rights, Changes

Rule 31
Transfer
1. An application for registration of a transfer under Article 17 of the Regulation shall contain:
(a) the registration number of the Community trade mark;
(b) particulars of the new proprietor in accordance with Rule 1 1 (b);
(c) where not all the registered goods or services are included in the transfer, particulars of the registered goods or services to which the transfer relates;
(d) documents duly establishing the transfer in accordance with Article 17 (2) and (3) of the Regulation.

2. The application may contain, where applicable, the name and business address of the representative of the new proprietor, to be set out in accordance with Rule 1 1 (e).

3. Transfers to any natural or legal persons who cannot be proprietors of Community trade marks pursuant to Article 5 of the Regulation shall not be registered.

4. The application shall not be deemed to have been filed until the required fee has been paid. If the fee is not paid or is not paid in full, the Office shall so notify the applicant.

5. It shall constitute sufficient proof of transfer under paragraph 1 (d):
(a) that the application for registration of the transfer is signed by the registered proprietor or his representative and by the successor in title or his representative; or,
(b) that the application, if submitted by the successor in title, is accompanied by a declaration, signed by the registered proprietor or his representative, that he agrees to the registration of the successor in title; or
(c) that the application is accompanied by a completed transfer form or document, as specified in Rule 83 1 (d), signed by the registered proprietor or his representative and by the successor in title or his representative.

6. Where the conditions applicable to the registration of a transfer, as laid down in Article 17 (1) to (4) of the Regulation, in paragraphs 1 to 4 above, and in other applicable Rules are not fulfilled, the Office shall notify the applicant of the deficiencies. If the deficiencies are not remedied within a period specified by the Office, it shall reject the application for registration of the transfer.

7. A single application for registration of a transfer may be submitted for two or more marks, provided that the registered proprietor and the successor in title are the same in each case.

8. Paragraphs 1 to 7 shall apply *mutatis mutandis* to applications for Community trade marks. The transfer shall be recorded in the files kept by the Office concerning the Community trade mark application.

Rule 32
Partial Transfers
1. Where the application for registration of a transfer relates only to some of the goods and services for which the mark is registered, the application shall contain an indication of the goods and services to which the partial transfer relates.

2. The goods and services in the original registration shall be distributed between the remaining registration and the new registration so that the goods and services in the remaining registration and the new registration shall not overlap.

3. Rule 31 shall apply *mutatis mutandis* to applications for registrations of a partial transfer.

4. The Office shall establish a separate file for the new registration, which shall consist of a complete copy of the file of the original registration and the application for registration of the partial transfer; a copy of that application shall be included in the file of the remaining registration. The Office shall also assign a new registration number to the new registration.

5. Any application made by the original proprietor pending with regard to the original registration shall be deemed to be pending with regard to the remaining registration and the new registration. Where such application is subject to the payment of fees and these fees have been paid by the original proprietor, the new proprietor shall not be liable to pay any additional fees with regard to such application.

Rule 33

Registration of licences and other rights

1. Rule 31 1 (a) (b) and (c), 2, 4 and 7 shall apply *mutatis mutandis* to the registration of the grant or transfer of a licence, to registration of the creation or transfer of a right *in rem* in respect of a Community trade mark, and to registration of enforcement measures. However, where a Community trade mark is involved in bankruptcy or like proceedings, the request of the competent national authority for an entry in the register to this effect shall not be subject to payment of a fee. 15 OF 26.

2. Where the Community trade mark is licensed for only part of the goods and services for which the mark is registered, or for only a part of the Community, or for a limited period of time, the application for registration shall indicate the goods and services or the part of the Community or the time period for which the licence is granted.

3. Where the conditions applicable to registration, as laid down in Articles 19, 20 or 22 of the Regulation, in paragraphs 1 and 2 above, and the other applicable Rules are not fulfilled, the Office shall notify the applicant of the irregularity. If the irregularity is not corrected within a period specified by the Office, it shall reject the applrcation for registration.

4. Paragraphs 1, 2 and 3 shall apply *mutatis mutandis* to applications for Community trade marks. Licences, rights *in rem* and enforcement measures shall be recorded in the files kept by the Office concerning the Communty trade mark application.

Rule 34

Special provisions for the registration of a licence

1. A licence in respect of a Community trade mark shall be recorded in the Register as an exclusive licence if the proprietor of the trade mark or the licence so request.

2. A licence in respect of a Community trade mark shall be recorded in the Register as a sub-licence where it is granted by a licensee whose licence is recorded in the Register.

3. A licence in respect of a Community trade mark shall be recorded in the Register as a licence limited as to the goods and services or as a territorially limited licence if it is granted for only a part of the goods or services for which the mark is registered or if it is granted only for a part of the Community.

4. A licence in respect of a Community trade mark shall be recorded in the Register as a temporary licence if it is granted for a limited period of time.

Rule 35

Cancellation or modification of the registration of licences and other rights

1. A registration effected under Rule 33 1 shall be cancelled at the request of one of the persons concerned.

2. The application shall contain:
   (a) the registration number of the Community trade mark; and
   (b) particulars of the right whose registration is to be cancelled.

3. Application for cancellation of the registration of a licence or another right shall not be deemed to have been filed until the required fee has been paid. If the fee is not paid or is not paid in full, the Office shall so notify the applicant. However, the request of the competent national authority for the cancellation of an entry where a Community trade mark is involved in bankruptcy or like proceedings shall not be subject to payment of a fee.

4. The application shall be accompanied by documents showing that the registered right no longer exists or by a statement by the licensee or the holder of another right, to the effect that he consents to cancellation of the registration.

5. Where the requirements for cancellation of the registration are not satisfied, the Office shall notify the applicant of the irregularity. If the irregularity is not corrected within a period specified by the Office, it shall reject the application for cancellation of the registration.

6. Paragraphs 1, 2, 4 and 5 shall apply *mutatis mutandis* to a request for the modification of a registration effected under Rule 33 1.

7. Paragraphs 1 to 6 shall apply *mutatis mutandis* to entries made in the files pursuant to Rule 33 4.

TITLE VI

Surrender

Rule 36
Surrender
1. A declaration of surrender pursuant to Article 49 of the Regulation shall contain:

(a) the registration number of the Community trade mark;

(b) the name and address of the proprietor in accordance with Rule 1 1 (b);

(c) where a representative has been appointed, the name and business address of the representative in accordance with Rule 1 1 (e).

(d) where surrender is declared only for some of the goods and services for which the mark is registered, the goods and services for which the surrender is declared or the goods and services for which the mark is to remain registered.

2. Where a right of a third party relating to the Community trade mark is entered in the register, it shall be sufficient proof of his agreement to the surrender that a declaration of consent to the surrender is signed by the proprietor of that right or his representative. Where a licence has been registered, surrender shall be registered three months after the date on which the proprietor of the Community trade mark satisfies the Office that he has informed the licensee of his intention to surrender it. If the proprietor proves to the Office before the expiry of that period that the licensee has given his consent, the surrender shall be registered forthwith.

3. If the requirements governing surrender are not fulfilled, the Office shall communicate the deficiencies to the declarant. If the deficiencies are not remedied within a period to be specified by the Office, the Office shall reject the entry of the surrender in the Register.

TITLE VII

Revocation and Invalidity

Rule 37
Application for revocation or for a declaration of invalidity
An application to the Office for revocation or for a declaration of invalidity pursuant to Article 55 of the Regulation shall contain:

(a) as concerns the registration in respect of which revocation or a declaration of invalidity is sought;

(i) the registration number of the Community trade mark in respect of which revocation or a declaration of invalidity is sought;

(ii) the name and address of the proprietor of the Community trade mark in respect of which revocation or a declaration of invalidity is sought;

(iii) a statement of the registered goods and services in respect of which revocation or a declaration of invalidity is sought;

(b) as regards the grounds on which the application is based,

(i) in the case of an application pursuant to Article 50 or Article 51 of the Regulation, a statement of the grounds on which the application for revocation or a declaration of invalidity is based;

(ii) in the case of an application pursuant to Article 52 (1) of the Regulation, particulars of the right on which the application for a declaration of invalidity is based and if necessary particulars showing that the applicant is entitled to adduce the earlier right as grounds for invalidity;

(iii) in the case of an application pursuant to Article 52 (2) of the Regulation, particulars of the right on which the application for a declaration of invalidity is based and particulars showing that the applicant is the proprietor of an earlier right as referred to in Article 52 (2) of the Regulation or that he is entitled under the national law applicable to lay claim to that right;

(iv) an indication of the facts, evidence and arguments presented in support of those grounds;

(c) as concerns the applicant, (i) his name and address in accordance with Rule 1 1 (b); (ii) if the applicant has appointed a representative, the name and the business address of the representative, in accordance with Rule 1 1 (e).

Rule 38

Languages used in revocation or invalidity proceedings

1. Where the application for revocation or for a declaration of invalidity is not filed in the language of the application for the registration of the Community trade mark, if that language is one of the languages of the Office, or in the second language indicated when the application was filed, the applicant for revocation or for a declaration of invalidity shall file a translation of his application in one of those two languages within a period of one month from the filing of his application.

2. Where the evidence in support of the application is not filed in the language of the revocation or invalidity proceedings, the applicant shall file a translation of that evidence into that language within a period of two months after the filing of such evidence.

3. Where the applicant for revocation or for a declaration of invalidity or the proprietor of the Community trade mark inform the Office before the expiry of a period of two months from receipt by the Community trade mark proprietor of the communication referred to in Rule 40 1, that they have agreed on a different language of proceedings pursuant to Article 115 (7) of the Regulation, the applicant shall, where the application was not filed in that language, file a translation of the application in that language within a period of one month from the said date.

Rule 39

Rejection of the application for revocation or for declaration of invalidity as inadmissible

1. If the Office finds that the application does not comply with Article 55 of the Regulation, Rule 37 or any other provision of the Regulation or these Rules, it shall inform the applicant accordingly and shall call upon him to remedy the deficiencies found within such period as it may specify. If the deficiencies are not remedied before expiry of the time limit, the Office shall reject the application as inadmissible.

2. Where the Office finds that the required fees have not been paid, it shall inform the applicant accordingly and shall inform him that the application will be deemed not to have been filed if the required fees are not paid within a period specified by the Office. If the required fees are paid after expiry of the period specified by the Office, they shall be refunded to the applicant.

3. Any decision to reject an application for revocation or for a declaration of invalidity under paragraph 1 shall be communicated to the applicant. Where the application is considered not to have been filed pursuant to paragraph 2, the applicant shall be informed accordingly.

Rule 40

Examination of the application for revocation or for a declaration of invalidity

1. If the Office does not reject the application in accordance with Rule 39, it shall communicate such application to the proprietor of the Community trade mark and shall request him to file his observations within such period as it may specify.

2. If the proprietor of the Community trade mark files no observations, the Office may decide on the revocation or invalidity on the basis of the evidence before it.

3. Any observations filed by the proprietor of the Community trade mark shall be communicated to the applicant, who shall be requested by the Office, if it sees fit, to reply within a period specified by the Office.

4. All communications under Article 56 (1) of the Regulation and all observations filed in this respect shall be sent to the parties concerned.

5. If the applicant, under Article 56 (2) or (3) of the Regulation, has to furnish proof of use or proof that there are proper reasons for non-use, Rule 22 shall apply *mutatis mutandis*.

Rule 41
Multiple applications for revocation or for a declaration of invalidity
1. Where a number of applications for revocation or for a declaration of invalidity have been filed relating to the same Community trade mark, the Office may deal with them in one set of proceedings. The Office may subsequently decide no longer to deal with them in this way.

2. Rule 21 2, 3 and 4 shall apply *mutatis mutandis*.

TITLE VIII

Community Collective Marks

Rule 42
Application of provisions
The provisions of these Rules shall apply to Community collective marks, subject to Rule 43

Rule 43
Regulation governing Community collective marks
1. Where the application for a Community collective trade mark does not contain the regulations governing its use pursuant to Article 65 of the Regulation, those regulations shall be submitted to the Office within a period of two months after the date of filing.

2. The regulations governing Community collective marks shall specify:
(a) the name of the applicant and his office address;
(b) the object of the association or the object for which the legal person governed by public law is constituted;
(c) the bodies authorized to represent the association or the said legal person;
(d) the conditions for membership;
(e) the persons authorized to use the mark;
(f) where appropriate, the conditions governing use of the mark, including sanctions;
(g) where appropriate, the authorization referred to in the second sentence of Article 65 (2) of the Regulation.

TITLE IX

Conversion

Rule 44
Application for conversion

1. An application for conversion of a Community trade mark application or a registered Community trade mark into a national trade mark application pursuant to Article 108 of the Regulation shall contain:

(a) the name and the address of the applicant for conversion in accordance with Rule 1 1 (b);

(b) where the applicant for conversion has appointed a representative, the name and the business address of the representative in accordance with Rule 1 1 (e);

(c) the filing number of the Community trade mark application or the registration number of the Community trade mark;

(d) the date of filing of the Community trade mark application or the Community trade mark and, where applicable, particulars of the claim to priority for the Community trade mark application or the Community trade mark pursuant to Articles 30 and 33 of the Regulation and particulars of the claim to seniority pursuant to Articles 34 and 35 of the Regulation;

(e) a representation of the mark as contained in the application or as registered;

(f) the specification of the Member State or the Member States in respect of which conversion is requested;

(g) where the request does not relate to all of the goods and services for which the application has been filed or for which the trade mark has been registered, an indication of the goods and services for which conversion is requested, and, where conversion is requested in respect of more than one Member State and the list of goods and services is not the same for all Member States, an indication of the respective goods and services for each Member State;

(h) where conversion is requested pursuant to Article 108 (4) of the Regulation, an indication to that effect;

(i) where conversion is requested pursuant to Article 108 (5) of the Regulation following a withdrawal of an application for registration, an indication to that effect, and the date on which the application for registration was withdrawn;

(j) where conversion is requested pursuant to Article 108 (5) of the Regulation following a failure to renew the registration, an indication to that effect, and the date on which the period of protection has expired, the period of three months provided for in Article 108 (5) of the Regulation shall begin to run on the day following the last day on which the request for renewal can be presented pursuant to Article 47 (3) of the Regulation;

(k) where conversion is requested pursuant to Article 108 (6) of the Regulation, an indication to that effect, the date on which the decision of the national court has become final, and a copy of that decision.

2. Where a copy of a court decision pursuant to paragraph 1 (k) is required, that copy may be submitted in the language in which the decision was given.

Rule 45
Examination of application for conversion
1. Where the application for conversion does not comply with the requirements of Article 108 (1) of the Regulation or was not filed within the relevant period of three months, the Office shall reject it.

2. Where the conversion fee has not been paid within the relevant period of three months, the Office shall inform the applicant that the application for conversion shall be deemed not to have been filed.

3. Where the other requirements governing conversion as provided for in Rule 44 and in other Rules governing such applications are not fulfilled, the Office shall inform the applicant accordingly and invite him to remedy the deficiency within a period specified by the Office. If the deficiencies are not remedied within that period, the Office shall reject the application for conversion.

Rule 46
Publication of application for conversion
1. Where the application for conversion relates to a Community trade mark application which has already been published in the Community Trade Mark Bulletin pursuant to Article 40 of the Regulation or where the application for conversion relates to a Community trade mark, the application for conversion shall be published in the Community Trade Marks Bulletin.

2. The publication of the application for conversion shall contain:
(a) the filing number or the registration number of the trade mark in respect of which conversion is requested;
(b) a reference to the previous publication of the application or the registration in the Community Trade marks Bulletin;
(c) an indication of the Member State or Member States in respect of which conversion has been requested;
(d) where the request does not relate to all of the goods and services for which the application has been filed or for which the trade mark has been registered, an indication of the goods and services for which conversion is requested;
(e) where conversion is requested in respect of more than one Member State and the list of goods and services is not the same for all Member States, an indication of the respective goods and services for each Member State;
(f) the date of the application for conversion.

Rule 47
Transmission to central industrial property offices of the Member States
Where the application for conversion complies with the requirements of the Regulation and these Rules, the Office shall transmit without delay the application for conversion to the central industrial property offices of the Member States specified therein, including the Benelux Trade Mark Office. The Office shall inform the applicant of the date of transmission.

TITLE X

Appeals

Rule 48
Content of the notice of appeal
1. The notice of appeal shall contain:
(a) the name and address of the appellant in accordance with Rule 1 1 (b);
(b) where the appellant has appointed a representative, the name and the business address of the representative in accordance with Rule 1 1 (e);
(c) a statement identifying the decision which is contested and the extent to which amendment or cancellation of the decision is requested.

2. The notice of appeal shall be filed in the language of the proceedings in which the decision subject to the appeal was taken.

Rule 49
Rejection of the appeal as inadmissible
1. If the appeal does not comply with Articles 57, 58 and 59 of the Regulation and Rule 48 1 (c) and 2, the Board of Appeal shall reject it as inadmissible, unless each deficiency has been remedied before the relevant time limit laid down in Article 59 of the Regulation has expired.

2. If the Board of Appeal finds that the appeal does not comply with other provisions of the Regulation or other provisions of these Rules, in particular Rule 48 1 (a) and (b), it shall inform the appellant accordingly and shall request him to remedy the deficiencies noted within such period as it may specify. If the appeal is not corrected in good time, the Board of Appeal shall reject it as inadmissible.

3. If the fee for appeal has been paid after expiry of the period for the filing of appeal pursuant to Article 59 of the Regulation, the appeal shall be deemed not to have been filed and the appeal fee shall be refunded to the appellant.

Rule 50
Examination of appeals
1. Unless otherwise provided, the provisions relating to proceedings before the department which has made the decision against which the appeal is brought shall be applicable to appeal proceedings *mutatis mutandis*.

2. The Board of Appeal's decision shall contain:
(a) a statement that it is delivered by the Board;
(b) the date when the decision was taken;
(c) the names of the Chairman and of the other members of the Board of Appeal taking part;
(d) the name of the competent employee of the registry;
(e) the names of the parties and of their representatives;
(f) a statement of the issues to be decided;
(g) a summary of the facts;
(h) the reasons;
(i) the order of the Board of Appeal, including, where necessary, a decision on costs.

3. The decision shall be signed by the Chairman and the other members of the Board of Appeal and by the employee of the registry of the Board of Appeal.

Rule 51
Reimbursement of appeal fees
The reimbursement of appeal fees shall be ordered in the event of interlocutory revision or where the Board of Appeal deems an appeal to be allowable, if such reimbursement is equitable by reason of a substantial procedural violation. In the event of interlocutory revision, reimbursement shall be ordered by the department whose decision has been impugned, and in other cases by the Board of Appeal.

Title XI

General Provisions

Part A

Decisions and communications of the Office

Rule 52
Form of decisions
1. Decisions of the Office shall be in writing and shall state the reasons on which they are based. Where oral proceedings are held before the Office, the decision may be given orally. Subsequently, the decision in writing shall be notified to the parties.

2. Decisions of the Office which are open to appeal shall be accompanied by a written communication indicating that notice of appeal must be filed in writing at the Office within two months of the date of notification of the decision from which appeal is to be made. The communications shall also draw the attention of the parties to the provisions laid down in Articles 57, 58 and 59 of the Regulation. The parties may not plead any failure to communicate the availability proceedings.

Rule 53
Correction of errors in decisions
In decisions of the Office, only linguistic errors, errors of transcription and obvious mistakes my be corrected. They shall be corrected by the department which took the decision, acting of its own motion or at the request of an interested party.

Rule 54
Noting of loss of rights
1. If the Office finds that the loss of any rights results from the Regulation or these Rules without any decision having been taken, it shall communicate this to the person concerned in accordance with Article 77 of the Regulation, and shall draw his attention to the substance of paragraph 2 of this Rule.

2. If the person concerned considers that the finding of the Office is inaccurate, he may, within two months after notification of the communication referred to in paragraph 1, apply for a decision on the matter by the Office. Such decision shall be given only if the Office disagrees with the person requesting it; otherwise the Office shall amend its finding and inform the person requesting the decision.

Rule 55
Signature, name, seal
1. Any decision, communication or notice from the Office shall indicate the department or division of the Office as well as the name or the names of the official or officials responsible. They shall be signed by the official or officials, or, instead of a signature, carry a printed or stamped seal of the Office.

2. The President of the Office may determine that other means of identifying the department or division of the Office and the name of the official or officials responsible or an identification other than a seal may be used where decisions, communications or notices are transmitted by telecopier or any other technical means of communication.

PART B

Oral proceedings and taking of evidence

Rule 56
Summons to oral proceedings
1. The parties shall be summoned to oral proceedings provided for in Article 75 of the Regulation and their attention shall be drawn to paragraph 3 of this Rule. At least one month's, notice of the summons shall be given unless the parties agree to a shorter period.

2. When issuing the summons, the Office shall draw attention to the points which in its opinion need to be discussed in order for the decision to be taken.

3. If a party who has been duly summoned to oral proceedings before the Office does not appear as summoned, the proceedings may continue without him.

Rule 57
Taking of evidence by the Office
1. Where the Office considers it necessary to hear the oral evidence of parties, of witnesses or of experts or to carry out an inspection, it shall take a decision to that end, stating the means by which it intends to obtain evidence, the relevant facts to be proved and the date, time and place of hearing or inspection. If oral evidence of witnesses and experts is requested by a party, the decision of the Office shall determine the period of time within which the party filing the request must make known to the Office the names and addresses of the witnesses and experts whom the party wishes to be heard.

2. The period of notice given in the summons of a party, witness or expert to give evidence shall be at least one month, unless they agree to a shorter period. The summons shall contain:

(a) an extract from the decision mentioned in paragraph 1, indicating in particular the date, time and place of the hearing ordered and stating the facts regarding which the parties, witnesses and experts are to be heard;

(b) the names of the parties to proceedings and particulars of the rights which the witnesses or experts may invoke under Rule 59 2 to 5.

Rule 58
Commissioning of experts
1. The Office shall decide in what form the report made by an expert whom it appoints shall be submitted.

2. The terms of reference of the expert shall include:

(a) a precise description of his task;

(b) the time limit laid down for the submission of the expert report;

(c) the names of the parties to the proceedings;
(d) particulars of the claims which he may invoke under Rule 59 2, 3 and 4.

3. A copy of any written report shall be submitted to the parties.

4. The parties may object to an expert on grounds of incompetence or on the same grounds as those on which objection may be made to an examiner or to a member of a Division or Board of Appeal pursuant to Article 132 (1) and (3) of the Regulation. The department of the Office concerned shall rule on the objection.

Rule 59

Costs of taking of evidence

1. The taking of evidence by the Office may be made conditional upon deposit with it, by the party who has requested the evidence to be taken, of a sum which shall be fixed by reference to an estimate of the costs.

2. Witnesses and experts who are summoned by and appear before the Office shall be entitled to reimbursement of reasonable expenses for travel and subsistence. An advance for these expenses may be granted to them by the Office. The first sentence shall apply also to witnesses and experts who appear before the Office without being summoned by it and are heard as witnesses or experts.

3. Witnesses entitled to reimbursement under paragraph 2 shall also be entitled to appropriate compensation for loss of earnings, and experts to fees for their work. These payments shall be made to the witnesses and experts after they have fulfilled their duties or tasks, where such witnesses and experts have been summoned by the Office of its own initiative.

4. The amounts and the advances for expenses to be paid pursuant to paragraphs 1, 2 and 3 shall be determined by the President of the Office and shall be published in the Official Journal of the Office. The amounts shall be calculated on the same basis as the compensation and salaries received by officials in grades A4 to A8 as laid down in the Staff Regulations of Officials of the European Communities and Annex VII thereto.

5. Final liability for the amounts due or paid pursuant to paragraphs 1 to 4 shall lie with:

(a) the Office where the Office, at its own initiative, considered it necessary to hear the oral evidence of witnesses or experts; or

(b) the party concerned where that party requested the giving of oral evidence by witnesses or experts, subject to the decision on apportionment and fixing of costs pursuant to Articles 81 and 82 of the Regulation and Rule 94. Such party shall reimburse the Office for any advances duly paid.

Rule 60

Minutes of oral proceedings and of evidence. 2 OF 19.

1. Minutes of oral proceedings or the taking of evidence shall be drawn up, containing the essentials of the oral proceedings or of the taking of evidence, the relevant statements made by the parties, the testimony of the parties, witnesses or experts and the result of any inspection.

2. The minutes of the testimony of a witness, expert or party shall be read out or submitted to him so that he may examine them. It shall be noted in the minutes that this formality has been carried out and that the person who gave the testimony approved the minutes. Where his approval is not given, his objections shall be noted.

3. The minutes shall be signed by the employee who drew them up and by the employee who conducted the oral proceedings or taking of evidence.

4. The parties shall be provided with a copy of the minutes.

5. Upon request, the Office shall make available to the parties transcripts of recordings of the oral proceedings, in typescript or in any other machine-readable form. The release under the first sentence of the oral proceedings shall be subject to the payment of the costs incurred by the Office in making such transcript. The amount to be charged shall be determined by the President of the Office.

Part C

Notifications

Rule 61

General provisions on notifications

1. In proceedings before the Office, any notifications to be made by the Office shall take the form of the original document, of a copy thereof certified by, or bearing the seal of, the Office or of a computer print-out bearing such seal. Copies of documents emanating from the parties themselves shall not require such certification.

2. Notifications shall be made
   (a) by post in accordance with Rule 62;
   (b) by hand delivery in accordance with Rule 63;
   (c) by deposit in a post box at the Office in accordance with Rule 64;
   (d) by telecopier and other technical means in accordance with Rule 65;
   (e) by public notification in accordance with Rule 66.

Rule 62
Notification by post
1. Decisions subject to a time limit for appeal, summonses and other documents as determined by the President of the Office shall be notified by registered letter with advice of delivery. Decisions and communications subject to some other time limit shall be notified by registered letter, unless the President of the Office determines otherwise. All other communications shall be ordinary mail.

2. Notifications in respect of addresses having neither their domicile nor their principal place of business nor an establishment in the Community and who have not appointed a representative in accordance with Article 88 (2) of the Regulation shall be effected by posting the document requiring notification by ordinary mail to the last address of the addressee known to the Office. Notification shall be deemed to have been effected when the posting has taken place.

3. Where notification is effected by registered letter, whether or not with advice of delivery, this shall be deemed to be delivered to the addressee on the 10th day following that of its posting, unless the letter has failed to reach the addressee or has reached him at a later date. In the event of any dispute, it shall be for the Office to establish that the letter has reached its destination or to establish the date on which it was delivered to the addressee, as the case may be.

4. Notification by registered letter, with or without advice of delivery, shall be deemed to have been effected even if the addressee refuses to accept the letter.

5. To the extent that notification by post is not covered by paragraphs 1 to 4, the law of the State on the territory of which notification is made shall apply.

Rule 63
Notification by hand delivery
Notification may be effected on the premises of the Office by hand delivery of the document to the addressee, who shall on delivery acknowledge its receipt.

Rule 64
Notification by deposit in a post box at the Office
Notification may also be effected to addressees who have been provided with a post box at the Office, by depositing the document therein. A written notification of deposit shall be inserted in the files. The date of deposit shall be recorded on the document. Notification shall be deemed to have taken place on the fifth day following deposit of the document in the post box at the Office.

Rule 65
Notification by telecopier and other technical means
1. Notification by telecopier shall be effected by transmitting either the original or a copy, as provided for in Rule 61 1, of the document to be notified. The details of such transmission shall be determined by the President of the Office.

2. Details of notification by other technical means of communication shall be determined by the President of the Office.

Rule 66
Public notification
1. If the address of the addressee cannot be established, or if notification in accordance with Rule 62 1 has proved to be impossible even after a second attempt by the Office, notification shall be effected by public notice. Such notice shall be published at least in the Community Trade Marks Bulletin.

2. The President of the Office shall determine how the public notice is to be given and shall fix the beginning of the one-month period on the expiry of which the document shall be deemed to have been notified.

Rule 67
Notification to representatives
1. If a representative has been appointed or where the applicant first named in a common application is considered to be the common representative pursuant to Rule 75 1, notifications shall be addressed to that appointed or common representative.

2. If several representatives have been appointed for a single interested party, notification to any one of them shall be sufficient, unless a specific address for service has been indicated in accordance with Rule 1 1 (e) 3. If several interested parties have appointed a common representative, notification of a single document to the common representative shall be sufficient.

Rule 68
Irregularities in notification
Where a document has reached the addressee, if the Office is unable to prove that it has been duly notified, or if provisions relating to its notification have not been observed, the document shall be deemed to have been notified on the date established by the Office as the date of receipt.

Rule 69
Notification of documents in the case of several parties
Documents emanating from parties which contain substantive proposals, or a declaration of withdrawal of a substantive proposal, shall be notified to the other parties as a matter of course. Notification may be dispensed with where the document contains no new pleadings and the matter is ready for decision Part D Time limits.

Rule 70
Calculation of time limits
1. Periods shall be laid down in terms of full years, months, weeks or days.

2. Calculation shall start on the day following the day on which the relevant event occurred, the event being either a procedural step or the expiry of another period. Where that procedural step is a notification, the event considered shall be the receipt of the document notified, unless otherwise provided.

3. Where a period is expressed as one year or a certain number of years, it shall expire in the relevant subsequent year in the month having the same name and on the day having the same number as the month and the day on which the said event occurred. Where the relevant month has no day with the same number the period shall expire on the last day of that month.

4. Where a period is expressed as one month or a certain number of months, it shall expire in the relevant subsequent month on the day which has the same number as the day on which the said event occurred. Where the day on which the said event occurred was the last day of a month or where the relevant subsequent month has no day with the same number the period shall expire on the last day of that month.

5. Where a period is expressed as one week or a certain number of weeks, it shall expire in the relevant subsequent week on the day having the same name as the day on which the said event occurred.

Rule 71

Duration of time limits

1. Where the Regulation or these Rules provide for a period to be specified by the Office, such period shall, when the party concerned has its domicile or its principal place of business or an establishment within the Community, be not less than one month, or, when those conditions are not fulfilled, not less than two months, and no more than six months. The Office may, when this is appropriate under the circumstances, grant an extension of a period specified if such extension is requested by the party concerned and the request is submitted before the original period expired.

2. Where there are two or more parties, the Office may extend a period subject to the agreement of the other parties.

Rule 72

Expiry of time limits in special cases

1. If a time limit expires on a day on which the Office is not open for receipt of documents or on which, for reasons other than those referred to in paragraph 2, ordinary mail is not delivered in the locality in which the Office is located, the time limit shall extend until the first day thereafter on which the Office is open for receipt of documents and on which ordinary mail is delivered. The days referred to in the first sentence shall be as determined by the President of the Office before the commencement of each calendar year.

2. If a time limit expires on a day on which there is a general interruption or subsequent dislocation in the delivery of mail in a Member State or between a Member State and the Office, the time limit shall extend until the first day following the end of the period of interruption or dislocation, for parties having their residence or registered office in the State concerned or who have appointed representatives with a place of business in that State. In the event of the Member State concerned being the State in which the Office is located, this provision shall apply to all parties. The duration of the abovementioned period shall be as determined by the President of the Office.

3. Paragraphs 1 and 2 shall apply *mutatis mutandis* to the time limits provided for in the Regulation or these Rules in the case of transactions to be carried out with the competent authority within the meaning of Article 25 (1) (b) of the Regulation.

4. If an exceptional occurrence such as natural disaster or strike interrupts or dislocates the proper functioning of the Office so that any communication from the Office to parties concerning the expiry of a time limit is delayed, acts to be completed within such a time limit may still be validly completed within one month after the notification of the delayed communication. The date of commencement and the end of any such interruption or dislocation shall be as determined by the President of the Office.

PART E

Interruption of proceedings

Rule 73
Interruption of proceedings
1. Proceedings before the Office shall be interrupted:

(a) in the event of the death or legal incapacity of the applicant for or proprietor of a Community trade mark or of the person authorized by national law to act on his behalf. To the extent that the above events do not affect the authorization of a representative appointed under Article 89 of the Regulation, proceedings shall be interrupted only on application by such representative;

(b) in the event of the applicant for or proprietor of a Community trade mark, as a result of some action taken against his property, being prevented for legal reasons from continuing the proceedings before the Office;

(c) in the event of the death or legal incapacity of the representative of an applicant for or proprietor of a Community trade mark or of his being prevented for legal reasons resulting from action taken against his property from continuing the proceedings before the Office.

2. When, in the cases referred to in paragraph 1 (a) and (b), the Office has been informed of the identity of the person authorized to continue the proceedings before the Office, the Office shall communicate to such person and to any interested third parties that the proceedings shall be resumed as from a date to be fixed by the Office.

3. In the case referred to in paragraph 1 (c), the proceedings shall be resumed when the Office has been informed of the appointment of a new representative of the applicant or when the Office has notified to the other parties the communication of the appointment of a new representative of the proprietor of the Community trade mark. If, three months after the beginning of the interruption of the proceedings, the Office has not been informed of the appointment of a new representative, it shall inform the applicant for or proprietor of the Community trade mark:

(a) where Article 88 (2) of the Regulation is applicable, that the Community trade mark application will be deemed to be withdrawn if the information is not submitted within two months after this communication is notified; or

(b) where Article 88 (2) of the Regulation is not applicable, that the proceedings will be resumed with the applicant for or proprietor of the Community trade mark as from the date on which this communication is notified.

4. The time limits, other than the time limit for paying the renewal fees, in force as regards the applicant for or proprietor of the Community trade mark at the date of interruption of the proceedings, shall begin again as from the day on which the proceedings are resumed Part F Waiving of enforced recovery procedures.

Rule 74
Waiving of enforced recovery procedures
The President of the Office may waive action for the enforced recovery of any sum due where the sum to be recovered is minimal or where such recovery is too uncertain Part G Representation.

Rule 75
Appointment of a common representative
1. If there is more than one applicant and the application for a Community trade mark does not name a common representative, the applicant first named in the application shall be considered to be the common representative. However, if one of the applicants is obliged to appoint a professional representative, such representative shall be considered to be the common representative unless the applicant named first in the application has appointed a professional representative. The same shall apply *mutatis mutandis* to third parties acting in common in filing notice of opposition or applying for revocation or for a declaration of invalidity, and to joint proprietors of a Community trade mark.

2. If, during the course of proceedings, transfer is made to more than one person, and such persons have not appointed a common representative, paragraph 1 shall apply. If such application is not possible, the Office shall require such persons to appoint a common representative within two months. If this request is not complied with, the Office shall appoint the common representative.

Rule 76
Authorizations
1. Representatives acting before the Office must file with it a signed authorization for inclusion in the files. The authorization may cover one or more applications or one or more registered trade marks.

2. A general authorization enabling a representative to act in respect of all trade mark transactions of the party giving the authorization may be filed.

3. The authorization may be filed in any language of the Office and in the language of the proceedings if that language is not one of the languages of the Office.

4. Where the appointment of a representative is communicated to the Office, the necessary authorization shall be filed within a period specified by the Office. If the authorization is not filed in due time, proceedings shall be continued with the represented person. Any procedural steps other than the filing of the application taken by the representative shall be deemed not to have been taken if the represented person does not approve them. The application of Article 88 (2) of the Regulation shall remain unaffected.

5. Paragraphs 1 to 3 shall apply *mutatis mutandis* to a document withdrawing an authorization.

6. Any representative who has ceased to be authorized shall continue to be regarded as the representative until the termination of his authorization has been communicated to the Office.

7. Subject to any provisions to the contrary contained therein, an authorization shall not terminate *vis-à-vis* the Office upon the death of the person who gave it.

8. Where several representatives are appointed by the same party, they may, notwithstanding any provisions to the contrary in their authorizationsp act either jointly or singly.

9. The authorization of an association of representatives shall be deemed to be an authorization of any representative who can establish that he practises within that association.

Rule 77
Representation
Any notification or other communication addressed by the Office to the duly authorized representative shall have the same effect as if it had been addressed to the Office by the duly authorized representative shall have the same effect as if it originated from the represented person.

Rule 78
Amendment of the list of professional representatives
1. The entry of a professional representative in the list of professional representatives, as referred to in Article 89 of the Regulation, shall be deleted at this request.

2. The entry of a professional representative shall be deleted automatically:
(a) in the event of the death or legal incapacity of the professional representative;
(b) where the professional representative is no longer a national of a Member State, unless the President of the Office has granted an exemption under Article 89 (4) (b) of the Regulation;
(c) where the professional representative no longer has his place of business or employment in the Community;
(d) where the professional representative no longer possesses the entitlement referred to in the first sentence of Article 89 (2) (c) of the Regulation.

3. The entry of a professional representative shall be suspended of the Offices own motion where his entitlement to represent natural or legal persons before the central industrial property office of the Member State as referred to in the first sentence of Article 89 (2) (c) has been suspended.

4. A person whose entry has been deleted shall, upon request pursuant to Article 89 (3) of Regulation, be reinstated in the list of professional representatives if the conditions for deletion no longer exist.

5. The Benelux Trade Mark Office and the central industrial property officies of the Member States concerned shall, where they are aware thereof, promptly inform the Office of any relevant events under paragraphs 2 and 3.

6. The amendments of the list of professional representatives shall be published in the Official Journal of the Office.

Part H

Written communications and forms

Rule 79
Communication in writing or by other means
Applications for the registration of a Community trade mark as well as any other application provided for in the Regulation and all other communications addressed to the Office shall be submitted as follows:

(a) by submitting a signed original of the document in question at the Office, such as by post, personal delivery, or by any other means; annexes to documents submitted need not be signed;

(b) by transmitting a signed original by telecopier in accordance with Rule 80;

(c) by telex or telegram in accordance with Rule 81;

(d) by transmitting the contents of the communication by electronic means in accordance with Rule 82.

Rule 80
Communication by telecopier
1. Where an application for registration of a trade mark is submitted to the Office by telecopier and the application contains a reproduction of the mark pursuant to Rule 3 2 which does not satisfy the requirements of that Rule, the required number of original reproductions shall be submitted to the Office in accordance with Rule 79 (a). Where the reproductions are received by the Office within a period of one month from the date of the receipt of the telecopy by the Office, the application shall be deemed to have been received by the Office on the date on which the telecopy was received by the Office. Where the reproductions are received by the Office after the expiry of that period and the reproduction is necessary for the obtaining of a filing date, the application shall be deemed to have been received by the Office on the date on which the reproductions were received by the Office.

2. Where a communication received by telecopier is incomplete or illegible, or where the Office has reasonable doubts as to the accuracy of the transmission, the Office shall inform the sender accordingly and shall invite him, within a period to be specified by the Office, to retransmit the original by telecopy or to submit the original in accordance with Rule 79 (a). Where this request is complied with within the period specified, the date of the receipt of the retransmission or of the original shall be deemed to be the date of the receipt of the original communication, provided that where the deficiency concerns the granting of a filing date for an application to register a trade mark, the provisions on the filing date shall apply. Where the request is not complied with within the period specified, the communication shall be deemed not to have been received.

3. Any communication submitted to the Office by telecopier shall be considered to be duly signed if the reproduction of the signature appears on the print-out produced by the telecopier.

4. The President of the Office may determine additional requirements of communication by telecopier, such as the equipment to be used, technical details of communication, and methods of identifying the sender.

Rule 81
Communication by telex or telegram
1. Where an application for registration of a trade mark is submitted to the Office by telex or by telegram and the application contains a reproduction of the mark pursuant to Rule 3 2, Rule 80 1 shall apply *mutatis mutandis.*

2. Where a communication is submitted by telex or telegram, Rule 80 2 shall apply *mutatis mutandis.*

3. Where a communication is submitted by telex or telegram, the indication of the name of the sender shall be deemed equivalent to the signature.

Rule 82
Communication by electronic means
1. Where an application for registration of a trade mark is submitted by electronic means and the application contains a reproduction of the mark pursuant to Rule 3 2, Rule 80 1 shall apply *mutatis mutandis.*

2. Where a communication is sent by electronic means, Rule 80 2 shall apply *mutatis mutandis.*

3. Where a communication is sent to the Office by electronic means, the indication of the name of the sender shall be deemed to be equivalent to the signature.

4. The President of the Office shall determine the requirements as to communication by electronic means, such as the equipment to be used, technical details of communication, and methods of identifying the sender.

Rule 83
Forms
1. The Office shall make available free of charge forms for the purpose of:
(a) filing an application for a Community trade mark;
(b) entering opposition to registration of a Community trade mark;
(c) applying for an amendment of an application or a registration, for correction of names and addresses and of mistakes and errors;
(d) applying for the registration of a transfer and the transfer form and transfer document provided for in Rule 31 5;

(e) applying for the registration of a licence;

(f) applying for renewal of the registration of a Community trade mark.

(g) applying for revocation or for a declaration of invalidity of a Community trade mark;

(h) applying for restitutio in integrum;

(i) making an appeal;

(j) authorizing a representative, in the form of an individual authorization and in the form of a general authorization.

2. The Office may make other forms available free of charge.

3. The Office shall make available the forms referred to in paragraphs 1 and 2 in all the official languages of the Community.

4. The Office shall place the forms at the disposal of the Benelux Trade Mark Office and the Member States' central industrial property offices free of charge.

5. The Office may also make available the forms in machine-readable form.

6. Parties to proceedings before the Office shall use the forms provided by the Office, or copies of these forms, or forms with the same content and format as these forms, such as forms generated by means of electronic data processing.

7. Forms shall be completed in such a manner as to permit an automated input of the content into a computer, such as by character recognition or scanning.

Part I

Information of the public

Rule 84

Register of Community Trade Marks

1. The Register of Community Trade Marks may be maintained in the form of an electronic database.

2. The Register of Community Trade Marks shall contain the following entries:

(a) the date of filing the application;

(b) the file number of the application;

(c) the date of the publication of the application;

(d) the name, the address and the nationality of the applicant and the State in which he is domiciled or has his seat or establishment;

(e) the name and business address of the representative, other than a representative falling within the first sentence of Article 88(3) of the Regulation; where there is more than one representative, only the name and business address of the first named representative, followed by the words and others, shall be recorded; where an association of representatives is appointed, only the name and address of the association shall be recorded;

(f) the reproduction of the mark, with indications as to its nature, unless it is a mark falling under Rule 3 1; where the registration of the mark is in colour, the indication "in colour" with an indication of the colour or colours making up the mark; where applicable, a description of the mark;

(g) an indication of the goods and services by their names, grouped according to the classes of the Nice Classification; each group shall be preceded by the number of the class of that classification to which that group of goods and services belongs and shall be presented in the order of the classes of that classification;

(h) particulars of claims of priority pursuant to Article 30 of the Regulation;

(i) particulars of claims of exhibition priority pursuant to Article 33 of the Regulation;

(j) particulars of claims of seniority of an earlier registered trade mark as referred to in Article 34 of the Regulation;

(k) a statement that the mark has become distinctive in consequence of the use which has been made of it, pursuant to Article 7 (3) of the Regulation;

(l) a declaration by the applicant disclaiming any exclusive right to some element of the mark pursuant to Article 38 (2) of the Regulation;

(m) an indication that the mark is a collective mark;

(n) the language in which the application was filed and the second language which the applicant has indicated in his application, pursuant to Article 115 (3) of the Regulation;

(o) the date of registration of the mark in the Register and the registration number.

3. The Register of Community Trade Marks shall also contain the following entries, each accompanied by the date of recording of such entry:

(a) changes in the name, the address or the nationality of the proprietor of a Community trade mark or in the State in which he is domiciled or has his seat or establishment;

(b) changes in the name or business address of the representative, other than a representative falling within Article 88 (3), first sentence, of the Regulation;

(c) when a new representative is appointed, the name and business address of that representative;

(d) alterations of the mark pursuant to Article 48 of the Regulation and corrections of mistakes and errors;

(e) notice of amendments to the regulations governing the use of the collective mark pursuant to Article 69 of the Regulation;

(f) particulars of claims of seniority of an earlier registered trade mark as referred to in Article 34 of the Regulation, pursuant to Article 35 of the Regulation;

(g) total or partial transfers pursuant to Article 17 of the Regulation;

(h) the creation or transfer of a right *in rem* pursuant to Article 19 of the Regulation and the nature of the right *in rem*;

(i) levy of execution pursuant to Article 20 of the Regulation and bankruptcy or like proceedings pursuant to Article 21 of the regulation;

(j) the grant or transfer of a licence pursuant to Article 22 of the Regulation and, where applicable, the type of licence pursuant to Rule 34;

(k) renewal of the registration pursuant to Article 47 of the Regulation, the date from which it takes effect and any restrictions pursuant to Article 47 (4) of the Regulation;

(l) a record of the determination of the expiry of the registration pursuant to Article 47 of the Regulation;

(m) a declaration of surrender by the proprietor of the mark pursuant to Article 49 of the Regulation;

(n) the date of submission of an application pursuant to Article 55 of the Regulation or of the filing of a counterclaim pursuant to Article 96 (4) of the Regulation for revocation or for a declaration of invalidity;

(o) the date and content of the decision on the application or counterclaim pursuant to Article 56 (6) or the third sentence of Article 96 (6) of the Regulation;

(p) a record of the receipt of a request for conversion pursuant to Article 109 (2) of the Regulation;

(q) the cancellation of the representative recorded pursuant to paragraph 2 (e);

(r) the cancellation of the seniority of a national mark;

(s) the modification or cancellation from the Register of the items referred to in subparagraphs (h), (i) and (j).

4. The President of the Office may determine that items other than those referred to in paragraphs 2 and 3 shall be entered in the Register.

5. The proprietor of the trade mark shall be notified of any change in the Register.

6. The Office shall provide certified or uncertified extracts from the Register on request, on payment of a fee.

PART J

Community Trade Marks Bulletin and Official Journal of the Office

Rule 85

Community Trade Marks Bulletin

1. The Community Trade Marks Bulletin shall be published in periodic editions. The Office may make available to the public editions of the Bulletin on CD-ROM or in any other machine-readable form.

2. The Community Trade Marks Bulletin shall contain publications of applications and of entries made in the Register as well as other particulars relating to applications or registrations of trade marks whose publication is prescribed by the Regulation or by these Rules.

3. Where particulars whose publication is prescribed in the Regulation or in these Rules are published in the Community Trade Marks Bulletin, the date of issue shown on the Bulletin shall be taken as the date of publication of the particulars.

4. To the extent that the entries regarding the registration of a trade mark contain no changes as compared to the publication of the application, the publication of such entries shall be made by way of a reference to the particulars contained in the publication of the application.

5. The elements of the application for a Community trade mark, as set out in Article 26 (1) of the Regulation as well as any other information the publication of which is prescribed in Rule 12 shall, where appropriate, be published in all the official languages of the Community.

6. The Office shall take into account any translation submitted by the applicant. If the language of the application is not one of the languages of the Office, the translation into the second language indicated by the applicant shall be communicated to the applicant. The applicant may propose changes to the translation within a period to be specified by the Office. If the applicant does not respond within this period or if the Office considers the proposed changes to be inappropriate, the translation proposed by the Office shall be published.

Rule 86
Official Journal of the Office

1. The Official Journal of the Office shall be published in periodic editions. The Office may make available to the public editions of the Official Journal on CD-ROM or in any other machine-readable form.

2. The Official Journal shall be published in the languages of the Office. The President of the Office may determine that certain items shall be published in all the official languages of the Community.

Rule 87
Data bank

1. The Office shall maintain an electronic data bank with the particulars of applications for registration of trade marks and entries in the Register. The Office may also make available the contents of this data bank on CD-ROM or in any other machine-readable form.

2. The President of the Office shall determine the conditions of access to the data bank and the manner in which the contents of this data bank may be made available in machine-readable form, including the charges for these acts.

Part K

Inspection of files and keeping of files.

Rule 88

Parts of the file excluded from inspection

The parts of the file which shall be excluded from inspection pursuant to Article 84 (4) of the Regulation shall be:

(a) documents relating to exclusion or objection pursuant to Article 132 of the Regulation;

(b) draft decisions and opinions, and all other internal documents used for the preparation of decisions and opinions;

(c) parts of the file which the party concerned showed a special interest in keeping confidential before the application for inspection of the files was made, unless inspection of such part of the file is justified by overriding legitimate interests of the party seeking inspection.

Rule 89

Procedures for the inspection of files

1. Inspection of the files of Community trade mark applications and of registered Community trade marks shall either be of the original document, or of copies thereof, or of technical means of storage if the files are stored in this way. The means of inspection shall be determined by the President of the Office. The request for inspection of the files shall not be deemed to have been made until the required fee has been paid.

2. Where inspection of the files of a Community trade mark application is requested, the request shall contain an indication and evidence to the effect that the applicant:

(a) has consented to the inspection; or

(b) has stated that after the trade mark has been registered he will invoke the rights under it against the party requesting the inspection.

3. Inspection of the files shall take place on the premises of the Office.

4. On request, inspection of the files shall be effected by means of issuing copies of file documents. Such copies shall incur fees.

5. The office shall issue on request certified or uncertified copies of the application for a Community trade mark or of those file documents of which copies may be issued pursuant to paragraph 4 upon payment of a fee.

Rule 90

Communication of information contained in the files

Subject to the restrictions provided for in Article 84 of the Regulation and Rule 88, the Office may, upon request, communicate information from any file of a Community trade mark applied for or of a registered Community trade mark, subject to payment of a fee. 11 OF 19. However, the Office may require the exercise of the option to obtain inspection of the file itself should it deem this to be appropriate in view of the quantity of information to be supplied.

Rule 91

Keeping of files

1. The Office shall keep the files relating to Community trade mark applications and registered Community trade marks for at least five years from the end of the year in which:

(a) the application is rejected or withdrawn or is deemed to be withdrawn;

(b) the registration of the Community trade mark expires completely pursuant to Article 47 of the Regulation;

(c) the complete surrender of the Community trade mark is registered pursuant to Article 49 of the Regulation;

(d) the Community trade mark is completely removed from the Register pursuant to Article 56 (6) or Article 96 (6) of the Regulation.

2. The President of the Office shall determine the form in which the files shall be kept Part L Administrative cooperation.

Rule 92

Exchange of information and communications between the Office and the authorities of the Member States

1. The Office and the central industrial property offices of the Member States shall, upon request, communicate to each other relevant information about the filing of applications for Community trade marks or national marks and about proceedings relating to such applications and the marks registered as a result thereof. Such communications shall not be subject to the restrictions provided for in Article 84 of the Regulation.

2. Communications between the Office and the courts or authorities of the Member States which arise out of the application of the Regulation or these Rules shall be effected directly between these authorities. Such communication may also be effected through the central industrial property offices of the Member States.

3. Expenditure in respect of communications under paragraphs 1 and 2 shall be chargeable to the authority making the communications, which shall be exempt from fees.

Rule 93

Inspection of files by or via courts or authorities of the Member States

1. Inspection of files relating to Community trade marks applied for or registered Community trade marks by courts or authorities of the Member States be of the original documents or of copies thereof, otherwise Rule 89 shall not apply.

2. Courts or Public Prosecutors' Offices of the Member States may, in the course of proceedings before them, open files or copies thereof transmitted by the Office to inspection by third parties. Such inspection shall be subject to Article 84 of the Regulation. The Office shall not charge any fee for such inspection.

3. The Office shall, at the time of transmission of the files or copies thereof to the courts or Public Prosecutors' Offices of the Member States, indicate the restrictions to which the inspection of files relating to Community trade marks applied for or registered Community trade marks is subject pursuant to Article 84 of the Regulation and Rule 88.

Part M

Costs

Rule 94

Apportionment and fixing of costs

1. Apportionment of costs pursuant to Article 81 (1) and (2) of the Regulation shall be dealt with in the decision on the opposition, the decision on the application for revocation or for a declaration of invalidity of a Community trade mark, or the decision on the appeal.

2. Apportionment of costs pursuant to Article 81 (3) and (4) of the Regulation shall be dealt with in a decision on costs by the Opposition Division, the Cancellation Division or the Board of Appeal.

3. A bill of costs, with supporting evidence, shall be attached to the request for the fixing of costs provided for in the first sentence of Article 81 (6) of the Regulation. The request shall be admissible only if the decision in respect of which the fixing of costs is required has become final. Costs may be fixed once their credibility is established.

4. The request provided for in the second sentence of Article 81 (6) of the Regulation for a review of the decision of the registry on the fixing of costs, stating the reasons on which it is based, must be filed at the Office within one month after the date of notification of the awarding of costs. It shall not be deemed to be filed until the fee for reviewing the amount of the costs has been paid.

5. The Opposition Division, the Cancellation Division or the Board of Appeal, as the case may be, shall take a decision on the request referred to in paragraph 4 without oral proceedings.

6. The fees to be borne by the losing party pursuant to Article 81 (1) of the Regulation shall be limited to the fees incurred by the other party for opposition, for an application for revocation or for a declaration of invalidity of the Community trade mark and for appeal.

7. Cost essential to the proceedings and actually incurred by the successful party shall be borne by the losing party in accordance with Article 81 (1) of the Regulation on the basis of the following maximum rates:

(a) travel expenses of one party for the outward and return journey between the place of residence or the place of business and the place where oral proceedings are held or where evidence is taken, as follows:

(i) the cost of the first-class rail- fare including usual transport supplements where the total distance by rail does not exceed 800 km;

(ii) the cost of the tourist-class air-fare where the total distance by rail exceeds 800 km or the route includes a sea-crossing;

(b) subsistence expenses by one party equal to the daily subsistence allowance for officials in grades A4 to A8 as laid down in Article 13 of Annex VII to the Staff Regulations of Officials of the European Communities;

(c) travel expenses of representatives within the meaning of Article 89 (1) of the Regulation and of witnesses and of experts, at the rates provided for in subparagraph (a);

(d) subsistence expenses of representatives within the meaning of Article 89 (1) of the Regulation and of witnesses and experts, at the rates provided for in subparagraph (b);

(e) costs entailed in the taking of evidence in the form of examination of witnesses, opinions by experts or inspectionup to ECU 300 per proceedings;

(f) cost of representation, within the meaning of Article 89 (1) of the Regulation,

(i) of the opposing party in opposition proceedings: up to ECU 250;

(ii) of the applicant in opposition proceedings: up to ECU 250;

(iii) of the applicant in proceedings relating to revocation or invalidity of a Community trade mark: up to ECU 400;

(iv) of the proprietor of the trade mark in proceedings relating to revocation or invalidity of a Community trade mark: up to ECU 400;

(v) of the appellant in appeal proceedings: up to ECU 500;

(vi) of the defendant in appeal proceedings: up to ECU 500; Where the taking of evidence in any of the abovementioned proceedings involves the examination of witnesses, opinions by experts or inspection, an additional amount shall be granted for representation costs of up to ECU 600 per proceedings;

(g) where the successful party is represented by more than one representative within the meaning of Article 89 (1) of the Regulation, the losing party shall bear the costs referred to in subparagraphs (c), (d) and (f) for one such person only;

(h) the losing party shall not be obliged to reimburse the successful party for any costs, expenses and fees other than those referred to in subparagraphs (a) to (g).

PART N

Languages

Rule 95

Applications and declarations

Without prejudice to Article 115 (5) of the Regulation,

(a) any application or declaration relating to a Community trade mark application may be filed in the language used for filing the application for a Community trade mark or in the second language indicated by the applicant in his application;

(b) any application or declaration relating to a registered Community trade mark may be filed in one of the languages of the Office. However, when the application is filed by using any of the forms provided by the Office pursuant to Rule 83, such forms may be used in any of the official languages of the Community, provided that the form is completed in one of the languages of the Office, as far as textual elements are concerned.

Rule 96

Written proceedings

1. Without prejudice to Article 115 (4) and (7) of the Regulation, and unless otherwise provided for in these Rules, in written proceedings before the Office any party may use any language of the Office. If the language chosen is not the language of the proceedings, the party shall supply a translation into that language within one month from the date of the submission of the original document. Where the applicant for a Community trade mark is the sole party to proceedings before the Office and the language used for the filing of the application for the Community trade mark is not one of the languages of the Office, the translation may also be filed in the second language indicated by the applicant in his application.

2. Unless otherwise provided for in these Rules, documents to be used in proceedings before the Office may be filed in any official language of the Community. Where the language of such documents is not the language of the proceedings the Office may require that a translation be supplied, within a period specified by it, in that language or, at the choice of the party to the proceeding, in any language of the Office.

Rule 97
Oral proceedings
1. Any party to oral proceedings before the Office may, in place of the language of proceedings, use one of the other official languages of the Community, on condition that he makes provision for interpretation into the language of proceedings. Where the oral proceedings are held in a proceeding concerning the application for registration of a trade mark, the applicant may use either the language of the application or the second language indicated by him.

2. In oral proceedings concerning the application for registration of a trade mark, the staff of the Office may use either the language of the application or the second language indicated by the applicant. In all other oral proceedings, the staff of the Office may use, in place of the language of the proceedings, one of the other languages of the Office, on condition that the party or parties to the proceedings agree to such use.

3. In the case of taking of evidence, any party to be heard, witness or expert who is unable to express himself adequately in the language of proceedings, may use any of the official languages of the Community. Should the taking of evidence be decided upon following a request by a party to the proceedings, parties to be heard, witnesses or experts who express themselves in languages other than the language of proceedings may be heard only if the party who made the request makes provision for interpretation into that language. In proceedings concerning the application for registration of a trade mark, in place of the language of the application, the second language indicated by the applicant may be used. In any proceedings with only one party the Office may on request of the party concerned permit derogations from the provisions in this paragraph.

4. If the parties and Office so agree, any official language of the Community may be used in oral proceedings.

5. The Office shall, if necessary, make provision at its own expense for interpretation into the language of proceedings, or, where appropriate, into its other languages, unless this interpretation is the responsibility of one of the parties to the proceedings.

6. Statements by staff of the Office, by parties to the proceedings and by witnesses and experts, made in one of the languages of the Office during oral proceedings shall be entered in the minutes in the language employed. Statements made in any other language shall be entered in the language of proceedings. Amendments to the text of the application for or the registration of a Community trade mark shall be entered in the minutes in the language of proceedings.

Rule 98

Certification of translations

1. When a translation of any document is to be filed, the Office may require the filing, within a period to be specified by it, of a certificate that the translation corresponds to the original text. Where the certificate relates to the translation of a previous application pursuant to Article 30 of the Regulation, such period shall not be less than three months after the date of filing of the application. Where the certificate is not filed within that period, the document shall be deemed not to have been received.

2. The President of the Office may determine the manner in which translations are certified.

Rule 99

Legal authenticity of translations

In the absence of evidence to the contrary, the Office may assume that a translation corresponds to the relevant original text Part O Organization of the Office.

Rule 100

Allocation of duties

1. The President of the Office shall determine the examiners and their number, the members of the Opposition Divisions and Cancellation Divisions, and the members of the Administration of Trade Marks and Legal Division. He shall allocate duties to the examiners and the Divisions.

2. The President of the Office may provide that examiners may also be members of the Opposition Divisions, Cancellation Divisions, and the Administration of Trade Marks and Legal Division, and that members of these Divisions may also be examiners.

3. In addition to the responsibilities vested in them under the Regulation, the President of the Office may allocate further duties to the examiners and the members of the Opposition Divisions, Cancellation Divisions and the Administration of Trade Marks and Legal Division.

4. The President of the Office may entrust to other members of the staff of the Office who are not examiners or members of any of the Divisions mentioned in paragraph 1 the execution of individual duties falling to the examiners, Opposition Divisions, Cancellation Divisions or the Administration of Trade Marks and Legal Division and involving no special difficulties.

TITLE XII

Reciprocity

Rule 101
Publication of reciprocity
1. If necessary, the President of the Office shall request the Commission to enquire whether a State which is not party to the Paris Convention or to the Agreement establishing the World Trade Organization accords reciprocal treatment within the meaning of Article 5 (1) (d), Article 5 (3) and Article 29 (5) of the Regulation.

2. If the Commission determines that reciprocal treatment in accordance with paragraph 1 is accorded, it shall publish a communication to this effect in the Official Journal of the European Communities.

3. Article 5 (1) (d), Article 5 (3) and Article 29 (5) of the Regulation shall take effect for the nationals of the States concerned from the date of publication in the Official Journal of the European Communities of the communication referred to in paragraph 2, unless the communications states an earlier date from which it is applicable. They shall cease to be effective from the date of publication in the Official Journal of the European Communities of a communication of the Commission to the effect that reciprocal treatment is no longer accorded, unless the communication states an earlier date from which it is applilable.

4. Communications referred to in paragraphs 2 and 3 shall also be published in the Official Journal of the Office.

Article 2
Transitional Provisions
1. Any application for registration of a Community trade mark filed within three months prior to the date determined pursuant to Article 143 (3) of the Regulation shall be marked by the Office with the filing date determined pursuant to that provision and with the actual date of receipt of the application.

2. With regard to the application, the priority period of six months provided for in Articles 29 and 33 of the Regulation shall be calculated from the date determined pursuant to Article 143 (3) of the Regulation.

3. The Office may issue a receipt to the applicant prior to the date determined pursuant to Article 143 (3) of the Regulation.

4. The Office may examine the applications prior to the date determined pursuant to Article 143 (3) of the Regulation and communicate with the applicant

with a view to remedying any deficiencies prior to that date. Any decisions with regard to such applications may be taken only after that date.

5. With regard to the application, the Office shall not carry out any search pursuant to Article 39 (1) of the Regulation, regardless of whether or not a priority was claimed for such application pursuant to Articles 29 or 33 of the Regulation.

6. Where the date of receipt of an application for the registration of a Community trade mark by the Office, by the central industrial property office of a Member State or by the Benelux Trade Mark Office is before the commencement of the three months period specified in Article 143 (4) of the Regulation the application shall be deemed not to have been filed. The application shall be informed accordingly and the application shall be sent back to him.

Article 3
Entry into force
This Regulation shall enter into force on the seventh day following that of its publication in the *Official Journal of the European Communities*.

This Regulation shall be binding in its entirety and directly applicable in all Member States.

Done at Brussels, 13 December 1995

For the Commission.
Mario MONTI
Member of the Commission

Commission Regulation (EC) No. 2869/95

of 13 December 1995
on the fees payable to the Office for Harmonization in the Internal Market
(Trade Marks and Designs)

THE COMMISSION OF THE EUROPEAN COMMUNITIES,

Having regard to the Treaty establishing the European Community,

Having regard to Council Regulation (EC) No. 40/94 of 20 December 1993 on the Community trade mark,[1] as amended by Regulation (EC) No. 3288/94,[2] and in particular Article 139 thereof,

Having regard to Commission Regulation (EC) No. 2868/95 of 13 December 1995, implementing Council Regulation (EC) No. 40/94 on the Community trade mark,[3]

Whereas Article 139 (3) of Regulation (EC) No. 40/94 (hereinafter "the Regulation") provides that the fees regulations shall be adopted in accordance with the procedure laid down in Article 141 of the Regulation;

Whereas Article 139 (1) of the Regulation provides that the fees regulations shall determine in particular the amount of the fees and the ways in which they are to be paid;

Whereas Article 139 (2) of the Regulation provides that the amounts of the fees shall be fixed at such a level as to ensure that the revenue in respect thereof is in principle sufficient for the budget of the Office for Harmonization in the Internal Market (trade marks and designs) ("the Office") to be balanced;

Whereas, however, in the Office's start-up phase, balance can be achieved only if there is a subsidy from the general budget of the European Communities, in accordance with Article 134 (3) of the Regulation;

Whereas the basic fee for the application for a Community trade mark shall include the amount which the Office must pay to each central industrial property office of the Member States for each search report provided by such offices in accordance with Article 39 (4) of the Regulation;

1 OJ No. L 11, 14.1.1994, p. 1.
2 OJ No. L 349, 31.12.1994, p. 88.
3 See p. 1 of this Official Journal.

Whereas to ensure the necessary flexibility, the President of the Office ("the President") should be empowered, subject to certain conditions, to lay down the charges which may be payable to the Office in respect of services it may render, the charges for access to the Office's data bank and the making available of the contents of this data bank in machine-readable form, and to set charges for the sale of its publications;

Whereas, in order to facilitate the payment of fees and charges, the President should be empowered to authorize methods of payment which are additional to those explicitly provided for in this Regulation;

Whereas it is appropriate that the fees and charges payable to the Office should be fixed in the same currency unit as is used for the budget of the Office;

Whereas the budget of the Office is fixed in ecus;

Whereas, moreover, the fixing of these amounts in ecus avoids discrepancies that may result from exchange rate variations;

Whereas payments in cash should be made in the currency of the Member State where the Office has its seat;

Whereas the measures envisaged in this Regulation are in accordance with the opinion of the Committee established under Article 141 of the Regulation,

HAS ADOPTED THIS REGULATION:

Article 1

General

The following shall be levied in accordance with this Regulation:

(a) fees to be paid to the Office as provided for in the Regulation and in Regulation (EC) No. 2868/95;

(b) charges laid down by the President pursuant to Article 3 (1) and (2).

Article 2

Article 2 Fees provided for in the Regulation and Regulation (EC) No. 2868/95

The fees to be paid to the Office under Article 1 (a) shall be as follows:

(in ecus)

1. Basic fee for the application for an individual mark (Article 26 (2); Rule 4 (a))	975
2. Fee for each class of goods and services exceeding three for an individual mark (Article 26 (2); Rule 4 (b)	200
3. Basic fee for the application for a collective mark (Articles 26 (2) and 64 (3); Rules 4 (a) and (42)	1,675
4. Fee for each class of goods and services exceeding three for a collective mark (Article 26 (2) and 64 (3); Rules 4 (b) and 42)	400

	(in ecus)
5. Opposition fee (Article 42 (3); Rule 18 1)	350
6. Fee for the alteration of the representation of a a trade mark (point 1 of Article 140 (2) and Article 44 (2); Rule 13 2)	200
7. Basic fee for the registration of an individual mark (Article 45; Rule 23 1 (a))	1,100
8. Fee for each class of goods and services exceeding three for an individual mark (Article 45; Rule 23 1 (b))	200
9. Basic fee for the registration of a collective trade mark (Articles 45 and 64 (3); Rules 23 1 (a) and 42)	2,200
10. Fee foe each class of goods and services exceeding three for a collective mark (Articles 45 and 64 (3), Rules 23 1 (b) and 42)	400
11. Additional fee for the late payment of the registration fee (point 2 of Article 140 (2), Rule 3)	25% *of the belated registration fee, subject to a maximum of 750*
12. Basic fee for the renewal for an individual mark (Article 47 (1), Rule 30 2 (a))	2,500
13. Fee for each class of goods and services exceeding three for an individual mark (Article 47 (1), Rule 30 2 (b)	500
14. Basic fee for the renewal for a collective mark (Articles 47 (1) and 64 (3), Rules 30 2 (a) and 42)	5,000
15. Fee for each class of goods and services exceeding three for a collective mark (Articles 47 (1) and 64 (3), Rules 30 2 (b) and 42)	1,000
16. Additional fee for the late payment of the renewal fee or the late submission of the request for renewal (Article 47 (3), Rule 30 2 (c))	25% *at the belated renewal fee, subject to a maximum of 1 500*
17. Fee for the application for revocation or for a declaration of invalidity (Article 55 (2), Rule 39 2)	700
18. Appeal fee (Article 59, Rule 49 1)	800
19. Fee for restitutio in integrum (Article 78 (3))	200
20. Fee for the conversion of a mark into a national trade mark application (Article 109 (1), Rule 45 2)	200

	(in ecus)
21. Fee for the recording of the whole or partial transfer of an application for a Community trade mark (Article 24 and point 4 of Article 140 (2); Rule 31 4 and 8)	200 *per entry, but, where multiple requests are submitted in the same application or at the same time, not to exceed a total of 1 000*
22. Fee for the registration of the whole or partial transfer of a registered Community trade mark (point 4 of Article 140 (2); Rule 31 4)	200 *per registration, but, where multiple requests are submitted in the same application or at the same application or at the same time, not to exceed a total of 1 000*
23. Fee for the registration of a licence or another right in respect of a registered Community trade mark (point 5 of Article 140 (2), Rule 33 1) or an Application for a Community trade mark (point 6 of Article 140 (2), Rule 33 4: (a) grant of a licence (b) transfer of a licence (c) creation of a right *in rem* (d) transfer of a right *in rem* (e) levy of execution	200 *per registration, but,where multiple requests are submitted in the same application or at the same application or at the same time,not to exceed a total of 1 000*
24. Fee for the cancellation of the registration of a licence or other right (point 7 of Article 140 (2), Rule 35 3)	200 *per cancellation, but, where multiple requests are submitted in the same application or at the same time, not to exceed a total of 1 000*
25. Fee for the alteration of a registered Community trade Mark (point 8 of Article 140 (2), Rule 25 2)	200

(in ecus)

26. Fee for the issue of a copy of the application for a Community trade mark (point 12 of Article 140 (2), Rule 89 5), a copy of the certificate of registration (point 3 of Article 140 (2), Rule 24 2, or an extract from the register (point 9 of Article 140 (2), Rule 84 6)	
(a) uncertified copy or extract	10
(b) certified copy or extract	30
27. Fee for the inspection of the files (point 10 of Article 140 (2) No. 10, Rule 89 1)	30
28. Fee for the issue of copies of file documents (point 11 of Article 140 (2) No. 11, Rule 89 5)	
(a) uncertified copy	10
(b) certified copy	30
plus per page, exceeding 10	1
29. Fee for the communication of information in a file (point 13 of Article 140 (2), Rule 90)	10
plus per page, exceeding 10	1
30. Fee for the review of the determination of the procedural costs to be refunded (point 14 of Article 140 (2), Rule 94 4)	100

Article 3

Charges laid down by the President

1. The President shall lay down the amount to be charged for any services rendered by the Office other than those specified in Article 2.

2. The President shall lay down the amount to be charged for the Community Trade Marks Bulletin and the Official Journal of the Office as well as any other publications issued by the Office.

3. The amounts of the charges shall be laid down in ecus.

4. The amounts of the charges laid down by the President in accordance with paragraphs 1 and 2 shall be published in the Official Journal of the Office.

Article 4

Due date for fees and charges

1. Fees and charges in respect of which the due date is not specified in the Regulation or in Regulation No. 2868/95 shall be due on the date of receipt of the request for the service for which the fee or the charge is incurred.

2. The President may decide not to make services mentioned in paragraph 1 dependent upon the advance payment of the corresponding fees or charges.

Article 5
Payment of fees and charges
1. Fees and charges due to the Office shall be paid
   (a) by payment or transfer to a bank account held by the Office,
   (b) by delivery or remittance of cheques made payable to the Office, or
   (c) in cash.

2. The President may allow methods of payment other than those set out in paragraph 1, in particular by means of deposits in current accounts held with the Office.

3. Determinations made pursuant to paragraph 2 shall be published in the Official Journal of the Office.

Article 6
Currencies
1. Payments or transfers to a bank account referred to in Article 5 (1) (a), by delivery or remittance of cheques referred to in Article 5 (1) (b) or any other method of payment allowed by the President pursuant to Article 5 (2) shall be made in ecus.

2. The payments in cash referred to in Article 5 (1) (c) shall be made in the currency of the Member State where the Office has its seat. The President shall determine the ecus equivalents in that currency on the basis of the exchange rate in force, which are fixed daily by the Commission and published in the Official Journal of the European Communities in accordance with Council Regulation (EC) No. 3320/94[4].

Article 7
Particulars concerning payment
1. Every payment must indicate the name of the person making the payment and must contain the necessary information to enable the Office to establish immediately the purpose of the payment. In particular, the following information shall be provided:

(a) when the application fee is paid, the purpose of the payment, namely "application fee";

(b) when the registration fee is paid, the file number of the application which is the basis for the registration and the purpose of the payment, namely "registration fee";

(c) when the opposition fee is paid, the file number of the application and the name of the applicant for the Community trade mark against which opposition is entered, and the purpose of the payment, namely "opposition fee";

[4] OJ No. L 350, 31.12.1994, p. 27.

(d) when the revocation fee and the invalidity fee are paid, the registration number and the name of the proprietor of the Community trade mark against which the application is directed, and the purpose of the payment, namely "revocation fee" or "invalidity fee".

2. If the purpose of the payment cannot immediately be established, the Office shall require the person making the payment to notify it in writing of this purpose within such period as it may specify. If the person does not comply with this request in due time, the payment shall be considered not to have been made. The amount which has been paid shall be refunded.

Article 8

Deemed date of payment

1. The date on which any payment shall be considered to have been made to the Office shall be as follows:

(a) in the cases referred to in Article 5 (1) (a), the date on which the amount of the payment or of the transfer is actually entered in a bank account held by the Office;

(b) in the case referred to in Article 5 (1) (b), the date of the receipt of the cheque at the Office, provided that the cheque is met;

(c) in the cases referred to in Article 5 (1) (c), the date of receipt of the amount of the cash payment.

2. Where the President allows, in accordance with the provisions of Article 5 (2), other methods of paying fees than those set out in Article 5 (1), he shall also lay down the date on which such payments shall be considered to have been made.

3. Where, under the provisions of paragraphs 1 and 2, payment of a fee is not considered to have been made until after the expiry of the period in which it was due, it shall be considered that this period has been observed if evidence is provided to the Office that the person who made the payment –

(a) in a Member State, within the period within which the payment should have been made:

(i) effected the payment through a banking establishment;

(ii) duly gave an order to a banking establishment to transfer the amount of the payment; or

(iii) dispatched at a post office or otherwise a letter bearing the address of the Office and containing a cheque within the meaning of Article 5 (1) (b), provided that the cheque is met;

and –

(b) paid a surcharge of 10% on the relevant fee or fees, but not exceeding ECU 200; no surcharge is payable if a condition according to sub-paragraph (a) has been fulfilled not later than 10 days before the expiry of the period for payment.

4. The Office may request the person who made the payment to produce evidence as to the date on which a condition according to paragraph 3 (a) was fulfilled and, where required, to pay the surcharge referred to in paragraph 3 (b), within a period to be specified by it. If the person fails to comply with this request or if the evidence is insufficient, or if the required surcharge is not paid in due time, the period for payment shall be considered not to have been observed.

Article 9
Insufficiency of the amount paid
1. A time limit for payment shall, in principle, be considered to have been observed only if the full amount of the fee has been paid in due time. If the fee is not paid in full, the amount which has been paid shall be refunded after the period for payment has expired.

2. The Office may, however, in so far as this is possible within the time remaining before the end of the period, give the person making the payment the opportunity to pay the amount lacking or, where this is considered justified, overlook any small amounts lacking without prejudice to the rights of the person making the payment.

Article 10
Refund of insignificant amounts
1. Where an excessive sum is paid to cover a fee or a charge, the excess shall not be refunded if the amount is insignificant and the party concerned has not expressly requested a refund. The President shall determine what constitutes an insignificant amount.

2. Determinations by the President pursuant to paragraph 1 shall be published in the Official Journal of the Office.

Article 11
Entry into force
This Regulation shall enter into force on the seventh day following its publication in the *Official Journal of the European Communities*.

This Regulation shall be binding in is entirety and directly applicable in all Member States.

Done at Brussels, 13 December 1995

For the Commission
MARIO MONTI
Member of the Commission

Commission Regulation (EC) No. 216/96

of 5 February 1996
laying down the rules of procedure of the Boards of Appeal of the Office for Harmonization in the Internal Market (Trade Marks and Designs)

THE COMMISSION OF THE EUROPEAN COMMUNITIES,

Having regard to the Treaty establishing the European Community,

Having regard to Council Regulation (EC) No. 40/94 of 20 December 1994 on the Community trade mark,[1] as amended by Regulation (EC) No. 3288/94,[2] and in particular Article 140 (3) thereof,

Whereas Regulation (EC) No. 40/94 (hereinafter "the Regulation") creates a new trade mark system allowing a trade mark having effect throughout the Community to be obtained on the basis of an application to the Office for Harmonizaiton in the Internal Market (Trade Marks and Designs) ("the Office");

Whereas for this purpose the Regulation contains in particular the necessary provisions for a procedure leading to the registration of a Community trade marks, as well as for the administration of Community trade marks, for appeals against decisions of the Office and for proceedings in relation to revocation or invalidity of a Community trade mark;

Whereas under Article 130 of the Regulation, the Boards of Appeal are to be responsible for deciding on appeals from decisions of the examiners, the Opposition Divisions, the Administration of Trade Marks and Legal Division and the Cancellation Divisions;

Whereas Title VII of the Regulation contains basic principles regarding appeals against decisions of examiners, the Opposition Divisions, the Administration of Trade Marks and Legal Division and the Cancellation Divisions;

Whereas Title X of Commission Regulation (EC) No. 2868/95 of 13 December 1995 implementing Council Regulation No. 40/94 on the Community Trade Mark[3] contains implementing rules to Title VII of the Regulation;

[1] OJ No. L 11, 14.1.1994, p.1.
[2] OJ No. L 349, 31.12.1994, p. 83.
[3] OJ No. L 303, 15.12.1995, p. 1.

Whereas this Regulation supplements those other rules, in particular as regards the organization of the Boards and the oral procedure;

Whereas before the beginning of each working year a scheme should be established for the distribution of business between the Boards of Appeal by an Authority established for that purpose;

Whereas to this end the said Authority should apply objective criteria such as classes of products and services or initial letters of the names of applicants;

Whereas to facilitate the handling and disposal of appeals, a rapporteur should be designated for each case, who should be responsible *inter alia* for preparing communications with the parties and drafting decisions;

Whereas the parties to proceedings before the Boards of Appeal may not be in a position or may not be willing to bring questions of general relevance to a pending case to the attention of the Boards of Appeal;

Whereas, therefore, the Boards of Appeal should have the power, of their own motion or pursuant to a request by the President, to invite the President of the Office, to submit comments on questions of general interest in relation to a case pending before the Boards of Appeal;

Whereas the measures provided for in this Regulation are in accordance with the opinion of the Committee established under Article 141 of the Regulation.

HAS ADOPTED THIS REGULATION:

Article 1

Allocation of duties and Authority competent to allocate

1. Before the beginning of each working year, duties shall be allocated to the Boards of Appeal according to objective criteria, and the members of each of the Boards and their alternates shall be designated. Any member of a Board of Appeal may be designated for several Boards of Appeal as a member or an alternate. These measures may, where necessary, be amended during the working year in question.

2. The measures referred to in paragraph 1 shall be taken by an Authority composed of the President of the Office as Chairman, the Vice-President of the Office responsible for the Boards of Appeal, the Chairmen of the Boards of Appeal and three other members of the Boards of Appeal elected by the full membership of those Boards, except the Chairmen, for the working year in question. The Authority may validly deliberate only if at least five of its members are present, including the President or the Vice-President of the Office and two Chairmen of Boards of Appeal. Decisions shall be taken by majority vote. In the event of a tie, the vote of the Chairman shall be decisive. The Authority may lay down its internal rules of procedure.

3. The Authority provided for in paragraph 2 shall decide on conflicts regarding the allocation of duties among different Boards of Appeal.

4. Until more than three Boards of Appeal have been set up, the Authority referred to in paragraph 2 shall consist of the President of the Office, who shall act as Chairman, the Vice- President of the Office responsible for the Boards of Appeal, the Chairman or Chairmen of the Boards of Appeal which have already been set up and one other member of the Boards of Appeal elected by ther full membership of the Board, except the Chairman or Chairmen, for the working year in question. The Authoritiy may validly deliberate only if at least three of its members are present, including the President or the Vice-President of the Office.

Article 2

Replacement of members

1. Reasons for replacement by alternates shall in particular include leave, sickness, inescapable commitments and the grounds of exclusion set out in Article 132 of the Regulation.

2. Any member asking to be replaced by an alternate shall without delay inform the Chairman of the Board concerned of his unavailability.

Article 3

Exclusion and objection

1. If a Board has knowledge of a possible reason for exclusion or objection under Article 132 (3) of the Regulation which does not originate from a member himself or from any party to the proceedings, the procedure of Article 132 (4) of the Regulation shall be applied.

2. The member concerned shall be invited to present his comments as to whether there is a reason for exclusion or objection.

3. Before a decision is taken on the action to be taken pursuant to Article 132 (4) of the Regulation, there shall be no further proceedings in the case

Article 4

Rapporteurs

1. The Chairman of each Board shall for each appeal designate a member of his Board, or himself, as rapporteur

2. The rapporteur shall carry out a preliminary study of the appeal. He may prepare communications to the parties subject to the direction of the Chairman of the Board. Communications shall be signed by the rapporteur on behalf of the Board

3. The rapporteur shall prepare internal meetings of the Board and the oral proceedings.

4. The rapporteur shall draft decisions.

Article 5
Registries
1. Registries shall be established for the Boards of Appeal. Registrars shall be responsible for the discharge of the functions of the Registries. One of the Registrars may be designated Senior Registrar.

2. The Authority provided for in Article 1 (2) may entrust to the Registrars the performance of functions which involve no legal or technical difficulties, particularly with regard to representation, the submission of translations, inspection of files and notifications.

3. The Registrar shall submit to the Chairman of the Board concerned a report on the admissibility of each newly-filed appeal

4. Minutes of oral proceedings and of the taking of evidence shall be drawn up by the Registrar or, if the President of the Office has agreed thereto, such other officer of the Office as the Chairman of the Board may designate.

Article 6
Change in the composition of a Board
1. If the composition of a Board is changed after oral proceedings, the parties to the proceedings shall be informed that, at the request of any party, fresh oral proceedings shall be held before the Board in its new composition. Fresh oral proceedings shall also be held if so requested by the new member and if the other members of the Board have given their agreement.

2. The new member shall be bound to the same extent as the other members by an interim decision which has already been taken.

3. If, when a Board has already reached a final decision, a member is unable to act, he shall not be replaced by an alternate. If the Chairman is unable to act, then the member of the Board concerned having the longer service on the Board, or where members have the same length of service, the older member, shall sign the decision on behalf of the Chairman.

Article 7
Joinder of appeal proceedings
1. If several appeals are filed against a decision, those appeals shall be considered in the same proceedings.

2. If appeals are filed against separate decisions and all the appeals are designated to be examined by one Board having the same composition, that Board may deal with those appeals in joined proceedings with the consent of the parties.

Article 8

Remission to the department of first instance

Where the proceedings of the department of first instance whose decision is the subject of an appeal are vitiated by fundamental deficiencies, the Board shall set aside the decision and, unless there are reasons for not doing so, remit the case to that instance or decide the matter itself.

Article 9

Oral proceedings

1. If oral proceedings are to take place, the Board shall ensure that the parties have provided all relevant information and documents before the hearing.

2. The Board may, when issuing the summons to attend oral proceedings, add a communication drawing attention to matters which seem to be of special significance, or to the fact that certain questions appear no longer to be contentious, or containing other observations that may help to concentrate on essentials during the oral proceedings.

3. The Board shall ensure that the case is ready for decision at the conclusion of the oral proceedings, unless there are special reasons to the contrary.

Article 10

Communications to the parties

If a Board deems it expedient to communicate with the parties regarding a possible appraisal of substantive or legal matters, such communication shall be made in such a way as not to imply that the Board is in any way bound by it.

Article 11

Comments on questions of general interest

The Board may, on its own initiative or at the written, reasoned request of the President of the Office, invite him to comment in writing or orally on questions of general interest which arise in the course of proceedings pending before it. The parties shall be entitled to submit their observations on the President's comments.

Article 12

Deliberations preceding decisions

The rapporteur shall submit to the other members of the Board a draft of the decision to be taken and shall set a reasonable time-limit within which to oppose it or to ask for changes. The Board shall meet to deliberate on the decision to be taken if it appears that the members of a Board are not all of the same opinion. Only members of the Board shall participate in the deliberations; the Chairman of the Board concerned may, however, authorize other officers such as registrars or interpreters to attend. Deliberations shall be secret.

Article 13

Order of voting

1. During the deliberations between members of a Board, the opinion of the rapporteur shall be heard first, and, if the rapporteur is not the Chairman, the Chairman last.

2. If voting is necessary, votes shall be taken in the same sequence, save that if the Chairman is also the rapporteur, be shall vote last. Abstentions shall not be permitted.

Article 14

Entry into force.

This Regulation shall enter into force the third day following its publication in the *Official Journal of the European Communities*.

This Regulation shall be binding in its entirety and directly applicable in all Member States.

Done at Brussels, 5 February 1996.

For the Commission
Mario MONTI
Member of the Commission

Statements for Entry in the Minutes of the Council Meeting at which the Regulation was adopted

1. Re Article 1(1)
"The Council and the Commission consider that the activity of retail trading in goods is not as such a service for which a Community trade mark may be registered under this Regulation".

2. Re Article 1(2)
"The Council and the Commission consider that the word "surrendered" in Article 1(2) means surrendered within the meaning of Article 49".

3. Re Article 4
(a) "The Council and the Commission consider that Article 4 does not rule out the possibility:
- of registering as a Community trade mark a combination of colours or a single colour;
- of registering in the future sounds as Community trade marks,

provided that they are capable of distinguishing the goods or services of one undertaking from those of other undertakings".

(b) "The Council and the Commission consider that the word "shape" is also intended to cover the three-dimensional form of goods".

4. Re Article 7(1) (e)
"The Council and the Commission consider that where goods are packaged, the expression "shape of the goods includes the shape of the packaging".

5. Re Article 8(1)(b) and 9(1)(b)
"The Council and the Commission note that "likelihood of association" is a concept which in particular has been developed by Benelux case-law".

6. Re Article 9

"The Council and the Commission consider that the reference to advertising in paragraph 2(d) does not cover the use of a Community trade mark in comparative advertising".

7. Re Article 12

"The Council and the Commission consider that the words "his own name" in subparagraph (a) apply only in respect of natural persons".

8. Re Article 14(2)

"The Council and the Commission consider that the reference to the law of Member States relating in particular to civil liability and unfair competition is to be construed as including passing-off. "Passing-off" is a term used in common-law countries such as the United Kingdom. It occurs when one person presents goods or services in a way which is likely to injure the business or goodwill of another person, for example by causing the public to believe that they are goods or services associated with that other person.

In order to succeed in an action for passing-off, a plaintiff must show that the way his goods or services are presented by the defendant is likely to cause confusion and that he is likely to be injured by that confusion; it is not, however, necessary to show that the defendant intended to mislead or confuse the public".

9. Re Article 15

"The Council and the Commission consider that use which is genuine within the meaning of Article 15 in one country constitutes genuine use in the Community".

10. Re Article 20

"The Council and the Commission consider that insofar as the national law of the Member State determined in accordance with Article 16 contains rules concerning the limits on the procedure for levy of execution in respect of a debtors assets, for example in the case of infringement of his rights of personality, these rules will also apply to the cases covered by Article 20".

11. Re Article 21

(a) "The Council and the Commission consider that insofar as the national law of the Member State determined in accordance with Article 21 contains rules concerning the limits on there measures which may be taken as regards a debtors assets in bankruptcy or like proceedings, for example in the case of infringement of his rights of personality, these rules will also apply to the cases covered by Article 21".

(b) "The Council and the Commission note that the principles of Articles 234 of the EEC Treaty apply to conventions concluded before the entry into force of the Regulation between one or mode Member States on the one side and one or more third countries on the other side".

12. Re Article 23(1)
"The Council and the Commission consider that Article 23(1) should not be interpreted as meaning that application of Article 53(3) to use of a Community trade mark by a licensee would be subject to registration of the licence".

13. Re Article 39(5)
"The Council and the Commission consider that, in the framework of the procedures provided for in Article 39(5), the central industrial property offices of the Member States are free to inform the proprietors of any earlier national trade marks or national trade mark applications cited in the national search report of the publication of the Community trade mark application".

14. Re Article 43(4) and Article 56(4)
"The Council and the Commission consider that these provisions do not exclude the possibility of the Office making proposals for a friendly settlement if it thinks fit".

15. Re Article 44(2)
"The Council and the Commission consider that the words "obvious mistakes" should be understood as meaning mistakes which obviously require correction, in the sense that nothing else would have been intended that what is offered as the correction".

16. Re Article 65(1)
"The Council and the Commission consider that, where the association which is proprietor of the Community collective mark consists of several member associations, the mark may be used not only by these member association but also by their members".

17. Re Article 66(2)
"The Council and the Commission consider that a collective mark which is available for use only by members of an association which owns the mark is liable to mislead within the meaning of Article 66(2) if it gives the impression that it is available for use by anyone who is able to meet certain objective standards".

18. Re Article 87(1)
"The Council and the Commission consider that the reference to national laws it to be understood as meaning that any restrictions in national laws applicable to administrative and legal co-operation between the courts or authorities of the State concerned will apply to such co-operation between the Office and the courts or authorities, but does not empower the Member States to introduce national laws treating administrative and legal co-operation between the Office and the courts or authorities of the State concerned in a different way from such co-operation between the courts or authorities of that State".

19. Re Article 86, last sentence
"The Council and the Commission consider that this sentence is to be understood as meaning that, while the inspection by the authorities mentioned will not be subject to the restrictions laid down in Article 84, this will not affect the restrictions on inspection by the public".

20. Re Article 89
"The Commission states its intention of carrying out, at the end of a period of three years from the date on which the Office begins to accept the filing of applications, and examination of the functioning of the manner of representation as laid down in Article 89 and if necessary of submitting to the Council and appropriate proposal, possibly for the introduction of a qualifying examination for entry on the list of professional representatives".

21. Re Article 90(1)
"The Council and the Commission consider that the aim of paragraph 1 is to render the provisions of the Convention on Jurisdiction and the Enforcement of Judgements in Civil and Commercial Matters applicable for the purposes of this Regulation, insofar as the provisions of the Regulations do not derogate therefrom. It is therefore unnecessary to refer in each Article in Title X to the provisions of the Convention or to incorporate them explicitly in the text of the Articles".

22. Re Article 91(1)
"The Council and the Commission consider that the functions assigned by the Regulation to Community trade marks courts cover only infringement and validity actions together with the provisional, including protective, measures referred to in Article 99".

23. Re Article 105(106)
"The Council and the Commission consider that, with the objective of avoiding frivolous or vexatious actions, account should be taken in particular or the need to avoid Article 105 being misused by differentiating the ownership of the trade marks on which the actions are based, and of the requirement that the decisions to stay judgement or, if appropriate, to decline jurisdiction should be taken at the outset and on the basis of the elements which the budget has at his disposal".

24. Re Article 108(1)
"The Council and the Commission consider that the words "The Community trade mark ceases to have effect cover the following cases: failure to renew the registration of the Community trade mark (Article 47), surrender of the Community trade mark (Article 49), revocation of the rights of the proprietor of the Community trade mark and declaration of invalidity of the Community trade mark (Article 54)".

25. Re Article 117

"The Council and the Commission consider that the acts of the President referred to in this Article are those which he performs under the powers conferred upon him by Article 118(2) of the Regulation, by the Implementing Regulation, by the fees regulations or by any other rules applying to Community trade marks".

26. Re Article 120 (6)

"The Council and the Commission consider that the term "information may also cover acts of the Office".

Proposal for a Council Decision

approving the accession of the European Community to the Protocol Relating to the Madrid Agreement Concerning the International Registration of Marks, adopted at Madrid on 27 June 1989

THE COUNCIL OF THE EUROPEAN UNION

Having regard to the Treaty establishing the European Community, and in particular Article 235, in conjunction with Article 228(2), second sentence, and Article 228)3), first sub-paragraph, thereof,

Having regard to the proposal from the European Commission,[1]

Having regard to the opinion of the European Parliament,[2]

Having regard to the opinion of the Economic and Social Committee[3]

Whereas Council Regulation (EC) No. 40/94 of 20 December 1993 on the Community trade mark, which is based on[4] Article 235 of the Treaty, is designated to create a market which functions properly and offers conditions which are similar to those obtaining in a national market; whereas in order to create a market of this kind and make system whereby undertakings can by means of one procedural system obtain Community trade marks to which uniform protection is given and which produce their effects throughout the entire area of the European Community;

Whereas following preparations initiated and carried out by the World Intellectual Property Organization with the participation of the Member States which are members of the Madrid Union, the Member States which are not members of the Madrid Union and the European Community, the Diplomatic Conference for the Conclusion of a Protocol Relating to the Madrid Agreement Concerning the International Registration of Marks (hereinafter referred to as "the Madrid Protocol") on 27 June 1989, at Madrid;

Whereas the Madrid Protocol was adopted in order to introduce certain new features into the system of the international registration of marks existing under

[1] *Missing in the Proposal.*
[2] *Missing in the Proposal.*
[3] *Missing in the Proposal.*
[4] OJ No. L 11, 14.1.1994, p. 1.

the Madrid Agreement Concerning the international Registration of Marks of 14 April 1891 as amended (hereinafter referred to as "the Madrid Agreement");[5]

Whereas the objectives of the Madrid Protocol are to ease the way for certain States, and in particular the Member States which are not currently parties thereto, to accede to the system of international registration of marks;

Whereas as compared to the Madrid Agreement, the Madrid Protocol introduced, in its Article 14, as one of the main innovations the possibility that an intergovernmental organization which has a regional office for the purpose of registering marks with effect in the territory of the organization may become party to the Madrid Protocol;

Whereas the possibility that an intergovernmental organisation which has a regional office for the purpose of registering marks may become a party to the Madrid Protocol was introduced in the Madrid Protocol in order to allow, in particular, for the European Community to accede to the said Protocol;

Whereas the Madrid Protocol has entered into force on 1 December 1995 and has become operational on 1 April 1996 and the Community trade mark system has also become operational on the latter date;

Whereas the Community trade mark system and the international registration system as established by the Madrid Protocol are complementary; whereas in order to enable firms to profit from the advantages of the Community trade mark through the Madrid Protocol and vice-versa, it is necessary to allow Community trade mark applicants and holders of such trade marks to apply for international protection of their trade marks through the filing of an international application under the Madrid Protocol and, conversely, holders of international registrations under the Madrid Protocol to apply for protection of their trade marks under the Community trade mark system;

Whereas the establishment of a link between the Community trade mark system and the international registration system under the Madrid Protocol would promote a harmonious development of economic activities, will eliminate distortions of competition, will be cost efficient and will increase the level of integration and functioning of the internal market; whereas, therefore, the accession of the Community to the Madrid Protocol is necessary in order for the Community trade mark system to become more attractive;

Whereas the European Commission should be authorised to represent the European Community in the Assembly of the Madrid Union after the accession of the Community to the Madrid Protocol; whereas the European Community will not express a view in the Assembly in matters relating solely to the Madrid Agreement;

Whereas the competence of the European Community to conclude or accede to international agreements or treaties does not derive only from explicit confer-

[5] The Madrid Agreement Concerning the International Registration of Marks as revised last at Stockholm on 14.7.1967 and as amended on 2.10.1979.

ral by the Treaty but may also derive from other provisions of the Treaty and from acts adopted pursuant to those provisions by Community institutions;

Whereas this decision does not affect the rights of the Member States to participate in the Assembly of the Madrid Union with regard to their national trade marks.

HAS DECIDED AS FOLLOWS:

Article 1

The Protocol Relating to the Madrid Agreement Concerning the International Registration of Marks, adopted at Madrid on 27 June 1989 (hereinafter referred to as "the Madrid Protocol"), is hereby approved on behalf of the Community with regard to matters within its competence.

The text of the Madrid Protocol is attached to this Decision.

Article 2

1. The President of the Council is hereby authorised to deposit the instrument of accession with the Director General of the World Intellectual Property Organization as from the date on which the Council has adopted the measures which are necessary for the establishment of a link between the Community trade mark and the Madrid Protocol.

2. The declaration, which is attached to this decision, shall be made in the instrument of accession.

Article 3

1. The European Commission is hereby authorised to represent the European Community at the meetings of the Assembly of the Madrid Union to be held under the auspices of the World Intellectual Property Organization and to negotiate matters, on behalf of the European Community, which fall under the competence which the Assembly has pursuant to Article 10 of the Madrid Protocol.

2. The position of the European Community will be drawn up by the European Commission and the Member States within the competent Council working party or at on-the-spot meetings convened in the course of the work carried out within the framework of the World Intellectual Property Organization.

Done at Brussels,

For the Council,

The President

Proposal for a Council Decision approving the accession of the European Community to the Protocol Relating to the Madrid Agreement Concerning the International Registration of Marks, adopted at Madrid on 27 June 1989

Declaration on the individual fee system

The President of the Council, when depositing this instrument of accession with the Director General of WIPO, shall attach the following declaration to the instrument of accession.

"The European Community declares that, in connection with each international registration in which it is mentioned under Article 3 *ter(1) or (2)* of the Madrid Protocol, and in connection with the renewal of any such international registration, it wants to receive, instead of a share in the revenue produced by the supplementary fee and complementary fee,

for an individual mark:

a designation fee of 2,075 ECU[6] plus, where applicable, 400 ECU for each class of goods or services exceeding three, or, where applicable,

a renewal fee of 2,500 ECU[7] plus, where applicable, 400 ECU for each class of goods or services exceeding three;

for a collective mark:

a designation fee of 3,875 ECU[8] plus, where applicable, 800 ECU for each class of goods or services exceeding three, or where applicable,

a renewal fee of 5,000 ECU[9] plus, where applicable, 800 ECU for each class of goods or services exceeding three".

Protocol

(omissis)

[6] The said fees are provisional; they will be diminished by the savings resulting from the international procedure, once they are known.

[7] See footnote 6.

[8] See footnote 6.

[9] See footnote 6.

Proposal for a Council Regulation (EC)

modifying Council Regulation (EC) No. 40/94 of 20 December 1993 on the Community Trade Mark to give effect to the accession of the European Community to the Protocol Relating to the Madrid Agreement Concerning the International Registration of Marks, adopted at Madrid on 27 June 1989

THE COUNCIL OF THE EUROPEAN UNION

Having regard to the Treaty establishing the European Community, and in particular Article 235 thereof,

Having regard to the proposal from the European Commission,[1]

Having regard to the opinion of the European Parliament,[2]

Having regard to the opinion of the Economic and Social Committee,[3]

Whereas Council Regulation (EC) No. 40/94 of 20 December 1993 on the Community trade mark ("the Community trade mark Regulation"),[4] which is based on Article 235 of the Treaty, is designed to create a market which functions properly and offers conditions which are similar to those obtaining in a national market; whereas in order to create a market of this kind and make it increasingly a single market, the said Regulation created the Community trade mark system whereby undertakings can by means of one procedural system obtain Community trade marks to which uniform protection is given and which produce their effects throughout the entire area of the European Community;

Whereas the Diplomatic Conference for the Conclusion of a Protocol Relating to the Madrid Agreement Concerning the International registration of Marks, adopted the Protocol Relating to the Madrid Agreement Concerning the International registration of Marks (hereafter referred to as "the Madrid Protocol") on 27 June 1989, at Madrid;

Whereas the Madrid Protocol was adopted in order to introduce certain new features into the system of the international registration of marks existing under the Madrid Agreement Concerning the International Registration of Marks of 14 April 1981 as amended (hereafter referred to as "the Madrid Agreement");[5]

[1] *Missing in the Proposal.*
[2] *Missing in the Proposal.*
[3] *Missing in the Proposal.*
[4] OJ No. L 11, 14.1.1994, p.1.
[5] The Madrid Agreement Concerning the International Registration of Marks as revised last at Stockholm on 14.7.1967 and as amended on 2.10.1979.

Whereas as compared to the Madrid Agreement, the Madrid Protocol introduced, in its Article 14, as one of the main innovations the possibility that an intergovernmental organization which has a regional office for the purpose of registering marks with effect in the territory of the organisation may become party to the Madrid Protocol;

Whereas the Madrid Protocol has entered into force on 1 December 1995 and has become operational on 1 April 1996 and the Community trade mark system has also become operational on the latter date;

Whereas the Community trade mark system and the international registration stream as established by the Madrid Protocol are complementary; whereas in order to enable firms to profit from the advantages of the Community trade mark through the Madrid protocol and vice-versa, it is necessary to allow Community trade mark applicants and holders of such trade marks to apply for international protection of their trade marks through the filing of an international application under the Madrid Protocol and, conversely, holders of internationals registrations under the Madrid Protocol to apply fro protection of their trade marks under the Community trade mark system;

Whereas the establishment of a link between the community trade mark system and the international registration system under the Madrid Protocol would promote a harmonious development of economic activities, will eliminate distortions of competition, will be cost efficient and will increase the level of integration and functioning of the internal market; whereas, therefore, the accession of the Community to the Madrid Protocol is necessary in order for the Community trade mark system to become more attractive;

Whereas, for the above reasons, the Council, acting on a proposal from the Commission,[6] approved the Madrid Protocol and authorized the President of the Council to deposit the instrument of accession with the Director General of the World Intellectual Property Organization (WIPO) as from the date on which the Council has adopted the measures which are necessary to give effect to the accession of the European Community to the Madrid protocol; whereas this Regulation contains these measures;

Whereas these measures shall be incorporated in the Community trade mark Regulation through the inclusion of a new Title on "International Registration of marks"; whereas for this reason, the legal basis of this proposal must be the same as the legal basis of the Community trade mark Regulation, i.e., Article 235 of the Treaty,

Whereas it is necessary to provide for rules applying to the filing of an international application at the International Bureau of WIPO through the intermediary of the Office for Harmonization in the Internal Market (trade marks and designs) (The "Harmonization Office");

[6] Commission proposal for a Council decision approving the accession of the Community to the Protocol Relating to the Madrid Agreement Concerning the International registration of marks, adopted at Madrid on 27.6.1989, doc. COM (96) 367 final.

Whereas the rules and procedures relating to international registrations designating the European Community shall, in principle, be the same as the rules and procedures which apply to Community trade mark applications and the protection of community trade marks; whereas according to this principle, international registrations designating the European Community shall be subject to examination as to absolute grounds for refusal, searches in the Register of Community trade marks and the registers of trade marks of those Member States which have informed the Harmonization Office of their decision to operate such a search and shall be subject to opposition in the same way as published Community trade marks; whereas international registrations designating the European Community shall be subject to the same rules on use and invalidation as Community trade marks; whereas such international registrations may be converted into national trade mark applications or into territorial extensions to Member States which are party to the Madrid Protocol or the Madrid Agreement where such international registrations are refused or cease to have effect.

HAS ADOPTED THE FOLLOWING REGULATION:

ARTICLE I

Council Regulation (EC) No. 40/94 of 20 December 1993 on the Community trade mark shall be amended as follows.

(a) The following Title shall be inserted after TITLE XII:

TITLE XII

International Registration of Marks

SECTION 1

General Provisions

Article 140

Application of provisions

Unless otherwise specified in this Title or in the Protocol Relating to the Madrid Agreement Concerning the International Registration of Marks, adopted at Madrid on 27 June 1989 (hereafter referred to as "the Madrid protocol"), and the Regulations adopted under the Madrid Protocol, this Regulation and any regulations implementing this Regulation adopted pursuant to Article 159 shall apply *mutatis mutandis* to applications for international registrations under the Madrid Protocol (hereafter referred to as "international application") based on an application for a Community trade mark or on a Community trade mark and to registrations of marks in the international register maintained by the International

Bureau of the World Intellectual property Organization (hereafter referred to as "international registrations" and "the International Bureau", respectively) designating the European Community.

Section 2

International Registration on the Basis of Applications for a Community Trade Mark and of Community Trade Marks

Article 141
Filing of an international application
1. International applications pursuant to Article 3 of the Madrid Protocol based on an application for a Community trade mark or on a Community trade mark shall be filed at the Office.

2. Where an international registration is requested based o a Community trade mark and the international application is filed before the registration of the mark as a Community trade mark, the international application shall be deemed to have been received on the date of registration of the Community trade mark.

Article 142
Form and contents of the international application
1. The international application may be filed in any of the languages allowed under the Madrid Protocol, provided that it is a language of the Office. The language of the international application shall be the language of the proceedings before the Office.

2. The filing of an international application shall be subject to the payment of a fee to the Office. in the cases to in Article 141(2) the fee shall be due on the date of registration. The application shall be deemed not to have been filed until the required fee has been paid.

3. The international application must comply with the conditions laid down in the Implementing Regulation.

Article 143
Recordal in the files and in the Register
1. The date and number of an international registration based on a Community trade mark application, shall be recorded in he files of that application. When the application results in a Community trade mark, the date and number of the international registration shall be entered in the register.

2. The date and number of an international registration based on a Community trade mark shall be entered in the Register.

Article 144
Request for territorial extension subsequent to the international registration
A request for territorial extension made subsequently to the international registration pursuant to Article 3 *ter*(2) of the Madrid Protocol may be filed in the language of the international application.

Article 145
International fees
Any fees payable to the International Bureau under the Madrid Protocol shall be paid direct to the International Bureau.

SECTION 3

International Registrations Designating the European Community

Article 146
Effects of international registrations designating the European Community
1. An international registration designating the European Community shall, from the date of its registration pursuant to Article 3(4) of the Madrid Protocol or from the date of the subsequent designation of the European Community pursuant to Article 3 *ter*(2) of the Madrid Protocol, have the same effect as an application for a Community trade mark.

2. If no refusal has been notified in accordance with Article 5(1) and (2) of the Madrid Protocol or if any such refusal has been withdrawn, the international registration of a mark designating the European Community shall, from the date referred to in paragraph 1, have the same effect as the registration of mark as a Community trade mark.

3. For the purposes of applying Article 9(3), publication of the particulars of the international registration designating the European Community pursuant to Article 147(1) shall take the place of publication of a Community trade mark application, and publication pursuant to Article 147(2) shall take the place of publication of the registration of a Community trade mark.

Article 147
Publication
1. The Office shall publish the date of registration of a mark designating the European Community pursuant to Article 3(4) of the Madrid protocol or the date of the subsequent designation of the European Community pursuant to Article 3 *ter*(2) of the Madrid protocol, the number of the international registration, and the date of publication of such registration in the Gazette published by the International Bureau.

2. If no refusal of protection of an international registration designating the European Community has been notified in accordance with Article 5(1) and (2) of the Madrid Protocol or if any such refusal has been withdrawn, the Office shall publish this fact, together with the number of the international registration and, where applicable, the date of publication of such registration in the Gazette published by the International Bureau.

Article 148
Seniority
The applicant for or the holder of an international registration designating the European Community may claim, in the international application or direct before the Office, the seniority of an earlier trade mark registered in a Member State, including a trade mark registered in the Benelux Countries, or registered under international arrangements having effect in a Member State, as provided for in Articles 34 and 35.

Article 149
Examination as to absolute grounds for refusal
1. International registrations designating the European Community shall be subject to examination as to absolute grounds for refusal in the same way as applications for Community trade marks.

2. Protection of an international registration shall not be refused before the holder of the international registration has been allowed the opportunity to renounce or limit the protection in respect of the European Community or of submitting his observations.

3. Refusal of protection shall take the place of refusal of a Community trade mark application.

4. Where protection of an international registration is refused by a final decision under this Article or where the holder of the international registration has renounced the protection in respect of the European Community pursuant to paragraph 2, the Office shall refund the holder of the international registration a part of the individual fee to be laid down in the Implementing Regulation.

Article 150
Search
1. Once the Office has received a notification of an international registration designating the European Community, it shall draw up a Community search report as provided for in Article 39(1).

2. As soon as the Office has received notification of an international registration designating the European Community, the Office shall transmit a copy thereof to

the central industrial property office of each Member State as provided for in Article 39(2).

3. Article 39(3), (4) and (5) shall apply *mutatis mutandis*.

4. The Office shall inform the proprietors of any earlier Community trade marks of Community trade mark applications cited in the Community search report of the publication of the international registration designating the European Community as provided for in Article 147(1).

Article 151
Opposition
1. International registrations designating the European Community shall be subject to opposition in the same way as published Community trade mark applications.

2. The period within which notice of opposition must be filed shall be nine months following the date of the publication pursuant to Article 147(1). The opposition shall not be treated as duly entered until the opposition fee has been paid.

3. Refusal of protection shall take the place of refusal of a Community trade mark application.

4. Where protection of an international registration is refused by a final decision under this Article or where the holder of the international registration has renounced the protection in respect of the European Community prior to a final decision under this Article, the Office shall refund the holder of the international registration a part of the individual fee to be laid down in the Implementing Regulation.

Article 152
Replacement of a Community trade mark by an International Registration
The Office shall, upon request, enter a notice in the Register that a Community trade mark is deemed to have been replaced by an international registration in accordance with Article 4 *bis* of the Madrid Protocol.

Article 153
Invalidation of the effects of an international registration
1. The effects of an international registration designating the European Community may be declared invalid.

2. The application for invalidation of the effects of an international registration designating the European Community shall take the place of an application for a declaration of revocation as provided for in Article 50 or for invalidation as provided for in Article 51.

Article 154

Conversion of an international registration into a national trade mark application or into a territorial extension to the Member States

1. Where an international registration designating the European Community has been refused or ceases to have effect, the holder of the international registration may request the conversion of his international registration designating the European Community into a national trade mark application or the conversion of his international registration designating the European Community into a territorial extension to a Member State party to the Madrid Protocol or the Madrid Agreement Concerning the International Registration of Marks, adopted at Madrid on April 14, 1981, as revised and amended (hereafter referred to as "the Madrid Agreement") under Article 3 *ter*(2) of the Madrid Protocol or Article 3 *ter*(2) of the Madrid Agreement. Article 108 to 110 shall apply, *mutatis mutandis*.

2. The national trade mark application or the territorial extension to a Member State party to the Madrid Protocol or the Madrid Agreement resulting from the conversion of an international registration designating the Community shall, notwithstanding Article 3 *ter* (2) of the Madrid Protocol and Article 3 *ter*(2) of the Madrid Agreement, enjoy in respect of the Member State concerned the date of the international registration pursuant to Article 3(4) of the Madrid Protocol or the date of the designation of the European Community pursuant to Article 3 *ter*(2) of the Madrid Protocol if the latter was made subsequently to the international registration, or the date of priority of that registration and, where appropriate, the seniority of a trade mark of that State claimed under Article 148.

3. The request for conversion shall be published.

Article 155

Use of a mark subject of an international registration

For the purposes of applying Articles 15(1), 43(2), 50(1)(a) and 56(2), the date of publication pursuant to Article 147(2) shall take the place of the date of registration.

Article 156

Transformation

1. Subject to paragraph 2, the provisions applicable to Community trade mark applications shall apply *mutatis mutandis* to applications for transformation of an international registration into a Community trade mark application pursuant to Article 9 *quinquies* of the Madrid Protocol.

2. When the application for transformation relates to an international registration designating the European Community the particulars of which have been published pursuant to Article 147(2), Articles 38 to 43 shall not apply.

Article 157
Languages
1. The language in which an international designating the European Community or a request for subsequent territorial extension to the Community was filed shall be considered to be the language of the application pursuant to Article 115.

2. The applicant for an international registration designating the European Community must indicate in his international application a second language which shall be a language of the Office the use of which he accepts as a possible language of proceedings for opposition, revocation or invalidity proceedings.

3. Where the requirement of paragraph 2 is not complied with, the language into which the international registration designating the European Community has been translated by the International Bureau shall be the second language as provided for in Article 115(3).

(b) A new sub-paragraph (iv) shall be added to Article 8(2)(a):

"(iv) trade marks registered under international arrangements which have effect in the Community;".

(c) Title XIII becomes Title XIV.

(d) Articles 140, 141, 142 and 143 shall be renumbered as follows:

Article 140 becomes Article 158
Article 141 becomes Article 159
Article 142 becomes Article 160
Article 143 becomes Article 161.

(e) The reference to Article 140 in Article 26(3) shall be replaced by a reference to Article 158.

(f) The reference to Article 141 in Article 139(3) and 140(3) shall be replaced by a reference to Article 159.

Article II
Entry into force
This Regulation shall enter into force on the date on which the Madrid Protocol enters into force with respect to the European Community. The date of entry into force of this Regulation shall be published in the Official Journal of the European Communities.

This Regulation shall be biding in its entirety and directly applicable in all Member States.

Done at Brussels,

For the Council

The President

General Provisions

1. Definition of Community trade mark

Irrespective of whether a mark is registered for goods or services, it will be referred to as a Community trade mark if it is registered in accordance with the Regulation (Article 1, par. 1). Both categories of marks, trade marks for goods and (trade) marks for services, are governed by the same set of rules. As set out in the preamble to the Regulation, the creation of a Community trade mark should enable enterprises to adapt their activities to the scale of the whole Community.[1]

The legal instrument of a Community trade mark should enable companies to make and distribute their goods or render their services under one and the same trade mark throughout the Community. However, this is easier said than done. Nowadays, for obvious reasons of cost, marketing and logistics, companies which are active on an international scale often try to opt for one trade mark for all their goods or services. However, in view of the countless trade marks in existence in the Community, both registered and unregistered, as well as other rights which have to be taken into account – trade names, copyrights, design rights in the case of three-dimensional marks – it is often very difficult to find a unique trade mark which can be used without objections from owners of earlier rights.

This situation will not change in the near future, because national trade marks will also continue to exist. In the Explanatory Memorandum to its original "Proposal for a Council regulation on Community trade marks" of November 1980,[2] the Commission expressed the view that "the creation of a Community trade mark existing alongside national rights is the only means whereby a common market in marked goods can eventually be achieved. The conflicts and hence the obstacles to the free movement of goods and services and to competition will diminish as more and more existing national trade marks are converted

[1] For consistency with the terminology of the regulation, the term Community instead of European Union is used.

[2] Doc. COM (80) 635 final/2, 27.11.1980, p. 23.

into Community trade marks and as new marks are increasingly registered as Community trade marks". However, considering the huge number of trade marks which have been registered in only one or a few Member States, national trade marks will not easily disappear.

The Community trade mark Regulation will make it possible to obtain *one* trade mark for the whole territory of the Community by means of *one* application submitted to *one* office under *one* procedure governed by *one* law.

The unitary character is an essential principle of the system. Consequently, all that may happen during the life of a registered Community trade mark will have equal effect throughout the Community: registration, transfer or surrender of the trade mark will automatically take effect in all Member States, and decisions regarding validity, use or rights conferred by a Community trade mark will have the same unitary effect (Article 1, par. 2).

The Commission had already expressed the view in the Explanatory Memorandum to its original Proposal of November 1980 that the unitary character of a Community trade mark was to be considered a fundamental principle of the Regulation which was not to be undermined and that derogations might therefore only be permitted in exceptional cases.[3] The proprietor of an earlier right such as an earlier trade mark, trade name or another industrial propriety right which exists under the law of an individual Member State, who has refrained from filing an opposition against the registration of a Community trade mark, may as yet oppose the use of the Community trade mark in the territory where his right is protected, be it in so far as the law of the Member State concerned so permits (Articles 106 and 107).

The proprietor of such an earlier right, being aware of the use of a later Community trade mark in the Member State where he can claim better rights, should not wait too long before taking action. If he has acquiesced, for a period of five successive years, in the use of a later Community trade mark, he will no longer be entitled to oppose the use of this later trade mark in respect of the goods or services for which his trade mark is protected, either by way of registration or otherwise, unless of course registration of the later Community trade mark was applied for in bad faith (Article 53, par. 2).

2. *The Office*

It will be clear that a central Office is needed which should guarantee the implementation of the Community trade mark system and its uniform application. To that end the Office for Harmonization in the Internal Market (trade marks and designs) has been established in Alicante, Spain (Article 2).

The Office fulfils a central role. It will receive the application for a Community trade mark which may be filed, at the choice of the applicant, either at the Office or at the central industrial property office of a Member State, or at the Benelux Trade Mark Office (Article 25). The national trade mark offices

[3] *Ibidem*, p. 25.

must send the applications to the Office in Alicante within two weeks from filing. The Office will check whether the application fulfils the minimal formal requirements for the accordance of a date of filing (Article 36). The Office will also carry out an examination as to absolute grounds for refusal (Article 38).

Furthermore, once the Office has recorded a filing date, it will make a search in the Community trade mark register in order to establish whether there are any identical or similar earlier Community trade marks which have been registered or registration has been applied for with respect to identical or similar goods (Article 39, par. 1). The Office must also transmit a copy of the Community trade mark application to the central industrial property offices in the Member States which have informed the Office of their decision to carry out a search in their own registers of national trade marks.

Such a national search report has to be submitted to the Office in Alicante within three months of the date of receipt of the Community trade mark application (Article 39 par. 2 and par. 3). The Office in its turn must send its own search report and the national search reports to the applicant as soon as possible (Article 39 par 5.). One month later, the Community trade mark application will be published and at the same time the Office must inform the proprietors of any earlier Community trade mark or Community trade mark application which it has cited in the Community search report of the publication of the Community trade mark application (Article 39 par. 6).

After publication, proprietors of earlier rights may file opposition to the registration of the Community trade mark within a period of three months. Such earlier rights may relate to registered national trade marks or Community trade marks but also to applications for such trade marks, non-registered trade marks, well known trade marks even if not registered,[4] or rights in other signs used in the course of trade of more than mere local significance, provided that such a sign confers on its proprietor the right to prohibit the use of a subsequent trade mark (Articles 42 and 8).

If there is no opposition or if the opposition is rejected by a definitive decision, the trade mark will be registered as a Community trade mark (Article 45). The Office will also decide on applications for revocation of a Community trade mark because of non-use, or in case the trade mark has become the common name in the trade for a product or service, or has become liable to mislead the public with respect to the nature, quality or geographical origin of the goods or services for which it has been registered (Article 50).

Furthermore, the Office will decide on applications for invalidation of a Community trade mark in case it has been registered in spite of the fact that it should have been refused on absolute grounds, for example, if the trade mark applied for is descriptive of the goods for which it is intended to be used and for that reason is devoid of any distinctive character (Article 51).

[4] Article 6 *bis* of the Paris Convention.

An invalidation action can also be brought by third parties, claiming better earlier rights either in a Community trade mark or a national trade mark or even on the basis of any other earlier right which, pursuant to the pertinent national law, confers on its proprietor the right to prohibit the use of the Community trade mark (Article 52). The proprietor of an earlier right which only applies to a particular locality may, however, not apply to the Office to have the Community trade mark declared invalid. The reason for this is given in the Explanatory Memorandum to the Proposal of November 1980.[5] The grant of the Community trade mark would be made considerably more difficult if the proprietor of such local right were also entitled to apply for a declaration that the Community trade mark was invalid. The owner of such a right may, however, oppose the use of the Community trade mark in the territory where he can claim legal protection under the law of the pertinent Member State (Article 107).

Decisions in connection with the procedures before the Office are taken by the Examiners, by the Opposition Division in case of an opposition to an application to register a Community trade mark application, by the Administration of Trade Marks and Legal Division which is, in particular, responsible for decisions in respect of entries in the register of Community trade marks, and by the Cancellation Division in relation to an application for the revocation or declaration of invalidity of a Community trade mark. Appeals from decisions of the Examiners and the aforesaid divisions should be brought before the Boards of Appeal of the Office (Article 125 seq).

It will be clear from the above that the role of the Office and its institutions will be important. The Office has to make sure that the Community trade mark system works in an effective and efficient way. The success of the system will depend to a great extent on the approach taken by the Office. Should it apply strict standards for distinctiveness and consequently set a high threshold for registration, or will the Office also allow the registration of trade marks which have a low degree of distinctiveness? The following guideline found in the Explanatory Memorandum to the Proposal of November 1980 may be of help: "When examining applications for trade marks, the Office is responsible for ensuring that the application of this rule does not complicate unnecessarily the registration of Community trade marks".[6]

3. The capacity to act

Both natural and legal persons may apply for and hence own a Community trade mark. Legal persons are covered by a broad definition: companies or firms and other legal parties shall be regarded as such if, under the terms of the law governing them, they are entitled to have rights and obligations and to accomplish legal acts (Article 3). Consequently, the legal status of such a person need not always equal a legal entity; it is sufficient that they are treated as such.

[5] *Op. cit.* footnote 2, p. 44.
[6] *Ibidem* p. 28.

4. Signs of which a Community trade mark may consist

One may conclude from the definition of a Community trade mark that there are two conditions which have to be fulfilled. A Community trade mark may consist of any sign, provided that such a sign can:

1. be represented graphically and
2. distinguish the goods or services of one enterprise from those of other enterprises.

The signs mentioned in this Article 4 are only examples, namely: "*particularly* words, including personal names, designs, letters, numerals, the shape of goods or of their packaging". This list is not exhaustive and consequently no type of sign is automatically excluded from registration. As stated in the Explanatory Memorandum to the original Proposal of November 1980: "It is designed to simplify the adaptation of administrative practices and court judgments to business requirements and to encourage undertakings to apply for Community trade marks".[7] In principle, solid colours or shades of colours and signs denoting sound, smell or taste are not excluded from constituting Community trade marks. The question is whether the Office will indeed allow the registration of such signs and if so, whether it will provide a uniform set of rules on how to indicate the contents of such trade marks so that at least no questions as to the interpretation of the publication will arise. The regulation in which the rules implementing the Council Regulation on the Community trade mark are laid down does not include a provision for filing sound, smell or taste trade marks. However, with regard to sound marks the Examination Guidelines provide that such trade marks may be applied for, provided that they can be represented graphically, such as by musical notation. Consequently, it will be questionable whether, for example, the manufacturer of the famous Harley Davidson motorcycles can apply for the protection of the distinctive growling noise of this engine as a trade mark. An application to that end was filed at the US Patent and Trade mark Office which accepted this trade mark for publication.

A sign can only be protected as a Community trade mark if it is capable of distinguishing the goods or services for which it is used. Coined words, which have no meaning and are not descriptive or generic for the goods for which they are used, are strong trade marks which can be properly protected and defended against younger identical or similar trade marks. However, many trade marks are more or less descriptive and consequently possess little or no distinctiveness. Such weak trade marks are difficult to protect and can thus hardly be defended against similar trade marks used for identical or similar goods. Whether a trade mark is to be considered distinctive will also depend on the way in which it is used and presented to the public. Consistent use may strengthen the trade marks character. Even relatively weak signs may so acquire distinctiveness and obtain trade mark character which make it possible to register and defend such signs as a Community trade mark.

[7] *Ibidem* p. 26.

Not only words but also designs, letters and numerals can be protected as Community trade marks. It will be clear that the way in which letters and numerals are used must make them distinctive in order to qualify for trade mark protection.

Personal names, first names and surnames, can also be protected as Community trade marks, but the owner of such a trade mark cannot prohibit a third party from using his own name, even if he is trading in the same or similar goods for which the Community trade mark has been registered. Such a use is considered to be in accordance with honest practices in commercial matters. However, he may not give his name the character of a trade mark and use it as a distinctive sign for the products he is marketing.

A separate category is that of three-dimensional trade marks: shapes of goods or of their packagings. Three-dimensional shapes can certainly fulfil the function of a trade mark. The Coca-Cola bottle, the outer appearance of the Lego brick, the shape of the Toblerone chocolate bar or the Philips triple head shaver are examples of distinctive shapes which identify the same products as originating from one source. They therefore qualify for trade mark protection.

5. Persons who can be proprietors of Community trade marks

As a consequence of the Agreement on Trade Related Aspects of Intellectual Property Rights (the TRIPs-Agreement), which is annexed to the Agreement establishing the World Trade Organization (WTO), Article 5 of the Regulation had to be changed. Article 3 of the TRIPs agreement provides that each Member of the WTO shall accord to the nationals of other Members treatment no less favourable than that it accords to its own nationals with regard to the protection of intellectual property. In order to comply with this obligation of national treatment, Article 5, par. 1 (b) and par. 1 (d) had to be amended so as to ensure that nationals of all WTO Members, even if the Member in question is not a party to the Paris Convention, receive the same treatment as accorded to nationals of Community Member States. With Council Regulation (EC) No. 3288/94 of 22 December 1994,[8] said paragraphs have been amended as follows: Article 5 (1) (b) shall be replaced by the following: *"(b) nationals of other States which are parties to the Paris Convention for the protection of industrial property, hereinafter referred to as "the Paris Convention", or to the Agreement establishing the World Trade Organization;"*. Article 5 (1) (d) shall be replaced by the following: *"(d) nationals, other than those referred to under subparagraph (c), of any State which is not party to the Paris Convention or to the Agreement establishing the World Trade Organization and which, according to published findings, accords to nationals of all the Member States the same protection for trade marks as it accords to its own nationals and, if nationals of the Member States are required to prove registration in the country of origin, recognizes the registration of Community trade marks as such proof."*

[8] OJ No. L349/83, 31.12.1994.

Nationals of both Member States and non-Member States are entitled to apply for and own Community trade marks. Nationals of non-Member States ("other States") which are parties to the Paris Convention for the protection of industrial property or to the Agreement establishing the World Trade Organization may also file applications for a Community trade mark without fulfilling any further requirement. Nationals of States which are not parties to the Paris Convention may also apply for a Community trade mark, provided that they are domiciled or have their seat or a real and effective industrial or commercial establishment within the territory of the Community or of a State which is party to the Paris Convention.

Even if they do not belong to this broad group of natural and legal persons, nationals of other countries may still apply for a Community trade mark, provided that the reciprocity rule exists between the Community and the State to which such a person belongs. This may also mean that a national of such a State has to prove that the trade mark for which an application for a Community trade mark has been filed is also registered in the State of origin. Finally, stateless persons shall be regarded as nationals of the country in which they have their habitual residence.

6. Means whereby a Community trade mark is obtained

Contrary to accepted practice in some Member States, where the law provides that rights in the trade mark can come into existence through first use, a Community trade mark can only be obtained by registration (Article 6). This is for obvious reasons of legal certainty.

It should be clear from the Community trade mark register which trade marks have been registered, so that anybody who wishes to introduce a new trade mark can make a reliable search before bringing his product on the market. However, it should be realized that in some Member States, national unregistered trade marks can be invoked against the use of a registered Community trade mark. In order to avoid unnecessary official filing fees, before applying for the registration of a trade mark, the applicant should make a search in the registers of national trade marks and the register of Community trade marks. It is even possible to carry out a further search as to unregistered trade marks and trade names. Several private bureaux offer such services, and the assistance of these bureaux can be of great help in selecting a new trade mark. Such a preliminary search by the trade mark owner himself makes the official search by the Office in Alicante and the national offices superfluous, the more so, because the official search does not cover unregistered trade marks and other signs which may form a bar against the registration and use of the applicant's trade mark. The search will take time, will raise the cost and will delay the publication of the Community trade mark application. For that reason several associations of trade mark owners have opposed the original proposals for a search, however without success.

Absolute Grounds for Refusal

I. Article 7. 1 a): Signs which do not conform to the requirements of Article 4

Article 4 provides that *"A Community trade mark may consist of any signs capable of being represented graphically, particularly words, including personal names, designs, letters, numerals, the shape of goods or of their packaging, provided that such signs are capable of distinguishing the goods or services of one undertaking from those of other undertakings."*

Therefore, all signs can potentially constitute a trade mark. Article 4 provides a non-restrictive list of examples of signs that can constitute trade marks; however, it presents both a content requirement and a form requirement.

1. Examples of signs

The law provides six examples of signs that can constitute trade marks:

a) *Words* and *personal names* that do not need to be presented in any special way (see below).

b) *Drawings*, except those that are too simple (see below), may constitute trade marks. Article 15.1 of the TRIPs Agreement also provides that figurative elements can distinguish goods or services of a company and thus constitute a trade mark.

c) *Numbers* and *letters* may constitute trade marks, unless they are too simple (see below).

d) The *shape* of the good or of its packaging can constitute a trade mark. For example, the triangular shape of their chocolate allows one to distinguish the goods of the Toblerone company. Article 15.1 of the TRIPS Agreement does not provide that a shape can constitute a trade mark; however, it does not forbid it. The shape must naturally satisfy certain conditions in order to be distinctive (see below).

e) Council Regulation No. 40/94 does not provide – including in Article 4 – the possibility of registering one or several *colours* as trade marks. Nevertheless, it is accepted in Europe that such signs can constitute trade marks. Moreover, Implementation Regulation No. 2868/95 of 13 December 1995 (Article 3.5) and the examination guidelines (Articles 3.7.1 and 3.7.4) permit the registration of a trade mark in colour, and Articles 8.2 and 8.3 of the examination guidelines mention the registration of colours.

f) Lastly, Article 15.1 of the TRIPS Agreement provides that *colour combinations* can constitute trade marks. Thus, although this Agreement does not oblige its member States to protect a single colour as a trade mark, even in a particular shade, it does not prohibit it.

2. The content requirement

Article 4 allows signs to be trade marks only if they *"are capable of distinguishing the goods or services of one undertaking from those of other undertakings."*

This is also what is provided in Article 15.1 of the TRIPS Agreement.

Distinctiveness is first assessed in view of the marked object, which is thus distinguished from other objects presented to the consumer. Thus, light bulbs marked "A" are distinguishable from light bulbs marked "B", when they are placed next to each other on the store shelves.

However, distinctiveness is also assessed on the basis of the origin of the objects marketed. The distinctive sign is constituted by the more or less subjective image the consumer has in mind concerning the company that markets this marked good.

Hence, not only is the object marketed distinguished from neighbouring competition but also, in the consumers mind, the trade mark carries properties acquired from the original company, and such properties in turn identify and personalise the company (see below concerning the various distinctive signs).

3. The form requirement

Article 4 of the Council Regulation imposes a requirement of form: *"the sign must be capable of being represented graphically."* This is what the Implementation Regulation provides in Articles 3.1 and 3.2 et seq. It is also required by Article 15.1 of the TRIPS Agreement, although it is worded differently: *"signs must be visually perceptible in order to be registered."*

a) We must assume that the words and letters are written in the Latin alphabet.

The presentation of a word in a different alphabet of any of the (official or unofficial) languages of the European Community must be possible. For instance, this is definitely the case of a word in Greek written in the Greek alphabet. The protection granted by registration should cover the visual aspect of the letters in that alphabet, as well as the meaning of the word in its original language. However, it is recommended that the word be filed in the Latin alphabet as well.

If the word is presented in the alphabet of a non-European Community language (for instance in Arabic or Japanese characters), should the protection be restricted to the visual aspect of the signs, and not cover the meaning of the word?

Would it be possible to file words in the phonetic alphabet?

b) Three-dimensional trade marks can be represented in two dimensions, thanks to perspective images, which can be either photographs or drawings, pursuant to Article 3.4 of the Implementation Regulation and Article 3.7 of the guidelines.

The above-mentioned legal texts provide that six perspective images can be included in the trade mark registration. In such case, it should be considered that the protection applies only to the full three-dimensional shape formed of all the perspectives filed, and not on one or more of the perspective images contained in the registration.

4. Other signs

Other signs can constitute trade marks since the list provided in Article 4 begins with the adverb "particularly" which is used to designate a few examples taken from a larger list.

Are sounds, smells and tastes capable of distinguishing goods or services of one company from those of other companies?

a) *Sound signs* are mentioned in Article 8.2 of the examination guidelines.

i) Musical phrases, such as radio or television show theme songs, or musical jingles clearly exercise a distinctive and attractive role in the consumers' minds.

Such sound signs can be graphically represented by means of the universal system of musical notes on a staff. The same is true of orchestrations and musical arrangements.

Of course, the trade mark right will then cover the musical content rather than the graphic representation of the staff registered as a trade mark, even though it may not necessarily be within the reach of those who cannot read music.

ii) Sounds and noises can also exercise a distinctive role.

This is undoubtedly the case of the MGM (Metro-Goldwyn-Mayer Lion Corp.) lion roar, when it is heard by the audience in a movie theatre or by television viewers.

According to Harley Davidson, the motorcycle manufacturer, the sound of its motors is characteristic and enables the consumer to distinguish its motorcycles from its competitors. Therefore, according to trade mark law, such a sound can exercise a distinctive purpose. However, if the sound results intrinsically from a technical feature of the motor, it then describes a characteristic of the good and should not be registered unless it has become distinctive through its use (see below Article 7.3).

It is admitted that sounds and noises can be scientifically represented by physico-acoustic means that are transcribed using numbers and curves in particular.

Of course, such a scientific representation would not be within everyone's reach. Consequently, should it be required that a trade mark registration include a written note defining and explaining the sounds and noises claimed, or even a recording of the sounds, a copy of which could be given to anyone wishing to hear it (the trade mark owner guaranteeing the proper state of such recording)?

b) *Olfactory signs*

It seems that smells can constitute perceptible signs capable of distinguishing goods or services of one company from those of other companies. Smells are emanations carried by a fluid (air or water) that are perceived by the olfactory apparatus. Aromas are odorous emanations which rise up from certain plant or animal substances. Currently, smells play an increasingly important role, not only in the area of perfume, but also in that of food products and other promotional activities. They are even used therapeutically or as stimulants.

i) Aromas alone cannot be appropriated since they are produced by nature. Thus, the aroma of chocolate must remain available to all those in the chocolate business.

However, perfumes are man-made compositions and could be protected by copyright (droit d'auteur) since, according to some, they can be original and bear the mark of their creators' personality.

It does not seem possible to appropriate fragrances per se as trade marks. This is because, as a rule, a fragrance used to designate a fragrance is not distinctive.

ii) A smell registered as a trade mark for flowers is in fact used to designate an essential feature of the good. Therefore, the sign would not be distinctive. The same should be true of a smell used to designate cosmetics or personal hygiene goods, as well as food products.

Nevertheless, certain smells may be arbitrary when connected with the designated good. This is the case for smells which are not essential to or a natural part of a good, such as the use of the salty and iodized smell of the sea or the ocean to designate clothing. Thus, reservations should be made for smells that are too plain, and smells should only be registered in a particular nuance.

Still, the distinctiveness of an olfactory sign is much clearer when it is attached to an object that usually does not have odorous qualities or properties. Therefore, a scent applied to embroidery threads would exercise a distinctive purpose.

iii) It seems possible to represent smells graphically. In fact, there are several ways to describe a smell: physico-chemical formulas, descriptions in analogue, spectrometric and even chromatographic forms – even though certain molecules have not yet been identified among the nearly 500,000 known substances.

Still, here again, the trade mark registration could be completed with a note describing the smell and including samples – guaranteed as being in good condition by the trade mark owner – from which extracts could be provided upon request.

c) *Gustatory signs*

Flavour is a quality perceived by the sense of taste. The beverage under the Coca-Cola trade mark has its own particular and individual flavour. To consumers, flavour is what distinguishes this beverage from other beverages. It also gives its origin and even allows instant identification and personalization of the Coca-Cola company.

However, usually, due to their lack of fame, flavours are not capable of identifying or personalizing the company that supplied the object. Moreover, flavours are indissociable from the object they are attached to; they even constitute the essential quality of foods or beverages, and such quality determines the consumers choice. Therefore, gustatory signs should never be distinctive.

It is only when the gustatory signs allow consumers to recognize and identify the origin of the object, especially given its long-standing and extensive use, that they could constitute a valid trade mark, since they render the object distinctive in comparison with competing foods and beverages.

II. Article 7.1 b): Trade marks that are devoid of any distinctive character

Article 6 *quinquies* B 2) of the Paris Convention allows States to deny registration of trade marks *"when they are devoid of any distinctive character."*

In the Council Regulation, this negative condition is tautological in relation to the substance condition imposed in Article 4 with regards to signs which must be capable of distinguishing the objects of one company from those of other companies.

We know that distinctiveness rests on the binary or arbitrary relationship between the object and the sign to which it is applied. It is not arbitrary to use the word *soap* to designate soap, whereas using the sign *soap* to designate automobiles is arbitrary and therefore distinctive. The examination guidelines (Articles 8.1.1 and 8.3) stress that the words *beer* and *wine* are not distinctive in designating beers and wines. In Article 8.4.2 of the examination guidelines, the Office illustrates the distinctive nature of a trade mark, when the sign is *"taken from a sector other than that to which the European Community trade mark application relates (...) in construction, an expression such as 4 x 3 designates product dimensions; however it would not be commonplace to describe"* beverages or other commercial retail products in a distinctive manner.

1) In Article 8.3 of its guidelines, the Office has noted that certain signs cannot be distinctive due to their plainness or their basic nature: for instance, a sign composed of one or two letters, of one or two numbers, of a circle or a square, of a single primary colour. To this one can also add the simple parallelepiped shape of a container to designate liquids. Indeed, such signs cannot be distinctive alone because, due to their banality, they cannot have any attractive power. Moreover, given the small number of such signs, if they were recorded, this might interfere with the freedom of industry and trade.

Nevertheless, in the examination guidelines, the Office has also noted that such signs can be distinctive if they are placed with unusual or nonsensical representations, in exceptional circumstances. This would also be the case when, because of the use that has been made of a simple sign – particularly a long-standing or extensive use – it becomes established in the consumers mind as an indication of origin. This should be true, for instance, of British Petroleums BP trade mark and of Master Cards twin circles.

Of course, the combination of non-distinctive elements can in itself be distinctive. This is often the case for bank trade marks, e.g., "Commerzbank."

2) The signs distinctiveness is not necessarily in its novelty or originality, because trade marks must be considered in the application of the sign to an object. Therefore, such sign need not be new or original in itself.

On the contrary, it is often said that, if a sign is original or new, it is *a fortiori* distinctive. Nevertheless, not all novelties are distinctive. When a new word is formed in accordance with linguistic and grammatical rules, it cannot be distinctive. Thus, the new word "telecopist" directly describes the person in charge of telecopies.

Furthermore, a shape can be new and original to present a vase or a bottle, but it will not be distinctive in designating a vase or a bottle since it designates a determining quality of the good. To the contrary, this new and original shape for the bottle is distinctive if it is used to contain perfume; it could therefore be registered as a trade mark to designate perfume.

3) The advertising sign could be registered as a trade mark, because it exercises an attractive and promotional role in order to ensure better communication between the marked object and its potential buyers. Thus, the advertising sign has a broader purpose as compared to the trade mark, whose role is to indicate the origin of the good or service.

The expression *"Just do it"* used by Nike in its various advertising campaigns to promote its sporting goods possesses an attractive character that consumers keep in mind. This has improved communication between the Nike company and the public.

4) The examination guidelines provide, in Article 8.1.4, that it is necessary to take into account those trade marks registered in countries where a similar examination has been carried out concerning distinctiveness.

5) Trade marks are sometimes said to possess a "weak" distinctive character. In fact, this means that, among the elements of which the trade mark is comprised, only a minority are distinctive and a majority are not.

For instance, the "piPPe" trade mark refers to pipes. It is distinctive in that the central letter P had been doubled and enlarged by comparison with the other letters. Therefore, the protection of the trade mark would be restricted to such double capital letters. A competitor could of course reproduce the word *pipe*, but it would infringe the trade mark rights if it reproduced the double capitals, since there is no reason or need for the competitor to reproduce the distinctive element.

It is with this transparency in mind that the European Communitys legal texts have provided the possibility of filing a disclaimer (Article 38.2 of the Council Regulation, Articles 1.3 and 11.2 of the Implementation Regulation and Article 8.13 of the examination guidelines). However, these texts are very rigid in the sense that the Office could refuse the registration of a trade mark on the grounds that the applicant had not *"waived all exclusive rights in this element that is not distinctive."* Such a disclaimer could induce a competitor to copy such element, even though it may not have been necessary or indispensable for the competitor to designate its goods or services.

It must be noted that, usually, a Judge of trade mark rights violations is in the best position to assess whether a trade mark is violated by another sign, and to define the exact scope of a registered trade mark. Therefore, the Office should be more liberal with regards to elements that are not distinctive, as well as neither necessary nor indispensable in designating the objects in question, for its is a question of simple fairness not to copy a prior competitor when such copy is neither necessary nor indispensable to designate ones activities or goods.

6) Article 12 of the Council Regulation wisely provides that the trade mark cannot prevent the use of a trade mark for descriptive purposes. Thus, Article 17 of the TRIPs Agreement authorizes, in spite of the existence of a trade mark registration, *"fair use of descriptive terms, provided that such exceptions take account of the legitimate interests of the owner of the trade mark and of third parties."* Article 12 of the Council Regulation indicates that such use must be made *"in accordance with honest practices in industrial or commercial matters."*

It should be noted that the authorized descriptive use must serve to designate the good itself or one of its characteristics. Moreover, the descriptive use of a trade mark must exclude its use alone, detached or highlighted, in an attractive manner; and the descriptive use implies the use of the trade mark in a description of the good and not in a context intended for catching the consumers attention. Thus, the French trade mark *femme* (meaning "woman"), designating perfumes, is distinctive when it stands alone and detached, in spite of the designation of the purpose of the good. The descriptive use of such trade mark, which would be authorized by virtue of Article 12, should therefore consist in taking up the word *femme*, not in an isolated way, but in context, such as in: "un parfum pour femmes" (a perfume for women).

Such descriptive uses will be admitted in the instructions for use related to goods, as well as in their presentation documents. However, the problem will be more delicate when the trade mark is used "descriptively" in a slogan to get the attention of clients.

III. Article 7.1 c): Descriptive signs

Article 7 of the Council Regulation provides that trade marks are denied registration when they *"consist exclusively of signs or indications which may serve, in trade, to designate the kind, quantity, intended purpose, value, geographical origin or the time of production of the goods or of rendering of the service, or other characteristics of the goods or service."*

This is almost exactly what the Paris Convention provides in Article 6 *quinquies* B 2). The Convention speaks of the place of origin of the goods instead of their geographical origin, but this does not seems to change the material meaning of these sections. However, the Council Regulation has added that if the trade mark designates other characteristics of the good or service, it shall be denied registration.

1) The descriptive nature of a trade mark is assessed "within the trade" in question. It is the application of the fundamental rule of speciality in trade mark law.

This is reiterated in Article 8.4.2 of the examination guidelines: if a sign is descriptive in a given area, it can lose its descriptive nature and become distinctive when it is applied in another area. However, the example provided in the guidelines is perhaps inadequate because, although the sign "4 x 3" designates product dimensions for construction materials, it is also descriptive to designate a dozen eggs in retail sales. However, the same sign "4 x 3" applied to beverages could then become distinctive.

2) In Article 8.4.1, the examination guidelines provide examples of descriptive signs of characteristics of goods and services:

a) to designate the kind of good, the guidelines mention the adjective "light" for low-tar cigarettes; and the same is true of the word "tobacco" in designating such goods;

b) to designate quality, the guidelines mention the word "superior," which is descriptive for all goods and services. The characteristic to use in assessing distinctiveness should be the one by which the consumer makes his/her choice. Thus, the expression "nearly unbreakable" in designating glassware is descriptive, whereas the adjective "unbreakable" is distinctive in designating meat, because it does not describe a characteristic of the good that might determine the consumer's choice to buy.

c) As mentioned in the guidelines, numbers spelled out in letters or written in digits often describe quantity;

d) The words "kitchen" or "bathroom" for cleaning products describe their uses.

e) The expression "the least expensive" describes the value of the good or service.

f) The guidelines explain that geographical origin is either the place (location, region or country) of production, or the place from which the public at issue might assume it comes. It has already been noted that the actual place of production could nevertheless be registered as a distinctive trade mark, provided the geographical name cannot mislead consumers as to the origin of the good, e.g., bananas marked "North Pole." However if, from the consumers point of view, the geographical name designates a good that has come from such a place, and whose qualities and characteristics result from the nature and people of the place in question, or if the place has a certain reputation (for instance Paris for fashion and perfume), then the geographical name cannot be registered as a trade mark to designate the good in such areas. Of course, the owner of the geographical name registered as a trade mark cannot prohibit anyone from using such geographical name in their mailing address or any other address.

g) The time of production of certain goods can constitute a determining quality in the buyers mind, such as, according to the examination guidelines, a specific year for wines or fresh produce "of the day." However, for other goods, the time of production is not determinant in the buyers mind and can be considered as a distinctive sign. An example of this is the name "Pastis 51" which designates the anise beverage which was first launched on the French market after World War II, and more precisely in 1951.

h) The examination guidelines give the example of the expression "unleaded" to designate gasoline, which is indeed another characteristic of the good. Therefore, if the sign designates a characteristic that is determining in the consumers mind, such a sign cannot be registered as a trade mark. The same is true of a sign attesting that the good complies with European or national quality standards.

3) If a sign is only evocative, can it be denied registration?
The wording of Article 7.1.c) seems to say it cannot since a sign must be denied registration when it "*may* serve (...) to designate [a] characteristic of the goods (...)."

Yet, in business, manufacturers and tradespeople need to evoke the good they are marketing to the public. Therefore, the trade mark must often spontaneously awaken in the publics mind an idea or image of the object – or of something directly related thereto.

Consequently, according to some people, a sign that evokes only one of the goods characteristics could be registered because, although it evokes the good, it does not necessarily designate a characteristic that determines the buyers choice.

The distinctiveness of an evocative sign will certainly be increased, as mentioned in Article 8.5 of the examination guidelines, if there are additional elements such as words, drawings or designs that do not designate the characteristics of the good for sale. Nevertheless, the guidelines state that representations such as bunches of grapes or vine leaves are still available for use by manufacturers and tradespeople in the area of wine products.

4) The descriptiveness of a word must be assessed based on the understanding of it that buyers may have. Still, it is true that two buyers may understand a word in different ways. This is the case of an English word that a Greek buyer does not know.

Community legal texts (Article 7.2 of the Council Regulation and Article 2.3 of the examination guidelines) require that descriptiveness be taken into account even when it only concerns "part of the European Community." The guidelines specify that it can be "any part of the European Community."

An examiner will therefore have to consider the official languages of the European Union (time will tell how the problem of new members joining the European Union – with their own language – will be resolved).

According to the examination guidelines (Article 8.1.3), an examiner will consult standard dictionaries of all eleven official languages of the Community, as well as specialized technical reference books.

If a word is descriptive in one language of part of a Member State, for instance in Welsh, would the Office not be entitled to deny registration of the descriptive sign which is common in the bona fide and established practices of Welsh trade?

IV. Article 7.1 d): Customary signs

The Office will refuse to register trade marks that are exclusively composed of signs or information which have become customary in common language or in the bona fide and established practices of trade. This was previously stated in Article 6 *quinquies* B 2) of the Paris Convention.

We know that a sign that is distinctive at the outset can lose its distinctiveness because the sign has been used in a commonplace manner, by professionals or by consumers, to designate the good in general and regardless of its origin. Such a sign can no longer be appropriated by only one company.

1) Customariness is assessed based on common language or on the bona fide and established practices of trade. If the sign is used in the common language of part of the Community, it cannot be registered. Here again, the Office will have to consider the eleven official languages, as well as regional languages.

Customariness must also be assessed by taking into account professionals and interested groups in addition to the general public.

Furthermore, customariness must be the result of long-standing use so that, if a sign is no longer fashionable or used, it could once more be registered as a trade mark.

Finally, if a trade mark contains other elements that are distinctive, it can be registered in order to protect such elements, even if it means the owner must file a disclaimer to acknowledge it is not entitled to claim an exclusive right in the customary element alone. Article 8.5 of the examination guidelines mentions the example of the letter “L” used to designate driving schools.

2) Article 50.1.b of the Council Regulation provides that the trade mark owner will lose its rights if, in consequence of its acts or inactivity, its trade mark has become the common name in the trade for a good or service in respect of which it is registered.

In order to avoid such loss of rights, a trade mark owner must show its intention not to let anyone use its trade mark to designate the good, regardless of its origin.

For example, the owner must be actively vigilant when the patent expires on the patented good named with a registered trade mark, and it can therefore be manufactured and marketed freely.

V. Article 7.1 e): Descriptive shapes

It is provided that the Office can refuse to register signs consisting exclusively of:
i) the shape which results from the nature of the goods themselves; or
ii) the shape of goods which is necessary to obtain a technical result; or
iii) the shape which gives substantial value to the goods;

The exclusion of such descriptive shapes applies both to the goods and to their packaging, which Article 4 considers as signs that are capable of distinguishing the goods of a company.

i) A shape that results from the nature of the goods themselves is denied registration, whereas Article 4 says that shapes can be used as a trade mark. How does one reconcile these two conditions?

It is certain that the known shape of a good cannot be registered as a trade mark to designate the good, i.e., the crescent shape of a *croissant* cannot be registered to designate baker's *croissants*.

However, when a shape known in one area is applied for the first time in another area, can it not be distinctive? For instance, a triangular shape cannot be registered to designate musical triangles, but it could be registered to designate chocolate products.

A newly created shape is not necessarily distinctive. For example, although new shapes for bottles cannot be registered as trade marks for bottles, the same new shapes can be registered as trade marks for perfume.

ii) The shape of goods must not be necessary to obtain a technical result.

Hence, the circular shape of a hoop cannot be registered to designate such toys.

The examination guidelines provide in Article 8.6 that although the pins of an electrical plug are necessary for it to function, the general shape of the plug is not a result of this technical requirement and that this can consequently be registered as a trade mark.

However, if several shapes are available to obtain the same technical result, could one of them be registered as a trade mark? Apparently not, especially if the shapes are simple, basic and in limited numbers, so as not to impede industry and trade.

iii) The Office will refuse to register a shape that gives substantial value to the goods.

One would think that the substantial value of a good would consist in the aspect of the good that determines the buyer's choice, such as the shape of a dress or a handbag, or the shape of a vase or an ashtray.

Indeed, the shape of a dress designates the kind or quality of the dress. It directly describes the good that is being marketed. It is therefore is not distinctive.

Once again, the shape of a bottle cannot be registered as a trade mark to designate bottles, but that it can be to designate perfume. This is because the shape of the bottle describes the bottle, whereas it does not describe the perfume. The shape of the bottle will not provide the perfume with its substantial value, even though the originality of such shape can create additional value, although only accessory. Furthermore, if the buyer purchases on the basis of the shape of the bottle, the trade mark remains valid to designate perfume.

The same should be true of the shape of the well-known LEGO construction set piece, which directly describes such a construction set piece. The shape gives substantial value to the good since the product is purchased precisely because of its shape. However, the shape of this piece applied to chocolate products is distinctive and can be registered as a trade mark to designate such chocolate products.

In the area of applied arts, the shape of the goods is usually the characteristic that best determines the buyers choice. Such is the case of the shape of Hermès' "Kelly" handbag and Rolex watches.

However, given their aesthetic aspect, these shapes have been protected by means of other rights, such as copyrights or registered designs. As such rights are temporary, can the shapes be appropriated as trade marks when they expire?

It seems that Article 7.1.e.iii does indeed prohibit a company from appropriating as a trade mark a shape that was previously protected by other means, and Article 7.3 of the Council Regulation does not allow the use of the shape to enter into play to render the shape distinctive.

Although the rule confirms that anything in the public domain can be freely reproduced, this rule is nevertheless strict with shapes which, in the consumers minds, remain or become the means of identifying the origin of the product and of personalizing the company that markets it. If Article 7.3 allows use to enter into play to render a shape distinctive when it was initially descriptive, this should also be the case for a shape that gives substantial value to the good, since this shape describes one of the characteristics of the good that determines the buyer's choice and, therefore, the shape is descriptive, like the other signs mentioned in Article 7.1 c).

Article 15.1 of the TRIPS Agreement admits that signs that are not inherently capable of distinguishing a good, for example a descriptive shape, can still be registered if they have become distinctive through use.

If it is admitted that a functional or technical shape cannot acquire distinctiveness through the use made of it, it seems harder to accept that the same exclusion is valid for those visual or aesthetic shapes which, due to their long-standing and extensive use, identify and personalize the company that markets them. In such a case, shape plays the essential part of the trade mark, in spite of its substantial value. In addition, the registration of such aesthetic shapes does not prevent the exploitation of other aesthetic shapes to satisfy the consumers' needs.

Moreover, if a competitor copies such an aesthetic shape, it generally is not merely by chance or coincidence. It is because it wants to take advantage of both the goodwill attached to this shape and the link that exists with the company identified and personalized by this shape. Therefore, the competitor should at least be required to take precautions so that buyers are not confused as to the origin of the product, for example, by requiring a clear and precise indication of the exact origin of the manufacturer or the actual retailer.

VI. Article 7.1 f): Trade marks which are contrary to public policy or to accepted principles of morality

Article 6 *quinquies* B 3) of the Paris Convention allows Union States to deny registration for trade marks which are contrary to public policy or to morality. The Council Regulation has included this provision but, in its French version, it has restricted it to *"bonnes moeurs,"* i.e., accepted standards of behaviour, which appears less extensive than morality.

The Paris Convention states that a trade mark may not be considered contrary to public policy for the sole reason that it does not comply with certain provisions of trade mark legislation, except if such provision itself relates to public policy.

It seems that these concepts of public policy and accepted principles of morality / *"bonnes moeurs"* are generally admitted and understood in the field of Intellectual Property.

Article 8.7 of the examination guidelines mentions the example of insults, of racist or blasphemous images, and agrees to register signs that are merely tasteless.

It should be noted that if a registered trade mark is not contrary to public policy or to accepted principles of morality, it can become so when it is exploited. Thus, although the French trade mark *Opium*, designating perfume, does not violate public policy, because it does not present the drug called "opium" in a favourable light and because it does not encourage the use of such narcotics, it would be preferable that the related advertising avoid suggesting intentionally any association with such poisons in order to better strike the imagination and catch the publics attention.

VII. Article 7.1 g): Deceptive trade marks

Article 6 *quinquies* 3 of the Paris Convention allowed Union States to deny registration for trade marks which might deceive the public. The Council Regulation illustrates the area of the deception by mentioning the nature, quality or geographical origin of the goods or services.

Yet the Council Regulation should also have mentioned other areas of deception, such as the kind, quantity, intended purpose, value and time of production, which it mentions in Article 7.1.c for descriptive signs.

Article 8.8 of the examination guidelines indicates that the deception must bear on a factor that is determining to buyers in their choice. Therefore, if a false assertion was made as to a secondary aspect of the good, the sign would not be denied registration.

The legal text prohibits all signs that might be deceitful, even if the trade mark has not caused any true deceptions. As stated in Article 8.8 of the guidelines, one should take into account "the nature of the trade and its clients" or of interested groups.

1) Article 7 of the Paris Convention provided that the nature of the goods to which a trade mark is to be applied shall in no case be an obstacle to the registration of the trade mark. This provision is reiterated in Article 15.4 of the TRIPS Agreement.

Therefore, a trade mark designating a drug can be filed and registered in the name of a person who does not have the required authorizations to manufacture and/or market such drug.

2) This provision on the nature of the products or services should be identical for trade marks comprised of family names.

When the family name identifies a person who is well-known in a given area, can it be registered as a trade mark to designate any object? Should Mr. Jacques Delors, former Chairman of the European Commission, be allowed to register his family name to designate a series of books on political economics, even though he did not write them, but only authorized them?

In law, it seems that one should distinguish between, on the one hand, material objects that are marked by their manufacturer or distributor and, on the other hand, the intellectual contents thereof that are identified by the name of their author and their title.

3) Article 50.1.c of the Council Regulation says that a trade mark can become deceptive. In such a case, if the deception ensues from its use by the trade mark owner, then the owner will lose its rights.

Could the Coca-Cola trade mark become deceptive if it was applied to a drink with a different taste from the one currently known by millions of consumers? Here again the terms and conditions of the trade marks exploitation should serve to avoid any risk of error.

VIII. Article 7.1 h): Official emblematic trade marks

The Office will refuse to register trade marks which are prohibited by Article 6 *ter* of the Paris Convention.

It refers to armorial bearings, flags and other emblems of States or international organizations, as well as their official signs and hallmarks indicating control and warranty.

IX. Article 7.1 i): Public emblematic trade marks

The Office will also refuse to register badges, emblems or escutcheons that are of particular public interest, even though they are not covered by Article 6 *ter* of the Paris Convention.

The examination guidelines do not provide any examples of the symbols that are of particular public interest. One could imagine that this would include the shape and colour of European highway signs, which could not be appropriated as trade marks to designate transport services. However, such signs could remain available in other areas, and such road signs could be distinctive to designate food products, for example.

X. Article 7.1 j): Geographical indications

The TRIPS Agreement provides in Article 22.3 that the registration of a trade mark must be denied when it contains a geographical indication with respect to goods not originating in the territory indicated, if use of the indication in the trade mark for such goods is of such nature as to mislead the public as to the true place of origin.

Article 22.4 of the same Agreement also indicates that the registration of a trade mark must be denied if although the geographical indication it contains is literally true as to the territory, region or locality in which the goods originate, it falsely represents to the public that the goods originate in another territory.

In application of this Agreement, the Council passed Regulation No. 3288/94 of 22 December, 1994, modifying the Community trade mark Regulation. Therefore, a paragraph j) was added to Article 7.1, denying registration for trade marks designating wines or spirits that contain a geographical indication identifying wines or spirits, when such wines or spirits do not have such origin.

In the examination guidelines, the Office provides in Article 8.11 that, in such situations, the examiner must ask the applicant to restrict the list of wines or spirits so as to comply with this requirement.

In this case, the geographical indication for wines and spirits originating in this locality will constitute an indication that may serve to designate the geographical origin of the goods. Therefore, it will be a descriptive indication, pursuant to Article 7.1 c), that must remain available to all wines and spirits producers and merchants of the given locality.

XI. Article 7.2: Absolute grounds in part of the Community

The Office must refuse to register a trade mark even if the grounds *"obtain only in part of the Community."*

This provision, which certainly limits the number of signs available as Community trade marks, is the necessary consequence of the uniform trade mark system in the European Union. It is logical to transpose the grounds that the Offices and Courts apply at a national level to an European level.

This provision also flows logically from the expansion of the national markets to the level of the European market.

From an intellectual point of view, however one might deplore the fact that such uniformity might lead to monotony in our purchase options.

XII. Article 7.3: The trade mark rendered distinctive through use

The Office may register a non-distinctive trade mark – descriptive or customary – if it has acquired distinctiveness through the use made of it.

This provision is derived from Article 6 *quinquies* C 1) of the Paris Convention, which provides that in order to assess whether a mark can be protected, one should take into account all facts, particularly the length of time the mark has been in use.

Indeed, the exploitation of an initially non-distinctive sign (whether it is descriptive or customary), particularly thanks to its long-standing and extensive use, can cause the consumer to identify the sign with a specific company and to recognize the origin of the good or service. Therefore, the sign acts essentially as a trade mark and deserves to be registered as a trade mark.

It is under such conditions that Article 15.1 of the TRIPS Agreement allows Member States to agree to register a sign that was not in itself capable of distinguishing a company's goods and/or services, if it has become distinctive through use.

1) Article 8.12 of the examination guidelines indicates the terms and conditions of the proof of acquisition of distinctiveness though use of the sign. This proof must bear on the place, period, extent and nature of the use. It can be presented in the form of documents from that period, such as catalogues, invoices and advertisements. Written statements, taken in compliance with national laws, can be used in support of the proof that distinctiveness has been acquired. The same is true of opinion surveys.

The acquisition of distinctiveness must be achieved throughout the Community, even if it is only by means of advertising campaigns. The guidelines state that the examiner must take into account the means used by the trade mark owner to communicate with its clients. It seems that this condition is more of an obligation of use intended to maintain trade mark rights, because distinctiveness must be rooted in the clients minds regardless of the trade mark owner's efforts.

2) As discussed previously, it is unfortunate that a non-functional descriptive shape cannot be registered as a trade mark once it has become distinctive through use, as authorized in Article 15.1 of the TRIPS Agreement.

XIII. Conclusion

Article 41 of the Council Regulation provides that third parties may submit written observations on the absolute grounds for refusal. This provision will be useful in finding out whether, in part of the Community, a sign is descriptive, customary or not distinctive in a given location.

Such third parties do not become parties in the proceedings before the Office, but their comments are passed on to the applicant, which can then respond with its own observations (Article 10 of the examination guidelines).

Relative Grounds for Refusal and Invalidity

The term "relative grounds for refusal", which is the title of Article 8 of the Regulation, relates to grounds on which registration of a Community trade mark may be refused, arising from some conflict with the rights of another party. These grounds, which are fully set out in Article 8, may be based either upon an "earlier trade mark" (under Article 8.1) or on certain other prior rights (Article 8.4); also included is the case where an agent or representative of the proprietor of a trade mark registers *the mark* without the proprietor's consent (Article 8.3).

It should be noted that the Office does not have the power to refuse registration *ex officio* on relative grounds. Article 39 requires the Office to make a search for prior Community trade mark registrations and applications which may be invoked under Article 8 (Article 39.1), and further provides for the national offices of Member States to make searches for conflicting national trade marks and applications (Article 39.3). However the only obligations of the Office, in respect of earlier rights, are to communicate the results of the searches to the applicant and to inform the proprietors of earlier Community trade mark's and Community trade mark applications cited in the Community search report (Article 39.5 & 6 respectively). Proprietors of trade marks and applications cited in national searches are not required to be notified. If the proprietor of a prior right wishes to prevent registration of the Community trade mark, he must give notice of opposition (under Article 42). Licensees of earlier trade marks, and persons authorized to exercise certain unregistered rights, may also oppose under Article 42. However opposition is not open to other parties. Although third parties – who may be natural or legal persons or any group or body representing manufacturers, producers, suppliers of services, traders or consumers (and thus *who* may be owners of prior rights) – are permitted to submit written observations, under Article 41, it is not clear *whether* any grounds other than absolute grounds for refusal may be raised in this manner. Under Article 41.1 it is permitted to submit written observations "explaining on which grounds under Article 7, in particular, the trade mark shall not be registered ex officio". It is possible that the words "in particular", are to be taken as an indication that other grounds may be raised, in addition to absolute grounds (under

Article 7). However it is thought that use of the words "ex officio" excludes relative grounds from the scope of this provision because, as mentioned above, the Office has no power to refuse, *ex officio*, on such grounds.

Once a Community trade mark *is* registered, it is possible to have the trade mark declared invalid on a number of "relative grounds for invalidity", as set out in Article 52, including grounds on which registration might have been opposed under Article 8, and on certain additional grounds. A Community trade mark may be declared invalid on application to the Office or on the basis of a counterclaim in infringement proceedings (Article 52.1). Although Article 52.1 does not itself *state* who may seek such a declaration, the effect of Article 55.1(b) is that the right to apply to the Office is confined to those who would have been entitled to oppose registration under Article 42.1. In the case of Article 52.2, which provides further grounds on which declarations of invalidity may be granted which are not available for opposition under Article 8, the applicant may be the owner of the prior rights relied upon or the persons entitled under the relevant national law of the Member State concerned to exercise the rights (Article 55.1(c)). Article 55 makes no reference to counterclaims seeking declarations of invalidity. Therefore it would appear that any person (natural or legal) who is a defendant to a claim for infringement may invoke, by counterclaim, any relative grounds for invalidity under Article 52. This is not excluded by Article 96 ("Counterclaims").

I. The relative grounds for refusal

1. The grounds

The relative grounds for refusal may be considered as *falling into* two main categories:

those which are based upon conflict with "earlier trade marks"; and

those which are founded upon another trade mark or similar right which is not registered.

As mentioned above, a further ground for refusal is available to the proprietor of a trade mark sought to be registered by an agent or representative of the proprietor who has applied for registration of the trade mark in his own name without the proprietor's consent (Article 8.3).

2. Meaning of "earlier trade mark"

The earlier trade marks, on which refusal of registration under Article 8 may be based, are defined in Article 8.2. They are: Community trade mark's, trade marks registered in a Member State or at the Benelux Trade Mark Office, and trade marks registered under international arrangements (i.e. the Madrid Arrangement or the Madrid Protocol) having effect in a Member State (Article 8.2(a)(i) to (iii)). It is a requirement that such marks have a date of application for registration which is earlier than the date of application for registration of the Community Trade Mark in question, taking account, where appropriate, of the priorities claimed for the trade marks (Article 8.2). Article 8.2(b) extends the definition of "earlier trade mark" to cover applications for any such trade marks "subject to their registration". Presumably this means that, where a ground of refusal based upon *a prior* application appears to be established, final refusal of registration of the Community trade mark will be deferred until the applicant's entitlement to registration has been determined. Article 8.2(c) specifies a third category of "earlier trade mark", namely trade marks which, on the date of application for registration of (or of the priority claimed for) the Community trade mark are "well known" in a Member State, within the meaning of those words in Article 6 *bis* of the Paris Convention.

3. Refusal based on "earlier trade marks"

Where the trade mark sought to be registered is identical to the earlier trade mark and the goods or services are identical to those which the earlier trade mark is protected, the Community trade mark application must be refused under Article 8.1(a). No likelihood of confusion need be shown to exist. Where the specifications of goods or services are not identical in totality, but merely overlap, this objection will apply to those items which are the same.

In any other situation, in which the trade marks are the same or similar and the goods or services covered by the trade marks are the same or similar, the ground of refusal will only be valid if there exists a likelihood of confusion on the part of the public in the territory in which the earlier trade mark is protected. Such likelihood of confusion includes the likelihood of association with the earlier trade mark (Article 8.1(b)). It should be noted that the word "protected" is used in subsections Article 8.1(a) and 8.1(b) to cover the case of the well-known trade mark, which is not necessarily registered in the Member State concerned. The third situation, in which the marks are identical or similar, but there is no similarity between the goods or services covered by the Community trade mark application and the earlier trade mark, is the subject of different rules, set out in Article 8.5. If the earlier trade mark has a reputation – in the case of a Community trade mark in the Community, and in the case of any other earlier national trade mark, in the Member State concerned – the Community trade mark application *must* be refused if it is shown that the use "without due cause of the trade mark applied for would take unfair advantage of, or be detrimental to, the distinctive character or the repute of the earlier trade mark". All these grounds for refusal require some further explanation.

4. Explanation of the grounds based upon earlier trade marks

Save for one point, no further explanation is required of the first ground for refusal, where the trade marks and the goods or services are identical. As already indicated, if the application is opposed it must be refused. The point which requires consideration is what is meant by "identical"? For example a question could arise as to whether a word represented in block capitals is identical to the same word represented in a different typeface; or whether a mark shown in red is identical to the same mark represented in black and white. If the Regulation is interpreted literally it would seem that such marks are only to be regarded as "similar". In practice this may not make much difference, because the Office (or a court in infringement proceedings) will usually find a likelihood of confusion in such cases. However such matters are important when the question of evidence is being considered because if reliance is placed on the identical nature of the marks, then no evidence is needed to show the existence of a likelihood of confusion.

Where there is no identity both of the trade marks *and* the goods or services, the position is not so straightforward. It is necessary to consider first the case in which the goods or services are identical or similar, and, secondly, the case in which they are not similar.

In the first case, as already mentioned, for the relative ground for refusal to apply there must exist a likelihood of confusion on the part of the public, which includes the likelihood of association with the (earlier) trade mark. The likelihood of confusion has to be determined in the light of *all* the relevant factors, which include the identity or similarity of the marks and the identity or similarity of the goods or services. There is no guidance as to when marks are "similar", and presumably this is purely a question of fact in each case. The same applies to the question of similarity of goods and services, as to which again no guidance is given. Some assistance may be derived from decisions under the old *United Kingdom* law (the Trade Marks Act 1938) as to whether goods or services were, or were not, "of the same description", but such decisions cannot in any way be conclusive. There is little doubt that it is permissible under Article 8(1)(b), in appropriate circumstances, to find that goods may be similar to services and *vice versa*. To some extent the question of similarity, of marks and of goods or services, must be a matter of degree, and the likelihood of confusion must generally be greater the more similarity there is in any given case. Also, the nature of the mark is clearly a relevant factor; there is in general a greater likelihood of confusion with more distinctive marks; this may be particularly significant where there is a lesser degree of similarity of goods or services.

The question of "association" may raise a technical problem of interpretation. In a document described as "Statements for entry in the minutes of the Council meeting at which the regulation is adopted" ("the Annex") – see paragraph 5 of the Annex – it is stated that "The Council and the Commission note that "likelihood of association" is a concept which in particular has been developed by Benelux case law". However the Annex, although published in the ECTA Law Book (ECTA; 1994) is technically, it would seem, a confidential document and it is open to doubt whether it should have official standing in a court or in the Office. Nevertheless a statement of the Benelux Court of Justice (Decision of 20 May 1983, case nr. A 82/5, Nederlandse Jurisprudentie 1984, 72 *Henri Julien B.V.* v. *Norbert Verschuere*), is helpful:

"There is similarity between a mark and a sign when, taking into account the particular circumstances of the case, such as the distinctive power of the mark, the mark and the sign, each looked at as a whole and in correlation, show such a resemblance phonetically, visually or conceptually that by this resemblance alone, associations between the sign and the mark are evoked."

Of course, the similarity of the goods or services is another factor to take into account. Subject to that, this seems to be a general approach which might be adopted, even without reference to the Annex.

In the third situation, where there is identity or similarity of marks, but the goods or services are not similar, then a different test is applied by Article 8.5, which is concerned with what, in some jurisdictions, is called "dilution". In such a case registration is to be refused where the earlier trade mark has a reputation (in the case of a Community trade mark, a reputation in the Community and in the case of a national trade mark, a reputation in the Member State concerned) and the use without due cause of the trade mark applied for "would take unfair advantage of, or be detrimental to, the distinctive character or the repute of the earlier trade mark" (Article 8.5). The effect of the words "without due cause" is not clear; they may simply mean in the absence of authority, such as some form of licence, or perhaps the absence of some otherwise legally justifiable reason for adopting the mark for the goods or services in question. The requirements of unfair advantage or detriment raise questions which will essentially be questions of fact, although the interpretation of these terms may also involve questions of law. Clearly the nature of the earlier trade mark will be a significant factor; an unusual or distinctive mark will generally enjoy a greater scope of protection. It is thought that Article 8.5 does not require proof of any particular degree of reputation, although the Office or the courts may well impose some minimum level of reputation, below which the provision will not be applied. What has to be considered in each case is whether, having regard to the marks themselves and to the nature of the goods or services covered by the earlier mark trade mark and by the application, the reputation of the earlier trade mark is such that either of the consequences, of unfair advantage or detriment, can be expected to follow.

The terms "unfair advantage" and "detriment", with reference to the "distinctive character" or the "repute" of the trade mark, need some further explanation. The distinctive character in this context may arise partly from the mark itself and partly from use. Repute may, perhaps, be looked upon as being broadly the same as goodwill. Taking unfair advantage involves what may be termed parasitic trading, or "riding on the back" of the reputation of the earlier trade mark. Detriment may occur by way of dilution of the trade mark, which may not involve any confusion or deception of the consumer, or it may be in the form of actual damage to the mark or the goodwill in it, for example if the defendant's goods or services are inferior or have some connotation which is derogatory.

5. Refusal based upon other earlier rights

Article 8.3 provides for opposition by the proprietor of the trade mark sought to be registered as a Community trade mark, where the applicant seeks registration without due authority. A licensee or authorised user may not oppose under this provision. Registration must be refused if the applicant is an agent or representative of the proprietor, seeking registration in his own name without the proprietor's consent, unless the agent or representative "justifies his action". It is difficult to see how such action could be justified where the proprietor has not given consent to the application. Perhaps these words might be applied in a case in which a proprietor had over a long period allowed the agent or representative to use the trade mark for goods or services which had no connection with the proprietor.

Article 8.4 provides that, upon opposition by the proprietor of a non-registered trade mark or of another sign used in the course of trade of more than mere local significance, a trade mark shall not be registered where and to the extent that, pursuant to the law of the Member State governing the sign, (a) rights to that sign were acquired prior to the date of application to register the Community trade mark or the date of priority claimed and (b) the sign confers on its proprietor the right to prohibit use of a subsequent trade mark. Under Article 42.1(c) persons authorised under the relevant national law to exercise the rights concerned may also oppose. This provision is intended to protect rights acquired in a mark through use, even if they are not registered. For example, a right to protect an unregistered trade mark, against use of an identical or similar mark in such a way as to deceive consumers, has long been recognised under the English common law, in the form of the tort of passing off, and similar rights may be given under unfair competition laws in some other Member States.

No explanation is given of the words "of more than mere local significance". It seems unlikely that trade marks used for goods would be regarded as having mere local significance in many cases, although the words could be applied to services of an essentially local nature, such as dry cleaning, taxi services and café or restaurant services and public houses. Whether a particular right, to an unregistered trade mark or sign, is within the scope of Article 8.4 must be determined in accordance with the relevant national law.

II. Relative grounds for invalidity

1. Grounds also available for opposition

Relative grounds for invalidity are provided by Article 52. Such grounds may be invoked either on application to the Office or on the basis of a counterclaim in infringement proceedings (Article 52.1). Some of these are identical to the grounds for opposition under Article 8. Thus earlier trade marks, within Article 8.2, may be invoked as grounds for a declaration of invalidity, where the conditions of Article 8.1 or 8.5 are fulfilled (see Article 52.1(a)). Under Article 52.1(b) a declaration of invalidity may be granted on the ground provided in Article 8.3, i.e. where an agent or representative of the proprietor obtains registration without the proprietor's consent and cannot justify his action in obtaining registration. Under Article 52.1(c) a declaration of invalidity may be granted on the basis of an unregistered national rights where the conditions of Article 8.4 are fulfilled.

2. Grounds not available for opposition

Article 52.2 provides certain additional grounds, on which a declaration of invalidity may be obtained, which are not available as grounds for opposition. These grounds arise where use of the Community trade mark may be prohibited pursuant to the national law governing the protection of "any other earlier right". Certain types of earlier rights are expressly mentioned, but they are preceded by the words "in particular", which indicates that other unspecified rights may also be covered. Those specified are: (a) a right to a name; (b) a right of personal portrayal; (c) a copyright; (d) an industrial property right. The last mentioned right would include a registered design or an unregistered design right. A right to a plant *variety* name would probably also be covered by Article 52.2.

3. Limitations on relative grounds for invalidity

Article 52.3 rules out the granting of a declaration of invalidity where the proprietor of the right referred to consents expressly to the registration of the Community trade mark before submitting the application or counterclaim for a declaration of invalidity. Article 52.4 prevents a proprietor of any of the rights referred to, who has previously applied or counterclaimed for a declaration of invalidity, from submitting a new application or counterclaim on the basis of any other such right which he could have invoked in support of the first application or counterclaim. Article 53 (limitation in consequence of acquiescence) imposes further restrictions on seeking declarations of invalidity. Article 53.1 applies, where the proprietor of an earlier Community trade mark acquiesces in the use of a later Community trade mark in the Community for a period of five successive years, being aware of such use. Article 53.2 makes similar provision, in the case of the proprietor of a national trade mark (under Article 8.2) or another earlier sign (under Article 8.4), who acquiesces in the use of a later Community trade mark in the Member State in which the right is protected. In such circumstances the proprietor of the earlier trade mark or right may not seek a declaration of invalidity in respect of the Community trade mark or oppose its use for the goods or services for which it has been used, unless registration of the Community trade mark was applied for in bad faith.

4. Partial invalidity

Article 52.5 applies Article 51.3 (concerned with absolute grounds for invalidity), which provides that if a ground for invalidity exists only in respect of some of the goods or services for which the Community trade mark is registered, the trade mark is to be declared invalid for those goods or services only.

Reputed Trade Marks

The significance of a trade marks advertising function has grown considerably within the past few years.[1] Increasingly, consumers orient themselves around an image originating from a trade mark, which in turn, often influences their purchasing decision. Therefore, many trade mark owners spend enormous amounts on marketing and advertising their marks. The successfully promoted trade mark represents economic value. Its positive image is often transferred to various products. Considering the variety of trade marks in todays market and the consumers short term memory, there is a substantial risk of losing a marks positive image. Moreover, the increasing risk of third parties actively infringing on a valuable mark can lead to even greater damage to that trade marks market value. Therefore, the owner of a mark must be provided with a large scope of protection against third party conduct which interferes with his prior protected rights.[2] On the other hand, this degree of protection cannot extend to all trade marks, because this would lead to an unnecessary limitation on the variety of trade marks available for other users. A balancing of these two interests requires a legally informed consideration between an owners interest in the goodwill of his mark on the one hand, and the freedom of other potential users to determine the marking of their products. The directives of the Community trade mark Regulation concerning the protection of reputed trade marks serve to balance these interests.

The reputed trade mark is a new legal term in Community law, for which there is no official definition so far. In the past, each Member State has developed its own set of judicial rulings concerning famous and reputed trade marks. The unification of these laws is one of the goals of the Community Trade Mark Regulation. The definition of the term "reputed trade mark" will depend upon a decision of the European Court of Justice. However, because there is no such ruling to date, a definition can only be gleaned through an interpretation of the wording in the Community trade mark Regulation. This will now be discussed from a German point of view.

1 Levin, GRUR Int. 1996, 454-461, Gielen/Strowel, Mitt. 1995, 198, 199.
2 Meister, WRP 1995, 366, 371.

II. The Community Trade Mark in the Community Trade Mark Council Regulation

1. The reputed trade mark as a relative ground for refusal, Article 42 (1) (a) in connection with Article 8 (5) Community trade mark Regulation

According to Article 42 (1) (a) and Article 8 (5) Community trade mark Regulation, in an opposition proceeding, within a period of three months following the publication of a Community trade mark application, an opposer may assert ownership of a reputed mark as a relative ground for refusal of the newly published mark. Article 8 (5) Community trade mark Regulation states as follows:

> *"Furthermore, upon opposition by the proprietor of an earlier trade mark within the meaning of paragraph 2, the trade mark applied for shall not be registered where it is identical with or similar to the earlier trade mark and is to be registered for goods or services which are not similar to those for which the earlier trade mark is registered, where in the case of an earlier Community trade mark the trade mark has a reputation in the Community and, in case of an earlier national trade mark, the trade mark has a reputation in the Member State concerned and where the use without due cause of the trade mark applied for would take unfair advantage of, or be detrimental to, the distinctive character or the repute of the earlier trade mark."*

Article 8 (5) refers to Article 8 (2) Community trade mark Regulation concerning the definition of a mark. According to this definition, there are Community and national marks as well as "well known" marks as defined under Article 6 *bis* Paris Convention (PC). The earlier national mark (either registered or pending registration) must have a reputation in the Member State concerned, i.e., the marks reputation and registration must be in the same state. If "well known" marks under Article 6 *bis* PC are not registered in a Member State and are not protected by that Member States national trade mark law, it is doubtful whether they can be considered as "national marks" by that state. However, these "well known" marks may still be considered "national"[3] within the framework of the Paris Convention, because membership in the Paris Convention gives even "unregistered" national marks protection in that Member State.

It is sufficient that the opposers reputed mark has a reputation in one of the Member States.[4] But because the mark must have a reputation in a specific state, that state has to be named by the opposer.

[3] Kur, GRUR 1994, 330, 340.
[4] Kur, GRUR 1994, 330, 340.

2. The reputed trade mark as a relative ground for invalidity, Article 52 (1) (a), Article 8 (5) Community trade mark Regulation

A reputed trade mark can further be alleged as a ground for invalidating a registered mark. However, this allegation must be raised in an application to the European Trade Mark Office (Article 2 Community trade mark Regulation), or on the basis of a counterclaim in infringement proceedings brought before at the National Community Trade Mark Courts
(Article 9 (1) Community trade mark Regulation).

3. The reputed trade mark as a ground for the protection in addition to the protection based on likelihood of confusion, Article 9 (1) (c) Community trade mark Regulation

According to Article 9 (1) (c), a proprietor is entitled to prevent all third parties from using, without his consent, any sign which is identical with or similar to his mark in the course of trade. Article 9 (1) (c) Community trade mark Regulation states as follows:

> *"The proprietor shall be entitled to prevent all third parties not having his consent from using in the course of trade any sign which is identical with or similar to the Community trade mark in relation to goods or services which are not similar to those for which the Community trade mark is registered, where the latter has a reputation in the Community and where use of that sign without due cause takes unfair advantage of, or is detrimental to, the distinctive character or the repute of the Community trade mark."*

The elements of this offence as provided in Article 9 (1) (c) Community trade mark Regulation are almost identical to those found in Article 8 (5) Community trade mark Regulation. The differences are that under Article 9 (1) (c) Community trade mark Regulation, a reputed trade mark can be raised against any similar sign. In Article 8 (5) Community trade mark Regulation however, a reputed trade mark can only be raised against a trade mark application. Article 9 (1) (c) Community trade mark Regulation does not permit an opposer to raise an opposition based on a national reputed trade mark. Contrary to Article 8 (5), Article 9 (1) (c) Community trade mark Regulation does not require a prognosis decision,[5] but a judgement based on actual circumstances, i.e. the concrete individual case. The other constituent elements of Article 8 (5) and Article 9 (1) (c) Community trade mark Regulation are identical.

[5] This can be concluded from the wording "would" in Article 8 (5) Community trade mark Regulation and from the fact that a pending mark does not have to be used in advance. In the context of Article 8 (5) Community trade mark Regulation, the decision does not depend on a possible prior usage of the mark. The prognosis decision does not have to be negative just because the actual usage of the sign up to that point has not lead to an infringement of the earlier mark.

Because the constituent elements are identical and because the nature of the interests involved are similar, it may be assumed that these constituent elements should be interpreted the same way. As such, in the context of this discussion there will be no further differentiation between Article 8 (5) and Article 9 (1) (c) Community trade mark Regulation.

III. The Meaning of a Trade mark Having a Reputation

1. *Historical origin of the Community trade mark Regulation*

The phrase, "trade mark having a reputation" was first referred to in the third draft of the Community trade mark Regulation. In the first draft of 27 November 1980,[6] extended trade mark protection required that the mark hava a "high reputation" in the entire community.[7] In an altered proposal[8] dated July 1984, it was not required that a mark have a "high reputation" in the entire community. Although the phrase "high reputation" was retained, the word "entire" in reference to the European Community was left out. The language, "trade mark having a reputation" was first used in the trade mark directive which was passed by the Council of the European Union on 21 December 1988.

This change in terms was preceded by adjudication[9] in several Member States, that recognised protection of a mark "having a reputation" besides that which was provided to a "famous" mark. Whether this change in terms was meant to reduce the grounds of protection under EC law is unknown, because both terms are new autonomous legal terms of Community law[10] that have not yet been discussed or clarified by a European Court of Justice ruling which would be decisive. Considering the adjudication in the Member States that differentiates between marks "having a reputation" and "famous" marks, it is likely that the change in terms was meant to indicate that the defining elements of the "reputed" trade mark should be less strict than the national "famous" marks.

2. *The varying translation of the defining terms in the five languages of the Office*

According to Article 115 (2) Community trade mark Regulation, the languages of the Office are English, French, German, Italian and Spanish. The languages are equally entitled. However, a literal interpretation of the specific wording of the Community trade mark Regulation in the five languages of the Office results in a difference in the meaning of the terms used. In particular English version

[6] Dokument KOM 80, 653 endg./2 27.11.1980, GRUR Int. 1981, 86, 87.

[7] Article 8 (b) of the proposal of 27.11.1980.

[8] Dokument KOM (84) 470 endg. of 31.7.1984.

[9] See for German Adjudication the "Dimple" Decision of the BGH in GRUR 1985, 550.

[10] See von Mühlendahl, GRUR Int. 1989, 353, who speaks of a new attempt at redefiniting the protection of reputed marks apart from the traditional "scope of similarity" protection. There shall be no relation to the traditional, older term of the "well known" trade mark.

speaks of "a mark having a reputation". This corresponds to the meaning of the French version "Marque jouit d'une renommée". However, the Italian and Spanish versions in contrast, focus on the "notoriety" of a mark: "Marchio communitario gode di notorieta" and "Marca notoriamente conocida", respectively. The German version in turn, speaks of a "bekannte (known) Marke".[11] While the terms, "reputation" and "renommée" aim at quality features (the reputation of a mark), the German term, a "known" mark, is directed at quantitative criteria (the notoriety of a mark). The Italian and Spanish versions seem to refer to Article 6 *bis* PC by using the words "notorietà" and "notoriamente conocida", respectively. These terms are also directed at quantitative criteria. These different literal interpretations in the five languages of the Office already show that the term, "reputed trade mark" is accentuated differently in the particular Member States. The wording of the Article therefore, cannot be called upon for a final interpretation even if one concludes that the different terms lead to the result that qualitative as well as quantitative elements will be required.

Following the passing of the Community trade mark Regulation in 1988, a Community trade mark Regulation Implementing Order was issued on 13 December 1995.[12] This order hints at a possible unification of the phrase "reputed trade mark". In German, the specific phrase in the Order concerning the "reputed trade mark" reads: "Marke, die Wertschätzung im Sinne des Article 8 (5) der Verordnung genießt", meaning "trade mark having a reputation".

The same applies to the Spanish version which reads "Marqua renombra a effectos del apparado 5 del articolu 8 del Reglamento". Only the Italian version still refers to the notoriety of the mark by saying "gode di notorieta". The new phrasing in the German and Spanish version are notable, because they differ from the Council Regulation and because they are obviously adjusted to the English and French versions. This indicates the probable interpretation that the Office and the European Court of Justice will provide even though a precise unified term still does not exist.

IV. Criteria for Assuming a Reputed Mark

Among other grounds of protection, one is the existence of a "reputed trade mark". A "reputed trade mark" is defined by qualitative and quantitative features. Both criteria are obligatory preconditions for the protection of a "reputed trade mark" the Community trade mark Regulation).[13] It is unclear whether more emphasis should be given to one or the other criteria, and in particular, whether the quantitative criterion must have a specific minimum level of mea-

[11] Office Journal 1/95, p. 74/75.
[12] Office Journal 2-3/95, p. 288, 289.
[13] Opposing opinion Ingerl, "Die Gemeinschaftsmarke", p. 85.

surable consumer recognition. (Consumers, as referred to herein, are only those who fall within a specific product/service consumer group, hereafter called "trade circles concerned"). As mentioned earlier, the term "reputed trade mark" is an autonomous legal term of Community Law, the preconditions and scope of which can only be determined by the European Court of Justice. As long as there is no binding interpretation of this legal term, one must refer to parallel decisions reached by national courts.[14]

1. Notoriety (quantitative criterion)

a) Degree of Notoriety

The notoriety of a mark is usually measured according to a survey of the "trade circles concerned". It is therefore quantifiable. This quantitative element has been important in German adjudication concerning the protection of "famous" and "known" trade marks. In German law, in order that a mark be recognised and protected as a "famous" mark, a greater than 80% recognition by the "trade circles concerned" is necessary.[15] Although no exact level of recognition has actually been established to determine a known mark, the German Supreme Court (BGH) has traditionally ruled that at least a 33% recognition level was necessary by the "trade circles concerned" for a mark to be considered as "known".[16] Specifically, the German Supreme Court has emphasised that the protection of a marks reputation does not only depend upon the degree of its notoriety, but substantially, also on other circumstances such as the peculiarity of the sign itself, the kind of goods distributed under the sign, their quality and prestige, and most of all, the relationship between the mark which is to be used in association with certain goods and the goods themselves.[17] Based on this reasoning, the German Supreme Court has remarked in its "Dimple" decision that a notoriety degree of less than 33% could also be sufficient, because the economic exploitability of a marks reputation does not only depend on a specific degree of its notoriety.[18]

According to the Community trade mark Regulation, the protection of a "reputed trade mark" does not only include protection against exploitation of reputation, but also against infringement of the distinctive character of a mark (danger of dilution), that has been reserved formally to the "famous" mark.

These two formerly separated categories[19] of marks are now combined in one legal term. Thus, it has been argued that the protection of a "reputed trade mark" should require a degree of notoriety in its "trade circles" of 80-90%, because this is the percentage required for the protection of a "famous" trade mark.[20]

[14] Pieper, GRUR 1996, 657, 658.
[15] BGH WRP 1991, 568, 570 – Avon.
[16] BGH GRUR 1985, 550, 551 – Dimple.
[17] BGH GRUR 1985, 550, 552 – Dimple.
[18] BGH GRUR 1985, 550, 552 – Dimple.
[19] In Germany: protection of the "known" mark under § 1 UWG; protection of the "famous" mark under §§ 823, 1004 BGB.
[20] Berlitz, "Das neue Markenrecht", 1997, No. 22.

However, this argument has little merit, because there is no reason why the simple combination of both categories should produce a higher evidentiary burden for the "known mark". On the contrary, the change of definition in the Community trade mark Regulation from "having a high reputation" to "having a reputation"[21] arguably indicates a reduced evidentiary burden than was previously required under national law. So far, there are no indications that the European Court of Justice will require a minimum percentage which would define in quantitative terms a notorious "community trade mark".[22]

b) The reputed trade mark compared with the other types or marks

According to German adjudication, there has traditionally been a graduated scale of a notoriety to define different kinds of marks. For instance, a minimum degree of recognition of approximately 20-30% is necessary for an unregistered mark to acquire prominence as a trade mark and therefore be protected under the German Trade Mark Act.[23] A "known" mark, in turn, in general must have a minimum recognition level of approximately 30%.[24] Next, in order to show the "acquired capacity to distinguish", the generally accepted level of notoriety has been 50-60%,[25] even though this percentage depends very much on the mark in question.[26] About the same percentage (60%) applies for the "well known" mark according to Article 6 *bis* PC. Finally, an 80 to 90% notoriety level is necessary for a "famous" mark.

Such a graduation of necessary consumer recognition does not appear in the new Community trade mark Regulation. It is believed however, that the criterion necessary[27] to define the Community trade mark Regulation "reputed" trade mark will be somewhere between the previous requirement to find that a mark had acquired prominence and therefore protected or that it had "acquired the

[21] In the German language version from "berühmte Marke" to "bekannte Marke".

[22] The official reasoning of the Ministerial Bill of the German Trade Mark Act states that there should be no requirement that the "reputed" mark have a higher degree of notoriety than marks which have acquired prominence are registered with the national trade mark office because they have acquired the capacity to distinguish.

[23] BGH GRUR 1960, 130 – Sunpearl; BGH GRUR 1963, 622 – Sunkist, see also BGH GRUR 1992, 72, 73 – quattro, where 60% was not sufficient for a descriptive sign to be protected as a trade mark.

[24] BGH GRUR 1995, 550, 551 – Dimple.

[25] BPatG GRUR 1972, 34 – Tabac; BPatG 1986, 671 – GFK; BGH GRUR 1990, 360, 361 – apropos Film II.

[26] For protection of colours the percentage has to be higher than 80%.

[27] In German legal literature, there is the opinion that a notoriety degree of 20% will normally not be sufficient, see Pieper, GRUR 1996, 429, 433; others mention the following minimum degrees: Sack, GRUR 1995, 81, 86: 30% may be sufficient; Boes/Deutsch, GRUR 1996, 168, 169: 30% in any case sufficient; Rößler, GRUR 1994, 559, 562: 33% sufficient; v. Schultz, GRUR 1994, 85, 88: 40% sufficient; Pagenberg, FG für Beier, p. 317, 322: 40% sufficient; Schweer, Die 1. Markenrechtslinie der EG, Diss. 1992, p. 114: 60-75%; Pieper, GRUR 1996, 657, 660: more than what is required for acquired prominence; Levin, GRUR Int. 1996, 454, 460: same degree as required for capacity to distinguish (secondary meaning).

capacity to distinguish" through secondary meaning.[28] Also, a clear line can not be drawn between the terms "reputed trade mark" and "well known trade mark" according to Article 6 *bis* PC, because the Italian and Spanish versions utilise the term "notorious" to indicate that they require the same precondition for a "reputed" mark as for a "well known" mark according to Article 6 *bis* PC. Because of the different requirements in the Member States, it is difficult to forecast whether the European Court of Justice will require a certain degree of notoriety for the "reputed" mark. At this moment, it is not possible to say whether there will be a graduation between different types of trade marks, such as the criterion that a "well known" mark (Article 6 *bis* PC) always require a higher notoriety than a "reputed" trade mark.[29]

2. Reputation (qualitative criteria)

Based on general opinion, the protection of the Community trade mark against those who would take unfair advantage of its reputation, presumes that it has a special reputation. In this context, it is controversial whether the criterion of repute should be viewed as an additional requirement,[30] or whether it should be viewed in combination with the notoriety requirement for the existence of a reputed trade mark. When regarding the English or French version of the Community trade mark Regulation, the legal term, "mark having a reputation" ("marque jouit d'une renommée") implies that the definition of "reputed" mark depends mainly on the repute the mark receives. Contrary to this, the German as well as the Italian and Spanish versions refer to quantitative criteria, leading one to infer that the question of a marks repute should be discussed only in the framework of impaired rights.

The point of view that the phrase "reputed" mark is neutral and a requirement on its own is justified[31] by two arguments: the requirement of repute is mentioned separately, and a repute is only necessary when considering the uses detrimental to a marks repute. The requirement of repute is not necessary when considering uses which are detrimental to a marks distinctive character.[32] These arguments, however, have little merit. In particular, according to the German adjudication on the subject to date, uses which are detrimental to a marks distinctive character also require a finding that a trade mark is of high repute.[33] As to the second argument, it is unpersuasive that because the German Supreme

[28] Levin, GRUR Int. 1996, 454, 461, who assumes, that a "well known" mark according to Article 6 *bis* PC will always meet the preconditions for a "reputed" trade mark.

[29] See Kur, GRUR 1994, 330, 339, who argues for an equalisation of the requirements of "notoriety" and "acquired prominence" (general adoption in the circle of users).

[30] Pieper, GRUR 1996, 429, 433; also apparently Levin, GRUR Int. 1996, 454, 460; Nordemann, "Wettbewerbs- und Markenrecht" 1995, No. 430 e.

[31] Pieper, GRUR 1996, 429, 433; Boes/Deutsch, GRUR 1996, 168, 169.

[32] Pagenberg, FG für F.K. Beier, p. 331.

[33] BGH GRUR 1959, 182, 186 – Quick; BGH GRUR 1966, 623, 624 – Kupferberg; BGH WRP 1991, 568, 570, 573 – Avon.

Court[34] has separated these two criteria in its past rulings, that this is to be continued for the "reputed" trade mark under the new European trade mark regulation. Rather, the "reputed" trade mark is different from the "known" mark. The phrase "reputed trade mark" is an autonomous legal term of the Community law based on a different premise. Specifically while the protection of the "known" mark developed through German court decisions which referred to the "good reputation" of a mark which in turn, required among other factors, a certain notoriety, the Community trade mark (in its German version) does not refer to reputation, but to notoriety which is to be assessed according to the capacity to distinguish and the repute of a mark. The good reputation factor is therefore integrated into the notoriety requirement.[35] The same can be concluded from the official reasoning of the Ministerial Bill of the German Trade Mark Act[36] which explicitly states that the notoriety of a mark depends on both, qualitative and the quantitative criteria.

A marks repute is a psychological factor, the full extent of which cannot be precisely quantified. It has yet to be seen what criteria or parameters the European Court of Justice will take into consideration in determining the repute of a Community trade mark. In general however, a mark is viewed as especially worthy if it has an expressive image[37] or goodwill.[38] The image or goodwill of a mark may, in turn, be viewed as measurable based on criteria such as quality, exclusivity or a relatively high price. On the other hand, it is possible that image and goodwill are moulded by irrational motivations so that the degree of a marks repute cannot be fully reconstructed. In the end, it is likely that a marks repute will mainly be determined by the extent of its commercial realisability.[39] Specifically, a mark receives a special repute when its reputation is so outstanding that its economically reasonable exploitation is also possible for other goods and services.[40] In this context, it must be questioned whether the repute of a mark is so great that an economic exploitation of its reputation seems reasonable within the trade circles of the opposed sign. In regard to instances of impairment or infringement such as those enumerated in Article 9 (1) (c) Community trade mark Regulation, this economic exploitation of a marks reputation is used in a case of "image transfer". Once an "image transfer" to non-obvious goods or services seems economically reasonable, the special repute of the mark in question cannot be denied. The strength of a marks repute depends upon the scope of the possible image transfer. An already existing image transfer, i.e., the economical exploitation of a mark for use on different goods or services can be taken as an indication of strong repute.

[34] BGH GRUR 1985, 550, 552 – Dimple.
[35] See Rößler, GRUR 1994, 559, 562.
[36] Bundestagsdrucksache 2/6581, p. 72.
[37] Kur, GRUR 1994, 330, 333; Boes/Deutsch, GRUR 1996, 168, 169.
[38] Ministerial bill of German Trade Mark Act, Drucksache 12/6581, p. 72; Levin, GRUR Int. 1996, 454, 460.
[39] Kur, GRUR 1994, 330, 333.
[40] BGH GRUR 1985, 550, 552 – Dimple.

3. General survey/correlation

Although the notoriety and repute of a trade mark are two criteria to be assessed separately from each other, both must be present to a certain extent in order for a reputed trade mark to exist. A general survey will always be necessary where the qualitative and quantitative criteria are in a correlation. For instance, a very high degree of notoriety can indicate such a high repute for the mark in question that no strenuous requirements should be demanded in examining the qualitative features. However, the correlation between repute and notoriety should not be interpreted to mean that an extremly high notoriety can compensate a hardly established repute.[41] On the other hand, a mark with high repute usually has at least a small notoriety within the trade circles, although this notoriety is not necessary. It appears possible in this respect that a mark which has been on the market only a short time could have a high repute, but due to its short life-span, it has not yet achieved a significant notoriety. On the whole, the question of whether a "reputed" trade mark exists will probably depend on the criteria of repute, with the quantitative criteria of notoriety serving only as an indicator to estimate the extent of repute.[42]

4. Trade circles concerned

According to Article 8 (5) and Article 9 (1) (c) Community trade mark Regulation, the Community trade mark must have a reputation in the Community. The wording is identical in all five language versions. Nevertheless, it is somewhat ambiguous in so far as one cannot tell whether the Community trade mark has to have a reputation in every single Member State or whether the reputation in just one Member State is sufficient.

For some insight into the proper interpretation of this wording, reference may be made to the historical origin of the Community trade mark. The first proposal of 1980 required that a trade mark have a high reputation within the entire community, i.e., in every Member State. The deletion of the word "entire" leads to the conclusion that "notoriety" in every Member State is not required. A further clue as to whether a mark must have notoriety in only one or more states can be gleaned from Article 8 (5) Community trade mark Regulation itself. Because of the equalisation of the "reputed" community trade mark with the national mark, one can infer that the mark need only to be known in a single Member State.[43]

Notoriety, and respectively, repute does not have to be established within the whole public of the Member State, but only within the concerned trade circles.[44]

[41] Opposing opinion Ingerl, "Die Gemeinschaftsmarke", p. 85.

[42] Kur, GRUR 1994, 330, 333.

[43] Opposing opinion Pieper, GRUR 1996, 657, 660, who advocates that notoriety in one Member state is only sufficient for national marks. See Levin, GRUR Int. 1996, 454, 456.

[44] Pieper, GRUR 1996, 657, 660; Boes/Deutsch, GRUR 1996, 168, 169.

V. Further Requirements for the Protection of a Reputed Trade Mark

1. Registered trade mark

According to Article 6 Community trade mark Regulation, only registered Community trade marks can be asserted in infringement proceedings (Article 9 Community trade mark Regulation). In examining the relative grounds of refusal according to Article 8 (5) Community trade mark Regulation, a prior national mark with a reputation in one Member State can be asserted against the opposed sign. Due to the reference in Article 8 (5) to Article 8 (2) Community trade mark Regulation, "well known" marks without registration in any Member State (according to Article 6 *bis* PC) can be asserted as well.

2. Usage

A trade mark can only[45] have a reputation when it is being used.[46] The Community trade mark Regulation does not explain whether the use of a trade mark as an indicator of origin is necessary, or whether use of a mark in a non-trade mark sense (i.e. as a descriptive term), is also an offence.[47] According to the ninth preamble paragraph of the council regulation,[48] actual use of the trade mark is the only requirement. According to the seventh preamble paragraph, the origin function in particular is to be guaranteed. Therefore, it may be assumed that the regulation only protects against third party usage of a sign as a trade mark or as an indicator of origin.[49]

3. Acts impairing the rights of a reputed Community trade mark

According to the wording of the Community trade mark Regulation, the impairment of a reputed trade marks rights takes place when the use of that mark without due cause takes unfair advantage or is detrimental to the distinctive character or the repute of the Community trade mark. Because of the specific use of the word "or" in the regulation, we can conclude that there are four different types of offences or activities against which the Community trade mark Regulation provides protection. These are as follows:

a) Taking advantage of a marks repute

Advantage is taken of the special repute of the Community trade mark when an image transfer occurs.[50] The image or the goodwill of the mark has to be exploited as a result of a transfer of this image or goodwill to another partys goods or services.

[45] A trade mark according to Article 6 *bis* PC does not have to be used in a Member State.
[46] Levin, GRUR Int. 1996, 657, 660.
[47] Pieper, GRUR 1996, 657, 660.
[48] Office Journal 1/95, p. 56.
[49] Pieper, GRUR 1996, 657, 660.
[50] Pieper, GRUR 1996, 429, 434; Pagenberg, FG für Beier, p. 317; Pieper, GRUR 1996, 657, 660.

b) Uses detrimental to trade marks repute

Although when an infringer takes unfair advantage of the repute of a Community trade mark, the focus is on the infringer's sign, when an infringers use is detrimental to a Community trade marks repute, the focus is on the Community trade mark. The repute of a mark is detracted when its positive image is impaired due to the awakening of a negative association with a so called "incompatible secondary use".[51] Detriment to repute usually takes place when a negative image[52] has been transferred from the goods or services with which the attacked sign is associated. This depends on the way in which the attacked sign is actually used. Given the different wording in Article 9 (1) (c) and Article 8 (5) with respect to the word "would", it is questionable whether just the "danger" of a detriment to a marks repute is sufficient[53] to create an offence. Whether or not a sign is detrimental to the repute of a trade mark is a theoretical conclusion, because the decision does not depend on an actual impairment realised by the trade circles. Therefore, the simple "danger" of a detriment to a marks repute, will not likely be sufficient to create an offence.

c) Uses detrimental to a marks distinctive character

By possessing a distinctive character, a sign possesses the ability to distinguish goods and services of one undertaking from those of another undertaking. A distinctive character is impaired when the third party users sign is very similar to the prior marks and the ability to distinguish the origin of the goods and services of the prior mark is impaired or diluted.[54]

d) Uses taking advantage of the marks distinctive character

It is questionable whether this offence has a scope of its own. Normally, the act of taking advantage of a marks distinctive character will be joined in an action based on a detriment to repute.[55] In most other cases, the detriment of the distinctive character will also be present where a party takes unfair advantage of the distinctive character of another mark. As far as this offence has a scope of its own, one will have to take into account the additional requirement that the use of the sign is "without due cause".

[51] Sack, GRUR 1995, 81, 84; Pieper, GRUR 1996, 429, 435.
[52] Pieper, GRUR 1996, 429, 435.
[53] Pieper, GRUR 1996, 429, 435.
[54] See Meister, WRP 1995, 366, 371, who is of the opinion that of "distinctive character" must be defined here other Meister than within the absolute ground of refusal. According to his opinion, negative consumer feedback is mainly responsible for diluting the distinctive character of a mark. Such negative feedback occurs when the consumer has had a bad experience with the transferred goodwill and transfers this back to the original product.
[55] See Pieper, GRUR 1996, 429, 434.

4. Notification of unfairness
A necessary element in finding an act detrimental to the distinctive character or repute of a Community trade mark, or of finding that advantage has been taken of the distinctive character or the repute of a mark is that these acts must be unfair. In order to determine unfairness, there must be a weighing of the interests involved and an evaluation of the specific facts and circumstances of the case. Whether this evaluation must include grounds of justification[56] (possible defences) is doubtful. The wording of the regulation states that questions concerning "unfairness", and possible grounds of justification must be considered separately. However, the fact that one element will influence the other has to be assumed. An infringement can hardly be called unfair if there is a legitimate ground of justification.

5. Grounds of justification
The impairment of rights has to be without a justified ground. Whether the European Court of Justice will regard consent as grounds for justification, or as a regulatory component is yet to be determined. There are no specific grounds of justification in the Community trade mark Regulation.

6. No similarity of goods or services
As a negatively formulated regulatory component, the protection of a "reputed trade mark" requires that the goods or services for which the trade mark is registered are not similar to those for which the attacked sign is used. This precondition must be set forth and proved by the owner of the reputed mark. If the goods and services are similar, the reputed trade mark falls under the protection of Article 9 (1) (b) Community trade mark Regulation.[57] In particular, there is no extension of the scope of Article 9 (1) (c) Community trade mark Regulation to the area of similarity of goods and services due to the word "association" in Article 8 (1) (b), because this is a dependant fact that only serves to determine likelihood of confusion.[58]

VI. Supplementary Legislation

According to Article 14 (2) Community trade mark Regulation, there is additional protection for the "reputed trade mark" in the national laws against exploitation of trade marks especially as found within the national unfair competition laws. The scope of Article 9 (1) (c) Community trade mark Regulation, does not exclude the implementation of national laws.

[56] Pieper, GRUR 1996, 657, 661; Levin, GRUR Int. 1996, 454, 460.
[57] Pieper, GRUR 1996, 657, 661.
[58] Pieper, GRUR 1996, 657, 662.

VII. Conclusion

The new European Trade Mark Law provides additional protection for reputed trade marks apart from the traditional scope of protection based on "likelihood of confusion". The interpretation of (Article 8 (5) and Article 9 (1) (c) Community trade mark Regulation) will depend upon the decisions and rulings of the European Court of Justice. This courts decisions will inturn influence national rulings, because all the national Trade Mark Acts refer back to the European Council Directive 89/104/EEC to approximate the laws of the Member States relating to trade marks. At the present time, without any European Court of Justice rulings on the regulation, the national courts depend on the wording of the Community trade mark Regulation and their own former adjudication. Different interpretations in Europe due to the different linguistic variations of the "reputed trade mark" definition have lead to different interpretation in the Member states. There is a tendency, however, to unify these linguistic variations. In particular the Implementing Order to the Regulation uses the new linguistic term, "reputation" also in its Spanish and German versions. This is a clear indicator that the definition of the reputed Community trade mark will mainly deal with the reputation of the mark, i.e. the qualitative criterion. The quantitative criterion of notoriety will likely only serve as an indicator of a marks reputation but not as a precondition with a fixed minimum degree of notoriety within the trade circles concerned.

International Exhaustion: The European Dimension

1. Introduction

Both Article 13 (1) of the Community trade mark Regulation and Article 7 (1) of the European Harmonization Directive have used the uniform wording for fixing the principle of exhaustion of trade mark rights, and so it is also laid down in Article 24 (1) of the New German Trade Mark Act. It is equally provided that a trade mark proprietor cannot prohibit use of his mark in relation to goods which have been put on the market in the Community under the trade mark by him or with his consent.[1] There is equally one exception to the basic rule where there exist "legitimate reasons" for the trade mark proprietor to oppose further putting the goods into commerce, e.g. if their condition has been changed or if they have been impaired after their first commercialization.

Unless there are "legitimate reasons" it is clear from the wording that trade mark rights are indeed exhausted when the goods have been put anywhere on the Common Market.[2] How should one construe the provision when it comes to the question of exhaustion beyond the Common Market? Is the failure to not mention the situation beyond the Common Market an indication that there is no principle of worldwide exhaustion of trade mark rights rather than only a territorial exhaustion on the Common Market? Or is the answer left open for subsequent judgments or legislation without any intention to come to a final decision at this stage? Both conclusions have their merits because the wording is not self-explanatory.

[1] Article 13 (1) Council Regulation (EC) No. 40/94 of 20.12.1993 on the Community trade mark;

Article 7 (1) First Council Directive of 21.12.1988 to approximate the laws of the Member States relating to trade marks 89/104 (EC) referred to as "Harmonization Directive";

Article 24 (1) Gesetz über den Schutz von Marken und sonstigen Kennzeichen (German Trade mark Act of 25.10.1994).

[2] Article 24 (1) German Trade mark Act extends the rule also to the European Economic Area. The extension is also true for the Council Regulation and the Directive. In our article, we simply refer to the "Common Market" to make things easier.

To give some guidance, it is our aim to spotlight the position in Germany first, have a glance at the harmonized European trade mark landscape and to finally focus on the Community trade mark asking whether there is a doctrine of international exhaustion of trade mark rights or only a territorial exhaustion on the Common Market.

2. German Trade mark Law: The "Levi Strauss" Case

In a judgment given on 14 December 1995 which is also known as the "Levi Strauss" case, the Federal High Court considered the question of international exhaustion of trade mark rights and concluded: "With the coming into force of the Trade mark Act the principle of international exhaustion of trade mark rights is no longer applicable." [3]

Before the Trade mark Act became effective on 1 January 1995 it was a well established rule under German case law for many years, in the absence of any written law, that the exclusive rights vested in the trade mark cease to exist in respect of those goods which the trade mark proprietor puts on the foreign market beyond the European Community. However, those actions were not regarded as justified which were to be seen as violating the essential functions of the trade mark to guaranty the trade mark as an indication of certain origin and, following from this, to guaranty a certain quality and identity of the goods designated by the trade mark. It was said that the trade mark right which was basically exhausted became revalidated when there is as action which does harm to the aforesaid essential functions of the trade mark, such as modifications and remanufacturing.[4]

In the "Levi Strauss" case, the defendant sold second-hand genuine "Levi Strauss" and "Levy's Jeans" which originated from the US and were bleached, coloured and some of them even cut to shorts. The defendant placed a notice in his retail store informing the customers that the offered jeans were used "Levy's" jeans from the US which had not been bleached by Levi Strauss. Levi Strauss complained against the commercial exploitation of its brand and claimed trade mark infringement, arguing that the aggressive chlorine substances negatively affected the quality of the original jeans.

It would have been easy for the Federal High Court to reject the defence that there was a case of international exhaustion of trade mark rights at all because the bleaching and cutting off of the jeans negatively affected their quality. The notice by defendant could not help him to avoid infringement. Therefore, even under the former doctrine and under the new law, due to the absence of "legiti-

[3] Federal High Court, 14.12.1995, GRUR Int. 1996, 726 – "Gefärbte Jeans"; the same view was also expressed by the Higher Regional Court of Munich, 12.10.1995, GRUR Int. 1996, 730 – "GT ALL TERRA" and the Regional Court Dusseldorf, 4.7.1995, GRUR Int. 1996, 732 – "Adidas-Import".

[4] Federal High Court, 22.1.1964, GRUR Int. 1964, 202 – "Maja"; Federal High Court, 2.2.1973, GRUR Int. 1973, 562 – "Cinzano"; Federal High Court, 19.1.1984, GRUR 1984, 545 – "Schamotte-Einsätze".

mate reasons" on the side of defendant, there was no justification for the defendant. Because of the quality of the colours used by Levi Strauss, the Court clearly stated that each bleaching and colouring could no longer safeguard that the jeans remain of the high quality derived from the original colouring process. No guaranty of the original quality means no exhaustion of trade mark rights.

Nevertheless, the Federal High Court made a ultimate ruling on the new provision of Article 24 (1) German Trade mark Act relating to the exhaustion of trade mark rights. The reasons for its conclusion that the exhaustion doctrine is now restricted to a first putting of the goods on the market in any of the Member States of the European Union are interesting enough:

- The Federal High Court stated that the German legislative body clearly transformed the provision of Article 7 (1) Harmonization Directive according to which the doctrine of international exhaustion valid until then was abolished in favour of a restricted exhaustion of trade mark rights in the European Economic Area only. This is indeed in accordance with the clear wording of the Official Grounds for Article 24 (1) Trade mark Act.[5]
- The so restricted exhaustion principle was also subject of Article 13 CTMR.
- The territorial exhaustion doctrine did neither violate European nor German constitutional law because the European Union has the means to negotiate and conclude mutual agreements with all countries and so to establish the principle of exhaustion *vis-à-vis* those countries. This was already discussed within the European Parliament proceedings.[6]
- The Court was fully aware of the protectionalism effect of its decision as the free movement of goods was no longer possible beyond the Common Market thus forming a certain trade barrier. However, the Court argued that the principle of international free trade clearly is a political matter, and it was bound by the wording of the new law.

In summary, the Federal High Court came to the conclusion that the provision of Article 24 (1) German Trade mark Act is definite in the sense that the new law repeals the former doctrine of international exhaustion in favour of a restricted European exhaustion. This view is accepted by most learned authors.[7] Critics, however, argue that the new section provides only for a minimum standard of "European" exhaustion, whereas it is open for jurisdiction whether to

[5] Amtliche Begründung, BT-Drs. 12/6581, in: Deutsches Markenrecht. Texte und Materialien, ed. von Mühlendahl, 1995, pp. 107 ss., p. 166 s.

[6] Cf. O.J. C 307/44, 63 of 14.11.1983.

[7] E.g., Nordemann, Funktionsverschiebungen im Markenrecht: Das Ende der Erschöpfungsdoktrin in Deutschland, Großbritannien und den USA?, DZWir 1995, pp. 315 ss.; Dreiss/Klaka, Das Neue Markengesetz, 1995, p. 41; Gaul/Bartenbach, Handbuch des Gewerblichen Rechtsschutzes, 5. ed. 1994, Band II, note R 476 s.; Pickrahn, Die Bekämpfung von Paralellimporten nach dem neuen Markengesetz, GRUR 1996, pp. 383 ss., p. 384; Klaka, Erschöpfung und Verwirkung im Licht des Markenrechtsreformgesetzes, GRUR 1994, pp. 321 ss., p. 324; Harte-Bavendamm/Scheller, Die Auswirkungen der Markenrechtsrichtlinie auf die Lehre von der internationalen Erschöpfung, WRP 1994, pp. 571 ss.

adhere to the doctrine of international exhaustion or not.[8] In particular it has been put forward that the interpretation of the Federal High Court overaccentuates the rights of trade mark owners and without cause repeals a doctrine which had worked well for many years.

In our view, the conclusion of the Federal High Court in the "Levi Strauss" case is reasonable. It is true, that the wording of Article 24 (1) German Trade mark Act is far from being clear[9] and definite. However, the provision cannot be understood out of its context. The section was made part of Chapter 4. of Part II. of the Act which deals with trade marks (apart from the registration formalities). Chapter 4. regulates the limitations of protection. The foregoing chapter 3. establishes the rights conferred and deals with cases of infringement. The basic rule is that the acquisition of trade mark protection confers on the proprietor exclusive rights therein (Article 14 (1) German Trade mark Act). This means that third parties are prohibited from using the identical mark for identical goods in the course of trade without the consent of the proprietor (Article 14 (2) German Trade mark Act). Article 24 (1) German Trade mark Act is one exception to this rule where the proprietor exposed his goods to the Common Market, and beyond this area the general rule of Article 14 German Trade mark Act is applicable: "exceptio firmat regulam (in casibus non exceptis)". Since the question of exhaustion was part of Parliamentary discussions it would have been necessary to have very strong indications within the Act that, despite the basic principle of Article 14 German Trade mark Act, the doctrine of international exhaustion should still prevail or at least the case be a not regulated matter. One cannot expect Parliament to solve all possible problems arising in the future, but one can expect Parliament to come to a final conclusion where the basic question was considered. This is the case here.

A very strong argument for the Federal High Court in the "Levi Strauss" case is also the reference to the Official Grounds for the new Act. The legislative body indeed wished to transform Article 7 (1) Harmonization Directive into national law and, therefore, only accepted the restricted "European" exhaustion approach as an act of transforming the Directive. However, was the German Parliament right when it felt it was bound by Article 7 (1) of the Harmonization Directive?

[8] E.g. Albert/Heath, Comment on the "Levi Strauss" case, GRUR 1996, 275; Loewenheim, Comment on the "Levi Strauss" case, LM Article 24 MarkenG Nr. 1; von Gamm, Zur Warenzeichenrechtsreform, WRP 1993, pp. 793 ss., p. 795.

[9] There is a clear linguistic mistake: Article 24 (1) Trade mark Act reads "The proprietor of a trade mark ... shall not be entitled to prohibit a third party from using the trade mark ... in relation to goods which have been put on the market by *him* or with *his* consent ...", and, construed verbally, the words "him or with his consent" refer to the third party and not to the proprietor as it was meant – "error in syllaba non nocet". Article 7 (1) Harmonization Directive, on the contrary, is precise on this.

3. European Harmonization Directive

Article 7 (1) of the Harmonization Directive reads:

> *"The trade mark shall not entitle the proprietor to prohibit its use in relation to goods which have been put on the market in the Community under the trade mark by the proprietor or with his consent."*

To fully understand the impact of this wording on the question whether or not the doctrine of territorial exhaustion has to be implemented into the national trade mark laws of the European Union Member States, it seems necessary to discuss the proceedings for adopting the Harmonization Directive.

During the proceedings to adopt the Directive one notes that the Proposal of the Commission submitted to the Council on 25 November 1980 provides in its Article 6 (1) that the trade mark shall not give exclusive rights to the proprietor to prohibit use of the mark in relation to goods which have been put into commerce by him or with his consent. This wording fully accepted the doctrine of international exhaustion. In this sense it is also made clear in the 8th recital of the Proposal that it makes no difference whether the goods have been put on the Common Market or beyond it to allow the exhaustion of trade mark rights, and this is based on the function of the trade mark to guaranty it as an indication of origin.[10] However, the proposed Article 6 (2) (a) established an exception to the above rule of Article 6 (1) where there are legitimate reasons on the side of the proprietor to oppose the commercialization of goods which have been put on the market outside the Common Market. This exception stands next to two further exceptions namely: where the conditions of the goods is changed or impaired (Article 6 (2) (b)) or where a third party fixed a new packaging to the goods (Article 6 (2) (c)). This means that more cases except the modification of the goods and new packaging where thought conceivable to limit importation of goods to the Common Market which were originally introduced into the market beyond. In this sense, this is a limited exception to the doctrine of international exhaustion provided for in Article 6 (1).

The Proposal was considered by the Economic and Social Committee which resulted in the Statement of the Committee of 23/24 September 1981. The Committee recommended introducing a further example of a "legitimate reason" to object to the importation of goods in cases where the third country beyond the Common Market in turn refuses imports from the Common Market in its territory.[11] This means a restriction of the doctrine of international exhaustion *vis-à-vis* those countries in which the proprietor basically retains his exclusive rights to prohibit importation of the goods although they have been put on the foreign market intentionally.

[10] OJ No. C 351/1 of 31.12.1980.

[11] OJ No. C 310/22, 24, sub. II. 6. b), of 30.11.1981.

The Resolution of the European Parliament of 12 October 1983 led to the wording which became final in its Article 6 (1). Further the former Article 6 (2) (a) of the Committee's Proposal was completely crossed out.[12] The Parliamentary Resolution pointed out that the harmonization of national trade mark law of the Member States was absolutely necessary as there may be cases of deception of the consumers as to the origin of goods stemming from conflicts at the frontier of the European Union.[13] The Modified Proposal of the Harmonization Directive of the Commission presented to the Council on 17 December 1985 establishes in its Article 6 (1) the wording of the final Article 7 (1) of the Harmonization Directive. It is said that the Commission follows the Economic and Social Committee as well as the Parliament to waive the introduction of the principle of international exhaustion. The modified 8th recital now provided that it followed from the principle of free circulation of goods that the proprietor of the mark must not oppose those goods which have been put on the market under his direction whereas the original text also referred to a putting into commerce beyond the Common Market.[14]

The history of the proceedings shows that the question of whether to introduce the doctrine of international exhaustion or a restricted version *vis-à-vis* certain countries or a territorial "European" exhaustion is something like a leitmotif. When Article 7 (1) of the Directive now says that there is a limitation of rights where the goods were marketed in the European Union it is indeed difficult to say that the Directive is not particularly definite on the international exhaustion question and only concentrates on the situation within the European Union.

Article 7 (1) of the Harmonization Directive would have not even have been necessary because the principle of exhaustion of trade mark rights within the European Union is a well established feature of the jurisdiction of the European Court of Justice (ECJ) under Article 36 of the EC Treaty. As early as in the "Centrafarm/Wintrop" case the ECJ concluded that it would be an obstacle to the concept of free movement of goods in the sense of Article 36 of the EC Treaty if the trade mark proprietor were allowed to object to the importation of those goods which were commercialized within the Common Market under his direction.[15] Therefore, there would be no room for any meaningful provision to be implemented into national law because the well-established jurisdiction of the ECJ is already effective in all Member States without any need to have it entered into the wording of national trade mark legislation.

The basic principle within the Directive is that the proprietor has the right to oppose the trade with goods to which his trade mark is affixed (Article 5

[12] OJ No. C 307/60 of 14.11.1983.

[13] *Loc. cit.*, 67, sub 2. – 4.

[14] EC Commission, KOM (85) 793 endg., 17.12.1985, V, 5.

[15] ECJ, 31.10.1974, GRUR Int. 1974, 456 – "Centrafarm/Wintrop"; ECJ, 17.10.1990, GRUR Int. 1990, 960 – "HAG II"; ECJ, 11.7.1996, GRUR Int. 1996, 1144, 1147 – "Bristol-Myers Squibb".

Directive). As the principle of international exhaustion was indeed subject of the proceedings to adopt the Directive it is therefore obvious to say that the Harmonization Directive does not provide for a doctrine of international exhaustion and rather restricts the principle of exhaustion to the Common Market.

Although this aims at the situation beyond the Common Market, one still would come to the conclusion that the EC Treaty provides for the power to make a final statement as to whether the Member States are free to have a doctrine of international exhaustion or not. Although one can question whether Article 110 of the EC Treaty is fully applicable, it would be difficult to argue that there are not at least the necessary implied powers to also regulate the situation beyond the European Union. There are two aspects: firstly, trade mark proprietors within the European Union would be put at a disadvantage as against those outside the European Union where the national law does not adhere to the principle of international exhaustion. Secondly, trade mark proprietors in certain Member States would be put at a disadvantage with regard to those trade mark proprietors in other Member States where there is no adherence to the principle of international exhaustion, if the former Member States provide so. Therefore, there are sufficient reasons to accept the necessary implied powers to finally decide whether there should be a concept of international or territorial exhaustion.

This view is confirmed by the European Commission in the answer of the responsible Commissioner to a Member of the European Parliament on 26 April 1994 concerning international exhaustion of rights. The question had arisen in conjunction with Council Directive 92/100/EC on Rental and Lending Rights and its Article 9 (2). The Commissioner stated that the wording of this provision allowed the owner of the right to object against parallel import from third countries because national legislation is bound not to adopt the principle of international exhaustion. The answer concludes with the note that this provision is in accordance with other Directives on intellectual property law and names the Harmonization Directive.[16]

Therefore, we come to the conclusion that it is reasonable to construe Article 7 (1) of the Directive in the sense that there is no doctrine of international exhaustion and rather the confirmation of a territorial exhaustion.[17] Since it is binding to adopt Article 7 (1) in the Member States we consider that the German Federal High Court[18] was correct in saying that Article 24 (1) of the German

[16] Answer of Mr. Vanny d'Archirafi of 26.4.1994 (E-3482/93 E-3483/93 and E-3484/93), GRUR Int. 1995, 205.

[17] This view also takes, e.g., Cohen Jehoram, International Exhaustion versus Importation Right: a Murky Area of Intellectual Property Law, GRUR Int. 1996, pp. 280 ss., p. 283; for a different view see, e.g., Loewenheim, Nationale und internationale Erschöpfung von Schutzrechten im Wandel der Zeiten, GRUR Int. 1996, pp. 307 ss., p. 314.

[18] The Austrian High Court came to the contrary view, 8.11.1994, GRUR Int. 1995, 810, 811 – Vorabstreiferblätter.

Trade mark Act does not provide for the principle of international exhaustion and rather restricts the exhaustion of trade mark rights to those goods which were put on the Common Market by the proprietor intentionally. Is the same also true for the Community trade mark?

4. The Position under Community Trade Mark Law

Article 13 (1) of the Community trade mark Regulation is in line with Article 7 (1) of the Harmonization Directive and reads:

"A Community trade mark shall not entitle the proprietor to prohibit its use in relation to goods which have been put on the market in the Community under that trade mark by the proprietor with his consent."

The history of Article 13 (1) of the Community trade mark Regulation is also in line with the history of Article 7 (1) of the Directive as outlined above and even more definite so as to underpin that there is no principle of exhaustion laid down in the Community trade mark Regulation.

The Proposal of the Commission presented to the Council on 25 November 1980 implemented the basic doctrine of international exhaustion in accordance with the Proposal concerning the Harmonization Directive of even date in its Article 11 (1). In its 8th recital this is confirmed, referring to the function of the Community trade mark to guaranty it as an indication of origin.[19] In the grounds for the Proposal it is said that, otherwise, the Community trade mark had a protecionalism effect and would lead to a trade barrier on the world market so that it seems necessary to implement the doctrine of international exhaustion.[20] The Economic and Social Committee had the same comments on this provision as on the parallel provision of the proposal for the Directive.[21] And then it came to the wording of the final provision such as in the case of the Directive.

Therefore, the history of Article 13 (1) of the Community trade mark Regulation makes it obvious that the introduction of the principle of international exhaustion was discussed but that in the end its implementation was dropped. This means that the wording of said provision has to be construed in the sense that exhaustion can only apply where the goods have been put into commerce within the Common Market but not beyond. Therefore, this is a maximum and not a minimum rule.

It has also to be noted that the provision of Article 13 (1) regulation has to be construed in its context. The basic rights confirmed by a Community trade mark are contained in Article 9 of the Community trade mark Regulation and, henceforth, the limitations of the effects concerning possible exhaustion under

[19] OJ No. C 351/5 31.12.1980.

[20] The protectionalism effect is highlighted by Beier/von Mühlendahl, Der Grundsatz der internationalen Erschöpfung des Markenrechts in den Mitgliedstaaten der EG und ausgewählten Drittstaaten, Mitteilungen der deutschen Patentanwälte 1980, pp. 101 ss., p. 102.

[21] OJ No. C 310/22, sub III. 2., 30.11.1981.

Article 13 (1) have to recognize the basic rule. Where there is no explicit case of any limitation, the general rule reveals. As to the wording, and knowing the history of this provision, one can not but admit that Article 13 (1) says there is only an exhaustion of trade mark rights when the goods where put on the Common Market. Unlike the situation in Germany where there was a deviating doctrine before the harmonization of German trade mark law, we have a completely new situation as regards the Community law which has no predecessors and therefore has to be construed autonomously. An autonomous interpretation can only come to the conclusion "yes" or "no" as regards international exhaustion and would not allow any intermediate answer.

It is also not too difficult to establish the necessary powers of the European Commission to decide whether to have the principle of exhaustion beyond the Common Market. Article 235 of the EC Treaty requires that the necessary action of the Commission by adopting a Council Regulation has to respect the objectives of the Community within the framework of the Common Market. Such objectives are a system which protects from distortion or competition or from the hindrance of a common European policy. Indeed, it would make a difference to proprietors of Community trade marks whether there is a principle of international exhaustion or not because those proprietors are dependant on the legal consequences of putting the goods into commerce outside the Common Market. It would also weaken the political position of the European Union if they did not have the possibility to enter into negotiations concerning the principle of international exhaustion with other countries or organizations. Therefore, it seems reasonable to conclude from Article 235 EC Treaty that the Commission had the necessary powers to make a definite decision on the doctrine of international exhaustion.

In summary, we conclude that it seems reasonable to say that neither under the Harmonization Directive nor under the Community trade mark Regulation is there a concept of international exhaustion, but rather an exhaustion of trade mark rights only if the proprietor exposed his goods to the Common Market.[22] Of course, others may come to the conclusion that things are different, either concerning the Directive or the Council Regulation. This would have interesting consequences.

5. What happens if there is a lack of symmetry?

When asking whether there exists a doctrine of international or territorial exhaustion we have an interesting situation: The provisions of the most national European (harmonized) trade mark laws, the Community trade mark Regulation as well as the Harmonization Directive are verbally uniform. However, there may still be different consequences because the wording is not so clear as to allow only one interpretation. Our interpretation comes to the conclusion that

[22] View also taken by Cohen Jehoram, *op. cit.*, p. 283.

the provisions of German trade mark law, the Harmonization Directive and the Community trade mark Regulation require identical interpretation so that there is indeed no "conflict" and therefore a symmetry between all laws. However, the case could be different, and in the following we give an outline of the various possibilities:

a) *First scenario:* The Community trade mark is not subject to international exhaustion. The Harmonization Directive provides that national law has to implement it in the sense that there is no doctrine of international exhaustion.

In this case, there is absolutely no lack of symmetry. The proprietors of trade marks in the various Member States as well as the proprietors of Community trade marks face the same situation; namely that the rights are only exhausted if the goods have been put on the Common Market. Proprietors of both national trade marks and Community trade marks have the legal measures to stop importation of goods from outside the Common Market which were disposed of either by the proprietor or with his consent. This would be the case according to our interpretation.

b) *Second scenario:* Community trade mark law is construed in the sense that there definitely is a principle of international exhaustion. Unlike this, the Harmonization Directive is construed in the sense that there is no principle of international exhaustion to be implemented into national law.

The consequence would be that the proprietor of a Community trade mark has less rights than a proprietor of a national trade mark because the latter would have the possibility to object to importation of goods from outside the Common Market. This would counteract the intentions for the Community trade mark Regulation because it is expressed that it would be desirable to have an internal market which offers conditions which are similar to those obtaining in a national market (first recital), and now they are less positive for the Community trade mark owner than under each national law. National trade marks then would not only be replaced by the Community trade mark (cf. 5th recital) but national trade marks would, in this case, grant even better protection than a Community trade mark.

c) *Third scenario:* The Community trade mark is subject to international exhaustion. The interpretation of the Harmonization Directive leads to the conclusion that it only imposes a minimum standard.

This means, that under each national law the introduction of the principle of international exhaustion is the genuine task of each Member State. Given the freedom to choice, it is most likely that there are non-uniform provisions in the various countries. This means, that Member State A is free to restrict exhaustion to the Common Market, whereas Member State B adheres to the doctrine of international exhaustion.

The proprietor of a trade mark in Member State A would have more rights than a proprietor of a trade mark in Member State B. This might be regarded as justified if one argues that there is no absolute need for national trade mark law to produce equal effects even after harmonization. However, the proprietor of a trade mark in Member State A would be in a better position than a proprietor of a Community trade mark, and we have here the consequences as outlined above b).

d) *Fourth scenario:* No doctrine of international exhaustion under Community trade mark law. Freedom for each Member State to apply a wider exhaustion principle as the one restricted to the Common Market. Also in this case we would have to face the fact that Member State A has a limited exhaustion principle restricted to the Common Market, and Member State B introduces the doctrine of international exhaustion.

In this case, the Community trade mark would give more rights than the national trade mark in Member State B. The Community trade mark would be more attractive. This, however, would fit into the system of Community trade marks and national trade mark law side by side. It would not undermine national law in Member State B and, therefore, not replace it (cf. 5th recital of the Council Regulation), but it would in fact induce a national undertaking to apply for Community trade mark protection if it considers it necessary to oppose against importation of goods from outside the Common Market.

It can be imagined that a trade mark proprietor in Member State A who wishes to take action against importation of goods from outside the Common Market faces the defence of a third party arguing that the goods in question were first imported into Member State B and, thus, brought on the Common Market in a justified manner. However, the clear wording of the trade mark law would be contrary to this defence. It is said that the doctrine of exhaustion only applies "in relation to goods which have been put on the market in the Community under that trade mark by the proprietor or with his consent". This means, that the proprietor and not any third party has to be the one who had put the goods on the market intentionally in the Community. Therefore, at least this defence would not lead to even more restrictions for the trade mark proprietor in Member State A. However, what remains is that he is in a worse position than the proprietor of a Community trade mark in relation to importation of goods.

e) The second and third scenarios would lead to consequences which are unfriendly towards the Community trade mark and, therefore, it has to be doubted whether this would be in accordance with the objectives of the Council Regulation. This would indeed underpin the reasoning that there is no principle of international exhaustion under Community trade mark Law if at least one Member State (such as the German Federal High Court has made clear) does not adhere to the doctrine of international exhaustion and restricts the exhaustion of trade mark rights to the commercialization of goods within the Common Market.

6. Conclusion

In our view, the better arguments indicate that uniformly under Community trade mark law and under the Harmonization Directive and henceforth under the national law of the Member States there is only a concept of territorial exhaustion of trade mark rights because exhaustion ends at the regional border of the Common Market. This allows political decisions *vis-à-vis* third countries or organizations concerning reciprocal regulations on the exhaustion of trade mark rights. The above scenario concerning eventual lacks of symmetry make it indeed desirable to look at the doctrine of international exhaustion not only in the context of either national or Community trade mark law but also to have regard to the consequences for the whole "European" system. More than other issues, the question of territorial or international exhaustion of trade mark rights is a matter where the objectives of European harmonization of trade mark laws and the implementation of the Community trade mark are at stake.

International Exhaustion: The Worldwide Dimension

1. Introduction

The following discourse refers to the principle of international exhaustion in trade mark law only and not to patents. The applicability and significance of this principle has to be determined for each intangible property right on its own pursuant to the legal provisions and purpose regulating such right.

The implementation of the European Council's First Directive No. 89/104/EEC to approximate the laws of the Member States relating to trade marks has started off the discussion whether Article 7 of the Directive actually aimed at a limitation of the principle of international exhaustion to the market of the European Union and of the European Economic Area or whether the Member States are still entitled to apply the principle of international exhaustion in the sense that the proprietor of a trade mark can not proceed against the import of original goods put on the market with his consent even in a third non-European country.

The recollection of the subsequent aspects might be useful to further a better understanding of the subject of this discussion.

2. The National Jurisprudence

In Germany the Supreme Court had ruled as early as in his judgement of 28 February 1902 in re "Kölnisch Wasser"[1] that a German trade mark serves only as a criterion of origin or distinctiveness which has the purpose to distinguish the goods of the trade mark owner from the goods of others and to prevent confusions with other goods, but that it is not destined to prevent illegal dispositions or the offering of the goods at a lower price than requested by the owner. The effect of a trade mark is exhausted after the goods have – either by the owner or by an authorized third party – in a lawful manner been marked with the trade mark and then placed on the market for the first time.

[1] RGZ 50, 229, 231/232.

Whereas the "Kölnisch Wasser" case had been a national matter (the defendant sold the original goods at a lower price than the retail price in Cologne fixed by the trade mark owner), the Supreme Court decided on 2 May 1902 in re "Mariani"[2] a case where the trade mark had been registered by the owner in France and in Germany and where the defendant offered in Germany the original wine produced and marked "Mariani" by the trade mark owner in Paris, which the defendant had bought from wholesalers in Paris. The exclusive licensee of the German trade mark right filed an action for forbearance to restrain defendant from selling "Mariani"-wine in Germany and argued that the French trade mark owner restrained his French wholesalers from exporting the wine and that defendant knew about this inhibition. The Court refused the complaint. The decision was based on the assumption that the trade mark right is not limited by the borders of the protecting state, but that there exists a unity and uniformity of the trade mark right if the same trade mark of the same person is protected in more than one country. Therefore, the Court also held that a buyer in another country of protection could rely on the fact, that the goods had lawfully been marked and put on the market in the trade mark owner's home country.

The Federal Supreme Court confirmed the result of this jurisdiction in his "Maja"-decision[3] of 22 January 1964. The plaintiff was the sole distributor and exclusive licensee of a Spanish soap-manufacturer who had registered the trade mark "Maja" among others in Spain and in Germany. The defendant purchased the original "Maja"-soap from Spanish wholesalers and imported it for resale in Germany. The Court rejected the suit and also the argument that the principle of territoriality has the effect that the trade mark right of the owner becomes only exhausted, if the goods are imported by the owner himself or by an authorized third party. The court accepted that the protection of a trade mark is limited to the territory of the granting state, but held at the same time that the principle of territoriality does not prevent a court from evaluating the question of illegality of a trade mark use within the domestic territory by balancing the mutual interests with due regard to actions of the owner abroad. The Court underlined that in Germany the main purpose of a trade mark is to designate the origin of goods from the enterprise of the trade mark owner, but not to protect the interest of the owner to regulate the distribution of the goods which he had placed on the market to different countries distinctly from one another. Otherwise, trade mark rights could be used to partition the market geographically along state borders and by this to fix prices and distribution channels, disregarding the prohibition of antitrust law or international or supra-national agreements on market organization.

In re "Cinzano",[4] decided by the Federal Supreme Court on 2 February 1973, the facts of the case were different: in "Maja" the Spanish owner of the German

[2] RGZ 51, 263, 276/268.
[3] BGH GRUR 1964, 372, 374/375.
[4] BGH GRUR 1973, 468, 470/471.

and Spanish trade mark had marked by himself the "Maja" soap in Spain, whereas in "Cinzano", it is the Spanish subsidiary and the French licensee of Francesco Cinzano & Cia. S.p.A., Turin, not the Italian mother company, which had branded the imported vermouth in their home countries with the mark "Cinzano". The German "Cinzano" trade marks had been registered by the German subsidiary with the approval of the Italian mother company. The defendant purchased Spanish and French "Cinzano" vermouth wines, which had been placed on the market in Spain by the subsidiary and in France by the licensee and imported the wines into Germany for sale. The German subsidiary filed suit to restrain defendant from offering the vermouth wines produced in Spain and in France under the mark "Cinzano" in Germany.

The Court rejected the action and held that plaintiff has to be treated under German trade mark law as if he had marked the Spanish and French "Cinzano" vermouth wines and had placed them himself on the Spanish and French market, because all companies derived the right to designate their products with the "Cinzano" trade mark from the Italian mother company. Therefore, the Court stated that the German subsidiary could not argue that the "Cinzano" designations by the Spanish and French companies had been illegal. Further, the Court expressed the view that the interest of a multinational concern to divide and isolate national markets can not make the further distribution of marked goods as unlawful, and that the purpose of the German trade mark is only to designate the origin of the goods. The Court defined in this context the real meaning of the "principle of exhaustion" as a metaphor of the rule that it is inconsistent with the limited purpose of the trade mark monopoly, to impede or even obstruct the further distribution of goods from the perspective of trade mark law, if the goods had been marked and placed on the market with the consent of the trade mark owner.

3. The European Court of Justice

In the European Union, the Court of Justice earlier, had the opportunity to decide on the relationship between the protection of intangible property rights by the Member States and the principle of free movement of goods and services as established by the EEC Treaty. In re "Grundig/Consten",[5] the Court of Justice held that Articles 36, 222 and 234 EEC Treaty do not protect the exercise of national industrial property rights from the reach of Community law and stated clearly that it is incompatible with the rules of competition of the Community, if the rights flowing from the trade mark law of the Member States are misused for purposes, which are in contradiction to the antitrust law of the EEC.

In "Centrafarm/Winthrop",[6] the Court of Justice applied the principle of exhaustion at EEC level and decided that it is inconsistent with the provisions of the EEC Treaty on the free movement of goods within the common market, if

[5] 1966 ECR 299.
[6] 1974 ECR 1183.

the owner of a trade mark obstructs the distribution of goods in a Member State in accordance with legal provisions of that state, if these goods have been placed on the market in another Member State under the same trade mark either by the owner himself or with his approval by a third party. The Court said it was irrelevant that there existed differences between the prices for sale in the country of export on the one hand and the country of import on the other and it rejected also the argument of the trade mark owner that he wanted to control the distribution of the branded pharmaceuticals to protect the general public from health hazards of defective products.

Further decisions developing the principle of exhaustion in the common market were, among others, the "HAG" judgements of the European Court of Justice. In "HAG I" the Court held in its decision of 3 July 1974 that it is a violation of the provisions on the free movement of goods in the Community, if the distribution of a product, which has in a lawful manner been marked with the trade mark in one Member State, is prohibited in another Member State with the argument that an identical registered trade mark existed in the other Member State. In re "HAG II",[7] the Court of Justice modified its earlier decision and held that the trade mark owner's consent is the decisive criterion for the exhaustion of a trade mark right provided that the essential conditions have been met, which have been made by the trade mark owner a pre-condition for the placement on the market. In the latter case, the trade mark owner can not block the import of goods, which with his consent, have been put on the market in another Member State. Also, it was confirmed by the Court of Justice in the "HAG II" decision that the main function of a trade mark is to guarantee the identity of origin of the branded product to the consumer and purchaser and to enable the discrimination of different products without doubt.

The Court of Justice and the Court of First Instance have apparently not applied the principle of international exhaustion in some cases. In re "EMI Records/CBS",[8] the Court of Justice stated that community law does not prohibit the owner of a trade mark in the Member States of the EEC to use the trade mark rights granted by the Member States to prevent a third party to import goods with an identical trade mark registered in a state outside of the EEC, if the exercise of the trade mark right of that Member State is not due to a cartel agreement or a concerted practice, which aims at the isolation or interior partition of the common market.

4. *National decisions concerning the First Council Directive to approximate the laws of the Member states relating to trade marks*

The First Council Directive No. 89/104/EEC to approximate the laws of the Member States relating to trade marks was implemented in Germany by the new Trade Mark Act of 25 October 1994, which replaced the earlier Trade Mark Act

[7] 1974 ECR 731.
[8] 1990 – 3 CMLR 571.

after its hundred anniversary. Section 24 of the new act refers to the exhaustion of trade mark rights and provides as follows:

"*1. The proprietor of a trade mark or of a trade designation shall not be entitled to prohibit a third party from using the trade mark or the trade designation in relation to goods which have been put on the market by him or with his consent in the Federal Republic of Germany, in one of the other Member States of the European Union or other contracting state of the convention concerning the European Economic Area under that trade mark or trade designation.*

2. Subsection 1. shall not apply where there exist legitimate reasons for the proprietor of the trade mark or of the trade designation to oppose the use of the trade mark or of the trade designation in connection with further commercialization of the goods, especially where the condition of the goods is changed or impaired after they have been put on the market."

A first decision relating to Section 24 was the judgement of the District Court Düsseldorf in re "adidas import"[9] of 4 July 1995. The case referred to the import of sport shoes labeled with the brand "adidas" by the US-American licensee of the applicant, the owner of the German trade mark "adidas". The applicant moved for an injunction arguing that the licensee under the licence agreement was only permitted to sell the shoes in the United States, Canada, the Bermudas and the Caribean. The District Court granted the injunction and held that the principle of international exhaustion is not any longer applicable since the entry into force of the new German Trade Mark Act and that an exhaustion of trade mark rights can only occur under the pre-conditions of Section 24 subparagraph 1 of the Trade Mark Act.

The Court of Appeals of Munich decided on 12 October 1995 in re "GT all Terra"[10] that the application for an injunction on the general importer for "GT all Terra" bicycles was justified although the respondent had purchased the imported goods from the United States, where they had been placed on the market by GT Inc., USA, the sole owner of the trade mark which was also registered in Germany. The Court of Appeals stated likewise that the principle of international exhaustion formally accepted by the jurisdiction of the Federal Supreme Court is no any longer applicable due to the provisions of the new Trade Mark Act. It stated that Section 24 subparagraph 1 of the Act is verbally nearly identical with Article 7 of the Council Directive No. 89/104/EEC and that under consideration of the history of Article 7, Section 24 subparagraph 1 of the Act can not be interpreted in the sense of international exhaustion.

[9] GRUR 1996, 66, 67/68.
[10] GRUR 1996, 137, 138/139.

The first decision of the Federal Supreme Court is the judgement in re "Dyed Jeans"[11] of 14 December 1995. The US-American plaintiff is the owner of several German "Levi's" and "Levi Strauß" trade marks. The defendants sold in their retail shops in Germany "Levi's 501", Jeans which they had bought in the United States and which had been – without the consent of the plaintiff – bleached, dyed and partially been shortened to shorts before they were exported to Germany. The jeans had not been modified with respect to the labels of the plaintiff affixed to the trousers and to the buttons and the rivets. The Court of Appeals of Stuttgart granted the action only to a limited extent, among others to the dying of "Levi's 501" jeans in shrill colours and rejected the suit with respect to new jeans, which the defendant had bought in the United States. As to the used and bleached jeans, the Court of Appeals stated that German trade mark law provides for the application of the principle of international exhaustion if the goods have also been placed on the market by the trade mark owner abroad. But that the owner keeps the right to prevent actions, which violate the function of origin and guarantee of the trade mark, if the purchaser interferes decisively in the character and condition of the product.

The Federal Supreme Court held that there was no need to base the decision in this case on Section 24 subparagraph 2 of the new Trade Mark Act, because the principle of international exhaustion is no longer applicable since the entry into force of the new Act. The Court took the view that the German legislator had drafted Section 24 subparagraph 1 of the Act in accordance with Article 7 of the Council Directive in the sense that the prior principle of international exhaustion in German trade mark law has been abandoned in favour of an exhaustion limited to the European common market. Further, the Court held that it is not within its competence to evaluate whether such reduced principle of exhaustion contravenes international trade. Rather, the limitation of the principle of international exhaustion would allow the European Union to terminate the non-uniform application of the principle of international exhaustion in such a way that it could enter with its important trading partners into agreements, which implement the principle of international exhaustion between the contracting partners.

5. The German Trade Mark Act

A look at the legislative history[12] of the new Trade Mark Act shows that the Federal Supreme Court was correct when it stated that the German legislator meant to conform with Article 7 of the Council Directive, when he intended to reduce the principle of international exhaustion to the market of the European Union and of the Contracting States of the Convention concerning the European Economic Area. The wording of Article 7 paragraph 1 does not reveal whether the German legislator was right or wrong in his interpretation of the scope of Article 7 of the Council Directive, which reads as follows:

[11] GRUR 1996, 271, 273/274.
[12] BT-Drucksache 12/6581 p. 81.

"Exhaustion of the rights conferred by a trade mark

1. *The trade mark shall not entitle the proprietor to prohibit its use in relation to goods which have been put on the market in the Community under that trade mark by the proprietor or with his consent.*

2. *Paragraph 1 shall not apply where there exist legitimate reasons for the proprietor to oppose further commercialization of the goods, especially where the condition of the goods is changed or impaired after they have been put on the market."*

The first draft of the Council Directive of 1979[13] did provide for the regulation of international exhaustion and did not include the addition "in the Community". According to reports,[14] the express recognition of the principle of international exhaustion has then been modified due to the demands of some Member States and of representatives of European industry. The present wording of Article 7 paragraph 1 was incorporated in the modified draft of the Council Directive of 17 December 1985. The comment to the draft only states that the Council has decided to do without the regulation of international exhaustion. There are no further explanations in the comment. Therefore, there are different from the proponents of an interpretation[15] of Article 7 paragraph 1 in the sense of an exhaustion restricted to the common market. Many writers in legal literature interpret Article 7 paragraph 1 as the regulation of a minimum standard, which does not preclude the Member States from providing in their trade mark laws for a further reaching principle of international exhaustion.[16]

6. Conclusion

There are several arguments which support the interpretation of Article 7 paragraph 1 in the sense of the formulation of a minimum standard and not of a restriction of the principle of international exhaustion applied earlier in Member States. The first being the wording of Article 7 paragraph 1, which does not exclude the application of the principle of international exhaustion by the Member States (the same is true for Germany with respect to the wording of Section 24 subparagraph 1 of the new trade mark law). A confirmation of the understanding that the Council Directive did not want to interfere with the trade mark regulations of the Member States in this respect may also be found in the actual implementation of the Directive in the Member States: whereas Spain did

[13] GRUR Int. 1980, 31, 32.

[14] Beier, GRUR Int. 1989, 604, 614 f.

[15] E.g. ,Klaka, GRUR 1994, 321, 325; Harte-Bavendamm/Scheller, WRP 1994, 571, 574/575.

[16] E.g., Beier, GRUR Int. 1989, 603, 614; Mailaender, Festschrift für Gaedertz, 1992, 369, 389; von Gamm, WRP 1993, 793, 795; Ingerl/Ronke, NJW 1994, 1247, 1253; Albert/Heath, GRUR 1996, 275, 276.

implement the Directive in the sense of national exhaustion only, Denmark and Austria have on the other side pursuant to the express declaration of their legislators left the application of the principle of international exhaustion to their jurisdictions.[17]

Furthermore, the enactment of the first Council Directive is based on Article 100 lit. a EEC Treaty, which grants to the European Community only the competence to adopt the measures for the approximation of the legal and administrative provisions of the Member States for the erection and functioning of a single market. This provision does not provide for the elimination of principles of the national trade mark laws with respect to their relationship with foreign countries outside the EEC provided there are no retroactive effects to the common market. Also, the European Court of Justice has in recent proceedings of preliminary ruling according to Article 177 EEC Treaty stated that Article 7 of the Council Directive regulates the exhaustion in a definitive sense with respect to goods which are placed on the market within the community and that it refers only to the harmonisation of the laws of the Member States in this field of application.[18]

The question of exhaustion relates to the interpretation of the criterion "placement of a labeled good on the market" and is therefore a question of the interpretation of national substantial trade mark law and not a problem of international private law. The enactment of the first Council Directive has not reduced the competence of the national legislators of the Member States and of their jurisdictions to regulate and to interpret this criterion[19] of substantial law.

Last but not least, it can not be in the spirit of the EEC Treaty to abolish the application of the principle of international exhaustion by Member States which aims at a worldwide free trade. The restriction to a principle of exhaustion only within the common market would be a serious paceback to the disadvantage of the European Union and of world economy.

[17] Cp. Alber/Heath, GRUR 1996, 276.

[18] European Court of Justice decision of 11.7.1996 in re "Eurim-Pharm" (WRP 1996, 867), "MPA Pharma" (WRP 1996, 874) and "Bristol-Myers Squibb" (WRP 1996, 880).

[19] Martinek/Semler/Habermeier, Handbuch des Vertriebsrechts, 1996, 929/930.

The Madrid System and the Community Trade Mark

INTRODUCTION

Enterprises interested in an effective protection of their trade marks in Europe, are now offered an unprecedented choice of registration systems. An enterprise can of course still simply apply for national registration of its mark in the countries of market potential. This may be an appropriate approach, if the enterprise is interested in protection in its own country or in a few countries only. If protection in several or even an important number of countries is sought, it will be cheaper and more efficient to use an international system.

The enterprise may apply for a Community trade mark, which covers all 15 States at present members of the European Union and has an important number of advantages in comparison to registering the mark in all or most of these countries nationally (respectively at the Benelux-Office as concerns Belgium, Luxembourg and the Netherlands).

It may also, based on a registration in the home country, apply for an international registration of the mark under the Madrid Agreement of 1891 and extend this registration, at its choice, to some or all of the member countries of this Agreement. Not all countries of the EU are members of the Madrid Agreement, which has 46 members. Most come from continental Europe, however countries such as China, Korea and Vietnam are also members. The member countries of the Agreement as of 1.1.1997 are listed at the end of this introduction. An enterprise interested in protection in some member countries of the EU, which are party to the Madrid Agreement, such as the Benelux countries, France, Germany, Italy and Spain, and in some other countries in eastern part of Europe, may therefore prefer to apply for an international registration covering its countries of interest. This has also certain advantages, which will be dealt with later. Additionally, the Protocol to the Madrid Agreement (the "Protocol"), concluded in 1989 in Madrid, introduces certain changes as compared with the Madrid Agreement (the "Agreement"). It was necessary to provide for these changes in order to accommodate certain countries which where not prepared to adhere to the Agreement in view of a number of features of that Agreement which did not fit with their national system of trade mark protection. The Protocol entered into force on 1 December 1995 and the Common Regulations under the Madrid Agreement concerning the international registration of marks and the Protocol relating to that Agreement (the "Common Regulations"), which were adopted on 18 January 1996, entered into force on 1 April 1996. The owner of an international registration can, since that date, designate under the Protocol member countries of the EU which are not party to the Madrid Agreement such as Denmark, Finland, Great Britain, Sweden, and also Norway (these 6 countries have ratified the Protocol before 31 December 1995 and therefore were party to the new system from the beginning on 1 April 1996; in the meantime Iceland has also ratified). It can also be expected that other countries, not being members of the Agreement, will in the future adhere to the Protocol thus considerably extending the number of countries which can be designated in an international application. This advantage of the Protocol will, however, only be fully of interest, when most, if not all of the present member countries of the Madrid Agreement have ratified the Protocol, thus allowing trade mark owners in the new Protocol countries to extend their international registrations to these countries and allowing trade mark owners from these member countries of the Madrid Agreement to also extend their international registrations to the new Protocol countries.

Another important event in the history of the Madrid system will be the ratification of the Protocol by the European Union (EU), expected to take place in 1998. As a result of the EU becoming a Contracting Party to the Protocol, the Community trade mark system will be linked to the Madrid system, and to make this possible, was another important reason for the conclusion of the Protocol. As a consequence it will be possible to base an international registration under the Protocol on a Community trade mark and also to extend an international registration, based on a national registration in one of the Contracting States, to the Community with an effect assimilated to an application for a Community trade mark. Thus one will be able to speak of four layers of protection available in Europe: the first being national registrations; the second being the Community trade mark; the third being the Madrid system under the Common Regulations and the fourth being the interface between the Community trade mark and the Madrid system.

This fourth layer of protection will allow a party to obtain under the Madrid system protection in a large number of countries with one single international registration and at the same time to profit from the advantages offered by the Community trade mark system. In view of the importance of these new possibilities they will be described below. First the Madrid system, as it functions under the Common Regulations, will be explained (sections 1-8). Thereafter the interface between the Community trade mark and the Madrid system, will be dealt with (section 9) and finally, the advantages and risks of the different choices will be described (section 10).

Member countries of the Madrid Agreement (A) and Contracting Parties to the Protocol (P) on 1 January 1997 (Total 52):

Albania (A), Algeria (A), Armenia (A), Austria (A), Azerbaijan (A), Belarus (A), Belgium (A), Bosnia and Herzegowina (A), Bulgaria (A), China (AP), Croatia (A), Cuba (AP), Czech Republic (AP), Democratic Peoples Republic of Korea (AP) Denmark (P), Egypt (A), Finland (P), France (A) ,Germany (AP), Hungary (A), Iceland (P) Italy (A), Kazakstan (A), Kyrgizstan (A), Latvia (A), Liberia (A), Liechtenstein (A), Luxembourg (A), Macedonia (A), Monaco (AP), Mongolia (A), Morocco (A), Netherlands (A), Norway (P), Poland (AP), Portugal (AP), Republic of Moldova (A), Romania (A), Russian Federation (A), San Marino (A), Slovakia (A), Slovenia, Spain (AP), Sudan (A), Sweden (P), Switzerland (A; from May 1, 97 also (P), Tajikistan (A), Ukraine (A), United Kingdom (P), Utzbekistan (A), Vietnam (A), Yugoslavia (A).

1. The Common Regulations

Both the Madrid Agreement and the Protocol are self-contained treaties. However, not only is the text of the Protocol to a large extent identical to that of the Agreement, they are both inter-linked. According to Article 1 of the Protocol, its contracting parties, even if they are not Contracting States of the Agreement, belong to the same union as the countries of the Agreement, and according to Article 10 they are members of the same assembly. Furthermore, the Common Regulations provide for one new system, allowing applications for international registrations using one single form under both treaties. The Common Regulations also provide for some changes under the Agreement, even in cases where only the Agreement applies. In view of that, the approach chosen below is not to first explain the Agreement and then to explain the differences of the Protocol. Instead, the new system as it functions under the Common Regulations is explained, referring to the differences between the application of the Agreement and the application of the Protocol in the context where such differences exist. In view of these differences it is of course important to know which rules, those of the Agreement or those of the Protocol, apply in a concrete case. This is explained in section 2.4.

The term "Article" refers in the following to the respective Articles in both the Agreement and in the Protocol. To the extent that an Article in either the Agreement or the Protocol is meant, this is expressly said. The term "Rule" refers to Rules of the Common Regulations.

2. International Registration

2.1. National basis

A prerequisite for the application for an international registration of a mark (trade mark or service mark) is a national basis. Under the Agreement (Article 1(2)) this must be a *registration* in the country of origin. Under Article 2 of the Protocol it can be an *application* in the Office of origin (this is the Office in the country of origin or in the Office in Alicante if the EU is the Contracting Party of origin). In order to use an identical terminology for both the Agreement and the Protocol in the following the term "Office of origin", which is the Office of the Contracting Party of origin, will be referred to irrespective of whether the Contracting Party of origin is a member country of the Agreement or a Contracting State of the Protocol or is party to both the Agreement and the Protocol, or whether the EU is the Contracting Party of origin (to the Protocol).

Under the Agreement the Office of origin is the Office of the country is where the applicant has a real and effective industrial or commercial establishment, failing which where he has a domicile, and failing which the country of which he is a national. Under the Protocol no such cascade of requirements exists. The Office of origin can be the Office of any Contracting Party of which the applicant is a national or where he is domiciled or where he has a real and effective industrial and commercial establishment (an "establishment"). For the Community evidently these requirements are fulfilled if the applicant fulfils them in any of the Member States. If one of these requirements is fulfilled in several Contracting Parties to the Protocol, where the applicant has registered his mark or applied for registration, he has a choice which of those to use as basis for his international application. Under the Agreement such choice is only given to the extent that the applicant has several establishments (e.g. the headquarters in one Contracting Party and a sales office in another). An affiliate company is not considered to be an establishment of the parent.

2.2. International application (Rule 9)

The application for international registration is effected by filing a prescribed form at the Office of origin, where the national or Community trade mark application was filed.

In the official international application form the mark, for which international registration is sought, must appear. The applicant may declare that the mark be considered as a mark in standard characters. In all other cases it is considered that the mark should be registered and protected as appearing in the international application form. Where colours are claimed, the mark must appear in the official form in the colours claimed, since the International Bureau registers and publishes the mark in colours. Three-dimensional marks must appear in a two-dimensional representation. Several views of the three-dimensional mark may be shown.

Furthermore the goods and services, in respect of which protection of the mark is claimed, must be indicated. They should be grouped in the appropriate classes of the International Classification of goods and services, each group being preceded by the number of the class, and presented in the order of the classes of the Nice classification. This list may be more restricted than the list in the basic registration or application. It may not however be broader or contain different goods or services.

The applicant may claim priority under Article 4 of the Paris Convention and this priority may also be claimed from the basic application or from the application from which the basic registration results. Condition for a valid claim is that the date of the application filed with the Office of origin is not earlier than six months before the date which the international registration will bear (see section 2.9).

Under the Agreement the application must be made in French. Under the Protocol the language is either English or French, depending on what is prescribed by the Office of origin. The Office can, however, also leave the choice to the applicant (Rule 6 1). The International Bureau will translate all data contained in the application which is governed by the Protocol or both by the Agreement and the Protocol, except the mark, for the purpose of recordal in the international register and publication in the international Gazette (Rule 6 4).

The applicant may furnish a translation of any of the text into English if the international application is in French, or into French if the international application is in English. This may be of particular interest for the applicant with respect to the list of goods and services.

The Office of origin checks and certifies that the particulars appearing in the international application correspond to the particulars appearing in the basic registration or (under the Protocol) in the basic application, mentions their date and number and also the date of the international application, signs and forwards the international application form to the International Bureau in Geneva (Article 3(1)).

2.3. Geographical extensions (Article 3 *bis* and 3 *ter*).

The effect of the international registration extends to those Contracting Parties which the applicant expressly requests. Of course, extensions can be requested only to those parties which are Contracting Parties to the same treaty as the Contracting Party in which the Office of origin is located. In other words, if the Office of origin is in a country which is (still) only party to the Agreement, the international application cannot be extended to exclusive Contracting Parties to the Protocol. Also, if the Office of origin is in a Contracting Party to the Protocol alone, the international application cannot be extended to countries being members of the Agreement only. It is expected, however, that most if not all of the present member countries of the Agreement, which have not yet ratified the Protocol, will soon do so and become Contracting Parties to the Protocol.

2.4. Which provisions apply?

Repeatedly different provisions have been referred to, depending on whether the Agreement or the Protocol applies. It is now time to explain, under which circumstances which rules apply.

For applicants with a national basic registration in a Contracting Party to the Agreement, which has not (yet) adhered to the Protocol, obviously only the provisions of the Agreement apply. Equally obviously the Protocol alone applies, if the application is based on a national or Community Trade Mark application or registration in a party to the Protocol, which is not at the same time party to the Agreement, such as Denmark, Finland, Great Britain, Norway, Iceland or Sweden (and of course the EU; it even cannot become a Contracting Party to the Agreement, which is concluded between States).

For applicants from Contracting States to the Agreement which have already become Contracting Parties to the Protocol, such as China, Germany or Spain, it depends on Article 9 *sexies* of the Protocol which provisions apply. According to this so-called "Safeguard Clause" the Protocol is not applied between Contracting States of the Agreement in their dealings with each other. If the owner of a basic registration from a Contracting Party of origin which is party to both the Agreement and the Protocol applies for an international registration effective for countries which are also parties to the Agreement, only the provisions of the Agreement apply. This means in essence that the applicant himself can decide which provisions he wishes in the concrete case to be applied. If he designates in his international application only Contracting Parties which are (only or also) Contracting Parties to the Agreement, the provisions of the Agreement (as modified by the Common Regulations) apply exclusively. If he designates only Contracting Parties to the Protocol, the provisions of the Protocol apply exclusively. If he designates Contracting Parties to the Agreement and at the same time Contracting Parties, which are only party to the Protocol, both sets of provisions apply. The provisions of the Protocol apply to the latter extensions, the provisions of the Agreement to the former. As a consequence, a number of choices, given by the Protocol, cannot be used in such cases. For example, the international application must be based on a registration in the Office of origin. If the applicant nevertheless bases his international application on a (national or Benelux or Community trade mark) application, the Office of origin will cancel all extensions to Contracting Parties to the Agreement, unless the applicant expressly requests to keep these extensions (and in that case the international application is dealt with as being premature; see below 2.7).

In conclusion the international application is exclusively governed by the Protocol if the Office of origin is the Office of a Contracting Party which is exclusively party to the Protocol, or if the applicant designates only Contracting Parties which are exclusively party to the Protocol. The international application is exclusively governed by the Agreement, if the Office of origin is the Office of a State only member of the Agreement or if the applicant designates only Contracting Parties which at least also are Contracting Parties to the Agreement (whether or not they are also party to the Protocol; Article 9 *sexies*). Both sets of rules will apply only, if the Office of origin is the Office of a Contracting Party to both the Agreement and the Protocol and if the applicant designates Contracting Parties exclusively party to the Protocol and also Contracting Parties which are only party to the Agreement or party to both the Agreement and the Protocol.

2.5. Fees (Article 8 and Rule 10)

The fees are payable for 10 years and the amount depends on which Contracting Parties have been designated and on the number of classes of goods and services covered by the application.

For each application a basic fee (653 Swiss Francs for an application in black and white; 903 Swiss Francs where the reproduction of the mark is in colour) must be paid which is to cover the expenses of the International Bureau. A supplementary fee of Swiss Francs 73 must be paid for each class of goods and services beyond three classes. A complementary fee of Swiss Francs 73 must be paid for the designation of each Contracting Party for which no individual fee is payable. Under the Protocol, Contracting Parties can opt for an individual fee, which may not be higher than the fee which would have to be paid for an application at the Office of the Contracting Party. According to Article 8(7) of the Protocol the Contracting Party, which opts for an individual fee, must diminish the corresponding amount of the national fee by the savings of the international procedure; however, practice shows that the amounts fixed are the same or not much less than the corresponding national fee. This fee is due, however, only for designations governed by the Protocol. It also covers the amount to be paid for the goods and services covered by the application. If the application is governed exclusively by the Protocol, no supplementary fee is therefore due. The calculation of the amount of fees can be a source of errors which may delay the international application. The most convenient way of payment is therefore to maintain a current account with WIPO and just to ask the International Bureau to debit the amount to be paid from this account.

2.6. Representation (Rule 3)

A distinction must be made between representation before the Office of origin (to which the international application form must be submitted) and representation before the International Bureau. If the applicant wants to be represented before the Office of origin, he has to follow the rules of that Office.

The applicant is not obliged to have a representative before the International Bureau. However, he may appoint a representative to act on his behalf, who may or may not be the same representative which he may use before the Office of origin. Unless the Common Regulations provide otherwise, a duly recorded representative may always sign in place of the applicant or holder. Any communication sent by him to the International Bureau shall have the same effect as if it had been sent by the applicant or holder. In principle the International Bureau will address to the representative any communication which, in the absence of a representative, would have been sent to the applicant or holder. Whenever in this text the applicant or holder is referred to, this should therefore be understood as a reference to the applicant or holder or the representative (if any).

The address of the representative must be in the territory of a Contracting Party which is (exclusively or also) bound by the treaty governing the application. If the application is governed by both the Agreement and the Protocol, the address of the representative can be in any Contracting Party.

The representative can be appointed in the application form or in a separate power of attorney, which can also be a general power of attorney. The International Bureau records the name and address of the representative in the International Register.

2.7. Premature request for international application (Rule 11 1)
A request for an international application is premature if it is filed on the basis of an application for a mark in the Office of origin where a basic registration is needed. This problem cannot arise if the international application is governed exclusively by the Protocol. Under the Agreement it has been a frequent practice to address an application for international registration to the Office of origin together with the application for the basic registration and to request that the Office presents the international application to the International Bureau once the basic mark is registered. In that case the Office will put the premature international application aside until it has registered the basic mark. The request is then deemed to have been received on the date on which the basic mark was actually recorded in the register of the Office of origin (which in fact is the earliest date possible). This established practice is now expressly recognised in Rule 11 1 (a) for applications exclusively governed by the Agreement. However, if the international application is governed by both the Agreement and the Protocol, the application is premature only as far as concerns the designations of Contracting Parties to the Agreement. As concerns designations of Contracting Parties which are exclusively party to the Protocol, the Office of origin can process them at once and give them a filing date. Rule 11 1 (b) therefore provides that the Office of origin in such case deletes all designations to Contracting Parties bound by the Agreement. If an applicant has designated a large number of States party to the Agreement and perhaps one or two Contracting Parties bound by the Protocol he may loose most of his designations. As a consequence he will have to make subsequent designations (see below 4) for these States, which will not enjoy the same registration date as the international registration.

If, in such a situation, the applicant wishes to avoid loosing the designations of Contracting Parties to the Agreement, he must explicitly request that the international application be treated as governed by both the Agreement and the Protocol once the basic mark is registered in the Office of origin. In that case Rule 11 1 (c) provides that the Office of origin will not delete the designation of any Contracting Party but will put aside the international application until it has registered the basic mark. The request for international application is then deemed to have been received by the Office of origin on the date on which the basic mark was actually recorded in the register of the Office of origin. The disadvantage of that solution is that for all designations of Contracting Parties bound exclusively by the Protocol the date of the international registration will not be, as it might have been, the date on which the Office of origin received the international application, but the date on which the basic mark is effectively registered (provided that the Office of origin forwards the international application within two months from that date to the International Bureau; see below 2.9). That disadvantage may be one which can be neglected if the applicant can request the priority of the date of the application for his basic registration (see 2.2 and 2.9).

2.8. Recordal at the international register, notification and publication (Rule 14)
Where the International Bureau finds that the international application conforms to the applicable requirements, it registers the mark in the International Register, which is maintained as an electronic data base, accessible by the public upon payment of a fee. It also sends a certificate to the holder, notifies the Offices of the designated Contracted Parties of the international registration, informs the Office of origin and publishes the international registration in the International Gazette. Recordal and publication include any declaration that the mark be considered as a mark in standard characters. If the mark is in colour, it is published in colour.

Recordal and notification will be in French if the international registration results from an application governed exclusively by the Agreement. In all other cases the international registration will be recorded in both English and French. The translation will be prepared by the International Bureau, which will take into account any translation of any text matter which may have been added to the international application by the applicant. If the International Bureau considers the proposed translation incorrect, it will correct it after inviting the applicant to make, within one month, observations on the proposed corrections. However, the mark, which is the subject of the international application, will not be translated by the International Bureau. Any translation of the mark which the applicant may give according to Rule 9 4 (b)(iii) will not be checked by the International Bureau.

If an international registration is not recorded in the International Register within three working days following the receipt by the International Bureau, all the data contained in the international application will be entered in the electronic data base, notwithstanding any irregularities that may exist. The data must be accompanied by a warning to the effect that the international application may contain irregularities.

2.9. Date of the international registration (Article 3(4))
The international registration which conforms to the applicable requirements will, as a rule, bear the date on which the international application was received (or deemed to have been received; see 2.7) by the Office of origin. When, however, such international application is not received by the International Bureau within a period of two months from the date on which it was received or deemed to be received by the Office of origin, the international registration will instead bear the date on which the application was received by the International Bureau.

If the applicant had claimed the priority of his basic application or of the application which led to the basic registration, and the respective date is not earlier than 6 months before the date of the international registration, the international registration will enjoy the priority of the basic application or of the application for the basic registration.

The date of the international registration may be later than the date on which the application form actually arrives at the International Bureau. This is true in cases of irregularities which influence the filing date, i.e. when important elements are completely missing (such as the reproduction of the mark, the indication of goods or services or the declaration of the Office of origin certifying certain facts in the international application form). Rule 15 1 (a) lists these irregularities which must be remedied by the Office of origin within three months. In these cases the international registration will bear the date on which the last of the missing elements has reached the International Bureau. However, if the date on which the (last) missing element has reached the International Bureau is within the above mentioned two-month period, the international registration will still bear the date on which the defective international application was received by the Office of origin.

3. Protection of the international registration

3.1. Effects of registration

The effects of the international registration extend according to Article 3 *bis* and 3*ter* to the designated Contracting Parties.

From the date of registration, the protection of the mark in each of the designated Contracting Parties is the same as if the mark had been deposited direct with the Office of that Contracting Party (Article 4(1)).

If no refusal is notified to the International Bureau or a refusal is subsequently withdrawn, the protection of the mark in the Contracting Party concerned is the same as if the mark had been registered as from the date of the international registration by the Office of the Contracting Party.

3.2. Period of validity (Article 6(1)).

Under the Protocol registration of the mark is effected for 10 years with the possibility of renewal for further periods of 10 years. Under the Agreement registration is effected for twenty years.

Under the Common Regulations fees can only be paid for a period of 10 years (Rule 10). In other words, in any designation of a Contracting Party made under the Agreement, the protection is for 20 years, subject to the payment of the second instalment of fees at the expiry of the first period of 10 years. Consequently, under the Common Regulations all international registrations are always protected for a period of 10 years.

3.3. Refusal of protection (Article 5 and Rules 16-18)

Each designated Contracting Party has the right to refuse the protection of the international registration in its territory. The refusal must be notified to the International Bureau within a prescribed time limit, failing which such refusal will not be considered. The normal time limit for the notification of the refusal is the period prescribed in national law. However a maximum period of one year from the date on which the international Bureau has sent the notification of extension of the international registration to the respective Office is provided under the Agreement. Under the Protocol, any Contacting Party may declare that the time limit of one year is replaced by 18 months. In that declaration the Contracting Party can also specify that a refusal of protection resulting from an opposition may be notified after the expiry of 18 month. Such Contracting Party may, with respect to any given international registration, notify a refusal of protection after the expiry of the 18-month time limit, but only if it has, before the expiry of the 18-months limit, informed the International Bureau of the possibility that oppositions with respect to this international registration may be filed thereafter. If such notification is made, that refusal may be notified within a time limit of not more than seven months from the date on which the opposition period begins.

Since such possibilities of extended time periods for notifications of refusal are given under the Protocol and not under the Agreement, Offices can make use of them only with respect to designations that are governed by the Protocol. It can be expected that most Contracting Parties to the Protocol, which are not parties to the Agreement, will opt for the possibility of extended time limits (since this is generally in their favour). If Contracting Parties bound also by the Agreement opt for this possibility they can, according to Article 9 *sexies*, make use of it only with respect to designations resulting from applications governed exclusively by the Protocol (i.e. made by applicants whose Office of origin is in a Contracting Party bound only by the Protocol). It is therefore not very likely that many States party to the Agreement will make use of this option.

The International Bureau records the refusal in the International Register together with the data contained in the notice of refusal and publishes it in the Gazette. Furthermore the International Bureau transmits a copy of the notification to the holder.

As a result of these provisions, the holder of an international registration will for all designations which are governed by the Agreement know after one year from registration whether his mark is protected in a given Contracting State or whether there is a possibility that protection will be refused and, if so, for what reasons. For all designations which are governed by the Protocol, the owner, after a period of 18 months, knows whether his mark is protected in a given Contracting Party or whether there is a possibility that protection will be refused. He will know all the reasons for which the Office may ex-officio refuse the designation. He will also know whether there is a possibility that oppositions may be filed at a later stage.

The procedure before the Office which has pronounced the refusal follows the applicable law of the Contracting Party concerned. It may be subject to review or appeal and it may lead to a final decision refusing, in whole or in part, or accepting protection of the international registration in that territory. Consequently, the holder has the same rights as if he had deposited the mark direct with the Office which has notified the refusal.

4. Subsequent designation (Article 3 ter and Rule 24)

4.1. Requirements and procedures

The holder of an international registration may at any time extend its protection to Contracting Parties not covered by it. This is in principle also true with respect to Contracting Parties which at the time of the international application were not yet bound by the treaty under which it was filed, a situation which applies automatically for all international registrations recorded before the entry into force of the Protocol and the Common Regulations, where extensions are intended to be made to Contracting Parties which are parties to the Protocol only. An exception to this principle is provided in Article 14. It allows any Contracting Party, when acceding to the Agreement or to the Protocol, to declare that the protection resulting from an international registration effected before the date on which the entry into force in that Contracting Party becomes effective cannot be extended to it. When acceding to the Agreement, Mongolia (in 1985), China and Cuba (in 1989) and Poland (in 1991) made such declarations. It can only be hoped that not many new Contracting Parties of the Protocol will make such a declaration. The Nordic countries and the United Kingdom have not made such a declaration and Poland, when ratifying the Protocol, has even withdraw its reservation under the Agreement.

The holder of the international registration must, at the time of the subsequent designation, be entitled, under Article 1(2) of the Agreement or under Article 2 of the Protocol, to designate a given Contracting Party. The respective details are contained in Rule 24.

Where the request is made at least to one Contracting State under the Agreement, it must be filed at the Office of origin, otherwise it can also be filed direct at the International Bureau (the respective contracting party to the Protocol can, however, declare that subsequent designations must be filed through its Office of origin). It must indicate the designated Contracting Party or Parties and whether all or some of the goods and services of the international registration are claimed. In the latter case, the goods and services must be indicated, for which the request is made (which may or may not be the same for all designations). Of course the goods and services cannot be other than those listed in the international registrations.

Furthermore fees are to be paid. These are the basic fee (300 Swiss Francs) and a complementary fee (Swiss Francs 73) or an individual fee, as the case may be, for each of the designated Contracting Parties.

If the international registration resulted from an international application which was governed exclusively by the Agreement and the subsequent designation is also governed by the Agreement (this is the case if the designated Contracting Party is bound only by the Agreement or by both the Agreement and the Protocol) the subsequent designation must be communicated to the International Bureau in French. In all other cases, the communication to the International Bureau can be made in English or French, independently from the language in which the international application from which the international registration resulted was communicated to the International Bureau.

4.2. Date of the subsequent designation.

If the holder presents a subsequent designation direct to the International Bureau and it complies with the applicable requirements, it shall bear the date of its receipt by the International Bureau. A subsequent designation presented to the International Bureau by the Office of origin bears the date on which it was received by the Office, provided that it has been received by the International Bureau within two months from that date.

4.3. Recordal, notification and publication

The International Bureau records the subsequent designation which conforms to the applicable requirements in the International Register and notifies the Office(s) of the Contracting Party(ies) that has or have been designated. It informs at the same time the holder and, if the request was presented by an Office, that Office.

Recordal, notification and publication of a subsequent designation governed by the Agreement will be in French where the international registration has been recorded and published in French. Where the holder of an international registration resulting from an international application governed exclusively by the Agreement (which was only recorded and published in French) designates for the first time a Contracting Party bound by the Protocol but not by the Agreement, the subsequent designation will be recorded and published in English and French. At the same time the whole international registration will be published in English and will be republished in French (Rule 6 3).

In all other cases the recordal and publication will be in English and French, indicating the language in which the international application was received by the Office (the notification will be in English or French). The necessary translations will be prepared by the International Bureau. As in the case of an international application the holder may annex to the request for subsequent designation a translation of any text matter contained in the request (Rule 6 4).

The designation as recorded will be entered in the electronic data base, which is accessible to the public. If a subsequent designation is not recorded in the International Register within three working days following the receipt by the International Bureau of the designation, the International Bureau will enter all the date contained in the subsequent designation, notwithstanding any irregularities that may exist. The data shall be accompanied by a warning to the effect that the subsequent designation may contain irregularities (Rule 33 2).

4.4. Period of protection

The period of protection of the subsequent designation is the same as the period of protection of the international registration. This means that the effective date of renewal of the international registration is the same for all designations contained in the international registration irrespective of the date on which the designations were recorded (Rule 31 2).

An exception is made in the case where an international registration was effected before the entry into force of the Protocol and the Common Regulations and the required fees have been paid for 20 years. If in such case a subsequent designation is requested during the first period of ten years, fees for that designation can, under the Common Regulations, only be paid for the current 10-year period of protection of the international registration. When the subsequent designation is recorded, the current term of protection of the international registration expires more than ten years after the effective date of the subsequent designation, but the fees paid cover the first ten-year period only. At the expiry of that period (this may be between one and nine years), fees for the second instalment are due (Rule 40 3), which are treated as renewal fees (see section 6.1).

4.5. Refusal of protection (Rule 24 8)

The refusal of protection by a designated Contracting Party of the subsequent designation in its territory follows the Rules for the refusal of protection of a designation contained in the international application (Rules 16 to 18 apply *mutatis mutandis*).

5. Changes of the international registration (Rule 25)

5.1. Change in name or address

A request for recordal of a change in name or address of the holder or of his representative can be presented to the International Bureau by the holder himself, using the official form established by the International Bureau or a form having the same contents and format (Rule 25 1 (a+b)) This constitutes an important change in comparison with the former Regulations under the Agreement where the holder could not make such a request direct to the International Bureau. The holder may make his request in English or French (except where the international registration has been published in French only; Rule 6 2). One request may relate to several international registrations recorded in the name of the same holder. The request for recordal of a change in name or address of the representative is free of charge. For the request for recordal of a change in name or address of the holder a fix fee of Swiss Francs 150 must be paid, independently of the number of registrations referred to.

5.2. Limitation, renunciation and cancellation

The holder can request the recordal of the following restrictions of the protection of his international registration or registrations:

a) a limitation of the list of goods and services, which may effect some or all of the Contracting Parties ("Limitation");

b) a renunciation of the protection in respect of one or several Contracting Parties, which has effect for all the goods and services listed ("renunciation");

c) the cancellation of his international registration in respect of all the designated Contracting Parties which may effect some or all of the goods and services (total or partial "cancellation").

These requests must be presented to the International Bureau by the Office of origin, where the change affects any of the Contracting Parties designated under the Agreement. In all other cases the holder may also present the request direct to the International Bureau, at his choice either in English or French.

The fee for recordal of a limitation is 177 Swiss Francs. Recordal of a renunciation or cancellation is free of charge.

The International Bureau records the limitation, renunciation or cancellation in the International Register and notifies accordingly the Offices of the designated Contracting Parties, in which the limitation or renunciation has effect or, in the case of a cancellation, all designated Contracting Parties. Furthermore, the relevant data are published in the Gazette and entered in the electronic data base, accessible to the public.

The recordal of a limitation or renunciation does not entail, as such, a change in the international registration as originally recorded in the International Register. In other words, the limitation or renunciation does not entail a cancellation of the goods and services concerned in the International Register. Only the effects of the protection of the international registration are limited or renounced in the Contracting Parties for which the limitation or renunciation has been recorded. This is true even in the case that a limitation of the list of goods and services has been recorded with effect for all designated Contracting Parties.

Consequently, the goods and services which had been the subject of a limitation or renunciation can, following a request of the holder, be recorded in a subsequent designation both for already designated and for new Contracting Parties.

The situation is different as far as concerns a cancellation. If a cancellation of the international registration is recorded for all goods and services, nothing remains on the Register. In case of recordal of a partial cancellation, the goods and services, for which such partial cancellation has been recorded, are eliminated from the Register. An international registration which is cancelled ceases automatically to have effect in the designated Contracting Parties.

The consequence of this difference is that, in the case of a total cancellation, no subsequent designation can be made for the international registration, since it does not exist any more. If the former holder wishes to protect his mark again he must file a new international application. In the case of a partial cancellation, the holder of the international registration cannot ask for any subsequent designation with respect to goods or services for which the international registration has been cancelled. If he wishes to protect his mark again for such goods and services he must file a new international application.

5.3. Change in ownership

The ownership of a trade mark may change for different reasons and in different ways (e.g. assignment, merger of two holders, inheritance, bankruptcy). In accordance with Article 9 of the Protocol, the Common Regulations do not distinguish between such different causes and use the uniform terminology "change in ownership". The former owner of the international registration is the "holder", since he is still registered as owner in the register, when a request for recordal of the change is made. The new owner is referred to as "transferee" or "new holder" once the change in ownership is recorded.

A change in ownership can refer to some or all of the goods and services covered by the international registration and to some or all of the designated Contracting Parties.

This terminology is different from that used in the text of the Agreement, as applied before the entry into force of the new Common Regulations (the term "transfer" was used for a change in ownership in respect of all goods and services and to all countries covered by the international registration; the term "partial assignment" was used for a change for some of the goods and services or for some of the designated countries, a term which is not very fortunate, since a partial change of ownership can result from other causes such as a court decision).

The change in ownership can only validly be made if the transferee is a person who is entitled to file an international application (Article 9 *bis*(2) Agreement, Article 9 Protocol). Furthermore, if the transferee is only entitled under the Agreement the change in ownership cannot be recorded with respect to designated Contracting Parties bound exclusively by the Protocol and if he is only entitled under the Protocol the change in ownership cannot be recorded with respect to designated Contracting Parties bound exclusively by the Agreement (Rule 25 3).

The request for recordal of a change in ownership must be presented to the International Bureau by the Office of origin or another interested Office where the change affects any of the Contracting Parties designated under the Agreement. In all other cases the holder may also present the request direct to the International Bureau, at his choice either in English or French. The International Bureau does not accept a request made by the transferee since it is not in a position to decide whether the purported new owner is indeed the new owner. The transferee must therefore direct his request to the Office of origin or the interested Office where he is entitled to file an international application.

One request may relate to one or several international registrations recorded in the name of the same holder, if the change in ownership is the same for all of them. However, the fee for recordal of a change in ownership is 177 Swiss Francs per international registration.

Provided the request is in order, the International Bureau records the change in ownership in the International Register and notifies the Offices of the designated Contracting Parties in which the change has effect and informs at the same time the holder and, if the request was presented by an Office, that Office (Rule 27 1).

Where a change in ownership is made in respect of some only of the goods and services or some only of the designated Contracting Parties, the change will be recorded under the number of the international registration concerned. Any part which has been transferred to the transferee will be recorded as a separate international registration, bearing the same number as the registration of which a part has been transferred, together with a capital letter (Rule 27 2).

The new separate international registration can itself be the subject of a total or partial change in ownership.

The international Bureau publishes the relevant data of the change in ownership in the Gazette and enters them in the electronic data base. Where the change in ownership does not affect all goods and services or all designated Contracting Parties, the International Bureau publishes the part of the international registration, which has been transferred (with the reproduction of the mark, the list of goods and the designated Contracting Parties concerned).

The validity of the change in ownership is governed by the law of each designated Contracting Party concerned. If, in a designated Contracting Party, an assignment is only valid if the business or goodwill to which the mark belongs is assigned together with the mark, it suffices according to Article 6 *quater* of the Paris Convention (to which Article 9*ter*(4) of the Agreement refers) for the recognition of such validity that the portion of the business or goodwill located in that Contracting Party has been transferred to the assignee, together with the exclusive right to manufacture or sell in that Contracting Party the goods bearing the mark assigned. In that context it is important to take into account that the GATT TRIPs Agreement provides in its Article 21 that an assignment can be validly made without transfer of the business to which the trade mark belongs (however, transfer of the goodwill may still be required). Where the change in ownership is for some of the goods and services only, the Office of a designated Contracting Party may not recognise the validity of the change if the goods and services included in the part transferred are similar to some of those remaining in the name of the holder (this possibility is expressly mentioned in Article 9 *ter* of the Agreement).

The Office of a designated Contracting Party which is notified by the International Bureau of a change in ownership affecting it may therefore declare that the change in ownership has no effect in its territory. The effect of such notification is that, with respect to that Contracting Party, the international registration remains in the name of the transferee.

5.4. Merger of international registrations

Where the same natural or legal entity becomes the holder of two or more international registrations of the same mark resulting from a partial change in ownership as recorded, that person can request the merger of these international registrations. The provisions concerning the request for a change in ownership and its recordal and publication apply *mutatis mutandis* (Rule 27 3). The international registration resulting from the merger will bear the number of the international registration of which a part had been transferred, together, where applicable, with a capital letter.

6. Renewal (Article 7 and Rule 30)

6.1. Renewal fee and fee for a second instalment

Under the Common Regulations, the fee for a prolongation of protection is always paid for a period of 10 years and, depending on the nature of the international registration (whether it results from an international application governed by the Agreement or by the Protocol, or by both the Agreement and the Protocol) that fee may be a renewal fee, a second instalment fee or both. A payment of fees for 20 years is therefore not possible, even if the international registration resulted from an international application governed exclusively by the Agreement. However, it does not matter, that under the Agreement the fee to be paid after the expiry of the first 10-year period of protection is a second instalment for the second period of 10 years and not a renewal fee. The reason is that according to Rule 10 the provisions of Rule 30 for renewals apply for these second instalments. Since the payment of the second instalment under the Agreement is under the Common Regulations treated as the payment of a renewal fee, all fees to be paid after the expiry of the first 10 years of protection of an international registration will, in the following, simply be referred to as renewal fees.

If an international registration had been effected before the entry into force of the Common Regulations and the fees have been paid for 20 years already, of course no further fees are due for payment during that period. The situation is only different if and to the extent that a subsequent designation has been recorded after the entry into force of the Common Regulations and the current term of protection of the international registration expires more than 10 years after the effective date of the subsequent designation (section 4.4). In that case fees will become due at the expiry of the first period of 10 years of protection of the international registration, but only the respective complementary or individual fee(s) for that or those subsequent designation(s) and not the fees for the international registration as such. The *procedure* for the payment of fees for such subsequent designations is basically the same as for renewals and payment of second instalments for international registrations and will be dealt with in that context (section 6.3).

6.2. Notice of expiry

Six months before expiry of the 10-year term of protection, the International Bureau reminds, the holder of the international registration and his representative, if any, of the exact date of expiry by sending an unofficial notice.

6.3. Payment of fees

To renew the international registration (or to assure its continued protection for the second period of protection), it is necessary and sufficient to pay on or before the date on which the renewal (or second instalment) is due the renewal fees, indicating the name of the holder, the number of the international registration and the purpose of the payment. These fees are exactly the same as the fees due for an international registration (section 2.5). Any payment received by the International Bureau more than three months before the due date is considered as having been received three months before that date. This is important in case of change of fees between the date of actual payment and the due date.

The payment can still be made within six months from the date on which the renewal fee was due, provided a surcharge is paid, which amounts to 50% of the basic fee.

The holder can renew his international registration for some only of the Contracting Parties covered. This is the only exception permitted by Rule 30 2 from the principle established in Article 7(2) that the renewal may not bring about any change in the international registration in its latest form. If the holder does not intend to continue protecting his international registration for all the goods and services listed, he must separately request a limitation (section 5.2) before renewing the international registration.

Even if renewal is possible by the mere payment of the amount of fees, the International Bureau has, for the convenience of the holder, an unofficial form at its disposal, which it sends to the holder and his representative together with the unofficial notice of expiry.

6.4. Recordal, notification and publication

The international Bureau records the renewal with the date on which it was due, notifies the Offices of the designated Contracting Parties and sends a certificate to the holder. Where an international registration is not renewed in respect of a designated Contracting Party, the International Bureau notifies the Office of that Contracting Party accordingly (Rule 31). The relevant data concerning the renewal are published in the Gazette and are entered in the electronic data base (Rules 32 and 33).

Where the international registration has been published in French, and no subsequent publication has been made in English (that is, at the date of the recordal no Contracting Party has been designated under the Protocol), the recordal, notification, publication and entry into the electronic data base in only in French. In all other cases the recordal, publication and entry into the electronic data base is in English and French. The notification is either in English or in French (Rule 6).

7. Dependence and transformation (Article 6)

7.1. Dependence and "central attack"

For a period of five years from the date on which the international registration was effected, the protection resulting from the international registration remains dependent on the protection afforded to the mark registered or applied for registration (basic application or basic registration) in the Office of origin. This dependence exists regardless of the reasons for a partial or total cancellation of the basic mark, such as abandonment by its owner, cancellation because of non-use (where the grace period is less than 5 years) etc. Despite this, Article 6 is, under the Agreement, generally known by the term "central attack" since it permits the owner of a prior mark which is registered in the Contracting Party whose Office is the Office of origin of the international registration, to defeat that international registration for all countries in which it exists by means of one single successful invalidation action against the basic registration with the result that the basic registration is completely or partially cancelled.

Under the Protocol, where an international application can be based on a basic application, there is an increased danger for the holder of the international registration of loosing its protection for the reason that the basic application ceases to have effect. This need not be a "central attack" in the traditional sense of an invalidation action. The basic application can be refused protection, totally or partially, for absolute grounds or due to the existence of a prior right cited ex-officio in the examination procedure, and also following an opposition of the holder of such earlier right in that territory. According to the wording of Article 6 of the Protocol, the protection resulting from the international registration can no longer be invoked, in whole or in part, if, before the expiry of five years from the date of the international registration, the basic application or the registration resulting therefrom, or the basic registration no longer enjoys legal protection because it has been withdrawn, has lapsed, has been renounced or has been the subject of a final decision of rejection, revocation, cancellation or invalidation in respect of all or some of the goods or services listed in the international registration. The same rules apply, if an appeal against a decision refusing the effects of the basic application, an opposition to the basic application or an action requesting the withdrawal of the basic application or the revocation, cancellation or invalidation of the registration resulting from the basic application or of the basic registration results, after the expiry of the five-year period, in a final decision of rejection, revocation, cancellation or invalidation. Of course, these consequences take only effect after the expiry of the five-year period, if the appeal, action or opposition had begun before the expiry of that period.

Where in accordance with these provisions of Article 6(3) the basic application or registration ceases in total or in part to have effect, the Office of origin notifies the International Bureau accordingly and requests the corresponding cancellation of the international registration. The International Bureau cancels the international registration totally or partially in the international register, transmits a copy of the notification to the holder and to the Offices of the designated Contracting Parties and publishes in the Gazette both the notification and the cancellation.

The dependence of the international registration is not absolute. It is possible to change the ownership of the international registration, during the five years of dependence, without changing the ownership of the basic application or registration. The former holder of the international registration can even transfer his registration to a third party, not being the new holder of the international registration, who need not qualify for an application for international registration. The international registration simply remains dependent for its protection on the protection of the original basic application or registration and the Office of origin remains the same. As a consequence, where the original or new holder of the basic mark fails to renew it or if it ceases to have effect for other reasons, the original or new holder of the international registration can no longer invoke its protection.

7.2. Transformation (Protocol Article 9 *quinquies*)

In order to soften these consequences it is possible, under the Protocol, for the holder of an international registration which is cancelled because the basic mark ceases to have effect, to apply for registration of the same mark, with the priority of the original international registration, with the Offices of all Contracting Parties, where the international registration had effect, within three months starting from the date of the cancellation of the international registration. Of course, all requirements of the applicable law must be fulfilled, in particular as far as concerns the payment of fees.

Since the Agreement does not provide for transformation, such transformation of the international registration into applications in the Contracting Parties is only possible for those extensions of the international registrations which where governed by the Protocol. This is the case for all designations if the Office of origin is the Office of a Contracting Party bound only the Protocol. Applicants from these Contracting Parties (e.g. Denmark, Finland, Great Britain, Norway, Sweden) can always transform all designations of their cancelled international registration into national applications. Applicants, whose Office of origin is that of a Contracting Party bound by both the Agreement and the Protocol, can only transform those designations which are governed by the Protocol (designations to Contracting Parties bound exclusively by the Protocol). This is a consequence of the Safeguard Clause of Article 9 *sexies*, and shows that the Safeguard Clause (which assures the payment of the cheap complimentary fees instead of individual fees and forces the respective Offices of the designated Contracting Parties to issue a refusal of protection within one year) is not always to the advantage of the holder of an international registration.

8. Facts in designated Contracting Parties affecting international registrations

8.1. Invalidation (Rule 19)

Where the effects of an international registration are invalidated in a designated Contracting Party and the invalidation is no longer subject to appeal, the Office of the Contracting Party, whose competent authority has pronounced the invalidation (this may be the Office itself, a board of appeal or a court) must notify the International Bureau accordingly. The International Bureau records the invalidation in the International Register, informs the holder, publishes the relevant date in the Gazette and enters the information in the electronic data base.

If the international registration was published in French and at the date of recordal no designation to a Contracting Party has been made under the Protocol, the notification, recordal, information of the holder and publication will be in French. In all other cases the Office can notify the invalidation, at its option, in English or French and the International Bureau will notify the holder in that language. Recordal and publication will be in English and French.

8.2. Restriction of the holders right of disposal (Rule 20)

The Office of any designated Contracting Party may inform the International Bureau that the holder's right of disposal has been restricted in respect of the international registration in the territory of that Contracting Party. Such information is optional. However, if it is given it must refer to the main facts concerning such a restriction and must be given in the language of the international application which resulted in the international registration. The Office must also inform the International Bureau of any partial or total removal of that restriction. Recordal, information of the holder, publication and entering into the electronic data base follow the same rules as outlined under section 8.1 for invalidation.

An example for such restriction would be that the extension of the international registration in a Contracting Party is given as security of the subject of a right *in rem*. However, a licence is not considered to be such a restriction.

8.3. Replacement of a national or regional registration by an international registration (Article 4 *bis*).

A mark that is subject of a national or regional registration in the Office of a Contracting Party is, under certain conditions, deemed to be replaced by an international registration of the same mark in the name of the same holder. These conditions are according to Article 4 *bis*(1) of the Protocol that all the goods and services listed in the national or regional registration are also listed in the international registration in respect of that Contracting Party and the extension (which may also be a subsequent designation) takes effect after the date of the national or regional registration.

Such effect is without prejudice to any rights acquired by virtue of the national or regional registration (for example, priority under Article 4 of the Paris Convention or Priority of use).

According to Article 4 *bis*(2) the Office, in whose national or regional register the mark is recorded is, upon request, required to take note in its register of the international registration. This formulation is sometimes interpreted to mean that a request is a mandatory requirement for the holder in order to benefit from such replacement. However, the wording of Article 4 *bis* clearly provides that, quite independently from such request, the international registration is deemed to replace the national or regional registration. It may therefore be in the interest of the holder to request that the Office takes note of the international registration in its register. The effect is that if the holder, having made such request, decides not to renew his national or regional registration he will retain the priority of that registration for the designation of his international registration in that Contracting Party.

Where the Office of a designated Contracting Party has taken note in its Register, following a request made by the holder with that Office, that a national or regional registration has been replaced by an international registration, that Office must notify the International Bureau accordingly. The International Bureau records the notified indications in the International Register, informs the holder, publishes the relevant date in the Gazette and enters them in the electronic data base. This is of course very important, because the notice in the national register will not serve as information source after the national or regional registration has lapsed.

The information of the International Bureau, the recordal, information of the holder, publication and entering into the electronic data base follow the same language rules as outlined under section 8.1 for an invalidation.

The provision of Article 4 *bis* and its possible consequences are often overlooked. In fact, the system as provided is not very fortunate. It would indeed be better if such effects only took place as a consequence of a request of the holder. The solution for a claim of seniority of an earlier national or regional right, as provided in Article 34 of the Community Trade Mark Regulation is no doubt preferable.

8.4. Division of the basic application or registration (Rule 23)
This new provision takes into account the possibility that an applicant for, or the holder of, a registration has, in application of the Trade mark Law Treaty and under certain conditions, the possibility to divide his application or registration into several applications or registrations by distributing among them the goods and services listed in the initial application or registration.

The division of the basic application or basic registration has no legal effect on the international registration, since it is possible to base an international application, and the registration resulting therefrom, on several applications or registrations of the basic mark in the Office of origin. Nevertheless Rule 23 provides for notification, recordal, transmittal of the notification and its publication during the five years of dependence of the international registration, in order to transmit, in the interest of the public, information, as accurate as possible, of the situation of the basic application(s) or registration(s) during this dependence of the international registration on that basis.

9. The Interface between the Madrid system and the Community Trade Mark
9.1. General overview
As explained in the introduction, the Community will probably become a Contracting Party to the Protocol in 1998 and it will be possible to base an international registration on a Community trade mark application or to extend the protection of an international registration to the Community by designating it. In the first case the international registration with all its designations will be exclusively governed by the Protocol. This means that enterprises established in member States of the Community which are party to the Agreement can opt for the possibilities offered by the Protocol (such as an application as basis and transformation in case of refusal) by choosing a Community trade mark application as basis for their international registration instead of a national or Benelux registration in the Office of the respective member State (both the Office in the respective member State and the Office in Alicante are for these enterprises Offices of origin in the meaning as explained above in section 2.1). In the second case the designation of the Community will also be governed by the Protocol.

As a consequence, the Safeguard Clause never applies. The rules are in principle the same as in the case of an international application based on an application e.g. in Denmark or Sweden or in the case that the applicant for an international registration designates one of these countries.

There is therefore no need to repeat the procedures for registration, refusal, changes, renewal etc. in detail; all what has been said in sections 1 to 8 can be referred to. However the interface of the two systems raises some particular questions which will be dealt with below. One question regards the interface of the rules of conversion (Article 108 and 109 Community trade mark Regulation), in the case of final refusal of a Community trade mark or designation to the Community, with the provisions of transformation (Article 9 *quinquies* Protocol), in the case of cancellation of the international registration as a result of its basis ceasing to have effect. Some of the aspects will have to be regulated in the Regulation which the Community will have to adopt in order to deal with the interface of its Community trade mark system with the Madrid system, and which is in preparation (Proposal for a Council Regulation dated 24.7.1996, in particular introducing a new Title XIII on international registration of marks).

9.2. Designation of the Community

Clearly, an international registration can extend to the Community if its basis is a national mark in a country, which is not member of the Community. However, a national mark in one of the member countries can also serve as a basis for an international registration designating the Community. There is no provision in the Community trade mark Regulation which would prohibit the cumulative application for registration of the same mark in a member State and as a Community trade mark. Articles 34 and 35 of the Regulation which allow a claim of seniority of an earlier national mark are even based on the assumption of such cumulative protection.

The Community will opt for the payment of an individual fee, which may be the same or somewhat less than the fees to be paid for a Community trade mark application. However, since the Madrid system does not provide for payment of the fees in several stages, it will be necessary to pay at once that individual fee which covers the application fee and the registration fee as provided in the Community trade mark Regulation and the Community will provide for the possibility of reimbursement of a part of the individual fee corresponding to the registration fee in case that the designation to the Community is refused protection (Article 149 (4) of the draft Regulation dated July 24, 1996).

9.3. Cancellation of the international registration

What happens if in such case the international registration is cancelled because the national basis ceases to have effect within the five years of dependence of the international registration? The extension of the international registration to the Community can be transformed, according to Article 9 *quinquies* of the Protocol, into a Community trade mark application with the priority of the international registration. It will have to be seen whether the Office in Alicante will in such case ask for a second full payment of the fees (the draft regulation is silent on this aspect).

Of course, registration of the transformed Community trade mark application cannot be taken for granted. The Community trade mark application may well be refused later on (perhaps for the same absolute ground which led to the refusal or cancellation of the basis in a Member State, or because of a successful opposition). In that case the enterprise, whose international registration was cancelled and whose subsequent Community trade mark application was refused protection, can still convert the Community trade mark application into national applications with the priority of the Community trade mark application, which at the same time is the priority of the former international registration. However, it may well have to pay fees for the third time.

9.4. Refusal of protection of the extension to the Community

It is also possible that not the national or regional basis cease to have effect, but the designation of the Community is refused protection by the Office in Alicante (or later ceases to have effect).

Clearly, it must be possible to convert the extension to the Community into national applications in those countries within the Community where the obstacle leading to its refusal does not exist. This is provided in Article 154 of the proposal for a Regulation dated July 24, 1996.

Under the assumption that the owner of the international registration has, following the refusal of protection of his designation to the Community, converted the designation in a number of national applications with the priority of the international registration, and assuming further that subsequently the international registration is cancelled because the national basis ceases to have effect within the period of dependence, the question arises whether this event affects the converted national applications. Article 6 of the Protocol provides that the protection resulting from the international registration can no longer be invoked if the national basis falls. This is a clear ex nunc effect. Consequently the conversions of the refused extension to the Community have validly taken place before the national basis ceased to have effect.

Following interventions of the interested circles, the Commission has taken the initiative to propose an additional possibility for the holder of an international registration, whose designation for the Community has been refused or ceased to have effect. Instead of being converted into national applications, the international registration, according to the proposed Article 154, can also be converted into later designations of the respective Member Countries under Article 3 *ter* (2) of the Madrid Agreement or the Madrid Protocol. Thus he retains the advantage of one single international registration for protection in the territory of the European Union.

9.5. Community trade mark as basis

Clearly, a Community trade mark application can serve as basis for an international registration extending to non-member States of the Community. However, for the reasons given in section 9.2, it must also be possible to extend the international registration to member States of the Community, of course only, if they are also a Contracting Party of the Protocol (this should soon be the case for all member States of the Community). Even if in reality the designation of a member State of the Community is not an extension of the territory for which protection is sought (since the Community trade mark-basis of course covers also that territory) this mere semantic problem cannot exclude the possibility of designating Member States of the Community.

9.6. Refusal of the Community trade mark application

If the Community trade mark application is refused protection, the international registration will also be cancelled. In that situation the most particular aspect of the interface between the two protection systems arises: Two sets of rules will apply in parallel, both allowing national applications, which safeguard priority.

The refused Community trade mark application can be converted in national applications in those Member States in which the ground for refusal does not exist.

The cancelled international registration can be transformed into national applications in all Contracting Parties to which the international registrations extended.

As mentioned before, it is possible, in an international registration which is based on a Community trade mark application, to designate member States of the Community. In such situation, if the Community trade mark application is refused protection, the applicant for the Community trade mark has in those Member States the choice to either convert his Community trade mark application or to transform his extension of the international registration. Both rules have advantages. The advantage of the Protocol may be, that transformation is even possible, if conversion is not possible because the ground for refusal of the Community trade mark exists (exclusively or also) in that Member State. The advantage of conversion may be that, if the applicant has claimed the seniority of an earlier national right, that seniority claim can also be made for the converted national application.

10. Advantages and risks of the different protection systems

In the introduction it has been said that an enterprise, interested in an effective protection of a trade mark in Europe, is offered an unprecedented choice of registration systems. The question is of course which choice is the most advantageous one. There is no straightforward answer to this question. The advantages and risks of the different possibilities must be considered in each concrete case. In the following only some typical situations can be looked at.

10.1. Protection in one or in a few countries

If an enterprise is interested in protection in its own country or in a few countries only, the appropriate approach may be to simply apply for a national registration of its mark in the countries of market potential.

10.2. Protection in the member countries of the Community

If an enterprise seeks protection in the majority or even in all of the member States of the Community the most appropriate means of protection is to apply for a Community trade mark. The reasons are the following:

a) Costs:

The registration of a Community trade mark amounts to 2075 ECU, covering up to three classes of goods or services, and the applicant needs, as the case may be, no representative or only one representative. Clearly, national registrations in 12 countries + the Benelux registration would be much more expensive. However, an international registration is also more expensive, even if in the future it can be extended to all Member States. The reason is that only 9 Member

States of the Community are party to the Agreement, where the cheap complementary fees (Swiss Francs 73 per country) apply. For the other 6 Member States individual fees will have to be paid, comparable to the national fees. Also, in case of a refusal of protection, the holder of an international registration needs a representative in each respective country.

b) Chances of registration:

Admittedly it will be difficult to achieve registration of a Community trade mark application. However, it will still be easier, to have a Community trade mark with effect for the whole Community registered than to register a mark in all 12 national Offices and in the Benelux Office. The reasons for that are that a good number of national Offices will, even within the framework of harmonised tests for trade mark infringement, continue to afford relatively wide protection to existing trade marks, whilst the Office in Alicante will tend to register Community trade marks rather than to refuse their registration. This argument applies to an international registration exactly as to national registrations , since its designations to the Member States of the Community are in the respective Offices dealt with in the same way as national applications.

If the Community trade mark application is refused, it can be converted into national applications. There is therefore no legal disadvantage, and only the additional costs for the lost Community trade mark application must be paid, an investment which can be neglected in comparison with the costs for national applications.

However, if the applicant of the Community trade mark succeeds in registration, he enjoys an important cost advantage and the following advantage:

c) Use to safeguard protection:

Use of the Community trade mark in the Community is sufficient to safeguard the registration. National registrations and designations of an international registration to member States of the Community must be used in the respective territories in order to safeguard their protection. This is a consequence of the Harmonisation Directive which provides for uniform use obligation provisions in all member States. The owner of a Community trade mark enjoys therefore an enormous advantage. This advantage alone is so important that it is justified to try the registration of a Community trade mark, even if in the case of its refusal additional costs must be invested.

10.3. Protection beyond the Community

If an enterprise intends to extend the protection of its trade mark beyond the Community no doubt the Madrid system is a very appropriate and advantageous means of protection. It saves costs at the registration stage, since with one international application a great number of countries can be designated and, to the extend that the Safeguard clause applies, the designations are much cheaper than the national fees. Furthermore, and this applies to all designations whether they are governed by the Agreement or by the Protocol, no agents fees must be paid, as it would be necessary if one tried the national route. The advantages of an international registration are even more apparent if one looks at the situation after registration. Changes of name and address and changes in ownership can be effected with one single act paying one single and very reasonable fee and the international registration can be renewed with effect for all designated Contracting Parties simply by paying the renewal fees.

10.4. Combination of both protection systems

If an enterprise intends to protect its trade mark in the Community and additionally in a number of other countries outside the Community the most convenient means of protection will be to combine both protection systems.

If there are good chances to register a Community trade mark, an enterprise which is situated in the Community may apply for such Community trade mark and additionally apply for the international registration of its trade mark, based on the Community trade mark application, and extend the international registration to all countries outside the Community of its market potential. If chances to achieve registration of a Community trade mark are not very good, the enterprise may instead apply for registration of a mark in its home country and base on this application or on its registration an international registration with extension to the Community as well as to all other countries of market potential. Using that approach the enterprise may even, additionally to the Community trade mark extension, also designate those member States of the Community which are member of the Agreement (provided their Office of origin is also member of the Agreement). This can be cost-advantageous, if the Community trade mark extension is refused protection. Instead of having to convert in national applications and to pay the national fees the enterprise can in these countries simply rely on its designations in the international registrations. This means of course that the enterprise has on the outset to make an additional investment amounting to Swiss Francs 73 multiplied by the up to seven designations (including the Benelux countries) which can be made paying the complementary fee under the Agreement. This consideration will not be pertinent if the proposal of the Commission is retained that conversion of a refused designation of the European Union can at the choice of the holder of the international registration be converted into designations of the member States under the Madrid System instead of having to convert into national applications.

For an enterprise which is situated outside the European Union the latter approach, which is to base an international registration on a mark in its Office of origin and to extend it to the Community as well as to other countries of interest, is the only one possible if it wants to take advantage of a combination of both protection systems. The reason is that a Community trade mark application would not qualify as basis for an international registration, which must be applied for registration or registered in the Office of origin (above section 2.1).

Of course, an enterprise can also decide not to combine the two protection systems. This means that it would, in order to be protected in the Community, apply for a Community trade mark and, in order to be protected in the other countries of its commercial interest, base an international registration on an application or registration of its mark in the Office of origin of the Contracting State in which it is exercising its business. However, if one takes the trouble to register a mark in the Office of origin and to apply for international registration of the mark, based on the registration in the Office of origin, in order to protect the mark in the countries of market potential, why apply separately for a Community trade mark in the Office in Alicante instead of designating the Community in the international registration?

Also, if the principal interest of an enterprise is in the Community and the chances for registration of a Community trade mark are good, and it therefore applies for the registration of a Community trade mark, why should it, in order to protect its mark in other countries, which are Contracting Parties of the Protocol, additionally apply for registration of its mark in the Office of the member State where it is situated, only to be able to base on this national application or (under the Agreement) registration, an international registration? The simpler and more logical way is in that case, to base an international registration on the Community trade mark application.

In conclusion it can be said that an enterprise which is interested in the protection of its trade mark both in the countries of the Community and in other countries which are Contracting Parties to the Madrid system for the international registration of marks, will in the future make use of that system and will be able to profit from the interface between the two protection systems which will be a consequence of the accession to the Protocol by the Community.

Transfer and License

1. Dealing with Community trade marks as national trade marks (Article 16)

Article 16 indicates, in so far as Articles 17 to 24 do not give another solution, which Member States law should deal with a Community trade mark as an object of property. The principal rule is that property questions are dealt with according to the laws of the Member State in which the holder has his seat or domicile and, where there is no such seat or domicile, where he has an establishment.

It should be noted that Article 16 (1) contains the wording "on the relevant date". Although the relevant date is not defined, it is clear that the relevant date means the date on which a certain act which deals with the Community trade mark as an object of property is carried out.

If Paragraph 1 is not applicable (for instance in the case of a US company with no establishment in the EU), paragraph 2 provides that the applicable law will be the law where the Office is located (Spain).

Article 16 (3) contains a provision for joint holders. If two or more persons are mentioned as joint proprietors in the register, paragraph 1 will be applicable to the joint proprietor first mentioned. If no joint proprietor is first mentioned, paragraph 1 shall apply to the subsequent joint proprietors in the order in which they are mentioned. If paragraph 1 does not apply to any of the joint proprietors, Spanish law will apply.

2. Transfer (Article 17)

Article 17 deals with each form of transfer to a third party.

As we have seen, Article 16 (1) states that "unless Articles 17 to 24 provide otherwise", a Community trade mark as an object of property shall be dealt with as a national trade mark of a Member State. It seems clear that Article 17 deals only with transfer in an incomplete way. In our opinion, the wording "unless the Articles 17 to 24 provide otherwise", means that, where these Articles are silent, the law of the relevant Member State (according to Article 16) is applicable. For instance, if the law of such Member State would require a valid agreement to enter into the assignment and/or consideration, such requirements must be met.

In this respect, it should be noted that the law governing such underlying agreement may be different from the law of the Member State according to Article 16. The law of that Member State only governs the assignment itself. In a case in which the law of such Member State requires a valid underlying agreement, the law governing the agreement itself will decide whether or not such agreement is valid.

According to the Memorandum of the Commission on the creation of a Community trade mark, the possibility of assigning a trade mark independently of the complete or partial transfer of a business meets a commercial need and is recognized in the trade mark laws of a growing number of countries. Paragraph 2 stipulates that a transfer of the whole of the undertaking shall be regarded to include the transfer of the Community trade mark except where there is agreement to the contrary or circumstances clearly dictate otherwise, to be determined in accordance with the law that governs the transfer and the law that governs the contractual obligation to transfer the undertaking. The law that governs the contractual obligation may be different from the law that governs the transfer.

Paragraph 4 may lead to problems in practice.

Article 7 contains the absolute grounds for refusal of a trade mark. According to Article 7 (1) (g), registration of trade marks which are of such a nature as to deceive the public, for the goods or service shall be not be registered. Article 17 (4) does not concern trade marks that are of such a nature to deceive the public, but trade marks where it appears from the transfer documents that because of said transfer the public is likely to be misled.

In the Memorandum of the Commission on the creation of a Community trade mark, it is stated that the Office should have the power, without being obliged to undertake a comprehensive examination of the validity of the assignment, to refuse to record an assignment if it is "obvious" that the use of the assigned mark will lead to deception of the public.

From the use by the Commission of the world "obvious", it can be concluded that the Office should exercise restraint in refusing the transfer of a Community trade mark.

It is difficult to imagine under what circumstances it may appear from the transfer documents that the public is likely to be misled by the transfer of a Community trade mark as such.

According to paragraph 6, the successor in title may not invoke the rights arising from the registration of the Community trade mark as long as the transfer has not been registered in the Register. If the Office would refuse to register a transfer on the basis of paragraph 3 and if the Community trade mark of that transferor is not otherwise surrendered or nullified, such refusal would mean that the original proprietor could still invoke the rights arising from his Community trade mark registration.

The contractual consequences of a refusal by the Office to register a transfer will be governed by the law that governs the transfer contract. Problems may arise in particular if the applicable contract law would regard the successor in title as the legitimate proprietor of the trade mark, even in the case the Office refuses to register the transfer.

If the Office refuses to register the transferor of the Community trade mark, both the transferor and the transferee may file an appeal against said decision with the Board of Appeal on the basis of Articles 57-62.

Rules 31 and 32 provide for the contents of an application for registration of a (partial) transfer.

3. Transfer of a trade mark registered in the name of an agent (Article 18)

Article 18 is complementary to Article 11, which stipulates that the proprietor of a Community trade mark may oppose the use of his Community trade mark by his agent or representative if the Community trade mark is registered in the name of the agent or representative, without the authorization of the proprietor, unless the agent or representative justifies his action. In this respect, proprietors of Community trade marks should always confirm instructions and the agents or representatives authority in writing.

Whether the agent or representative may justify his action depends on the law of the relevant Member State (Article 16) or the law that governs the agency agreement.

As the aim of this provision is to protect the interests of the proprietor of the trade mark, the agent or representative should only be able to justify his action in exceptional clear-cut circumstances.

4. Rights in rem (Article 19)

This Article provides for the bare minimum and therefore the law of the relevant Member State will play an important role.

Article 19 should be read in conjunction with Article 23 which provides that such rights with respect to a Community trade mark shall only have the effect *vis-à-vis* third parties after entry in the Register.

Many questions have to be resolved by the law of the relevant Member State, for instance, concerning the formalities which have to be fulfilled in order to establish a valid security right or right *in rem*. Does the holder of the security right have the right to start infringement proceedings; is an award for damages in infringement proceedings (automatically) covered by the security right? How is the security executed? Is there an obligation to carry out a public auction? It is clear that before accepting security it will be important to find out which is the relevant Member State according to Article 16.

The national law of the Office (Spanish law) provides for the following with respect to rights *in rem* (of which usufruct seems to be the most important) and security rights:

a) The usufruct over a registered trade mark confers on the holder the right to exploit and carry out acts and authorise third parties to carry out such acts during the period of the validity of the usufruct. The usufruct may be constituted by *mortis causa* or *inter vivos* acts, in which case it may either be through a gift or an agreement to constitute the usufruct. The same rules that apply to transfer may be applicable. Contrary to the transfer of a Community trade mark, which should be in writing, freedom of form between the parties applies for usufruct, although registration at the Spanish Patent and Trade Mark Office is required for it to be effective for third parties; this registration should be made by public document and with prior evidence of payment of the tax for wealth transfers and documented legal acts.

b) Trade marks may effectively be subject to real security rights; in particular they may be subject to a chattel mortgage regulated under the Chattel Mortgage and Pledge Without Displacement Law of 1954. The chattel mortgage is the only right *in rem* security to which an industrial property right may be subject. In effect, it is a real security specifically adapted to the special characteristics of these rights.

In order to be effective, a chattel mortgage must be created by a public document (with a description of the secured debt and the object of the mortgage) and registered at the Chattel Mortgage and Pledge Without Displacement Registry. In addition, the Spanish Patent and Trade Mark Office should be notified of the creation of the chattel mortgage.

5. Levy of execution (Article 20)

Article 20 makes sure that the unitary character of the Community trade mark is preserved by giving exclusive jurisdiction to the courts of the relevant Member State according to Article 16. This seems a practicable and sensible solution as also the material law of a Member State will govern a Community trade mark.

It is not entirely clear if Article 20 also allows for preservation measures such as seizure of the Community trade mark before proceedings have commenced. We feel that this is possible if the law of the relevant Member State provides for such a measure. Such measures should be obtained from the courts of the relevant Member State as Article 20 (2) should be considered as giving exclusive jurisdiction also with respect to such matters which are in effect preliminary measures for levies of execution.

It is also clear that a levy of execution will only be possible with respect to judgments acknowledged by the Member State whose laws are applicable according to Article 16.

It should be noted that Spanish law does not have any special rules for levies of execution of trade mark rights, but the general rules on movable assets apply. Such levy can be created by a judicial order issued for the execution of a judgment or also as a preliminary measure. Notification to the Spanish Patent and Trade Mark Office is necessary in order to be effective against third parties.

On the basis of Article 23 Spanish Courts will hold a levy of a Community trade mark to be valid *vis-à-vis* a third party if registration at the Office has taken place.

Under Spanish law the execution of the levy is carried out by public auction followed by registration (in the case of a Community trade mark) at the Office.

6. Bankruptcy or like proceedings (Article 21)
For the same reasons that just one jurisdiction deals with levies, one jurisdiction also deals with Community trade marks in bankruptcy proceedings.

Article 20 and 21 do not contain a solution for situations in which a Community trade mark is already subject to a levy of execution when bankruptcy proceedings are started. In general this will not be a problem, as in practice the bankruptcy proceedings will often be started in the Member State whose laws are applicable to the Community trade mark under Article 16, as will normally be the place where the holder is established. If this is not the case, it seems logical that after bankruptcy has been declared the levy of executions is lifted, as this levy is in effect replaced by the levy in the bankruptcy. Another solution would be that the Community trade mark remains outside the bankruptcy assets, and the creditor in the levy of execution would then be in a privileged position which would run against the Community-wide accepted principle of the *paritas creditorum*.

7. Licensing (Article 22)
Paragraph 1 states that the Community trade mark may be licensed for some or all of the goods or services for which it is registered and for the whole part of the Community.

It should be noted that Article 13 (Exhaustion of rights conferred by a Community trade mark) means that if a licensee has put a product on the market with the consent of the right holder, such product can freely circulate in the EU market. The same consequence follows from the free movement of goods (Articles 30-36 of the EU Treaty). A license granted for part of the Community means therefore that if the product has been put on the market by the licensee for which the license has been granted, the proprietor cannot stop further sale into non-licensed EU countries. On the other hand, if the licensee should sell outside his assigned territory, there would be no consent and therefore paragraph 2 stipulates that the proprietor may invoke the rights conferred by this Community trade mark if the licensee contravenes a provision in his licensing contract with regard to the territory in which the trade mark may be affixed.

It is clear that Article 85 of the EU Treaty remains applicable to license agreements, and Article 22 is silent on questions such as whether or not a licensee can be forbidden to make passive sales to non-licensed countries. If such will be allowed, it is clear that the sales are made with the consent of the proprietor and that consequently such products may be sold throughout the Community.

According to paragraph 2, the proprietor may invoke the rights conferred by his Community trade mark against a licensee who contravenes any provision in his licensing contract with regard to its duration, the form covered by the registration in which the trade mark may be used, the scope of the goods or services for which the license is granted, the territory in which the trade mark may be affixed, or the quality of the goods or of the services provided by the licensee. In the majority of the Member States, contravention of the aforementioned contractual provisions would already constitute a trade mark infringement under national law. Strange enough, Paragraph 2 does not explicitly entitle the proprietor to invoke his trade mark rights if the licensee does not pay the royalties due (in time). The law that governs the license agreement will decide under what conditions the non-payment of royalties will constitute a breach of contract and what remedies the proprietor will have.

According to Paragraph 3, if nothing different is agreed, the licensee is not entitled to bring proceedings for infringement. The exclusive licensee may commence proceedings if the proprietor, after having been given notice of the infringement, fails to do so within an appropriate period. It will be clear that such proceedings can only be brought with respect to infringement in the licensed territory.

Paragraph 3 does not make clear what an appropriate period is. If a new infringement has been discovered and preliminary measures are possible, but have to be taken quickly in order not to loose the possibility of such preliminary measures, the "appropriate" period could be very short and may be only a matter of days. In order to prevent disputes between the proprietor and the licensee, the appropriate period should be defined in the license agreement.

As concerns Paragraph 4, the Community trade mark Regulation has no special provision with respect to damages and therefore, Article 98 (2) is applicable. Article 22 (4) is not entirely clear. Does Article 22 (4) entitle a licensee to ask for damages even if the law applicable under Article 98 (2) does not provide for such a possibility, or does Article 22 (4) only provide for the possibility of intervention in infringement proceedings (even if the procedural rules of the Court which hears the infringement action do not provide for such intervention) if the applicable law (under Article 98 (2)) provides for the possibility for a licensee to obtain damages? Although the text seems to make the second interpretation more plausible, we feel that Article 22 (4) also establishes the right for a licensee to obtain damages. A situation where the law to be applied by the Court with respect to infringements is different from the law of the Court is the exception, and therefore we assume that it was the intention not only to establish the right of intervention but also to establish the right for the licensee (also the non-exclusive licensee) to ask for damages, even if the law applicable to the acts of infringement under Article 98 (2) does not provide for such a right.

No commentary is given of Paragraph 5.

With respect to applications for the registration of the license, Rules 32 and 33 provide special provisions.

8. Effects vis-à-vis third parties (Article 23)

Paragraph 1 does not resolve difficult legal questions about, for instance, the position where the proprietor has granted (for the same territory and goods or services) two exclusive licenses and at the time of the second grant the first exclusive license was unregistered. What happens if the second license is registered first? It seems clear that the first license does not have effect *vis-à-vis* the second licensee. Does that mean that the first licensee has only a contractual claim against the proprietor but can no longer exercise his license or that the first licensee can continue with the exercise of his license but has to accept the second licensee on the market? This last solution does not seem to be the correct one as that would mean that the second license in effect loses his exclusivity. What happens if the first exclusive licensee registers his license after the second one is concluded but before this is registered? These complicated questions will have to be resolved by applying the law governing the Community trade mark pursuant to Article 16 and are inevitable as long as the registration itself is not a requirement for a valid transfer, license etc. per se.

Paragraph 1 contains an exception with respect to a third party who knew of the act (which was not entered in the Register) at the time of the acquisition of his rights. It will often be very difficult to prove such subjective knowledge. A more objective standard such as "knew or should have known" seems to give a more just result.

As concerns Paragraph 2, it seems strange that the transfer of the whole of the undertaking is judged to be a universal succession. In the case of a universal succession because, for instance, the proprietor has died, it is difficult to see problems with respect to third parties as such third parties can only acquire rights from the heirs. If a complete undertaking is transferred, the legal entity to whom the undertaking belonged remains in existence (and is registered as the owner of the right) Why should a third party who (not knowing of the transfer of the undertaking) acquires rights lose such rights *vis-à-vis* the new owner of the whole undertaking who could simply have made an entry in the Register but did not do so?

According to Paragraph 3 the effects *vis-à-vis* third parties of a levy of execution shall be determined by the law of the relevant Member State according to Article 16.

With respect to Paragraph 4 it is noted that, in view of Article 21, it seems only sensible to have the effects *vis-à-vis* third parties in a bankruptcy governed by the same law as that pursuant to Article 21 (1). However, the consequence is that the holder of a right *in rem*, security or (exclusive) license has certainty about the survival of his right in a bankruptcy of the proprietor only if under the laws of all Member States (all of which could – if the country where bankruptcy proceedings are first brought – be applicable) the rights of such holder are respected. With rights *in rem*, including security rights, this seems plausible, but there is a lot of certainty under the laws of the different Member States regarding licenses in bankruptcy.

9. *The application for a Community trade mark as an object of property (Article 24)*

This Article understandably applies the same rules to applications for Community trade marks as for Community trade marks themselves.

Entitlement

I. Criteria used to establish entitlement

The question of entitlement is dealt with in Article 5 of the Community trade mark Regulation which determines who may apply for and hence own a Community trade mark.

Article 5 ("Persons who can be proprietors of Community trade marks") reads as follows:

> *"1. The following natural or legal persons, including authorities established under public law, may be proprietors of Community trade marks:*
> *(a) nationals of the Member States; or*
> *(b) nationals of other States which are parties to the Paris Convention for the protection of industrial property, hereinafter referred to as "the Paris Convention", or to the Agreement establishing the World Trade Organization; or*
> *(c) nationals of States which are not parties to the Paris Convention who are domiciled or have their seat or who have real and effective industrial or commercial establishments within the territory of the Community or of a State which is party to the Paris Convention; or*
> *(d) nationals, other than those referred to under subparagraph (c), of any State which is not party to the Paris Convention or to the Agreement establishing the World Trade Organization; and which, according to published findings, accords to nationals of all the Member States the same protection for trade marks as it accords to its own nationals and, if nationals of the Member States are required to prove registration in the country of origin, recognizes the registration of Community trade marks as such proof.*
> *2. With respect to the application of paragraph 1, stateless persons as defined by Article 1 of the Convention relating to the Status of Stateless Persons signed at New York on 28 September 1954, and refugees as defined by Article 1 of the Convention relating to the Status of Refugees signed at New York on 31 January 1967, shall be regarded as nationals of the country in which they have their habitual residence.*

> *3. Persons who are nationals of a State covered by paragraph 1(d) must prove that the trade mark for which an application for a Community trade mark has been submitted is registered in the State of origin, unless, according to published findings, the trade marks of nationals of the Member States are registered in the State of origin in question without proof of prior registration as a Community trade mark or as a national trade mark in a Member State."*

If one compares these criteria on entitlement with the criteria used in Article 58 of the 1973 European Patent Convention[1] one could come to the conclusion that the Community trade mark Regulation is relatively restrictive on entitlement.[2] *However*, compared with other international agreements relating to trade marks, the Community trade mark Regulation legislation has been in fact extremely generous regarding entitlement:[3]

- To start with, both natural and legal persons are entitled.
- Furthermore, legal persons are covered by the very broad definition contained in Article 3 of the Community trade markR.[4]
- "Authorities established under public law" are specifically mentioned as being covered by the notion of "legal persons" with respect to possible proprietorship of Community trade mark in Article 5(1) "in limine".
- Finally, entitlement to acquire a Community trade mark is not restricted to European Community nationals or persons who are domiciled or have their seat or an establishment within the Community territory, but extends also to nationals and persons who are domiciled or established in practically all countries of the world, with very few exceptions.

It is therefore clear that only in a very few cases will a natural or legal person not be in a position to own a Community trade mark. Nothing else, except for the nationality condition, is required from the applicant for a Community trade mark. He need not be the proprietor of the company which is meant to use the trade mark and neither need he have the intention to use the trade mark applied for. Obviously, the fact that the applicant may be a "natural or legal person", without any further indication, leads to the conclusion that entitlement to acquire Community trade marks is not limited to business people or companies

[1] Article 58 of the Munich Convention on the granting of European Patents ("Entitlement to file a European patent application") provides that "A European patent application may be filed by any natural or legal person, or any body equivalent to a legal person by virtue of the law governing it."

[2] As does Carlos Fernández Novoa ("El Sistema Comunitario de Marcas", Madrid, 1995; page 45).

[3] Article 1(2) of the Madrid Agreement concerning the International Registration of Marks of April 14, 1891 as well as Article 2(1) of the Protocol Relating to the Madrid Agreement Concerning the International Registration of Marks, adopted at Madrid on 27.6.1989, restrict entitlement to nationals, and assimilated persons, of contracting States.

[4] Article 3 of the Community trade mark Regulation provides that "For the purpose of implementing this Regulation, companies or firms and other legal bodies shall be regarded as legal persons if, under the terms of the law governing them, they have the capacity in their own name to have rights and obligations of all kinds, to make contracts or accomplish other legal acts and to sue and be sued."

but refers to a much wider universe which covers persons not carrying out commercial activities.[5] No proof is required of being in business, nor of prior use of the mark, nor of anything else except that one is "a person" in the widest sense and a national of a relevant country.

International organizations:
At the request of the agents acting on behalf of the International Mobile Satellite Organisation (INMARSAT), the Office had to give its views on whether international organisations are entitled to own Community trade marks. Even though the reading of Article 5 seems to require that applicants need to be "nationals" of a particular State, it is obvious that it was not the intention of the author of the Regulation to exclude such organizations, when they trade, from being the proprietors of Community trade marks at their request. The reply of OHIM to the representatives of INMARSAT was as follows:

"According to Article 5(1) of the Regulation natural or legal persons, including authorities established under public law, may be proprietors of Community trade marks, provided that they are nationals of a State mentioned in subparagraphs (a) to (d) of that Article. In the case of a legal person, that determination is made on the basis of the place of business or seat of the legal person. According to the interpretation of the Office, an international organization can be proprietor of Community trade marks under Article 5 at least in the case where its seat is based in one of the States mentioned in subparagraphs (a) to (d) of Article 5(1). The place of the seat of an international organization can, for example, be determined according to the Convention by which the international organization is established.

Consequently, when an international organization has its seat in one of the Member States Article 5(1)(a) or in one of the other States which are parties to the Paris Convention or to the Agreement establishing the World Trade Organization Article 5(1)(b) or in a State (which is not party to either the Paris Convention or to the Agreement establishing the World Trade Organization) which, according to published findings by the European Commission, accords to nationals of all the Member States the same protection for trade marks as it accords to its own nationals Article 5(1)(d), it can be a proprietor of a Community trade mark pursuant to the Regulation."

[5] In fact, the President of the OHIM agreed to grant the very first Community trade mark application numbers, upon request, to certain non-profit making public and private organisations, namely:

Community trade mark number 1: "AIPPI" of the "Association Internationale pour la Protection de la Propriété Industrielle".

Community trade mark number 2: "ECTA" of the "European Communities Trade Mark Association".

Community trade mark number 3: "MAGISTER LUCENTINUS" of the University of Alicante.

Community trade mark number 4: "FICPI" of the "Fédération internationale des conseils en propriété industrielle".

Community trade mark number 5: "INTA" of the New York based "International Trade Mark Association".

To end this introduction, it should just be added that the legal significance of the question of entitlement is not limited to the moment of submission of the application, when the OHIM examines "ex officio", "inter alia", if the applicant is entitled. On the contrary, the entitlement issue is relevant throughout the life of the Community trade mark given that, if an entitlement ceases to exist, this is a ground for revocation of the Community trade mark.[6]

II. Persons entitled to be proprietors of Community trade marks

A. Nationals of one of the 15 Member States

Defining who is a national of each one of the Member States is to be decided according to the individual legislation of the 15 Member States of the European Community.

Natural persons: entitlement derives here from nationality alone; therefore no residence requirement has to be met. Of course, whilst residents will be entitled to apply personally, Member States' nationals who are resident outside of the European Union will need to act through a professional representative.[7]

Legal persons: unlike the situation concerning natural persons, where the holding of a given passport is the indisputable evidence of the corresponding nationality, doubts may sometimes arise as to the actual nationality of legal persons in cases where they are incorporated in certain territories having connections with one or other of the Member States. This is the case, for instance, with islands having links with the United Kingdom and belonging to the British Commonwealth.

Legal persons incorporated in the following territories are entitled to apply for and own Community trade marks:

- The Faeroe Islands, to which Denmark extended the application of the Stockholm Act revising the Paris Convention with effect from 6 August 1971;
- All French overseas departments and territories, as they were expressly mentioned as included in French membership of the Paris Convention;
- Holy See, which became a Party to the Paris Convention on 29 September 1960;
- Liechtenstein, member of the Paris Convention since 14 July 1933, and member of WTO since 1 January 1995;

[6] Carlos Fernández Novoa, *op. cit.*, chapter seven, No. 7.03.

[7] Article 88 of Community trade mark Regulation provides that:

"1. Subject to the provisions of paragraph 2, no person shall be compelled to be represented before the Office.

2. Without prejudice to paragraph 3, second sentence, natural or legal persons not having either their domicile or their principal place of business or a real and effective industrial or commercial establishment in the Community must be represented before the Office in accordance with Article 89 (1) in all proceedings established by this Regulation, other than in filing an application for a Community trade mark; the Implementing Regulation may permit other exceptions."

- Monaco, member of the Paris Convention since 29 April 1956;
- The Netherlands Antilles and Aruba, as they were expressly mentioned as included in Dutch membership of the Paris Convention; the Antilles were mentioned again in Dutch membership of the WTO;
- San Marino, member of the Paris Convention since 4 March 1960;
- The Canary Islands, Ceuta and Melilla which are autonomous Communities of the Kingdom of Spain;
- Gibraltar, and the Falkland Islands; and also the Isle of Man, to which the United Kingdom extended the application of the Stockholm Act revising the Paris Convention with effect from 1983, and Hong Kong which became full member of the WTO on 1 January 1995.

B. Nationals of States which are Parties Member of the Paris Convention or of the Agreement establishing the World Trade Organization 5(1)(b)[8, 9]

[8] As at 1.1.1996 the States Party to the Paris Convention for the Protection of Industrial Property (1883), revised at Brussels (1900), Washington (1911), The Hague (1985), London (1934), Lisbon (1958) and Stockholm (1967), and amended in 1979, are the following:

Albania, Algeria, Argentina, Armenia, Australia, Austria, Azerbaijan, Bahamas, Bangladesh, Barbados, Belarus, Belgium, Benin, Bolivia, Bosnia and Herzegovina, Brazil, Bulgaria, Burkina Faso, Burundi, Cameroon, Canada, Central African Republic, Chad, Chile, China, Congo, Costa Rica, Côte d'Ivoire, Croatia, Cuba, Cyprus, Czech Republic, Republic of Korea, Denmark, Dominican Republic, Egypt, El Salvador, Estonia, Finland, France, Gabon, Gambia, Georgia, Germany, Ghana, Greece, Guinea, Guinea-Bissau, Guyana, Haiti, Holy See, Honduras, Hungary, Iceland, Indonesia, Iran, Iraq, Ireland, Israel, Italy, Japan, Jordan, Kazakstan, Kenya, Kyrgyzstan, Latvia, Lebanon, Lesotho, Liberia, Libya, Liechtenstein, Lithuania, Luxembourg, Madagascar, Malawi, Malaysia, Mali, Malta, Mauritania, Mauritius, Mexico, Monaco, Mongolia, Morocco, Netherlands, New Zealand, Niger, Nigeria, Norway, Paraguay, Peru, Philippines, Poland, Portugal, Republic of Korea, Republic of Moldova, Romania, Russian Federation, Rwanda, Saint Kitts and Nevis, Saint Lucia, Saint Vincent and Grenadines, San Marino, Senegal, Singapore, Slovakia, Slovenia, South Africa, Spain, Sri Lanka, Sudan, Suriname, Swaziland, Sweden, Switzerland, Syria, Tajikistan, The Former Yugoslav Republic of Macedonia, Togo, Trinidad and Tobago, Tunisia, Turkey, Turkmenistan, Uganda, Ukraine, United Kingdom, United Republic of Tanzania, United States of America, Uruguay, Uzbekistan, Venezuela, Vietnam, Yugoslavia, Zaire, Zambia and Zimbabwe.

[9] As at 1 July 1996, the list of Members of the World Trade Organization is the following:

Antigua and Barbuda, Argentina, Australia, Austria, Bahrain, Bangladesh, Barbados, Belgium, Belize, Benin, Bolivia, Botswana, Brazil, Brunei Darussalam, Burkina Faso, Burundi, Cameroon, Canada, Central African Republic, Chile, Colombia, Costa Rica, Côte d'Ivoire, Cuba, Cyprus, Czech Republic, Denmark, Djibouti, Dominica, Dominican Republic, Ecuador, Egypt, El Salvador, European Community, Fiji, Finland, France, Gabon, Germany, Ghana, Greece, Grenada, Guatemala, Guinea, Guinea-Bissau, Guyana, Haiti, Honduras, Hong Kong, Hungary, Iceland, India, Indonesia, Ireland, Israel, Italy, Jamaica, Japan, Kenya, Korea, Kuwait, Lesotho, Liechtenstein, Luxembourg, Macau, Madagascar, Malawi, Malaysia, Maldives, Mali, Malta, Mauritania, Mauritius, Mexico, Morocco, Mozambique, Myanmar, Namibia, Netherlands – for the Kingdom in Europe and for the Netherlands Antilles, New Zealand, Nicaragua, Nigeria, Norway, Pakistan, Paraguay, Peru, Philippines, Poland, Portugal, Qatar, Romania, Rwanda, St Kitts and Nevis, St Lucia, St Vincent and the Grenadines, Senegal, Sierra Leone, Singapore, Slovak Republic, Slovenia, South Africa, Spain, Sri Lanka, Suriname, Swaziland, Sweden, Switzerland, Tanzania, Thailand, Togo, Trinidad and Tobago, Tunisia, Turkey, Uganda, United Arab Emirates, United Kingdom, United States of America, Uruguay, Venezuela, Zambia and Zimbabwe.

Here again the fulfilment of the nationality requirement must be analysed in accordance with the respective national legislation. This requirement must be fulfilled when the application for a Community trade mark is made.

In the case of persons having more than one nationality, it shall suffice that one of their nationalities is of a State which is a party to one of the two Treaties. In cases where there is a plurality of applicants for one or several Community trade marks, it will be required that absolutely all of them have a nationality entitling them to own such trade marks.

The reference in Article 5(1)(b) "in fine" to the "Agreement establishing the World Trade Organization" was added to the Community trade mark Regulation prior to the actual opening of the OHIM in order to take account of European Community Membership of the WTO since 1 January 1995 and, by extension, of the legal obligation to extend the principle of national treatment to nationals of Member States of this Organization, since Article 3 of the TRIPs Agreement provides that each member shall accord to the nationals of other members treatment no less favourable than that it accords to its own nationals with regard to the protection of intellectual property.[10]

Legal persons incorporated *inter alia* in the following territories are entitled to apply for and own Community trade marks:

- Bahamas, member of the Paris Convention;
- Barbados, member of the Paris Convention and WTO;

[10] The first three recitals of Council Regulation (EC) No. 3288/94 of 22.12.1994 amending Regulation (EC) No. 40/94 on the Community trade mark for the implementation of the agreements concluded in the framework of the Uruguay Round read as follows:

"Whereas the Agreement establishing the World Trade Organization (hereinafter, the 'WTO Agreement') was signed on behalf of the Community; whereas the Agreement on Trade-Related Aspects of Intellectual Property Rights (hereinafter, the 'TRIPs Agreement'), annexed to the WTO Agreement, contains detailed provisions on the protection of intellectual property rights whose purpose is the establishment of international disciplines in this area in order to promote international trade and prevent trade distortions and friction due to the lack of adequate and effective intellectual property protection;

Whereas in order to ensure that all relevant Community legislation is in full compliance with the TRIPs Agreement, the Community must take certain measures in relation to current Community acts on the protection of intellectual property rights; whereas these measures entail in some respects the amendment or modification of Community acts; whereas these measures also entail complementing current Community acts;

Whereas Regulation (EC) No. 40/94 creates the Community trade mark; whereas Article 5 of Regulation (EC) No. 40/94 defines the 'Persons who can be proprietors of Community trade marks' by referring notably to the Paris Convention for the protection of industrial property and requires reciprocal national treatment from countries which are not parties to the Paris Convention; whereas Article 29 of Regulation (EC) No. 40/94, concerning the right of priority, also needs to be amended in this respect; whereas in order to comply with the national treatment obligation in Article 3 of the TRIPs Agreement, these provisions should be modified to ensure that nationals of all WTO Members, even if the Member in question is not a party to the Paris Convention, receive a treatment no less favourable than that accorded to nationals of Community Member States."

- Cyprus and Malta, members of the Paris Convention and WTO;
- Suriname, member of the Paris Convention and WTO;
- Cook Islands, Nine and Tokelan;[11]
- Puerto Rico.[12]

C. Persons domiciled or who have an establishment within the territory of the European Union or of a State party to the Paris Convention

The third category of persons who can be proprietors of Community trade marks comprises those who, although not nationals of any of the Paris Convention countries, are domiciled or have their seat or a real and effective industrial or commercial establishment within the territory of the Community or of a State which is party to the Paris Convention.

Since Council Regulation (EC) No. 3288/94[13] surprisingly did not modify Article 5(1)(c), only those persons who are domiciled or have an establishment within the territory of the European Union or of a State party to the Paris Convention benefit from the provisions of Article 5(1)(c). Therefore, those persons who are either domiciled or have an establishment in a WTO country do not benefit from treatment as to nationals of the relevant territories as regards Community trade mark entitlement.

Persons falling within this third category of entitlement are required to be domiciled or to have a "real and effective" industrial or commercial establishment in the European Union or Paris Convention Territory. The key question here is then to define what is understood by such notions of domicile and of real and effective establishment.

1. *Notion of domicile:* In a legal sense, the domicile of somebody is the place of his permanent residence. Consequently, the domicile requirement implies two conditions:

- residence, real and non fictitious and;
- permanent nature of that residence, which excludes from the notion of domicile all kinds of temporary or brief stays in a country without any intention of establishing one's lasting residence in it.

[11] To which New Zealand's accession to the Stockholm Act of the Paris Convention extends, with the exception of Articles 1 to 12.

[12] The United States of America extended the application of the Stockholm Act of the Paris Convention to all territories and possessions of the United States of America, including the Commonwealth of Puerto Rico, as from 25.8.1973.

[13] Amending Regulation (EC) No. 40/94 on the Community trade mark for the implementation of the agreements concluded in the framework of the Uruguay Round (OJ EC No. L 349, 31.12.1994, page 83).

2. *Notion of real and effective establishment:*[14] Since it is only required that it be "an" establishment and not the only or the main establishment, it will suffice when it is a branch of the firm. However, the establishment has to be real and effective and, therefore, fictitious and temporary establishments set up only for the purpose of applying for a Community trade mark would not qualify. Likewise, mere houses or representatives' offices would not qualify. In any case, the OHIM will have to analyse and determine these issues on a case by case basis.

3. *Applicable to both domicile and establishment:* It is the laws of the country in which the Community trade mark applicant claims to have his establishment or domicile which will be considered to determine whether the domicile or establishment exists or not.

D. Nationals of countries according national treatment to European Union nationals

The fourth category of persons entitled to own Community trade marks is that of natural and legal persons who, not belonging to any of the previous categories, are nationals of countries which accord to nationals of all European Union Member States the same protection for trade marks as that accorded to their own nationals.

This group of persons is entitled to own Community trade marks by virtue of the principle of reciprocity.

Rule 101 of the Implementing Regulation,[15] on "Publication of reciprocity", provides that, where necessary, the President of OHIM will request the European Commission to enquire whether a given country accords reciprocal treatment to Community nationals. If such is the case, the Commission will publish its findings in the "C" series of the Official Journal of the European Communities indicating the date from which it is retroactively applicable.

During the first year of operation of the OHIM, that is during 1996, only one such communication – concerning Taiwan – was published.[16] The conclusions reached by the Commission were the following:

– "Taiwanese nationals may become proprietors of a Community trade mark under Article 5(1)(d) of the Community trade markR.

[14] The condition of having a real and effective industrial or commercial establishment is also required by Article 3 of the Paris Union Convention when it equates certain categories of persons with the nationals of the Union countries.

[15] Commission Regulation (EC) No. 2868/95 of 13.12.1995 implementing Council Regulation (EC) No. 40/94 on the Community trade mark (OJ OHIM No. 2-3/95, page 258).

[16] OJ EC No. C 335/3 of 9.11.1996.

- Applicants for a Community trade mark need not prove the prior registration in Taiwan of the trade mark for which they have filed Community trade mark applications.
- These findings shall take effect on 1 April 1996."

Another reciprocity enquiry was also requested by the President of the OHIM to the Commission concerning Bermuda. No communication has yet been published.

Further reciprocity enquiries have also been requested by the President of OHIM to the Commission concerning Bermuda, Andorra and the British Virgin Islands. No communications have yet been published.

On the other hand, once it was concluded that legal persons incorporated in the Channel Islands (Jersey and Guernsey) cannot be proprietors of Community trade marks pursuant to Article 5(1)(a) of the Community trade markR, the Commission initiated enquiries of its own motion in order to establish whether the Channel Islands accord reciprocal treatment.

E. Stateless persons and refugees

Article 5(2) provides that stateless persons and refugees shall be regarded as nationals of the country in which they have their habitual residence, with respect to the application of paragraph 1.

For the notion of stateless person, the Regulation refers to the Convention relating to the Status of Stateless Persons,[17] whose Article 1(1) defines "stateless person" as a person whom no State regards as its national in application of its legislation.

For the definition of refugee, reference is made to Article 1 of the Convention relating to the Status of Refugees.[18] Paragraph A of Article 1 provides that, for the purposes of the Convention, the term "refugee" applies to any person:

- regarded as refugee in virtue of the Agreements of 12 May 1926 and 30 June 1928, or in application of the Convention of 28 October 1933 and 10 February 1938 and of the Protocol of 14 September 1939, or even in application of the Constitution of the International Organisation for Refugees;
- who, in consequence of events having taken place before 1 January 1951, and fearing for good reasons to be persecuted due to his race, religion, nationality, membership of a given social group or political opinions, finds himself outside of the country of his nationality and who, due to that fear, does not wish to request the protection of such country.

[17] Signed at New York on 28.9.1954 following the Conference of United Nations on the Status of Stateless Persons held from the 13 to 23 September 1954. The Convention entered into force 6.6.1960, pursuant to Article 39.

[18] Signed at Geneva on 28.7.1951.

III. Procedural aspects

Rule 10 of the Implementing Regulation provides that where, pursuant to Article 5 of the Regulation, the applicant is not entitled to be the proprietor of a Community trade mark, the Office shall notify the applicant thereof. The examiner concerned should also notify the Legal Department of OHIM, which will consider whether the process of adding the country to the list referred to in point 3.4.1(d) of the Examination Guidelines should be initiated. This list includes those countries according national treatment and thus benefiting from reciprocity.

In all cases, the Office shall specify a period within which the applicant may withdraw the application or submit his observations.

Where the applicant fails to overcome the objections to registration, the Office shall refuse the application. Such a decision of the examiner is subject to appeal.[19]

If a Community trade mark were awarded by mistake to a person who was not entitled, the trade mark could be declared invalid.[20]

As a final point in this chapter, it should be mentioned that, although in practice it is not very likely, it is theoretically possible for a trade mark granted to an entitled person to be revoked later on, when the initial entitlement ceases to exist.

This can be due to various circumstances, such as:

- loss of nationality or the owner's change of residence;
- abandonment of the European Union, the Paris Convention or the World Trade Organization by his country;
- or to the fact that the owner's country ceases to accord reciprocity to European Community nationals.

[19] Article 57(1) of the Community trade mark Regulation provides that: "An appeal shall lie from decisions of the examiners... It shall have suspensive effect.

[20] Article 51(1) of the Community trade mark Regulation provides that: "1. A Community trade mark shall be declared invalid....(a) where the Community trade mark has been registered in breach of Article 5..."

Rights Conferred

1. Introduction

The Community legislator confers on the holder of a Community trade mark an exclusive right, the scope of which is defined negatively, listing in article 9 the cases where use of the trade mark is forbidden by third parties.

Article 9 of the Community trade mark Regulation distinguishes between cases of identical reproduction of the trade mark which are prohibited per se, and simple cases of imitation, for which a likelihood of confusion on the part of the public is required between the junior sign and the Community trade mark. The principle of specificity, according to which the trade mark is only protected for the registered products and services, applies in both cases. Nevertheless, a wider protection is granted to Community trade marks which are well known in the Community.

The list of prohibited acts includes: the use of the sign on products or packaging, the importation or exportation of products under that sign, and the use of the sign in business papers and advertising.

2. Unfairness and trade mark law

2.1. If one tries to identify general principles in the field of intellectual property one has to start from the basic assumption that each businessman should behave fairly.[1] This means that he must act fairly in relation with his competitors and therefore also in the relationship with his customers. (Fairness toward competitors and honesty toward customers are simply the two faces of the same coin because he who behaves unfairly against the competitors, tries to obtain more customers, and he who behaves unfairly toward customers, diverts customers from his competitors).[2]

[1] Beier, "L'esigenza di una legislazione sulla concorrenza sleale", Foro Padano 1987, II, 155. See also Brown, "Design Protection: an overview", 34 UCLA L. Rev. 1341, 1357 (1987).

[2] Similarity but not identically, see: Schricker, "Twenty-Five Years of Protection Against Unfair Competition", in IIC Vol. 26 No. 6/1995, 782, 786.

If this is the general principle, in view of the complexity of the modern system, it is convenient or even necessary to identify some typical acts which are unfair per se, and therefore prohibited without any specific evaluation of particular circumstances and without applying any rule of reason. In fact, it is totally uneconomic to resolve every question with an evaluation case by case of the unfairness of the behaviour of the enterprises.[3]

2.2. For instance when a patent is granted and valid, the infringement of that patent is prohibited as being unfair per se. However, even in this area, an evaluation of fairness is almost always in most instances necessary: for instance the doctrine of equivalency can not probably be applied without an evaluation of the equitable elements.[4] This necessity of regulating typical conduct is also present in the trade mark area. Violation of a registered trade mark may be unlawful per se, without an evaluation of specific circumstances. Or it may be unlawful if special circumstances are present. It is the author's opinion that most of those special circumstances may be unified under the element of unfairness.

3. Article 9 (1)
(Rights conferred by a Community trade mark)

3.1. Article 9 (1) of the Community trade mark Regulation confers on the holder certain exclusive rights with regard to third parties. As indicated above, the exclusive right of the holder is defined in negative terms, granting him the possibility to prohibit certain behaviour by third parties, in the course of trade and in the absence of his consent, which will be examined below. Clearly, the rights of prohibition are subject to the absence of the holder's consent.[5]

3.2. Article 9 (1) of the Community trade mark Regulation defines different aggressions to a trade mark, which can be prohibited by the holder.[6] However, such cases can be easily summarised under the common principle of unfairness:

i) The first instance is the identical reproduction of a trade mark for the same goods. Article 9 (1) (a) provides that the trade mark holder can prevent the use

[3] Franzosi, Trade Mark Law from a European Prospective, Book of Speeches, Köhl, ERA Conference, 1995.

[4] Osaka Koto, Saibansho, 29.3.1996; Franzosi, "Il brevetto quale tutela", Milan, 1996, p. 185; Equitable consideration not ruled out by *Markman* v. *Westview Instruments Inc.*, (US Supreme Court 1996, 38 U.S.P.Q. 2D (BNA) 1461) and *Hilton Davis Chemical Company* v. *Warner-Jenkinson Company Inc.*, 35USPQ 2d. 1641 (Fed. Cir. 1995 en banc).

[5] Vanzetti, "La nuova legge marchi, Codice e commento alla riforma", Milan, 1993, p. 15, rightly considers that this qualification is redundant and appears obvious, if one assumes that "consent" means simply unwillingness to invoke exclusivity for the trade mark. "Consent" in this case has another meaning, that is: a type of contractual consent not to invoke the exclusive rights with respect to one or more third parties, a consent which the provision confirms is valid and rules out that it may be revoked at will.

[6] The Community trade mark Regulation distinguishes between identical reproduction and imitation. The first is forbidden, without having to take into account the likelihood of confusion, while imitation requires the demonstration that there is a risk of confusion; identical approach under Article 13 (A) (1) Benelux Trade Mark Law and Article 17 e) Italian Trade Mark Law.

of signs "identical with the Community trade mark in relation to goods or services which are identical to those for which the Community trade mark is registered". The infringement in this case is not subject to any conditions other than that of identical reproduction.[7] Such act is unfair per se. Such typical unfairness normally constitutes in the national laws the basis not only for a civil action but also for a criminal complaint;[8]

ii) The second case, regulated by Article 9 (1) (b), provides the infringement of a Community trade mark by the use of (not so) identical or similar signs concerning (not so) identical or similar goods or services,[9] where it generates a likelihood of confusion on the part of the public, which also includes a likelihood of association.[10]

If we correctly place the system within the framework of the general principle of fairness, it results evidently that it is not necessary to make two evaluations (namely, similarity of trade marks and similarity of goods) but one single evaluation of unfairness, where the two elements are considered together. Perhaps a short distance between signs compensates a bigger distance between the products and vice versa. The evaluation to be made is whether the behaviour of the imitator, evaluated in abstract, should be considered unfair. This is more important than a millimetric measurement of the distance between signs and goods;

iii) The third case is the violation of a well-known trade mark. In fact, the principle of trade mark specificity mentioned above includes an important derogation when the sign has acquired a certain fame or notoriety over a period of use. Article 9 (1) (c) forbids the use by third parties of an identical or similar sign to the registered trade mark even for non similar goods or services, when

[7] This is now expressly provided in Article 16.1 of the Trade-Related Aspects of Intellectual Property Rights (TRIPs) 1994, according to which an infringment is present if the trade mark and the sign and their corresponding goods/services are identical or in the case where the trade mark and the sign and their goods/services are sufficiently similar to each other. In the first situation, there is undoubted infringment. In the second situation, it is necessary to weigh the similarities against each other to determine infringement.

Article 20 of the Canadian Trade Mark Law established that the exclusive right of the owner of a registered trade mark is considered violated by a party which sells, distributes or advertises goods or services marked with a confusing trade mark. Under Canadian law, there is no presumption of risk of confusion if the junior trade mark is identical to the senior trade mark, but only provides for a presumption of violation in the case where the junior mark is confusing. The provision of Article 20 is, however, consistent with Article 16.1 of TRIPs.

[8] In Italy, see Article 473 Italian Criminal Code; in France, L 716-9/11 Code de la Propriété Intellectuelle; in Germany, § 374 StPo; in the United Kingdom, Article 92 of the Trade Marks Act 1994; in Portugal, Article 264 of the Portuguese Industrial Property Code.

[9] Unlike the first situation, this second hypothesis looks at the case of i) similarity of signs for similar goods and services, or ii) identical signs for similar goods and services or iii) similarity of signs for identical goods or services.

[10] Section 10 (2) of the United Kingdom Trade Mark Act 1994 provides that "a likelihood of confusion includes a likelihood of association". However, it is still unclear what this means in the United Kingdom (e.g., *Wagamama Limited* v. *City Center Restaurants Plc. and Another*, 1995 FSR 713). In *British Sugar Plc.* v. *James Robertson & Sons Limited* (1996, 9 RPC 281) it was held that the requirement for likelihood of confusion was quite distinct from the requirement of similarity.

the registered trade mark enjoys a reputation in the country concerned.[11] Why? Simply because such use is unfair, and has the double effect of attributing to the infringer the favourable evaluation of the trade mark having reputation and also of diminishing ("Verwasserung") the value of the well-known trade mark.

The protection of well-known trade marks is again an application of the principle of unfairness mentioned before. Therefore, the author does not believe that one first have to evaluate whether the trade mark is reputed and then to establish whether there has been a violation, but simply that one must evaluate whether the behaviour of the infringer has been an unfair attempt to take advantage of another. The trade mark can be considered reputed when the use of said (or similar) trade mark by an infringer is done to take advantage of the reputation of the reputed trade mark.[12]

iv) The fourth case is the attack on the reputed trade mark with the effect of diluting said sign. This case is another face of the same coin mentioned under iii): a dilution of the reputed trade mark is made when the infringer wishes to take undue advantage of the reputation of the first trade mark, even if there is no risk of confusion. As matter of fact, it is the same Article 9 (1) (c) which forbids the use of a sign without any particular reason that has the effect of taking unfair advantage of, or is detrimental to, the distinctive character or reputation of a trade mark reputed in the Community.[13]

In the first two hypotheses examined above (Article 9 (1) (a) and (b)), the principle of trade mark specificity applies. In other words, the mark is protected only when it applies to goods and services for which the mark has been registered, or to similar goods and services. In the other two hypotheses, specificity is abandoned.

[11] Some authors (B.van Reephingen, "Le Règlement (C.E.) No. 40/94 sur la marque communautaire", J.T. Droit Européen, 16.2.1995, No. 16) criticise the introduction of the clause which provides for special treatment of trade marks with a reputation in the Community. They argue that this new category of trade mark – established by the harmonisation Directive – is not really necessary, given that the concept of a "well-known trade mark" (Article 6b of the Paris Convention) already exists as a mark which is known to a large section of the public (not only at the level of manufacturer, importer and wholesaler – Brussels Court of Appeal, 2.5.1990, Ing. Cons., 1990, 214, *Panoxyl/Pannogel*). A further category of "mark of great repute" also exists and both definitions give the holder wider protection than the principle of trade mark specificity examined above (Comm. Brux. 5.1.1988, Ing. Cons. 1988, p. 28, *Rolls Royce/Rolls* (beer)). According to these authors, the trade mark with a Community reputation would thus fall between the simple trade mark and the well-known trade mark.

[12] Vanzetti, quoted at footnote 5, p 86.

[13] This provision is the transposition of Article 13 (A) (2) of the Benelux Trade Mark Law on trade marks (See Antoine Braun & B. van Reephingen, Chron Jur., "Les signes distinctifs", 1987 – 1991, J.T. 1992, p. 538, No. 76) into Community law. It is interesting to examine the discussion on this clause when it was introduced into the Directive. According to the Benelux delegations, the clause was fundamental for the trade mark holder. Opponents (Memorandum on the creation of the EEC trade mark, point 108) argued that this clause would lead to an extension of the monopoly of the trade mark holder which would go beyond the actual needs of trade mark protection. However, the first opinion, according to which the trade mark protection should be extended to goods and services which are not similar, prevailed.

4. Article 9 (2)
(The Content of the Exclusive Rights in the Community trade mark)
Article 9 (2) of the Community trade mark Regulation contains a non-exhaustive list of those acts which the trade mark owner is entitled to prevent third parties from carrying out in the course of trade, thus illustrating the content of the exclusive rights conferred by the trade mark.

Such list is indicative of a fairly broad range of trade mark use, and thus of trade mark infringement, which encompasses, as well as the usual cases of putting products on the market and supplying services with that mark, a series of less evident examples.

The list contains the following hypotheses:

(a) *affixing the sign*. This sub-paragraph includes in the exclusive rights the mere affixing of the sign to the goods or to their packaging, which is prohibited only in case it is done for commercial purposes. The trade mark owner can oppose the affixing of the sign, irrespective of whether the goods are then marketed in his territory.[14]

[14] According to Article 36 of the EC Treaty, the trade mark owner can prevent a parallel importer from marketing a product in another Member State by hte trade mark owner himself or with his consent, if the importer has given to the product a new packaging. However, the trade mark owner cannot oppose the importation: i) when he acts only to affect national markets in the EU; ii) when it is proved that the new packaging does not alter the original product; iii) if the the author of the packaging is clearly indicated on the the packaging itself; iv) when the new packaging does not damage the reputation neither of the trade mark nor of its owner; v) if the importer, before selling the product with the new package, informed the trade mark owner (European Court of Justice, *Eurim-Pharm Arzeinmittel GmbH c. Beiersdorf AG, Boehringer Inglheim Ingelheim KG and Farmitalia Carlo Erba GmbH*, C-71/94, C-72/94, 11 July 1996).

In the case *Hagens* (29.6.1982, Jur., 1981-1982, p. 40), the Benelux Court of Justice held that the owner of the trade mark has the right to oppose to the use of his trade mark considered as the «usage de cette marque ou de ce signe par une personne, concernant ses propres marchandises ou services, pour en favoriser le commerce ou la prestation, ou pour désigner sa propre entreprise». Therefore, the carrier who transports an infringing trade mark, should not be hold liable for infringement, even if he is aware of the judge's interdiction on trading such products.

In the same sense, the doctor who prescribes medicine is not considered as using such medicine, *Tandéril*, Benelux Court of Justice, 9.7.1984, Jur. 1984, p. 1. However, the person who renews and trades a product is considered liable for infringement, *Valeo*, Benelux Court of Justice, 6.11.1992, Jur., 1992, p. 1.

Finally, it is infringement to fill a form of packaging, which is marked with a certain trade mark, with a product which does not belong to the owner of such trade mark, *Shell*, Benelux Court of Justice, 20.12.1993, Jur., 1993, p. 1.

The use of an identical sign for identical products or services is not always considered as infringement. In fact, the use of the name, the address, and of indications concerning the kind, the quality, the destination, the value, or the geographical origin of the product is permitted if it is made according to the good commercial practice. Therefore, each indication concerning the trade mark should be limited to informative purposes *Polyglot*, Benelux Court of Justice, 16.6.1995, R.W., 1995-1996, p. 253, Ing.-Cons., 1995, p. 243).

Following on this statement is the principle of the exhaustion of trade mark rights. Although Community legislation and case-law applies exhaustion to cases where the goods were initially placed on the market in a EU Member State, there has been no lack of national decision asserting the principle of a worldwide exhaustion.[15]

Moreover, it is interesting to note that if we assume that the Internet address can act as trade mark, then the use of such address can be considered as affixing the sign.[16]

(b) *offering, putting on the market, stocking*. The term "offering" should be interpreted in the broad sense and considered to cover sales offer, donation or even a simple display for sale. However, the offer must be distinguished from the use of the trade mark in advertising. When offered, the trade mark has the direct function of distinguishing the good from the other goods of the same type, both as regards their features and their origin. Whereas, when used in advertising, the trade mark has on one hand the same function of informing the consumer and of inducing him to purchase the goods, but, on the other hand, there may be different consequences as concerns the loss of the trade mark for lack of use.

[15] See M. Franzosi, *"Grey Market – Parallel Importation as a Trade Mark Violation or an Act of Unfair Competition"*, 21 IIC, p. 194 *seq.* (1990). A survey of the application of the principle of exhaustion by the law courts in Europe is given by BEIER, *"The Doctrine of Exhaustion in EEC Trade Mark Law – Scope and Limits"*, 10 IIC, 20 *et seq.* (1979). In the USA see especially *Champion Spark Plug Co.* v. *Sanders*, 331 US 125 (1947); *Monte Carlo Shirt Inc.* v. *Daewoo Intl. Corp.*, 707 F.2d. 1054 (9th Cir 1983). In Italy, the principle of exhaustion was clearly expressed by the Supreme Court in the judgment of 4.4.1970, No. 914, 1970 Giur. It., I, 1, 1175; and by the Turin Court of Appeal, 25.2.1967, Foro Padano 1967, I, 468, in the *Rolex case*. Contrary Monza Tribunal, 27.11.1992, Giur. comm. 1996, 145. See G. Tesauro, *"La jurisprudence de la Cour de justice sur le droit de la "propriété intellectuelle"*, in Book of Speeches of the International Conference on Intellectual & Industrial Property, Athens 11-13 April 1994. Mangini, *"Competition and Monopoly in Trade Mark Law. An EEC Perspective"*, IIC, 591 *et seq* (1980). A worldwide dimension of the exhaustion principle was then given in *Veil Ceramics & Glass Inc.* v. *Dash* (F.2d, USPO2d – 3rd Circ. 1989); *K Mart Corp.* v. *Cartier Inc.*, US Supreme Court, 31.5.1988. In Italy, see Prato District Court, 28.9.1985 – *Fruit of the Loom case*, Giur. Dir. Ind. 768. See also the High Court of Tokyo of 23.3.1995, in *Jap Auto Products Kabushiki Kaisha and Another* v. *BBS Kraftfahrzeug Technik AG* (S. Yamamoto, *"A Reversal of Fortune for Patentee and Parallel Importers in Japan"*, in EIPR, 1995, 7, 341). For further information, see the chapter on the exhaustion of trade mark by Prof. Heinz Goddar and Andreas Ebert-Weidenfeller of the present book.

[16] As a matter of fact, Internet addresses and Internet domain names provide an Internet user with more than just the location of a source of interactive information, as they can also serve as trade marks. In the case *MTV Networks* v. *Curry*, a former MTV video jockey, Adam Curry, registered the domain name "mtv.com" while working for MTV Networks (MTVN). Promptly after Curry's departure, he was sued by MTV Networks for trade mark infringement, among other things, for refusing to stop using the "mtv.com" Internet address (See *MTV Networks* v. *Curry*, 867 F Supp 202, SDNY – 1994).

The offering of goods on the Internet should be wholly assimiliated to a regular contract.[17] If the parties are communicating directly across the Internet, it is likely that the standard offer and acceptance rules apply. On the contrary, if the parties are comunicating through a third party, such as an on-line service provider, the offer and acceptance are disciplined by the postal rules. In fact, in the latter case it is reasonable to assume that the parties will have implicitly or explicitly agreed to trust the transmission of their offer and acceptance to the third party, namely the service provider.

To put on the market means any act which put the goods into circulation for the first time. This includes pre-sale preparatory acts, such as displaying goods for sale, sales proposals, material advertising or advertising in catalogues indicating a price. According to this interpretation, it is controversial whether, after a declaration of banckruptcy, the goods which fall under the bankruptcy (and therefore be destined to a sale). Clearly, they are no longer under the control of the owner (but of the banckruptcy).

The mere stocking of goods for commercial purposes is equivalent to offering the goods or putting them on the market, as is offering or supplying the goods under the sign.[18] Persons who are not involved in the marketing of the product, but are aware of the illicit origin thereof and nevertheless keep or conserve such product, can be liable for carrying out these acts. Stocking is punished whether the goods are stored in owned, rented or even loaned premises and in the latter case the owner of the premises can also be liable as co-offender if he is aware of the unlawful act.

(c) *importing, exporting*. Importation of the goods under the sign is prohibited, irrespective of intent to market them in the State concerned, which would therefore appear to cover temporary imports,[19] reinforcing the above mentioned worldwide exhaustion theory.

[17] The Internet is a sphere of communication which is not exempt from the general rules of trade mark law. In the case *Playboy Enters* v. *Frena*, 839 F Supp 1552, 1559-61 (MD Fla 1993), the court assumed that trade mark law applied to Defendant George Frena's subscription computer bulletin board service that distributed unauthorised copies of Plaintiff Playboy Enterprises Inc's ("Playboy") copyrighted photographs bearing Playboy's federally registered Playboy and Playmate trade marks. As regards trade mark disputes over the Internet domain names, Playboy alleged in another case, *Playboy Enterprise Inc* v. *Imagnet Inc*, Civ. No. 95 Civ 5859 (HB) (SDNY August 1995) trade mark infringement based on Imagnet's use of the domain name "playmate.com".

[18] In Belgium and in the Netherlands, the use of the trade mark must be proportioned to the volume of the stock, otherwise the dealer could be held guilty for wrongly attracting consumers, using the trade mark unlawfully, as the stock does not correspond to the capacity of the trade mark user to satisfy the consumer's demand (see Article 23, 9°, of the Belgian Law of 14.7.1991, and Article 6:194 of the Dutch Civil Code).

[19] The European Court of Justice granted to the importer of pharmaceutical goods the right of replacing the original packaging with a new one, bearing the owner's trade mark, in accordance with the legal requirements of the importing country, *Hoffman-La Roche*, 23.5.1978, Rec., 1139.

There is trade mark infrigement only if the act of infringement is made in the course of business, in the sphere of a company activity, of a profession or any other activity which is not generally exercised in the private field and which has the purpose of realizing an economical advantage, *Tandéril, cit.*

Exportation of goods is also listed, confirming that the mere affixing of the sign is unlawful where the products are not to be marketed in the territory.

(d) *using sign on business papers and in advertising*. The use of the sign on business papers and advertising (including radio and television) is put on an equal footing.[20] Such use is becoming more and more common. This was already included in the exclusive rights under some national laws.[21] Indeed in the new UK Trade Mark Act the use of the spoken word may amount to infringement; the Community trade mark Regulation does not expressly provide for this however.

The provisions of Article 9 (2) are to be read in conjunction with Article 12 of the Community trade markR, which states that the registrant cannot prevent third parties from using certain terms such as its own name and address, the product's utility or geographical origin or even a trade mark where this is necessary to indicate the intended use of a particular product (notably car spare parts).[22]

Article 9 (2), is in line with recent decisions of the Benelux Court which interprets the Benelux Trade Mark Act.[23]

5. *The Basic Principles in Comparison between Signs*

Various problems may arise in evaluating the scope of protection of a trade mark.

The problem of infringement of a registered Community trade mark requires a distinction. National Court decisions have constantly affirmed two principles, namely that:

i) in evaluating infringement of a registered trade mark by a junior trade mark used in the market, a comparison has to be made between the senior trade mark as registered and the junior trade mark as used; but also that;

ii) in evaluating infringement the comparison has to be made having under the eye the junior trade mark and in the memory the recollection of the senior trade mark.

[20] The dealer who is marketing a product or providing a service with a certain trade mark can use such trade mark in advertisement. This right, which however has to to strictly limited to the marked product, was recognised by the Benelux Court of Justice, see *Daimler-Benz*, Jur., 20.12.1993, p. 65.

[21] E.g., it is a new element in the UK Trade Mark Act 1994.

[22] Following the Directive, national laws have largely copied the wording of Article 9 (2), with some alterations. Article 1(2) of the Italian Law is identical. The German Trade Mark Act of 1995 (BGBl. 1995 I, p. 156) is more comprehensive in that at Section 14 (4) it forbids those same acts set forth in Article 9 (2) which are preparatory to the commission of the offence as an "indirect" infringement of the trade mark – here the use of the trade mark in connection with the respective products or services need not be proven, since it will suffice that likelihood exists that a "direct" infringement of the trade mark may be committed. (The new UK Trade Mark Law includes, in addition, provisions on comparative advertising, see draft EC Directive in OJ 1991, C180/15).

[23] Of particular note is a decision of 20.12.1993 (Rec. 1993, p. 65) which held that the use by an unauthorised distributor of the Mercedes-Benz mark in its advertising was unlawful, in that it gave the public the impression that the mark was being used predominantly for advertising purposes or that the distributor was gaining benefit from the name or goodwill of the mark, and thus from then on damaging its advertising function.

These principles are clearly conflicting (the recollection of the senior trade mark may be – and usually is – different from the registered trade mark) but constantly (and the author suggests concurrently) affirmed.

It is the author's opinion that there is only one manner to reconcile the two principles.

From the point of view of trade mark law, the first principle applies. From the point of view of unfair competition law, the factual position of a name in the trade has to be taken into consideration, so that the second principle applies.

If the trade mark law is a part of the unfair competition law, the two principles above outlined are simultaneously applicable. If it is not a part of the unfair competition law, it must be considered nevertheless that in the judicial practice, the two counts of trade mark violation and unfair competition are normally brought forth, so that the two principles are applied jointly.

The confusion could be phonetic, visual, conceptual ("begripsmatig"). These are not three different classes of confusion, but simply aspects in which the unfairness can be demonstrated. A translation of a trade mark could also be an infringement if there is confusion in the mind of the public.

A principle which is not always applied correctly is that the plaintiff's trade mark has to be considered in its globality, taking into consideration all of its aspects. Even descriptive expressions or figures contained in the trade mark may play a certain role in the evaluation of confusion and therefore unfairness. Their role is simply more minor than the role of distinguishing elements. But it is not legitimate to eliminate descriptive characters from the trade mark and concentrate on the characteristic aspects of the trade mark (what in Italy is called "il cuore" or "il tipo").

As for the moment of evaluating confusion, this depends on the procedural laws of each countries. There are countries in which the judge has to decide on the facts submitted at the time of the writ of summons, or at the closing of the acquisition of facts ("conclusions") or at the time of the decision.

Another point is the size of the public which has to be considered when evaluating confusion: is confusion of a small part of the public sufficient? If the dominant principle is unfairness, it is clear that unfair behaviour leading to confusion of a small part of the public is unfair. But confusion of a small group of people may show that it was not intentional, constant and paramount.

6. Evaluation of Confusion in Trade Mark Law

6.1. General Rules for Comparison

Judgement of the risk of confusion depends on the specific characteristics of different cases and remains under the competence of national jurisdictions.[24] While the case of identical signs does not present particular problems, the judgement of confusion between similar signs is the object of important case-law at national level which will be examined further.

[24] In the case opposing Audi AG's trade mark *Quattro* to Deutsche Renault AG's trade mark *Espace Quadra*, the German Federal Supreme Court raised the question before the European Court of Justice whether the prohibition of the use in Germany of the trade mark Quadra used for a long time in France and abroad was in accordance with Article 30 and 36 of the EC Treaty concerning the prohibition of restrictions on trade between Member States. This question was raised because a car manufacturer in Germany claimed the rights in the trade mark *Quattro* according to the laws of that Member State, even though this mark had the recognisable meaning of a numeral and a significant role in the automobile industry. The European Court of Justice confirmed that in the absence of EC harmonisation in the field of industrial property rights, the requirements for the grant of industrial property rights were determined by national laws. The protection of the denomination *Quattro* had therefore to be determined by national law within the limits established by Article 36 of the EC Treaty which allows trade restrictions justified on the ground of protection of industrial and commercial property, provided that such protection does not constitute the means of arbitrary discrimination or disguised restrictions on trade between Member States. Such exceptions to Article 30 of the EC Treaty are justified for the safeguarding of rights which constitute the subject-matter of that property (Case 119/75, *Terrapin (Overseas) Ltd.* v. *Terranova Industrie CA Kapferer & Co.*, [1976] ECR 1039) i.e., in the case of trade marks namely to protect the trade mark owner against the risk of confusion with the help of which third parties wish to take advantage of the status and reputation of the owner's mark (Case 1674, *Centrapharm BV* v. *Winthrop BV* [1974] ECR 1183; Case 10/89, *CNL-Sucal NV* v. *Hag CF AG* [1990] ECR 3711). The Court further reiterated that the determination of rules for establishing the risk of confusion remains the responsibility of national law subject to the restrictions imposed by Article 36 of the EC Treaty. Since there were no indications that German Courts applied the requirements for creating a trade mark and determining its scope of protection in a discriminatory or deliberately restrictive manner, the Court concluded that national rules establishing an exclusive right to use the word *Quattro* and prohibiting use of similar names such as *Quadra* to avoid confusion could not be seen as an inadmissible trade barrier (Case C-317/91, *Audi AG* v. *Deutsche Renault AG*, European Court of Justice 30.11.1993).

The decision of the European Court of Justice is furthermore confirmed by the Council Directive of 21.12.1988 to approximate the laws of the Member States related to trade marks according to which the assessment of the likelihood of confusion will remain with national authorities. This situation will remain even in the case of Community trade marks. Since jurisdiction over the infringement of Community trade marks will remain in the exclusive jurisdiction of the Community trade mark Courts (Article 92 of the Council Regulation (EC) No. 40/94 of December 1993 on the Community trade mark).

On this question see also Gert Würstenberg, Determination of Risk of Confusion in Trade Mark Infringement Proceedings in the European Union, The *Quattro* Decision in [1994] 7 EIPR; Beier, "Ziele und Gedanken des europäischen Markenrechts" in [1976] GRUR Int. 363 – 373; Loewenheim, "Warenzeichen- und Gemeinschaftsrecht", [1977] GRUR 428 – 430.

In most countries (if not all), some general rules have been developed in order to assess the likelihood of confusion between two marks and some criteria for comparison have been established which will have more or less weight depending on the case. Most decisions will refer to some of these criteria and it is rare that the judge refers to more than a few in analysing any single case.[25]

6.1.1. The Trade Marks to be Compared

In case a registered trade mark is infringed by a trade mark in the market the comparison has to be made between the trade mark as registered and the infringing mark as used. The risk of confusion must be judged on the basis of the senior trade mark as registered and at the moment of registration, without taking into account the way in which it has been used, or the existence of other factors such as presentation, price and the regulation of the products.[26]

[25] In the USA, however, the Courts tend to apply and balance numerous factors before concluding where there is or is not a risk of confusion between marks. In *Ross Cosmetics Distribution Centers Inc.* v. *United States*, the US Court of International Trade (34 USPQ) 2d Volume 34, No. 11, at 1758) had to examine whether the plaintiff's packages for its bath oil products could be confused with several well-known trade marks. The Court applied and balanced multiple factors, i.e., (1) the degree of resemblance; (2) the similarity of the marketing method and channels of distribution; (3) the likelihood of a senior user expanding into the field of a junior user, where the goods are not directly competitive; (4) the degree of distinctiveness of the mark; (5) the characteristics of prospective purchasers and the degree of care they exercise; (6) the intent of the alleged infringer and (7) evidence of actual confusion. Applying this list of factors and examining the use of the well known marks and the general look and feel of the packaging of the plaintiff's products, the Court sustained the Custom's finding of likelihood of confusion.

We can also refer to the decision opposing the registered trade mark *Who's Who in the World* for a biographical directory distributed to libraries and biographies to the names *Who's Who Worldwide Registry* and *The Who's Who of American Business Leaders* for an occupational directory, in which the Court concluded that it was unlikely that the marks could be confused, after having examined the eight factors laid down in *Polaroid Corporation* v. *Polarad Electric Corporation* (287 F. 2d 492) to assess the likelihood of confusion, i.e., (1) the strength of the mark (which was not considered relevant in this case) (2) the degree of similarity (the titles were not considered substantially similar) (3) the proximity of the products (which was considered unlikely) (4) the likelihood that the prior owner will "bridge the gap": principle intended to protect the plaintiff who may intend to enter in the defendant's market in the future (which was not the case here since the books were different even if directed to the same market) (5) actual confusion (for which no evidence was offered) (6) good faith in adopting the defendant's mark (the fact to take advantage of the expression "Who's Who" was not prohibited since it was not protectable) (7) the quality of the defendant's products (which were considered inferior) (8) the sophistication of the buyers (the publishers would sell to professional buyers who would not not be easily confused (*Reed Publishing (USA) Inc.* v. *Who's Who Worldwide Registry*, District Court, ED New York No. CV 92-3959 (DFJ).

[26] In France, Plasseraud, Dehaut, Plasseraud, "Marques", Ed. Lefebvre, 1994, p. 240; Cass. com. 10.5.1988, RDPI 1988 No. 19 p. 103; Cass. com. 7.6.1988, Annales 1989 p. 27; Cass. com. 23.1.1990, D. 1993.114; CA Paris 25.1.1988, Annales 1989 p. 125. In Germany, Baumbach Hefermehl, Warenzeichengesetz, 12 Auf., § 31, 29; Sana/Scosana, GRUR 1993, p. 272. In Switzerland, BGE 100 II 416, 1974. In Italy, Vanzetti/Di Cataldo, Manuale di diritto industriale, 1996, p. 191.

6.1.2. The Memory of the Consumers
Much national case law affirms the principle that the comparison has to be made between the junior trade mark and the image of the senior trade mark which exist in the memory of the consumer. However, as mentioned above (point 6.1.1) the general principle states that the first element of comparison is the senior trade mark as registered. Now one suggests that the image of the senior trade mark in the memory of the consumers is to be considered. It is difficult to see how two principles can co-exist as they oppose each other.

6.1.3. The Overall Impression of the Trade Mark
In assessing confusion between a simple mark and a complex mark, it is necessary to proceed on the basis of a summary rather than an analytical examination. In other words, all the elements of the sign on the first impression that they may have are to be taken into account, and not on the exclusive basis of the element having the most distinguishing force[27](see however point 6.1.4. below).

The Swedish Court of Appeal protected a registered trade mark even if the used mark was not entirely identical with the registration. Reversing the decision of the City Court of Stockolm, the Court concluded that McDonald's Corp. used mark *Big Mac* was not different from the registered form *Big Mac* since the differences referred to elements which did not change its distinctive character. The Supreme Court confirmed this decision. The Court considered that the visual and audible differences were not important. Even if the word "Big" is more emphasised in the mark when written in two words, most Swedish speak English and would be able to distinguish the two elements even if they were put together (*McDonald's Corp.* v. *Max AB*, Supreme Court; in [1992] 8 EIPR D-161).

[27] The Swiss case law held that for an evaluation of the danger of confusion it has to be considered that the memorised image is vague due to the course of time, since the consumer generally does not have both signs before his eyes at the same time, see BGE 93 II 265 (1967) *Brisemarine/Blue Marine* – likelihood of confusion affirmed; BGE 95 II 194 (1969) *Tobler Mint/Polar Menthe* – likelihood of confusion denied.

See Italian Supreme Court, 22.1.1992 No. 782, Gir. Ann. Dir. Ind. 1993, No. 3017; in Germany, BGH GRUR 1976, 353 – *Colorboy*; GRUR 1991, 319 – *Cliff Hurrican/Hurricane*; GRUR 1986, 72 – *Tabac/Tabacco d'Harar*; BGH GRUR Int. 1996, Heft 1, 60; in France, see case law: Cour de Paris, 22.10.1964, Ann. 1965, p. 204; Cour de Paris, 11.12.1975, Ann. 1976, p. 161; Cour de Nîmes, 12.10.1982, Ann. 1983, p. 106; Cour de Cassation, 15.4.1986, Ann. 1987, p. 60; in Australia, *The Shell Company of Australia Ltd v. Esso Standard Oil (Australia) Ltd* (1963) 109 CLR 407; in Switzerland, BGE 88 II 381, 1962 – *Tobler-o-Rum/Torero-Rum*.

The Supreme Court of Finland held that the question of confusing similarity of the trade names of companies must be decided upon the total impression which the trade names make among the persons who use the services of the parties. The Court found that the name *Papula Rein Lahtela Oy* is not confusingly similar with *Leena Rein & Pirjo Lahtela Oy*, even though both companies are intellectual property agents as their clients should be able to note the dissimilarity in the parties' trade names (*Leena Rein & Pirjo Lahtela Oy* v. *Papula Rein Lahtela Oy*, Supreme Court, 30.3.1990, KKO 1990: 41).

The generic part of the trade mark is not to be excluded in the comparison of two trade marks. In a case opposing the trade mark *Rives* for drinks to the trade mark *Cocoribe*, also for drinks, the Spanish Supreme Court considered that the trade marks should be compared as a whole without disregarding the generic element and concluded that they were incompatible (*Destileria de Guadalete SL* v. *National Distillers & Chemical Corporation*, First Chamber, Supreme Court, 29.6.1993, Aranzadi No. 5225, 6682.

6.1.4. Similarities Are More Important Than Differences

Generally speaking, similarities are considered more important than differences.[28] Likelihood of confusion therefore should only be accepted if it is the common elements which give the infringed trade mark its distinctiveness.[29]

Also, the US Court of Appeals for the Federal Circuit reversed the decision of the US Patent and Trade mark Office which had refused registration of the mark *Varga Girl* for calendars because it could be confused with the previous registered trade mark *Vargas* for calendars and other materials without regard to the word "girl" considered as merely descriptive (In re Hearst Corp., US Court of Appeals for the Federal Circuit Newman J, 25 USPQ 2d 1238 (Fed. Circ. 1992)). On the contrary, the Court held that the component "girl" made a significant contribution to the appearance, sound and commercial impression of the mark Varga Girl.

However, in a Norwegian case, the Court found that by an overall evaluation the impression of the defendant's label, *Monte Carlo* and the plaintiff's label *Casino* for the same type of beverage, were so similar that risk of confusion was held to exist. The two marks *Casino* and *Monte Carlo*, although different, had a common connotation (moreover, the products were marketed in identical standard bottles where the distinguishing element is the label), *Nora Mineralvann A/S* v. *A.S. Brusetten*, 1 June 1987, Uttalelser fra Konkurranseutvalget, No. 28).

Austrian case law affirms that in the case where the trade marks are composed of more than one word, only one word is normally noted and that determines the overall impression (OPM 11.12.1991, BPI 1992, 206 *W Linea Wally's/Bally*).

[28] In Germany, see BGH GRUR 1993, 118 – *Corvaton/Corvasal*; GRUR 1995, 216 – *Oxygenol II*; in Austria, PGH 5.7.1961, PBI 1962, 78, *Marcel Guerlain maison fondée* en 1923 Paris – Guerlain. See however: NA 5.9.1984, PBI 1986, 147, *Jean Pascal/Jean Patou*. In France, Cour de Paris, 17.12.1951, Ann. 1952, p. 7; Cour de Paris, 13.7.1974, Ann. 1974, p. 129; Cour de Paris 5.7.1983, Ann. 1983, p. 150; in Benelux, Tribunal de Liège, 9.6.1982, Ing. Cons., 1982, p. 154; Prés. arr. Breda, 16.12.1988, B.I.E., 1989, 188; Prés. Comm. Charleroi, 11.2.1994, Ing. Cons., 1994, p. 249. In Italy, Tribunal of Rom, 29.11.1972, Giur. Ann. Dir. Ind., 1972, 208; Court of Appeal of Florence, 13.12.1972, *ibidem*, 1972, 213; Tribunal of Milan, 5.10.1978, *ibidem*, 1078.

[29] The City Court of Helsinki considered that the product name *Känniset* could be confused with the trade mark *Känni-Kalat* used for sherry-spiced Baltic herring and granted an injunction against its use. The Court considered that the catchword in the product name *Känniset* i.e., Känni, was identical to the plaintiff's registered trade mark *Känni-Kalat*, in which the word Känni represented the distinctive part of the trade mark; the prefix "set" in the defendant's product named *Känniset* was not independently distinctive. (Moreover, the product marketed by the defendants was in practice almost identical to the plaintiff's and its marketing was directed to the same group of consumer (*ÅAke Törnroos* v. *Railo Olavi Niemi & Riitta Anna-maija Häyrynen*, City Court of Helsinki, 3.6.1992; in [1994] 10 EIPR D-260).

The US Court in *Express Funding, Inc.* v. *Express Mortgage, Inc.* US 34 USPQ 2d Vol. 34, No. 12 at 1801, concluded that the marks *Express Funding* and *Express Mortgage* for mortgages services, at the wholesale and retail/wholesale level respectively, were likely to cause confusion among consumers. The Court confirmed that the most significant or dominant feature must be given greater effect in order to determine the similarity between the two marks. To determine whether the marks would be confusingly similar to the public, they must be viewed in their entirety. The Court found that the element *Express* was the dominant feature because the remainder of the marks were genuine terms, distinguishing their marks from other marks. The plaintiff's and defendant's marks could therefore be confused.

6.2. Criteria For Comparison

6.2.1. Importance of Distinctiveness for Scope of Protection

The more a trade mark is known, the greater is the chance that the consumer can relate his recollection of the older trade mark to the recent trade mark.

A lot of emphasis is generally placed on the distinction between "strong" and "weak" marks (even by decisions that do not explicitly formulate the principle).[30] Strong marks are generally those which "do not reveal anything about the type of product they distinguish", imaginative marks (e.g. KODAK for films), or otherwise contrived marks. Weak marks on the other hand are conceptually linked to the product in some way, have otherwise poor distinctive capacity, or "while not being identified with the generic name, easily suggest the product they distinguish".[31] The difference is vital for the scope of protection conferred. It is well-established that a strong mark enjoys wider protection – thus even substantial variants of it, where they leave the essential identity of the type intact, will be

---

There are also cases where the differentiating features of a trade mark will make the strongest impression. In a case before the South Africa Supreme Court (*Lotto S.p.A.* v. *National Converter Industries (Pty) Ltd.*, Supreme Court of South Africa, (BR Du Plessis, J), 23.3.1994), the Court concluded that there was no risk of confusion between the appellant's device mark and the respondent's device even if both were bound by a central parallelogram and relating to the same goods, because the differentiating features resulting from the "general impression or total effect" of the trade marks (i.e., the angular shape in the first case and the rounded shape in the other) made the visual impression strongest.

The right to the trade mark is also affected when a particular word or title is found literally and in a recognisable form in another trade mark, even if another term is added (see for example, the trade mark *Anti-Monopoly* which was prohibited because of its similarity with the trade mark *Monopoly*, Hoge Raad, 24.6.1977, B.I.E., 1978, p 39).

Prefixes are normally considered more important than suffixes in the evaluation of confusing similarities. In a case opposing the trade mark *Libene* to the registered trade mark *Libeno* in respect of cosmetics, the Norwegian Patent Office, however, decided after an overall evaluation of the marks that there was no risk of confusion nor that the public would believe that the products had the same origin. Moreover, the suffixes Ene and Eno differ both visually and phonetically so much that the two marks would be distinguished by the consumers (Beiersdorf AG's Application, Opposition by Astra AB, Patent Office 1st Division, 7.2.1995; in [1995] 4 EIPR D-102).

See also the German case law: BGH GRUR 1965, 183, 185 – *Derma*; GRUR 1990, 453 – *L-Thyroxin*.

[30] For example, French jurisprudence does not recognise explicitly the criterion by which a trade mark is considered strong or weak (Cour de Paris 6.7.1971, Ann. 1972, p. 34; TGI Paris 20.12.1982, PIBD 1983, No. 318, III, 53; TGI Paris 28.2.1994, PIBD 1994, No. 568, III, 330). Thus, in France, all registered trade marks benefit from the same level of protection. The judge does examine, however, whether the older trade mark has a distinctive character, taken on its own or in one of its elements (cfr. TGI Paris 1.12.1969, PIBD 1970, No. 38, III, 123; TGI Paris 16.12.1971, PIBD 1972, No. 83, III, 153; Court of Paris 20.5.1986, Ann. 1987, p. 45; Court of Orléans 13.9.1988, Ann. 1990, p. 18; TGI Paris 9.11.1988, RDPI No. 22, p. 73). On this point, see J. Baumgartner, "Le risque de confusion en matière de marques", Lausanne, 1970, p. 60.

[31] So the Italian Supreme Court, Cassazione 2.8.1990, decision No. 7768, Giur. Ann. Dir. Ind., 1990, 2476, e.g., the *Seven Up* mark.

infringements.[32] Weak marks only need slight changes to prevent infringement, since the expressive element at the core must remain at the disposal of everyone.[33]

[32] Di Cataldo, I segni distintivi, 1993, p. 73 (e.g., *Rochas/Simon Rochas* for perfumes, *Inver/Invercolour* for paints). In Italy, the following trade marks were considered "strong": *Fruit of the loom* (Tribunal of Rom, 31.8.1979, Giur. Ann. Dir. Ind., 1979, 1209); *Buondì* (Court of Appeal of Venice, 30.9.1977, Giur. Ann. Dir. Ind., 1977, 970); *Wrangler* (Tribunal of Naples, 4.4.1986, Giur. Ann. Dir. Ind., 1978, 2031) and were considered infringed by *Fruit goods for you, Bonny* and *Wyngler jeans*. See also Italian Supreme Court, 13.10.1975, decision No. 3279, Giur. Ann. Dir. Ind., 1975, 690.

In Austria, in the same sense: OGH 14.6.1994, 4 Ob 61/94, 12 – V – *Alpha Motor/Alfa*. In Germany, BGH GRUR 1988, 635, 636 – *Grundcommerz*. In Benelux, Arrêt *Juicy* Fruit, 5.10.1982, Ing. Cons., 1982, 221. In Swiss, Federal Tribunal, ATF 73 II 188 (1947), *Alpina/Alps*.

The Canadian Federal Court affirms in Miss Universe, Inc. c. Bohna (1994, [1995] 1 C.F. 614 (C.A.F.) that "the more a trade mark is known, from the point of publicity and use, the greater is its protection".

[33] In Italy, the following trade marks were considered "weak": *Fluimucil* (Court of Appeal of Milan, 12.1.1979, Giur. Ann. Dir. Ind., 1979, 1159); *Bergamon* (Court of Appeal of Rom, 27.10.1980, Giur. Ann. Dir. Ind., 1980, 1344); *Amplifon* (Tribunal of Catania, 17.5.1976, Giur. Ann. Dir. Ind., 1976, 833); *Playboy* (Court of Appeal of Milan, 19.6.1973, Giur. Ann. Dir. Ind., 1973, 353) and were considered not infringed by *Lisomucil, Bergasol, Udifon, Playmen*. Moreover, the Italian Courts have held that *Donna/Donna Più* for women's magazines, *Dermax/Dermadex* for dermatitis medicines do not create confusion. See also, Supreme Court, 28.10.1982, decision No. 5633, Giur. Ann. Dir. Ind., 1982, 1474; 20.11.1982, decision No. 6262, *ibidem*, 1982, 1477.

In Austria: OPM 21.6.1989, PBI 1990, 88, *Supersan/Sanco and Sosanco*; OGH 14.6.1977, 4 Ob 330/77, ÖBI 1977, 126, *His/h.i.s.*

Similarly, the Danish Supreme Court considered that the trade mark *Mars Gold* did not infringe the trade marks *Gold Nougat*, *Gold Toffee* or *Golden bar* and that there was no risk of confusion. The Court found that the plaintiff had established the non-distinctive word "Gold" as a trade mark – albeit weak – for chocolate. However, the word "Gold" made up a part of a compound trade mark (see below), the significant part of which was the other word "Mars". (*Toms Chokolade AS* v. *Master Foods AS*, Supreme Court, 18.12.1992, UfR 1993 at 158; in [1993] 8 EIPR D-180). In Germany, BGH GRUR 1989, 349, 350 – *Roth- Händle-Kentucki/Cenduggy*.

The Swiss Federal Tribunal in the case Clix/Clip (ATF 80 II 174 (1954), affirmed *"Celui qui choisit une marque qui rappelle une designation de choses appartenet au domaine public et qui constitue de ce fait une marque dite faible, doit en supporter les conséquences"*. Therefore the likelihood of confusion between the trade marks *Clix and Clip* for Zip was excluded.

The Benelux Court of Justice, in the decision *Juicy Fruit*, 5 October 1982 (Jur., 1981-1982, p. 20) affirmed the principle according to which the resemblance between two signs *"peut dépendre du pouvoir qu'a ce signe d'éveiller dans l'esprit du public des associations avec les marques; qu'il suit de ce qui précède qu'un rapport existe bien entre le pouvoir distinctif de la marque et l'étendue de la protection qui s'y attache; qu'en effet, une marque dotée d'un pouvoir distinctif faible, qui remplit donc la fonction prémentionée moins bien qu'une marque à pouvoir distinctif plus grand, se rappellera moins facilement au souvenir du public par l'emploi d'un autre signe. (...) Le pouvoir distinctif d'une marque contribue à déterminer l'étendue de la protection qui s'y attache en ce sens qu'à mesure que ce pouvoir distinctif s'affaiblit, il doit exister une ressemblance plus grande entre la marque et un signe pour pouvoir qualifier ce signe de ressemblant"*.

It is said that the risk of confusion is greater in the case of a well-known trade mark, especially where the goods to which the well-known trade mark and the infringing mark referred to are similar.[34] However, one may also argue that the well-known trade mark should be given a minor protection as it is unlikely that the consumer could be deceived or confused by the imitation. In fact, there are at least two reasons for giving wider protection to well-known trade marks; firstly to avoid dilution and secondly to protect consumers from being bombarded by too many similar trade marks.

[34] By applying unfair competition principles, the Spanish Supreme Court considered that there was a similarity and therefore a risk of confusion between the plaintiff's registered trade marks *Baileys* and its label and the label of the whisky bottles, which the defendant manufactured and sold under the name *Seget*. The Court took into account the fact that the registered trade mark was well-known in the market and deserved special protection. Therefore, the infringer, by imitating the registered trade mark of the original holder, took advantage of his sales efforts (*R and A Baileys & Co. Ltd.* v. *Licorera Albedense SL*, Supreme Court (first Chamber) 19.5.1993, Editorial Aranzasi 3804, at 4857; in [1994] 1 EIPR D-13).

Furthermore, the English High Court of the Vice Chancellor in *Guccio Gucci S.p.A.* v. *Paolo Gucci*, (16.10.1990) recognises the good will of luxury brand names and confirms that a man who has the same name as a famous brand has no absolute right to use it on his goods. In this case, Paolo Gucci, one of Guccio Gucci's grand-children planned to mark a range of goods from ties, furs and underwear to table lamps and car interiors with a shield device and the words *Paolo Designed by Paolo Gucci* and to sell these goods through up-market retail outlets in the UK. Paolo Gucci claimed that in the United States, even if he had been prohibited from using his name as a trade mark, he had been permitted to use the slogan *Designed by Paolo Gucci* in conjunction with another trade mark according to some strict guidelines laid down by the Court. The Vice-Chancellor granted injunctions for trade mark infringement and passing off (and noticed that Paolo Gucci was not complying with the US guidelines). The Vice-Chancellor, considering the strength of the brand name *Gucci*, concluded that the use by Paolo Gucci of the mark *Gucci* could cause confusion among customers as to the origin of the goods. He based its conclusions on its own visual comparison between the get-up used by Gucci and Paolo Gucci, a market survey carried out on the shopping streets of London, Bath and Manchester interviewing approximately 1,200 people, on evidence of potential customers and trade witnesses like Chanel, Ralph Lauren, Mary Quant and Dunhill. The case also confirms that a defendant cannot plead the use of his own name as a defence to a passing off action where the name is being applied to goods. It is interesting to note that this position is in some contrast to that in the United States (in [1991] 1 EIPR D-14 and see the Comment by A. Carboni, in [1991] 2 EIPR 65).

Likewise, the registration of the mark *Dominique Arpels* for jewellery goods was denied to the person of the same name in Hong Kong (*Dominique Arpels* v. *Van Cleef and Arpels SA*; in [1993] 1 EIPR D-8) since it could be confused with the well-known trade mark *Van Cleef & Arpels* for the same goods. The judge came to this conclusion after comparing the marks as a whole and considering the facts of the case, i.e.: the respective goods were likely to be sold in the same type of outlet and the potential customers were the same even if

Dominique Arpels' design were more modern and could be cheaper. Furthermore, due to the previous family relations, there was an assumption that a connection between the marks would be made (Dominique Arpels's great uncle, Louis Arpel, worked as a jewellery designer with Van Cleef for 12 years before establishing his own jewellery design business) and the name "Arpels" retained sufficient significance to be recognised on its own as the Van Cleef & Arpels trade mark. It was held that the additional care that a purchaser of expensive jewellery was likely to give was not sufficient to remove the likelihood of confusion between the marks.

The Hong Kong Court of Appeal also considered that there was a very high risk of confusion between the mark *Borsalini* and the well-known trade mark *Borsalino* for the same kind of goods with the consequence that the public could be seriously inconvenienced if both marks were registered and despite the honesty of the concurrent use by the respondent (*Borsalino Giuseppe & Fratello S.p.A.* v. *Wong Wai Sum*, HKMP No. 2443 of 1992; in [1993] 9 EIPR D-210).

See also American case, *Nina Ricci SARL* v. *ETF Enterprises Inc.* (Court of Appeals, Federal Circuit, 15.11.1989, 12 USPQ 2d 1901) where the registration of the mark *Vittorio Ricci* for the same or related goods as *Nina Ricci* was rejected as it was considered to be likely to cause confusion.

The German Federal Supreme Court justifies the greater protection afforded to well-known trade marks on the presumption that purchasers who are used to a well-known trade mark pay little attention to the differences and therefore, the risk of confusion is higher (BGH GRUR 1988, 635, 636 Grundkommerz). See however: BGH GRUR 1989, 349, 350 – *Roth-Händle- Kentucky/Cenduggy*. It must be noted that § 14, II, No. 3 of the German Trade Mark Act of 1995 is newly introduced to protect the mark against the use of identical or similar signs for non-similar goods/services, in the case where the mark is "well-known" in the domestic market and the junior sign is used of in an unfair way which exploits or distorts the distinctiveness of the senior mark. This provision, arguably, replaces German case law according to which "famous marks" enjoyed protection against diluition and "well-known" marks enjoyed protection against unfair distortion or exploitation of the reputation. This new provision could even broaden such protection by requiring only lower degrees of notoriety.

Also in Denmark, well-known marks are said to possess a wider scope of protection, *Ipalco/Icopal* (Law Reports 1970/ 69H); *Lego/Logos*.

Under Austrian law, the protection of well-known trade marks is limited to confusion of the signs and the similarity of the goods (OGH 27.3.1957 ÖBI 74, *Solodent/Solo*). Therefore, the use of a sign which is already used by others for different goods does not give rise to risk of confusion. Nevertheless, under certain circumstances, for example, when the use of the junior trade mark can potentially devalue the senior trade mark, the senior trade mark is protected. OGH 23.11.1955, 3 Ob 564, ÖBI 1956, 17, "Nimm DARMOL du fühlst dich wohl" – "Täglich UNDERBERG und du fühlst dich wohl – Magenbitter".

It is interesting to note that, from time to time, Mexican courts have extended protection to well-known trade marks in situations involving goods that are not similar (e.g., *Cadillac* as applied to automobiles and clothing; *Omega* as applied to watches and to machinery and tools; *Marlboro* as applied to tobacco products and to clothing; *Chanel* as applied to perfume and clothing, G.E. as applied to electric equipment and hardware and plumbing supplies. See H. Rangel-Ortiz, "Protection of well-known Marks in Mexico", The Trade Marks Reporter Vol. 78, No. 2, March-April 1988, p. 219.

The Swedish Supreme Court in a case on interlocutory injunction (NJA 1995, p. 635, *Galliano*) stated that a member state is allowed to extend protection also to products or services that were not identical with or similar to those, for which the trade mark had been registred but that doing so, a more strict standard regarding the similarity of the trade mark and the sign may be applied.

6.2.2. Sound Sight and Meaning

Confusion may also arise from phonetic similarity,[35] visual similarity,[36] and similarity of meaning.[37] Consideration should be taken of the "phonetic or

[35] The marks *Rysta/Aristoc* have been considered confusingly similar in the UK. Likewise, in Australia, *Revise/Levi's* both for jeans are found to be phonetically similar (*Wingate Marketing Pty Ltd.* v. *Levi Strauss & Co* (1994) 121 ALR 191).

In France, the Court of Paris considered the existence of a phonetic risk of confusion between the trade marks *Skip* and *Keep 3000* (Court of Paris 6.12.1988, Ann. 1990, p.18). By the same token, the Tribunal de Grande Instance de Paris decided that there was a risk of confusion between *Millemont and Richemont* (TGI 25.10.1991, PIBD 1992, No. 517, III, 147; the Paris Court decided for the risk of confusion between the trade marks *T.E.A.* and *Tesa* (Court of Paris 6.12.1988, Ann. 1990, p. 18); and the Court of Aix-en-Provence decided for the risk of confusion between *Jaz* and *Maz* (Court of Aix-en-Provence 1.3.1974, Ann. 1974, p. 264).

The Spanish Supreme Court considered that there was no sufficient phonetic similarity between the defendants name *Nutrec*, SA and the plaintiff's registered trade mark and trading name *Nutrexpa*, SA (*Nutrexpa, SA* v. *Nutrec, SA*, Supreme Court (1st Chamber), 16.5.1995, Aranzadi 4080, at 5435 and onward; in [1996] 1 EIPR D-25).

In South Korea, the Supreme Court decided that the trade mark *Gliss* was not confusingly similar with the country *Greece* either from the point of view of appearance or phonetics, IIC Vol. 20 No. 2/1989 p. 268.

Differences between languages can influence the decision on whether there is any risk of confusion or not. For example, the Supreme Administrative Court of Finland (2.2.1995, 5574/94) reversed the decision of the Finnish Patent Office and its Board of Appeal, considering that between the trade marks *Navy* and *Nany* there was no risk of confusion even if related to similar goods, because in the Finnish language a difference of one letter only serves to keep the meaning of short words apart from each other (moreover the court established that in this case there were major differences in the pronunciation of the trade marks in question), in [1996] 4 EIPR D-101.

The assessment of the risk of confusion between two marks due to their pronunciation will therefore differ depending on the language of the country in which the comparison will be made. The case of Japan seems to be the most complicated for foreign trade marks owners since the Japanese pronunciation differs totally from the occidental one as it does not use alphabets. John Kakinuki in his interesting article "Topics in Japanese Trade mark Law" (in [1994] 3 EIPR 103) examines this problem and gives some rules used in Japanese case law to assess similarity between two marks (i.e., based on the similarities/differences between syllables, vowels and consonants depending on their pronunciation in Japanese and on the total impression of the marks) and offers some interesting examples distinguishing between *"short"* and *"long marks"*. For example the marks *Dunhill/Runhill*, *J'aime/Shame*, *Librium/Levelume*, *Blistex/Britex* have been considered to be similar.

[36] In France the following trade marks have been regarded as visually confusing: *Brig* and *Brio* (Court of Paris, 7.3.1975, Ann. 1975, p. 247) and *Alagan* and *Allergan* (TGI Paris, 6.11.1991, PIBD 1992, No. 517, III, 153).

[37] As an example of meaning, a recent case found confusion in the UK between *Ocean Pearl/Sea Pearl*. The Hungarian Metropolitan Court (Aramis Inc's Aplication to register Ocean Surge, Metropolitan Court; in [1996] 1 EIPR D-13) also considered that the mark *Ocean Surge* could be confused with *Ocean* both for cosmetics goods. Confusing similarity lays in the first element of the mark, i.e., "Ocean" which is well-known to the average Hungarian consumer and does not present difficulties in interpretation. As far as the second element is concerned, i.e., "Surge", it will have no meaning for non English speakers who will only remember the first element "Ocean" and, for English speakers, they will believe that the product might be a variant of another marked with the "Ocean" word element.

graphic impression" that will normally be produced among consumers instead of searching for their deep and detailed meaning.[38] Problems may arise when marks having a phonetic similarity refer to different commercial activities. Some decisions prefer to deny confusion in such cases,[39] others affirm it.[40]

Semantic confusion has also been considered.[41] The risk of confusion can also be made up of more than one of these possibilities: phonetic, visual and semantic similarities[42] and from a graphic representation of a verbal element,[43] or vice versa.[44]

There are no reliable rules in Switzerland in deciding if the meaning of the word may cause confusion. In *Alps/Alpina*, the coinciding meaning was decisive for the affirmation of the likelihood of confusion (BGE 73 II 186 f. 1947) whereas in *Quick/Blick* (BGE 87 II 44, 1961), the different meaning of the words was the crucial factor for the denial of the likelihood of confusion.

The risk of confusion arising from meanings is not shared by every country, for example, the words *Tornado/Cyclone* used in the AIPPI survey on the Evaluation of Confusion, was found to cause confusion in the United States but not in Finland (AIPPI, Montreal 1995, Report Q 127, p. 105 and 111). See also footnote 46 on translation.

[38] In *Nutrexpa, SA* v. *Nutrec, SA* (Spanish Supreme Court (1st Chamber), 16.5.1995, Aranzadi 4080, at 5435 and onward), the Court compared the entirety of the syllables and letters forming the words of the trade marks in question, giving less value to those elements with a weaker differentiating function than those elements which have a special distinguishing effect.

[39] The Spanish Supreme Court of Justice considered that there was no visual risk of confusion between the defendant's trading name *Dobleuve, SL* and the plaintiff's trade mark *DOBLE-V* (*Hiram Wlaker Europe, SA* v. *Dobleuve, SL*, Supreme Court (3rd Chamber), 14.7.1995, Aranzadi 5892 at 7880). The Court considered that even if they had a phonetic similarity, they referred to different commercial activities; in [1996] 3 EIPR D-79).

[40] The Danish Maritime and Commercial Court considered that there was a risk of confusion between the device of a manufacturer of tools, used for a company logo, and the registered trade mark device by another manufacturer of drills, for drills and other tools, because they were visually similar even if they had a different meanings (*Sneholt & Nielsen A/S* v. *The Patent Appeal Board*, 22.3.1994, UfR 1994, p. 602; in [1994] 11 EIPR D-287).

[41] For example the synonyms (e.g., *Coup de Coeur/Coup de Foudre*, TGI Paris, 10.7.1986, PIBD 1986, III, 396), or use of the same idea (e.g., *Subito/Pronto*, Court of Paris, 9.3.1955, Ann. 1955, p. 160).

[42] For example *Biscuit/Biscotte* (TGI Paris, 16.9.1988, PIBD 1989, No. 449, III, 92).

The Spanish Supreme Court has thus considered that the trade mark *Pla natal* did not infringe the trade mark *Prenatal* as they differ in their structural composition, in the phonetic and were pronounced in a different way; they also differ visually as they were written in different type letters and had different colours (*Prenatal SA* v. *José P*, Supreme Court (First Chamber) 22.10.1992, Aranzadi 8593, 11296; in [1993] 7 EIPR D-161).

[43] For example, the name *Tour Eiffel* represented by an image of the Eiffel Tower (Court of Paris, 19.5.1993, PIBD 1993, No. 551, 111, 553).

[44] The title *Aigle* instead of an image of an eagle (Court of Aix-en-Provence, 20.5.1935, Ann. 1936, p. 14).

There is no hierarchy in the various risks of confusion and there are no fixed rules as to which element – sound, sight or meaning – should prevail, as this will vary from case to case.[45]

[45] For Italy, between *Cassera/Carrera*, confusion was found due to strong similarity in both phonetic and graphic term but not between *Chicco/Chico* due to the different figurative element. See also Italian Supreme Court, 13.2.1980, No. 1043, Giur. Ann. Dir. Ind., 1980, No. 1252; Court of Appeal of Milan, 22.12.1987, *ibidem*, 1987, No. 2222; Italian Supreme Court, 6.3.1995, No. 2578, *ibidem*, 1995, No. 3195. The judgement of the likelihood of confusion between marks must be made "comprehensively and synthetically, with a unitary and overall examination and appreciation of all the salient features of the mark; phonetic, visual"(Court of Modena 8.11.1985, Giur. Ann. Dir. Ind., 1985, No. 1966).

For German case law, see, BGH GRUR 1959, 183 – *Quick/Glück*; GRUR 1992, 130, 132 – *Bally/Ball*; GRUR 1975, 487 – *WMF-Mondmännchen*; GRUR 1976, 143 – *Biovital*; GRUR 1979, 853 – *Lil*.

In Australia, see *Deeko Australia Pty Ltd.* v. *The Decor Corporation Pty Ltd.* (1988) AIPC 90-479 where it said that in the case of services offered over the telephone, aural similarity would have more weight, however, where the goods are selected by the customers with little intervention by sales staff, visual differences would carry more weight.

In some countries, e.g., Denmark, Sweden and the United States, it is said that visual impression is the most important criteria in evaluating confusion, this is followed by phonetic impression. Meaning is less important for the evaluation of confusion.

In Denmark, the meaning of these words: *Crown/Corona*; *Lui/H.i.s*; *Deres/Yours*; *Den lille Havfrue/The Little Mermaid*, do not have much weight as they are visually and phonetically different. In Sweden, sight similarity was found to cause confusion in *Bi/BiC* and *Tenderelle/TEND*; in the United States, visual similarity is found between *Quirst/Squirt*; *Cattier/Cartier*; likewise in Canada where a finding of confusion based solely on similarity of meaning are rare.

However, under Austrian case law, the meaning of the word is said to be the most important element, NA 20.1.1981, Nm 4/79, PBI 1981, 118, *Panda/Pansan*; OPM 9.2.1983, PBI 168, *Mary's/ Mars*; 12.1.1994, Om 9/93, Immunine – Imukin; 27.4.1988, PBI 1989, 22, *Taffeta/Taft*. For example, in an Austrian Supreme Court case, the actual meaning of words in a mark was held to create adequate distinctiveness, despite visual and phonetic similarity, *Herholz/Wertholz*; in [1989] 7 EIPR D-117.

The German Federal Supreme Court has recently raised a preliminary question to the European Court of Justice asking if there is a risk of confusion between *wenn/bild* as the two marks have the same meaning although there are not visually similar (BGH, GRUR 1996, 198 – *springende Raubkatze* – Vorlagebeschluß).

In Switzerland, the Federal Court stated that the overall impression consisting of sound, sight and meaning had to be regarded as a whole but that the consumer kept the sound and the meaning more easily in mind, *Lego/Logi* (SMI I 1985, S.70).

6.2.3. Translations

Article 6 *bis* (1) of the Paris Convention not only provides for protection of well-known trade marks against reproduction or imitation, but also protects them against translation "liable to create confusion", notwithstanding the fact that the marks are not registered. As far as it concerns normal trade marks (not well-known), national jurisdictions generally recognise protection against the confusing translation of a trade mark.[46]

6.2.4. Family Trade mark

In Germany, confusion regarding a series of trade marks is in general only be considered under the double requirement that the marks being compared have the same or essentially the same prefix or suffix, and that this has distinguishing character for the user.[47] Also in the UK family marks with distinctive common elements are given stronger protection; if a trader owns several marks with a common prefix or suffix, and no other trader owns a mark of this type for the goods in question, he probably has exclusive rights in the prefix or suffix.[48]

[46] Translation into one of the Benelux languages is considered a form of imitation (Article 13 (C) Benelux Trade Mark Law). In Benelux, as far as other languages are concerned, it is up to the court to judge if there is an actual resemblance between the senior trade mark and the junior translation; for example, *She* was judged to be a copy of the Dutch title *Zij* (The Hague 28.6.1973, B.I.E., 1974, 163; Pres. Comm Bxl, 26.9.1975, Ing.cons, 1975, 254); Resemblance was affirmed between *Zeeslag and Battaglia navale* (The Hague, 5.1.1977, B.I.E., 1978, 244).

Germany protects trade marks from such kind of infringement. Examples of translations in which German Courts have found likelihood of confusion are *Lion/Löwe*; *Spring Garden/Frühlingsgarticleen*; *Ranger/Farmer*; *Botschafter/Ambassadeur*.

Similar protection is found in Canada, the United States and Switzerland; in Canada, confusion is found between *Rouge Royale/Royal Red*; *Mouton Noir & Design/Black Sheep & Design*; *Left Bank & Design/Rive Gauche*; in the United States, confusion was found between *Good Morning/Buenos Dias*.

In Switzerland, confusion was found between *Blaustern/Star* (BGE 63 II 285, 1937) and furthermore, the likelihood of confusion of wordmarks in only one of the four Swiss national languages is sufficient to render the younger mark inadmissible for the whole country, *Compact/Compactus* (BGE 84 II 317, 1958).

In Austria, translation is protected only if such translation is within the knowledge of the average Austrian consumer (OPM 27.4.1988, PBI 1989, 22, *Taffeta/Taft*; OGH 5.10.1976, 4 Ob 364/76, ÖBI 199, 40, *Grotta Azzurra/ Blaue Grotte* for a restaurant).

However, Denmark does not afford such protection to translation, the Danish Court did not find confusion between *Mars Gold/Guld-Barre*.

[47] A case in which confusion was found in Germany involved a series of medicinal and pharmaceutical products carrying the prefix *"Abbo-"* and another series in the same field with the prefix *"Abo-"* (BGH GRUR 1989, 350).

[48] See *McDonald's Corporation, USA and McDonald's Restaurant Denmark* v. *Allan Bjerrum Pedersen, cit.* footnote 22. In the United States, family mark in general enjoy heightened protection, e.g., *McSleep/McDonald*; *Phone-r-Us/Toy "r" Us*.

6.2.5. Conditions under which the senior trade mark has been used

a) Elements which were not registered with the trade mark, because they were not distinctive, will be taken into consideration in judging the risk of confusion, but not distinctive elements which were not registered.[49]

b) If the trade mark law cannot be invoked, the solution may be found by application of other rules, such as the rules of unfair competition.[50]

Similarly, in Canada and Japan, the McDonald's family of marks is protected where the prefixes Mc & Mac used by third parties are held to be confusing. Similarly, in Austria (OMP 10.2.1993, ÖBI 1994, 27, where the word MacChinese was found to cause confusion with trade marks which have the prefix "Mc" or "Mac", for example, McPizza, McChicken, Big Mac). See also: OPM 27.6.1990, PBI 1991, 119, *Lady Boss/Boss*; 24.4.1991, PBI 1991, 193 – Alpo.

The Maritime and Commercial Court of Copenhagen considered that there was a risk of confusion between the American well-known trade marks of *McDonald's* initiating with "Mc" (McChicken, McRib, McPizza, etc.) and the Danish trade mark *McAllan* initiating with the same prefix, since the goods sold by the defendant were similar to those of McDonald's. The Court moreover held that McDonald's trade marks were well-known in Denmark and connected to McDonald's, and that Allan Pedersen's use of the prefix "Mc" was likely to damage the distinctiveness and the reputation of these trade marks (*McDonald's Corporation, USA and McDonald's Restaurants Denmark* v. *Allan Bjerrum Pedersen,* Maritime and Commercial Court of Copenhagen, 24.8.1995; in [1995] 12 EIPR D-336).

In Finland, protection is acquired if the common element of a family mark is distinctive, e.g., *Topilar/Topipan*.

In Switzerland, the common elements of serial marks enjoy particular protection, BIC-poche, BIC-cristal; BIC-IMAC, BIC-Clic/BIG-PEN (BGE 87 II 38, 1961). A family mark has a wide protection as even if the plaintiff only owns one single mark, likelihood of confusion is affirmed if the defendant's mark creates the impression that it is a family mark of the plaintiff, *Annabelle/Annette* (BGE 102 II 126,1976).

[49] Article 12 of the Benelux Trade Mark Law provides that a distinctive sign cannot be protected as a trade mark if it is not registered.

This principle can be illustrated by a Swedish case opposing the device trade mark *MTV Music Television* to the application of registration of a device mark *MTV. Music Television* for similar goods; the first device included a disclaimer of "the text in the mark", and the application included a disclaimer of the elements *"MTV"* and the words "music television". The Patent Office considered that both mark devices were not confusingly similar and granted the application. On appeal of the opponent, the Court of Patent Appeals held that the opponent's trade mark registration did not provide protection for the unregistrable words "music television" or the combination of letters *"MTV"* and thus concluded that there was no risk of confusion. A dissenting judge however concluded that the opponent's trade mark registration included "the text" of the trade mark and concluded that there was a risk of confusion since both marks offered a highly similar overall impression. On appeal, the Supreme Administrative Court confirmed the position of the dissenting judge based on the overall impression of the marks, reversed the decision of the Court of Patent Appeals and rejected the application; in [1992] 6 EIPR D-122).

[50] Reference can be made to an Italian case in which the Pretore of Verona granted an order prohibiting the company Lidl Italia S.r.l. from using the packaging for selling and marketing its toothpaste *Sindramed*, since it could be confused by a non-specialised customer with the well-known Farmaceutici Dott. Ciccarelli toothpaste *Pasta del Capitano*, as it constituted an act of unfair competition based on Article 2598 of the Civil Code)(Farmaceutici Dr. Ciccarelli S.p.A v. Lidl Italia s.r.l., Pretura di Verona, 21.9.1992; in [1992] 11 EIPR D-238).

6.3. Other Elements of Evaluation

6.3.1. Confusion of Whom?

The risk of confusion must generally exist in the mind of the average consumer (i.e. the buyer of the product in question) of average attention who does not have the two trade marks in front of him at the same time.[51]

While the Spanish Trade Mark Law 32/1988 of 10.11.1988 does not offer adequate protection to famous brand names, Article 12 of the new Spanish Law 3/1991 of 10.1.1991 on Unfair Competition prevents the act of "exploiting another's reputation"; in [1991] 8 EIPR D-154).

Reference can also be made to a New Zealand case (*ICI Australia Operations Pty Ltd.* v. *Benjamin Moore & Co.*, Smellie J (1993) 4 NZBLC 103,068; in [1994] 5 EIPR D-113). ICI was the registered owner of the trade mark *Regal* for external house paints. Then, ICI decided to cease the use of that name and to use it for car paint. They were also reconsidering the possibility of using it for a relaunch of home paints. The defendant, a well established US company entered the New Zealand market and started to market house paints under the same name *Regal*. Moreover, the defendant used advertising material coming from the US which indicated that Regal was a registered trade mark of him (cfr. small capital R in a circle). ICI therefore sued Benjamin Moore, alleging trade mark infringement, passing off and breach of unfair competition rules, seeking an interlocutory injunction. The judge concluded that there was no trade mark infringement or passing off and declined to give an interlocutory injunction, because there was no risk of confusion since persons engaged in the trades of either house painting or car painting would not be confused and it was difficult to conceive that the average intelligent amateur purchaser of paints would be misled either. The judge however considered that the use of material indicating that *Regal* was a registered trade mark of Benjamin Moore would mislead and deceive the New Zealand public into accepting that Benjamin Moore had such registered trade mark in New Zealand, and constituted an infringement of the rules of unfair competition. Moreover, it constitutes an offence under the Trade Marks Act which relates to false representations as to the registration of trade marks. The judge therefore granted an order restraining such conduct.

See also the *Coca-Cola* decision of the Swiss Supreme Court (5.7.1990, ATF 116 II 463). The Court found that even if Coca-Cola could not invoke protection under trade mark law, it could still invoke the law against unfair competition (passing off) and the protection of its name and private sphere against the use of the Coca-Cola logo on bedclothes; in [1991] 10 EIPR D-200. In other jurisdictions, the Courts would have denied protection under the unfair competition principle due to the non competitive nature of the business.

Likewise, in *Semenzato Vittorio* v. *Omera SpA,* the defendant's industrial machine which had identical technical features to that of the plaintiff and the defendant's trade mark, Plurimatic, were not held to be slavish copying such as to cause confusion with the plaintiff's machine and trade mark, Multimatic, as the purchasers are technically qualified enough to distinguish one product from another. The Italian Court, instead held the defendant guilty of unfair competition, based on the fact that it had unfairly exploited the plaintiff's technical and commercial achievements through copying and selling the machine at a lower price; in [1990] 3 EIPR, D-47.

[51] See Court of Paris, 24.3.1973, Ann. 1973, p. 37; Court of Paris 14.6.1974, Ann. 1974 p. 259; Court of Paris, 31.5.1978, Ann. 1980, p. 90; and Court of Paris, 5.2.1985, Ann. 1986, p. 26. In the same sense in Austria: OGH 3.10.1994, PBI 1905, 28. See also: BGH GRUR 1971, 305 – Konservenzeichen II, when evaluating the risk of confusion on the food market, potential purchasers can also be taken into consideration.

6.3.2. Which Part of the Public[52]

The principle that the existence of a risk of confusion is affirmed when a non irrelevant part of the public is confused is often repeated. But it is also clear that confusion of a small part of the public is unfair and it should be sanctioned. In fact, it is not acceptable that a small part of the public, even if it is small, should be deprived of protection, nor is it acceptable that the entrepreneur should lose a small part of his sale for the reason that one of his competitors uses an identical or similar trade mark which confuses only that small group of people. A solution must be found.

The name *Neutralia* used by the subsidiary companies of the L'Oréal Group in the UK for hypo-allergenic products has been considered infringing the well-known registered trade mark *Neutrogena* in the UK used for hypo-allergenic skin preparations. In considering whether deception or confusion had been proven the Judge took into account the evidence gained from real witnesses, i.e., complaints following a Neutralia television advertisement showing the confusion between the two products and evidence given by individuals in person ("live" witnesses) considered as "real consumers" (*Neutrogena Corporation and Neutrogena (UK) Ltd.* v. *Golden Ltd and L'Oréal (UK) Ltd*, Jacob J, High Court, 19.5.1995; in [1995] 8 EIPR D-231). See also, John M. Benjamin, Purely Cosmetics The Neutrogena Passing-Off Case in [1995] 12 EIPR 604.

In another case concerning the appearance of a prosthetic cushion, the High Court affirmed that likelihood of deception or confusion of the ultimate consumer was an essential element of passing-off actions ("look- alikes"), and in this case deception as to the source. In the present case, however, there was no likelihood of deception since the consumer would buy the cushion in question for what it was and not in relation of a particular trade origin. Moreover, the cushion of the plaintiffs were expensive and were presented differently. Furthermore, they were bought with the intervention of healthcare professionals and there was no sufficient evidence proving that they would buy by source (*Hodgkinson & Corby Ltd and Roho Inc.* v. *Wards Mobility services Ltd.*, Jacob J, 20.7.1994; in [1994] 11 EIPR 494).

[52] The Australian Court held that likelihood of confusion of the whole public is not necessary and the standard adopted was that of persons of ordinary intelligence and memory (The Shell Company of Australia Ltd, footnote 20) and potential buyers of goods are not to be credited with any high perception or habitual caution (*Australia Woollen Mills Ltd.* v. *F.S. Walton & Co. Ltd.* (1937) 58 CLR 641), furthermore, infringement is deemed to have occurred when confusion is likely to occur in "a substantial protion of the public" or "in a not inconsiderable number of cases", *Southern Cross Refrigerating Company* v. *Toowoomba Foundry Pty Ltd* (1954) 91 CLR 592.

The Irish court held that a substantial member of purchasers must be or likely to be confused (*Coca-Cola Co.* v. *F. Cade & Sons Ltd.* [1957] I.R. 196. In the same sense, in Germany: BGH GRUR 1992, 110, 111 – *dipa/dib*. In France, see on this point, J. Baumgartner, "Le risque de confusion en matière de marques", Lausanne, 1970, p. 106.

The American Courts instead used the survey results to find confusion on the public. Confusion of 15% of survey respondents has been held sufficient to find infringement (Beefeater gin with sign of the *Beefeater restaurant*) but confusion of 7.6% of survey respondent is insufficient (*Miracle Whip/Yogowhip*).

In Norway, confusion on the public is affirmed, when a non insignificant part of it is mislead (Rettens Gang, 86, 1010).

The Sri Lankan Supreme Court gave a wide meaning as to what constitutes the public. It held that when the possiblity of deception or confusion of the name used is proved, the public is defined to mean the public present, prospective, local or foreign – the public at large,

If there is little confusion, this could depend on the infringing trade mark or reasons unrelated to the trade mark. If the public is confused due to the use of the trade mark, then trade mark law is to be applied. But, as we see from above, confusion of a small part of the public is not considered relevant. The small confused part of the public remains without any protection. If the public would be confused in any case independently from the trade mark, then trade mark law cannot be applied.

The solution must be sought in other area of the law and must be found in the rules of unfair competition. The behaviour leading to confusion of a small part of the public must be evaluated in the light of the general principle of unfairness.

6.3.3. Relevancy of kind of products

In the case of specific products, such as medicines, the likelihood of confusion will be assessed differently and will depend on the likelihood of confusion in the mind of professional purchasers in the field instead of normal purchasers.[53]

---

even if the customers were from two different countries and the quality of the goods – which in this case was tea – exported were different. It does not matter whether the goods were dispatched to the same destination or to two different destinations, *M.S. Hebtulabhoy & Co. Ltd.* v. *Stassen Exports Ltd & Another*; in [1989] 7 EIPR D-127.

[53] It is interesting to refer to some Canadian case law in which this matter was discussed with regard to applications for an interlocutory injunction brought before the Trial Division of the Federal Court in cases of distribution of look-alike pills that were available only by prescription. In the case *Searle Canada Inc.* v. *Novopharm Ltd.* (Federal Court of Appeal, Stone, Linden and McDonald JJA, 15.6.1994; in [1994] 11 EIPR D-285), the defendants started to sell tablets having the same active ingredient, verapamil, in 80-120-milligram tablets of identical appearance, size and shape to the corresponding tablets of the plaintiffs. The plaintiffs used the trade mark *Isoptin* for their products, where the defendants used the mark *Novo-Veramil* (even if the tablets did not bear these marks, the pharmacist would have put the appropriate trade mark on the label). The plaintiffs sued the defendants according to the Canadian Trade Marks Act for risk of confusion. A motion seeking an interlocutory injunction was brought before the Trial Division of the Federal Court. The judge concluded that the plaintiffs had raised a serious issue to be tried and that neither party had demonstrated that it would suffer substantially more irreparable harm than the other should the injunction be granted or refused. In assessing the merits, the judge referred to previous decisions in the Province of Ontario in cases of passing-off according to which, where medicines are sold under prescription, it is necessary for the plaintiffs to show that there is a likelihood of confusion of doctors, dentists or pharmacists. The judge considered that in the present case such risk of confusion was unlikely and dismissed the motion for an interlocutory injunction. The Supreme Court of Canada (in *Ciba-Geigy Canada Ltd.* v. *Apotex Inc.*, 1992] 3 SCR 120; 44 CPR (3d) 289; in [1993] 5 EIPR D-131) overruled in the meantime the decisions in the Province of Ontario that had been relied on by the Federal Court motions judge. The Supreme Court ruled that the likelihood of confusion of patients must also be considered in a passing off action relating to prescription drugs. The decision of the Federal Court motions judge was appealed to the Federal Court of Appeal which dismissed the appeal since the plaintiff's evidence did not make clear whether patients associate a particular get-up with the drug's effect or with its commercial origin.

Different approaches are taken if trade marks for medicinal products are involved. In certain cases, likelihood of confusion will be less easily accepted,

---

In its comment to this decision, William L. Hayhurts refers also to another similar case opposing Ciba-Geigy Canada Ltd. against the same Novopharm Ltd. (decided on 21.7.1994), but in which the motions judge concluded that there was a risk of confusion of patients and that the supply of look-alike pills would cause irreparable damage to the plaintiff and therefore granted an interlocutory injunction. It is interesting to note how the judge came to these conclusions (the tablets of the plaintiff were of 100 milligrams and had a different shape and colour). He considered, on one hand, that health-care providers such as doctors and pharmacist would not be confused as to the origin of the look-alike tablets of the same drug if supplied by the defendant. But, on the other hand, evidence of likelihood of confusion of patients came, not from patients directly, but from experienced health-care professionals who testified about their experience with the perception and reactions of patients when supplied with pills of a particular get-up.

Hayhurst also refers to the case *Dalgety Spillers Goods Ltd.* v. *Food Brokers Ltd.* before the English High Court ([1994] FSR 335 at 370 (HC)) relating to instant snacks, in which the judge concluded that, in a case like this where the judge's experience as a shopper can be taken to be typical of an ordinary purchaser, evidence is inadmissible from persons professing to have marketing expertise as to the likelihood of confusion of an ordinary purchaser. Such evidence would therefore be admissible where the judge's experience may not be typical as in cases where goods are sold in a specialist market and Hayhurst concluding that it would be unsafe to rely solely on the personal assessment of the likelihood of confusion of the judge in the case of prescriptions drugs.

Besides medicinal products, the likelihood of confusion is also less easily accepted in other specialised cases like financial services, up-market spirits and liqueurs and lenses sold to opticians. In *Shire Trust Ltd.* v. *Hambros Bank plc*, both the plaintiff and defendant offered financial services and the defendant's services were packaged under the acronym SHIRE. The English High Court held that there was no risk of confusion as the defendant's product was aimed at a sophisticated market and available only for very large sums, and the possibility seemed remote that customers would enter into the defendant's contract without becoming aware that the product was unconnected with the plaintiff's; in [1990] 4 EIPR D-77.

Likewise for up-market spirits and liqueurs in *Cointreau and Cie SA* v. *Pagan International*, the South African Court held that the defendant's label did not so nearly resemble the plaintiff's trade mark label as to be likely to deceive or cause confusion (the plaintiff's label mark was rectangular in shape with the name *Cointreau* prominently displayed in the upper third of the label and extending diagonally across it, whilst the defendant's label was also rectangular in shape with a border around the edges and the word *Triplice* in the upper third and extending diagonally across it, the product of parties is orange-based liqueur), for the reason that the average purchaser of these liqueurs was likely to have a degree of sophistication and intelligence; in [1989] 7 EIPR D-125.

In Essilor International "Compagnie General d'Optique", *France* v. *The Ministry of Trade* and Industry, confusion of similarity was dismissed between the plaintiff's trade mark *Orma* for eye glass lenses and the defendant's trade mark *Forma*, where the defendant was a manufacturer of margarine and had apparently registered its mark for eye glass lenses as well. The Court reasoned that the purchasers of the lenses, being opticians, are a very conscientious and trade minded group of specialists; in [1989] 6 EIPR D-10. A similar approach is adopted in Switzerland in *Sihl/Cosil* packaging materials for bulk purchasers (BGE 92 II 276, 1966).

because the doctor, dentist or pharmacist are specialised;[54] on the other hand, a higher threshold against confusion will be called for, since confusion of medicines can compromise the safety of patients.[55]

6.3.4. Decisive Moment of Confusion

The relevant time for judging confusion differs from country to country. In Italy, it is the date on which the summons was served, and in other countries, the developments during the course of the proceedings will be taken into account, and the relevant time is that of the decision.[56]

[54] This is shown in the case Xylocain/Celecain (BGE 84 II 445, 1958) in Switzerland and in Germany, *Corvaton/Corvasal*, footnote 21). The German case law shows a tendency to apply particular rules in the field of medicine, which resulted in minor protection of pharmaceutical trade marks. For example, it is an affirmed principle that the purchaser of cosmetic products places particular attention on the trade mark in order to purchase the desired product (BGH GRUR 1958, 81, 83 – Thymopect). See also BGH GRUR 1968, 550 – Poropan; BPatG Mitt. 1988, 177 – *Portasan/Tobasan*. The same tendency is found in the Austrian case law (OMP 10.6.1970, PBI 113, *Provascul/Proscalun*; NA 22.2. 1990 PBI 1991, 60, *Bramyc/Bromuk*; 12.12.1990, PBI 1991, 169, *Schick Confort plus/Contour Plus*).

Reference can also be made to the Belgium case in which the claim by the owner of the trade mark *Panoxyl* for pharmaceutical products for acne against the defendant's trade mark *Pannogel* for the same product was rejected by the Commercial Court of Brussels, because of the generally accepted rule that the resemblance ought not to be judged too severely, owing to the professional ability of physicians and chemists to distinguish the products and their origin. The Brussels Court of Appeal however reversed this decision since the products were available to the public without prescription and advertising for them was allowed under certain conditions. The Court concluded that there was a risk of association between the two marks since they were phonetically and graphically similar. This decision limits therefore the traditional rule concerning pharmaceutical products to circumstances under which the products are normally available only on prescription, (Stiefel Laboratoires & Laboratoris Stiefel Belgium v. Pannoc Chemie, Brussels Court of Appeal, 2.5.1990, Ingénieur-Conseil, 1990, at 214; in [1991] 6 EIPR, D-110).

[55] The Italian Court held that, when "drugs that can be sold exclusively on prescription, and only drugs which are actually sold on prescription" are involved, the interested level of public is the higher one. Likewise, a higher threshold is held by the Australian court in Rheumaton Trade Mark [1978] RPC 406.

However, this is not true for all countries as the practice in Sweden shows a slight tendency to lower the threshold when evaluating the likelihood of confusion, *Digibind/Digitrin*.

Likewise, recent case law in France, applies normal criteria in evaluating the risk of confusion even in conflicts between pharmaceutical trade marks (TGI Paris, 23.6.1988, A. 1990, p. 300; Court of Appeal of Paris, 7.4.1992, RDPI 1993 No. 46, p. 55).

This approach is also found in Denmark, where pharmaceutical products do not receive special treatment in the evaluation of confusion.

[56] See in Italy, Court of Appeal of Rome, 27.9.1993, *Philip Morris/Marlboro Sound*, in Giur. Ann. Dir. Ind., 1994, No. 3068; in Germany, BGH GRUR 1960, 130, 134 – *Sunpearl II*; GRUR 1963, 626 – *Sunsweet*; similar criterion is adopted in Switzerland.

6.3.5. Fraudulent Intent

Although it is affirmed that fraudulent intent is not required,[57] the intent to deceive may be regarded as a presumption of successful deception. Moreover, fraudulent intent is relevant in calculating damages and in assessing validity of the junior trade mark.

7. The Likelihood of Association

See Prof. Charles Gielen: Likelihood of Association hereafter.

In the Canadian case *Bally* v. *Vallys* (*Bally Shuhfabriken AG/Bally's Shoe Factories Ltd.* v. *Big Blue Jeans Ltd. Ltée.*, Federal Court of Canada, Trial Division (Rouleau J), 17.2.1992; in [1992] 6 EIPR D-112), the Federal Court of Canada, Trial Division, held that the date to be taken into consideration to determine the risk of confusion in the opposition proceedings was that of the Registrar's decision. In the present case, the Court confirmed the Registrar's decision according to which the trade mark *Vallys* for jeans and other clothing could not be confused with the well-known trade mark *Bally* for footwear, leather goods, clothing and accessories since the defendant's wares were inexpensive and were sold through dissimilar retail establishments.

[57] The American Court held that proof of intent is not required, but when submitted, is given great weight and creates a presumption that the intended deceit will succeed: *Valcream/Brylcream*.

In the Australian LEVI'S case (*Wingate Marketing Pty Ltd.* v. *Levi Strauss & Co*, *op. cit.*) the court indicated that the intent to deceive may be relevant to the question of whether there is deception but there is no established rule in Australian Trade Mark Law that the existence of an intention to deceive gives rise to a presumption of deception.

For the German Federal Supreme Court, the concept of risk of confusion is an objective concept: BGH GRUR 1952, 35 – *Ardia/Widia*. German courts consider fraudulent intent as presumption of risk of confusion.

Collective Trade Marks

A. Notion

The notion of Community collective marks has been legally defined in Article 64: a Community collective mark is a Community trade mark which is described as such when the mark is applied for and is capable of distinguishing the goods or services of the members of the association which is the proprietor of the mark from those of other undertakings.

B. Purpose of the Community Collective Mark

The Community collective mark shall enable the members of an association to mark their goods and services in a uniform manner. The purpose of the Community collective mark is to protect certain statements having distinction capacity for the entirety of the members of the association.

The financial benefit of the Community collective mark arises from the cost-savings of each member of the association who does not have to administer and enforce his own marks. This task is fulfilled by the association which also ensures that its members comply with the rules governing the use of the collective mark. It is obvious that the function of trade marks of ensuring a certain quality of goods or services is of particular importance for collective marks which proclaim the quality or the characteristics of goods and services being safeguarded by regulations.[1]

[1] See Article 65 containing the association's duty to submit regulations governing the use of the mark.

C. History[2]

The EC-Commission early on recognized the necessity of a regulation on collective marks. Already in its "Memorandum" on the creation of a Community trade mark of 1976[3] it was stated (No. 69 and 71):

"As the Community law on trade marks shall be open to companies from all industries in the same way, in addition to the traditionally protected trade marks, there have to be further categories of trade marks comprising marks for services as well as association marks and warranty marks. [...] These marks will be of increasing importance in the future. In the Common Market these marks will play an important role as instruments for promotion of sales, standardizing and development of quality products and measures of consumer information. Especially for small and mid-sized companies the joint use of marks is the only way of expanding their activity into the entire market." (our translation).

When the discussion for harmonization of trade mark law started, the necessity of separate provisions on Community collective marks was in dispute. Although it was said that the question of ownership of Community marks by associations could be solved within the framework of general rules on ownership, early drafts already provided a separate section on collective marks. Until the proposal of the Commission of 1984,[4] the drafts and proposals contained an explicit regulation on Community warranty marks and Community collective marks, e.g. Article 102 of the Draft on a Council Regulation on Community Marks of 1978.[5] Since the Draft Bill for a Regulation of 1988[6] the provisions on the Community collective mark have been included.

From that time on there were also included provisions on the protection of geographical indications of source. Although some of the Member States opposed a Community collective mark comprising both collective and warranty aspects at the same time, this solution seemed to be better than to distinguish between marks which solely serve to identify the collective source of a good or service and "certification marks"[7] known in some Member States.

[2] See with regard to the general development of the law on Community trade marks, Albert, Florian, Die Neuordnung des Markenrechts – Bericht über das 10. Ringberg-Symposium of 16 to 21.9.1996, soon to be published in GRUR int. 1997 No. 4 or 5.

[3] See "Denkschrift der EG Kommission über die Schaffung einer EWG-Marke" of 6.7.1976, Dok. SEC. (76) 2462, supplement 8/76 of the EC-Bulletin, published in GRUR int. 1976, p. 481.

[4] Dokument (84) 470 endg., Abl. EG 1984 No. C 230, S. 1, Article 86.

[5] Document No. III/D/753/78-DE of July 1978, working document No. 11 of the working group "Community Trade Mark", printed in GRUR Int. 1978, 452.

[6] Document 5865/88 of the Council of Ministers of 11.5.1988, altered proposal of a Council Regulation on the Community Trade Mark – consolidated text, published in GRUR Int. 1989, p. 388.

[7] These are especially known in Great Britain, see Article 50 Trade Marks Act 1994; Armand, Ruth/Norman, Helen, Blackstone's Guide to the Trade Marks Act 1994, London. Blackstone 1994; White, Thomas A./Jacob, Rubin, Kerly's law of Trade Marks and Trade Names, 12th ed., London 1994.

D. Applicable rules

Pursuant to Article 64 para. 3, the general rules on Community marks apply to Community collective marks save Articles 65 to 72 do not provide otherwise. In the following we discuss only provisions differing from the regulation provided for the Community individual trade marks.

E. Ownership

Pursuant to Article 64 para. 1 sentence 1, a Community collective mark can be owned by an association. The type of association meant by this provision can be concluded from sentence 2 of this provision: associations of manufacturers, producers, suppliers of services, or traders which, under the terms of the law governing them, have the capacity in their own name to have rights and obligations of all kinds, to make contracts or accomplish other legal acts and to sue and be sued may apply for Community collective marks.

It is questionable whether this includes umbrella organisations and leading associations whose members are associations which fall within the scope of the entities of possible proprietors of Community collective marks. There is no convincing argument to distinguish such umbrella organisations and leading associations from other associations of manufacturers, producers, suppliers of services or traders by their involvement in commercial business. Consequently, they have expressly been included into parallel national provisions.[8] However, mixed associations having as members manufacturers and traders as well as consumers do not fall within the scope of the entities which can be proprietors of Community collective marks.

Furthermore, legal persons governed by public law may apply for Community collective marks, pursuant to Article 64 para. 1.

With regard to ownership the Regulation refers to the national law which has to be applied to the entity who wishes to register a collective mark.

By virtue of Article 3, European economic interest groupings (EEIG) may apply for a Community collective mark irrespective of the fact that they do not have legal personality.[9]

In addition to the requirement of being one of the associations or legal persons mentioned above, the proprietor of a Community collective mark has to be involved in commercial business. This can be concluded from the wording of Article 64 para. 1 sentence 2 which mentions associations of manufacturers,

[8] This has been explicitly clarified in section 98 of the German Trade Mark Act 1994.

[9] See Article 1 para. 2 of the Regulation on European economic interest groupings of 25.7.1984, published in Abl. EG No. L 199 of 31.7.1985.

producers, suppliers of services, or traders. By contrast the registration of a Community individual mark does not require any participation in commerce.[10]

The requirements regarding the ownership of a Community collective mark will be examined ex oficio in the course of the application proceedings, pursuant to Article 66 para. 1, Article 37. It constitutes a ground for refusal if these requirements are not satisfied, pursuant to Article 66 para. 1. If the collective mark is registered in spite of that failure to comply with Article 64, this constitutes an absolute ground for invalidity under Article 51 para. 1 Lit. a) or, if the proprietor ceases to satisfy this requirement, a ground for revocation, pursuant to Article 50 para. 1 Lit. d).[11] However, it does not constitute a requirement for protection under a Community individual mark or a Community collective mark that the proprietor has a business.

Members of an association which itself cannot be the proprietor of a Community collective mark can jointly apply for and own a Community individual mark. An individual mark can be owned by a group of persons jointly. This can be concluded from Article 16 para. 3 of the Regulation on Community trade marks, rules 1 para. 4, 75 of the Implementing Regulation No. 2868/95.

In addition to entities domiciled in the Member States, associations and legal persons governed by public law domiciled in other states mentioned in Article 5 can apply for a Community collective mark. Thus, a wide circle of applicants has access to protection of Community collective marks.

F. Registration

The association has to describe the Community collective mark as such, pursuant to Article 64 para. 1 sentence 1.

It constitutes a peculiarity of the registration of a Collective mark that, in addition to the further requirements of Article 26, an applicant for a Community collective mark has to submit regulations governing the collective mark, according to Article 65 para. 1. These regulations govern the authorization to use the mark, the conditions of membership of the association and, where they exist, the conditions of use of the mark including sanctions (see Article 65 para. 2). The application has to contain the statements as provided for by rule 43 para. 2 of the Implementing Regulation (Regulation No. 2868/95 of the Commission (EC)[12]):

[10] See with regard to the consequences Schönfeld, Thomas, Die Gemeinschaftsmarke als selbständiger Vermögensgegenstand eines Unternehmens, Baden-Baden 1994; under the German Trade Mark Act 1994 the German legislator abandoned the requirement that the trade mark had to be linked to a business. A critical view held by Meister, Herbert, Die Verteidigung von Marken, WRP 1995, 366 and 1007.

[11] See the parallel provisions in the German Trade Mark Act, Section 36 para. 1 No. 4, para. 2, 50 para. 1 No. 2, 49 para. 2 No. 3.

[12] Printed in BlPMZ 1996 pp. 111 – 132.

- name of the applicant and address of his (registered) place of business;
- purpose of the association or purpose of the foundation of the public law entity;
- organs entitled to represent the association or the legal person;
- conditions of membership;
- persons entitled to use the mark;
- in the case being, the conditions to use the trade mark including sanctions;
- if applicable, the possibility to become a member of the association, pursuant to Article 65 para. 2 sentence 2.

The regulations have to be submitted within a term of two months from the day of application (see rule 43 para. 1 of the Implementing Regulation).

The application can be submitted either directly to the Office for Harmonization in the Internal Market at Alicante or to the BENELUX Trade Mark Office or to the national trade mark offices. The national trade mark offices will only take care of the transfer of the application to the Office for Harmonization and will not examine if it fulfils the legal requirements.

G. Legal effects of the Community collective mark

The Community collective mark is based on the principle of unit. By virtue of a single registration the proprietor obtains a unitary trade mark right with equal effects in all Member States of the European Union.[13] This is true for both the Community collective mark and the Community individual mark. They equally have unitary effect for the whole EC territory. This is laid down in Article 1 para. 2 of the Regulation, according to which Community trade marks can only be registered with effect within the entirety of the EC territory and that they shall not be transferred or surrendered or be the subject of a decision revoking the rights of the proprietor or declaring it invalid, nor shall its use be prohibited, save in respect of the whole Community.[14]

[13] The principle of unity of the Community mark was considered by the EC Commission to be the most important principle and was also the most disputed one, see Denkschrift der EG-Kommission über die Schaffung einer EWG-Marke vom 6.7.1976, Dok. SEC (76) 2462, Beilage 8/76 zum Bulletin in der EG, published in GRUR Int. 1976, p. 481, No. 60 ff.; Beier, Friedrich-Karl, Entwicklung und Grundzüge des europäischen Markenrechts, EuR 1982, p. 92, (94); Boucourechliev, Arguments en faveur d'un droit communautaire des marques, RIPIA 1977, 145.

[14] See with regard to the Regulation on trade marks in general: Ingerl, Reinhard, Die Gemeinschaftsmarke, Stuttgart 1996 (Jenaer Schriften zum Recht); Kuscko, Guido, Die Gemeinschaftsmarke, Wien 1996; Klaka, Rainer/Schulz, Andreas, Die europäische Gemeinschaftsmarke, Wien 1996, Pagenberg, Jochen/Munzinger, Peter, Manual on the European Community Trade Mark, Köln/Berlin/Bonn/München 1996.

H. Special provisions on Community collective marks on geographical indications of origin

I. Privilege of registration of geographical indications of origin

In derogation from Article 7 para. 1 lit. c), the Community collective mark may consist exclusively of signs and statements indicating the geographical source of goods or services, pursuant to Article 64 para. 2. This provision was subject to the most disputed rules on collective marks to which many reservations were made in the course of the elaboration process.[15] This is partly due to the very different national rules in this field.[16]

Pursuant to this regulation under Community law, all geographical indications of source can be registered as collective marks. Article 64 para. 2 does not contain any further requirements for registration. Special prerequisites like proof of reputation or a certain quality of the marked good which arise from the geographical surroundings are not to be considered for registration.[17] It is up to the association to provide for the conditions of use by adopting a Regulation, pursuant to Article 65. This Regulation may either exclusively refer to the geographical source or link the geographical source with a quality standard.

Problems arise from having to distinguish geographical indications of source from generic names which cannot be registered.[18] Pursuant to Article 7 para. 1

[15] Mühlendahl, Alexander von, Das neue europäische Markenrecht; in: Festschrift 100 Jahre Markenamt 1994, p. 215, (227); Tilmann, Winfried, Kennzeichenrechtlicher Schutz von Herkunftsangaben, in Festschrift Gewerblicher Rechtsschutz und Urheberrecht in Deutschland, Volume II, Weinheim 1991, p. 1007, (1014).

[16] Especially in French law there is no privilege with regard to geographical indications of source, see Lefebvre, Francis, Marques, Paris 1994, No. 1222, 1131; Berg, Günter, Die geographische Herkunftsangabe – ein Konkurrent für die Marke?, GRUR int. 1996, p. 425, (429) speaks of a map split up between countries with registered indications of source and countries with geographical collective and warranty marks; Beier, Friedrich-Karl/Knaak, Roland, The Protection of Direct and Indirect Geographical Indications of Source in Germany and the European Community, IIC 1994, p. 1, (14) with further references with regard to the situation in the EU Member States.

[17] Harte-Bavendamm, Henning, Ende geographischer Herkunftsbezeichnungen?, GRUR 1996, p. 717, (727); Beier, Friedrich-Karl/Knaak, Roland, Der Schutz der geographischen Herkunftsangaben in der Europäischen Gemeinschaft, GRUR int. 1993, p. 602, (605) with regard to the insofar unaltered accepted proposal on the Regulation on Community Trade Mark.

[18] This problem also exists in the Member States. In Section 126 para. 2 of the German Trade Mark Act 1994 the German Legislator consciously did not deliver any criterion to distinguish geographical indications of source from generic names. In the statement of reasons to the Draft Bill it is stated that this task should be left to the courts. The German legislator wanted to avoid that "for the transformation of a geographical indication of source into a generic name a different standard would be applied in German and European law", BT-Drucksache 12/6581, 118 oder PMZ, Sonderheft zum neuen Markengesetz, 1994, p. 112.

lit. d), generic names have to be understood as "trade marks which consist exclusively of signs or indications which have become customary in the current language or in the bona fide and established practises of the trade". These generic names do in fact refer directly or indirectly to a geographic location, but, applying generally accepted standards, they have never had the function of indications of source or lost this function subsequently. They cannot be used to mark goods or services, according to Article 64 para. 2, because they lack distinction capacity. It is still open which set of criteria will be applied by the Office of Harmonization in Alicante and the European Court of Justice (ECJ) which have, according to Article 63,[19] jurisdiction with respect to the registration of Community collective marks, in order to distinguish generic names which cannot be registered from geographical indications of source.[20] It is questionable whether the requirement of distinctiveness has to be decided merely on the facts existing in that country where the geographical indication originated or on the facts existing in other Member States as well. This is decisive in those frequent cases in which the indications will be considered geographical indications of origin in some countries whereas they are considered mere generic terms in others.[21] In this field the ECJ has not yet rendered a binding decision. The ECJ has held the principle that, for reasons of legal certainty, the interpretation of provisions of Community law has to be autonomous and uniform and independent from corresponding national law. The rules of interpretation known to most of the national legal systems is applied as a standard.[22]

[19] See with regard to the key role of the ECJ concerning the interpretation of the terms of Community law on trade marks, Meyer, Andreas, Das deutsche und französische Markenrecht nach der Umsetzung der Ersten Markenrichtlinie (RL 89/104/EWG), GRUR int. 1996, p. 592, (599).

[20] Conclusions can be carefully drawn from the practise of the Commission with regard to the registration under the Council Regulation (EC) No. 2081/92 of 14.7.1992: The Commission allowed for example registration of the names for cheese Esrom (Dänemark), Feta (Griechenland), Roncal (Spanien), Roquefort (Frankreich), Gorgonzola (Italien), Noord-Hollandse Gouda (Niederlande), Quejo Serpa (Portugal), White and blue Stilton Cheese (Großbritannien) and others, whereas registration was denied for Camenbert, Emmentaler, Brie, Mozzarella, Cheddar and others as they are no longer names of locality linked with quality. With regard to the registration of the name "Feta", Denmark has transformed this word into a generic term from a long time ago since legal action has been taken. No German cheese made it into that protected list. However, "Nürnberger Lebkuchen" and "Lübecker Marzipan" are protected.

[21] With reference to the possibilities of registration under Regulation 2081/92, several Member States claimed that "Ungarische Salami", "Dortmunder Bier", "Bayerisches Bier" oder "Mozzarella" were generic names, see Harte-Bavendamm, Henning, Ende geographischer Herkunftsbezeichnungen, GRUR 1996, p. 717, (718) with further references.

[22] See with regard to the interpretation of EC provisions in general, Zuleeg, Manfred, in: Groeben/Thiesing/Ehlermann, Kommentar zum EWG-Vertrag, 4th ed., Baden-Baden 1994, Article 1; Geiger, Rudolf, EG-Vertrag, Kommentar,", 2nd ed. München 1995, Article 164.

With regard to the difficult distinction between geographical indications of origin and generic names neither the grammatical interpretation[23] nor the historical interpretation[24] of Article 64 para. 2, Article 7 para. 1 lit. d) assists further because these provisions do neither explicitly state any facts for distinction nor there exist meaningful documents showing their genesis.

In the decision "Turrón de Alicante"[25] the ECJ held that community law is an obstacle to national protection of geographical indications of source only if the geographical indication has been transformed into a generic name in the country where it originated.[26] Some legal authors derived therefrom the view that the distinction between generic names and indications of origin depends on the situation in the country of origin.[27] However, it can only be concluded from this decision that protection of indications of origin is no infringement of Community law if the indication has not changed into a generic name in the country of origin. This does not hinder the Community organs to take the view that the situation in the other Member States is of importance based on the argument that the protection within the entire EEC territory is concerned.[28]

This reasoning could be backed up by a systematic interpretation of the Community law.[29] The Regulation No. 2081/92 on the protection of geographical indications and designations of origin for agricultural products and foodstuffs contains a more precise distinction between generic names and geographical indications of origin.[30] Pursuant to Article 3 para. 3 of that Regulation, the

[23] Also in Community law the wording of a provision is the starting point and the limitation of interpretation, see Zuleeg, Manfred, *op. cit.* (Fn.), Article 1 No. 30.

[24] Due to the restrictive practise of publishing documents concerning the elaborating process, the historical interpretation of EC rules is rather difficult. In this respect it is also noteworthy that the ECJ is not in favour of a strict commitment to the individual ideas of the legislator, ECJ decision of 22.6.1972 – Murry Slg. 1973, 333.

[25] ECJ decision of 10.11.1992, RS C-3/91, published in GRUR int. 1993, 76.

[26] This case focused on the question of whether a French producer was allowed to sell sweets under the name "Turrón de Alicante" and "Turrón de Jijon", which are Spanish geographical indications protected under a French-Spanish agreement. The producers claimed that these names had been transformed into generic names in France and were thus governed by the rules of free trade of goods, pursuant to Article 30, 36 of the Treaty.

[27] See as to the parallel question under the Regulation Tilmann, Winfried, Grundlage und Reichweite des Schutzes geographischer Herkunftsangaben nach der VO/EWG 2081/92, GRUR Int. 1993 S. 610.

[28] This view holds Gorny, Dietrich, Markenrecht und geographische Herkunftsangaben bei Lebensmitteln, GRUR 1996, p. 447, 451; dissenting Knaak, Roland, Der Schutz geographischer Herkunftsangaben im neuen Markengesetz, GRUR 1995, p. 103, 106 who thinks it desirable that the laws and situation in the state of origin be decisive; see in this sense Tilman, Winfried, *op. cit.*, (footnote 44) p. 616.

[29] Whereby the rules of Community law have to be construed in accordance with other rules. See Zuleeg, Manfred, *op. cit.*, p. 32.

[30] Official Bulletin of the European Communities, 1992, No. L 208/1-8, published in GRUR Int. 1992, p. 750; as to the relationship between the Regulation 2081/92 and the Regulation on Community trade marks see H. IV.

situation in other Member States and the relevant rules of national law or Community law are of relevance in addition to the situation in the state where the name originated and the territories where the products are sold.[31]

II. Compulsory admission to the association

The possibility to register geographical indications of source as collective mark, which constitutes an exception to Article 7 para. 1 lit. c), has been systematically linked to the compulsory admission on request in favour of such persons whose goods or services originate from the concerned geographical region, Article 65 para. 2 sentence 2. The Regulation under sec. 65 para. 1 has to establish that persons whose goods and services originate from that region have the right to join the association.

III. Limited exclusivity

Pursuant to Article 64 para. 2, the scope of protection for registered geographical indications of source is limited. The proprietor is not entitled to prohibit a third party from using such signs or indications in commerce, provided he uses them in accordance with honest practices in industrial or commercial matters. In particular, the mark may not be invoked against a third party who is entitled to use a geographical name. This article ensures that non-members of the association have the right to use the registered geographical indication of source, provided this use is in compliance with the concept of good morals.

Although it remains open, in this respect, under which conditions the EC-organs will assume fair use limiting the rights established in Article 9 the interpretation of Article 64 para. 2 sentence 2 will have to be orientated according to the purpose of the provision. The purpose of compulsory admission and limitation of proprietor rights with regard to geographical indications of source registered as collective marks is to prevent monopolization of geographical indications. The legal protection arising from the registration of geographical indications shall not be misused to damage the legitimate interests of non-organized outsiders. There is also no constraint to join an association being the proprietor of a Community collective mark. Conflicting interests may exist with regard to geographical collective marks which are linked to certain quality standards, the so-called qualified geographical indications of source: the members of the association, on the one hand, have an interest in controlling which goods are labelled with a geographical indication of source. Outsiders, on the other

[31] Heine, Joachim Friedrich, Das neue gemeinschaftliche System zum Schutz geographischer Bezeichnungen, GRUR 1993, p. 96, 99.

hand, might have an interest in producing comparable goods of a different quality. Not to forget the consumer who, on the one hand, wants to buy goods for a low price, but, on the other hand, is also interested in an ensured quality which he/she expects from an indicated geographical source.

The privilege of Article 64 para. 2 sentence 2 does not include the right to imitate the individual character in which the geographical indication is registered.[32] Furthermore, an effective protection of the reputation of the collective mark requires that the quality of non-members' goods and services is not inferior to the quality standard laid down in the regulation of the association.

IV. Relationship of Articles 64 – 72 to Council Regulation (EC) No. 2081/92 of July 14, 1992 on the protection of geographical indications and designations of origin for agricultural products and foodstuffs

The EC Regulation No. 2081/92 establishes a new legal framework of registered rights for geographical indications and designations of origin for agricultural products and foodstuffs.[33] Unlike the EC Regulation on Community trade marks, the Regulation No. 2081/92 exclusively gives protection to such products the properties of which correspond to their geographical origin.[34] As far as these products fulfil the requirements of registration, pursuant to that Regulation, a broad scope of protection can be obtained: protection against use of the indication for comparable goods if advantage is taken of its reputation, protection against any other, especially misleading use, protection against use with dislocalizing supplements and even protection against transformation into a generic name.[35] As a prerequisite of this protection the indication has to be registered with the Commission.[36]

It is the predominating opinion that the protection established by the Regulation (EC) No. 2081/92 and the protection established by the Regulation on Community trade marks exist independently from each other side by side because they emanate from secondary Community law enjoying the same legal rank.[37] Article 142 of the Regulation on Community trade marks explicitly

[32] See with regard to the parallel problem under German Trade Mark Law, Knaak, Roland, Der Schutz geographischer Herkunftsangaben im neuen Markengesetz, GRUR 1995, p. 103, (108).

[33] See with regard to this Regulation in general, Harte-Bavendamm, Henning, Ende der geographischen Herkunftsbezeichnung?, GRUR 1996, 717 with further references.

[34] This correspondence is especially clear with regard to mineral waters from locally bound sources. These constitute a big part of the registered products.

[35] See Article 13 of the Regulation (EC) No. 2081/92.

[36] See Article 6 of the Regulation (EC) No. 2081/92.

[37] Harte-Bavenamm, Henning, Ende der geographischen Herkunftsbezeichnung?, GRUR 1996, 717 with further references.

establishes that the Regulation No. 2081/92 remains unaffected.[38] It results from the principle of unitary and consistent interpretation of Community law that enforcement of a Community collective mark which is also within the scope of application of the Regulation No. 2081/92 is not misleading as such and that the proprietor of a registration under the Regulation No. 2081/92 is entitled to use the designation of origin.[39]

Due to the fact that registration and maintenance of a Community collective mark depends on other prerequisites than the registration under the Regulation No. 2081/92 and that the scope of protection is not identical it can be expected that there will be registrations of collective marks even within the scope of applicability of the Regulation No. 2081/92.[40]

I. Danger of misleading (Article 66 para. 2)

Comparing Article 7 para. 1 lit. g) and Article 66 para. 2 it can be concluded that the Community collective mark is subject to a stricter standard with regard to the danger of misleading than those of the individual mark. Pursuant to Article 66 para. 2, an application shall be refused if the public is liable to be misled as regards the character or the significance of the mark, in particular if it is likely to be taken to be something other than a collective mark whereas, pursuant to the general provision in Article 7 para. 1 lit. g), a mark shall not be registered if it is of such nature as to deceive the public, e.g. as to the nature, quality or geographical region of the goods or service. The wording of Article 66 para. 2 is broader by including the significance of the mark and in particular a misleading appearance on its character as a collective mark.

[38] However, the coexistence of national trade mark laws and the Regulation No 2081/92 is in heavy dispute, see Beier, Karl-Friedrich/Knaak, Roland, Der Schutz geographischer Herkunftsangaben in der Europäischen Gemeinschaft, GRUR int. 1993, p. 602 who even questions the legality of the Regulation; Tilmann, Winfried, Ausschließlicher Schutz für geographische Herkunftsbezeichnungen nach der EG-VO 2081/92, GRUR 1996, p. 959 with further references; Mühlendahl, Alexander von, Der Schutz gegoraphischer Herkunftsangaben in der Europäischen Gemeinschaft nach der Verordnung No. 2081/92 of 24.7.1992, ZLR 1993, p. 187; Meyer, Hagen, Verordnung (EWG) No. 2081/92 with regard to the protection of geographic indications and designations of origin.

[49] Harte-Bavendamm, Henning, Ende der geographischen Herkunftsbezeichnung?, GRUR 1996, p. 717, (728).

[40] Harte-Bravendamm, Henning, Ende der geographischen Herkunftsbezeichnung?, GRUR 1996, p. 717, (728); for another assessment see Knaak, Roland, Der Schutz geographischer Herkunftsangaben nach im neuen Markengesetz, GRUR 1995, p. 103, (112).

J. Enforcement of defense rights

Pursuant to Article 70 para. 1, the provisions of Article 22 para. 3 and para. 4 concerning the rights of licensees as regards infringement proceedings shall apply to every person who has authority to use a Community collective mark.

The proprietor of a Community collective mark shall be entitled to claim compensation on behalf of persons who have authority to use the mark where they have sustained damage as a consequence of unauthorized use of the mark, pursuant to Article 70 para. 2. Therefore, no assignment of damage claims is needed.

K. Preservation of rights by use of the Community collective mark

With regard to the requirement of use, pursuant to Article 15,[41] the use of the collective mark by any person who has authority to use it is sufficient to preserve the rights arising form the collective mark if all other conditions of use of the collective mark are equally fulfilled. The use of the collective mark by the members of the association will be attributed to the association. Pursuant to the wording of that provision, the use of the collective mark by one single member of the association is sufficient. During the elaboration process this was opposed on the argument that the purposes of the collective mark, e.g. cost saving and promotion of effectiveness of the marketing methods, could only be reached by the use of the collective mark by more than one member, thus preventing the preservation of a hidden individual mark.[42] This argument was abandoned later on. It is the purpose of the Community collective mark to serve as distinction of goods and services of the members of the association. Hence, the use of the mark by "any person who has authority to use it" is considered sufficient to preserve the proprietor's rights.[43]

Of course, the use of the collective mark by its proprietor, i.e. by the association, fulfils the requirements of compulsory use as well.[44]

[41] With regard to the compulsory use in general see Ralf Hackbarth, Grundfragen des Benutzungszwanges im Gemeinschaftsmarkenrecht, Schriftenreihe zum gewerblichen Rechtsschutz, Band 86, Köln/Berlin/Bonn/München 1993.

[42] See Hackbarth, *op. cit.*, p. 170.

[43] Ingerl, *op. cit.* (footnote 8), p. 121, 122.

[44] This has been explicitly clarified in Section. 100 para. 2 of the German Trade Mark Act; see with regard to the identical provision of the proposal for a Regulation on Community trade marks Hackbarth, *op. cit.*, p. 172.

L. Special grounds for invalidity

In addition to the grounds for invalidity, pursuant to Article 50, 51 and 52, the Regulation on the revocation of the collective mark, in Article 71 and for invalidity in Article 72, provides particular grounds for invalidity. Particular attention has to be attributed to Article 71 lit. a): The proprietor's rights by virtue of a Community collective mark shall be revoked if the proprietor does not take reasonable steps to prevent the mark from being used in a manner incompatible with the conditions of use, where these exist, laid down in the Regulation governing use, amendments to which have, where appropriate, been mentioned in the register. The association being proprietor of the Collective mark therefore has to safeguard the respect of the underlying Regulation.[45]

M. Distinction between Community collective marks and Community individual marks

Community collective marks and Community individual marks differ with regard to the principles by which ownership and the entitlement to use the registered mark are ruled: Even though, pursuant to Article 64 para. 1 sentence 1, the registered association is the proprietor of the collective mark it is the essential characteristic of the collective mark that it will not be used by the proprietor himself but first and foremost by the members of the association and only possibly by the association itself. The right of use is governed by the Regulations to be submitted, according to Article 66. Unlike the individual mark, the collective mark does not have the function of pointing to an individual business the origin of the labelled goods or services but to a group of users. The possibility to register a collective mark includes the practical necessity to use a trade mark for many unaffiliated companies.

It is true that an association would be able to obtain a similar legal effect by licensing an individual mark to its members.[46] However, it is an advantage of the collective mark to enable the members of the association to use the mark without having to enter into a license agreement. The right to use a collective mark is automatically granted to the members of the association by virtue of membership. Hence, the users have a better legal position in front of the proprietor of the mark than a licensee.[47]

[45] The German legislator speaks in Section 105 para. 2 of the German Trade Mark Act (1994) of "does not take suitable measures to prevent ..." instead of "tolerates ..." which was contained in the former provision solving this problem. The German legislator did not want the trade mark to be deleted because of pure inactivity.

[46] See with regard to the parallel provisions in the former German trade mark law: Althammer, Werner, Warenzeichengesetz, § 17 No. 1, 4th ed. Köln/Berlin/Bonn/München 1990, (5th edition in preparation).

[47] See with regard to the parallel provision under German law: Nordemann, Wettbewerbs- und Markenrecht, 8th Edtion, Baden-Baden 1995, No. 434.

N. Relationship between Community collective marks and national collective marks

I. National Rules on collective marks in the Member States

In all EU Member States the legal systems contain rules on collective marks.

The Member States are not obliged to provide protection for collective marks by virtue of EC law. The EC Directive on Trade Marks of 1988[48] which has to be transformed into national law, pursuant to Article 189 sentence 3 of the Treaty, does not contain an obligation to harmonise national law on collective marks. Article 15 of this Directive leaves the adoption of the rules on collective marks up to the Member States.

Furthermore, there is no obligation to provide for the registration of collective marks under the TRIPS agreement.[49] With regard to that agreement the European Community (and the US and Japan) which wanted to insert an obligation to introduce collective marks into the agreement did not prevail.[50]

However, in all EC Member States collective marks enjoy protection by virtue of Article 7 *bis* of the Paris Convention.

Nevertheless, due to the fact that this provision contains only rudimentary rules,[51] the rules on protection of collective marks differ widely in the Member States.[52]

[48] Council Directive (EC) of 21 December 1988 on the harmonization of the rules on trade marks of the Member States (89/104/EWG), Abl. Nr. L 40 of 11.2.1989, published in GRUR Int. 1989, 294.

[49] Trade-Related Aspects of Intellectual Property Rights. This Agreement is an appendix to the WTO Agreement, published in GRUR Int. 1994, 128.

[50] Kur, Annette, TRIPS und das Markenrecht, GRUR Int. 1994, 987 (No. 47).

[51] Tilmann, Winfried. Die geographische Herkunftsangabe, München 1976, p. 325 is of the opinion that the notion "marques collectives" was consciously chosen in order to cover different types of marks.

[52] Country reports of the AIPPI Year Books of 1980/II and 1993/iv (Association Internationale pour la Protection de la Proprieté Industrielle).

As to the national rules on collective marks see:

a. Austria: §§ 62-68 of the Markenschutzgesetz (MSchG) of 1970 as last amended by the Act 1993/109

b. Benelux: Article 19-28 of the Benelux Merkenwet (BMW) of 1.1.1971 as last amended 2.12.1992

c. Denmark: §§ 1-13 of the Lov om varemærker (vml) of 6.6.1991, in force since 1.1.1992

d. Germany: §§ 97 – 106 of the Markengesetz of 25.10.1994, in force since 1.1.1995 as last amended 19.7.1996

e. Finland: §§ 1-8 of the Tavaramerkkilaki of 1964 as last amended 22.12.1995

f. France: Article L. 715-1-L.715-3 of the Loi des marques (CPI) of 4.1.1991, in force since 28.12.1991, now "Livre VIIÓ of the Code de la popriété intellectuelle of 1.7.1992

g. Greece: Article 25 of the Nomos peri sematom of 1994, in force since 1.11.1994

h. Great Britain: Article 49 of the Trade Marks Act (TMA 1994) of 21.7.1994, in force since 31.10.1994

i. Ireland: Article 54 of the Trade Marks Act (TMA 1996) of 16.3.1996, in force since 1.7.1996

II. Relationship between the National Rules on trade marks and Community law on trade marks

The preamble of the Regulation (No. 40/94) states explicitly:

"Whereas the Community law relating to trade marks nevertheless does not replace the law of the Member States on trade marks; whereas it would not in fact appear to be justified to require undertakings to apply for registration of their trade marks as Community trade marks; whereas national trade marks continue to be necessary for those undertakings which do not want protection of their trade marks at Community level".

This general concept of coexistence of European and national laws was developed within the process of harmonization on patent law[53] and applied to trade mark law as well.

This does, however, not change the fact that the two systems of protection are interdependent in many ways. With regard to this relationship the rules on conflicting marks (Article 8), on the priority of a national application (Article 34, 35), on the transformation of a Community mark into a national application (Article 109 and following), on the prosecution of Community mark infringements (Article 14) and on the competence of national administrative bodies (Article 91) have to be observed.[54]

The companies still have the choice either to register one or more national trade marks or to register the mark under the Regulation on trade marks with effect on the entire EEC-territory.[55]

---

j. Italy: Title I of the Legge marchi of 21.6.1942 as last amended 13.3.1996, in force since 28.12.1992

k. Portugal: Article 175 of the Código da propriedade industrial (cpi) of 24.1.1995, in force since 1.6.1995

l. Sweden: § 1ff of the Varumärkeslag (VML) of 1960 as last amended by the Act SFS 1995:1277, 1278

m. Spain: Article 58-61 of the Ley de Marcas (LM) of 10 November 1988, in force since 12.6.1989

[53] Mühlendahl, Alexander von, Das künftige Markenrecht der Europäischen Gemeinschaft, GRUR Int. 1989, p. 353; Albert, Florian, Die Neuordnung des Markenrechts – Bericht über das 10. Ringberg-Symposium of 16 to 21.9.1996, soon to be published in GRUR int. 1997 No. 4 or 5.

[54] Kucsko, Guido, Die Gemeinschaftsmarke, Wien 1996, p. 15; Einem, Christoph von/Lorenz Kerstin, Die neue EU-Gemeinschaftsmarke, WiB 13/1996, p. 553 (559); Leroux, Isabelle, La procédure d'opposition et les leins avec les marques nationales, in: La marque communautaire, RIPIA 4e trim. 1995, p. 69; Muhlberg Hans, Claiming Seniority for Community Trade Marks, 19 TM World 1995, p. 23.

[55] Harte-Bavendamm, Henning/Bomhard, Verena von, Strategische Aspekte der Gemeinschaftsmarke, WRP 1996, S.534; Combaldieu, Jean Claude, Pourqoi une marque communautaire?, in: La marque communautaire, RIPIA 4e trim. 1995, p. 79; Meyer, Ilse, Internationale Marke oder Gemeinschaftsmarke?, ecolex 1994, 693; with regard to a combination of a Community mark and an international registration, see Kunze, Gerd F., Die Verzahnung der Gemeinschaftsmarke mit dem System der internationalen Registrierung von Marken unter der gemeinsamen Ausführungsverordnung zum Madrider Markenabkommen und dem Madrider Protokoll, GRUR Int. 1996, p. 627.

O. Fees

The fees to be paid for registration and maintenance of Community collective marks are governed by the Regulation (EC) No. 2869/95 of the Commission of 13th December 1995 on the fees to be paid to the Office for Harmonízation in the Internal Market (trade marks and designs):

1)	application fee	ECU	1.675,–
2)	class fee (for each class starting from the 4th class)	ECU	400,–
3)	registration fee	ECU	2.200,–
4)	class fee (registration)	ECU	400,–
5)	extension fee	ECU	5.000,–
6)	class fee (renewal)	ECU	1.000,–
7)	reinstatement fees	ECU	200,–

Likelihood of Association

1. Introduction

The criterion on the basis of which conflicts between trade marks or a trade mark and another sign are to be judged is whether there is likelihood of confusion including likelihood of association. This criterion can be found first of all in the first Council Directive of 21 December 1988 to approximate the laws of the member states relating to trade marks.[1] It can furthermore be found in the Council Regulation (EC) No. 40/94 of 20 December 1993.[2]

The aim of the Directive is to harmonize trade mark laws in Europe in order to avoid disparities which may impede the free movement of goods or the freedom to provide services.

An internal economic market, such as the European Union, should not have different laws protecting trade marks. According to the Directive all fifteen member states of the European Union should in the meantime have in the meantime adapted their laws to the Directive. The Protocol changing the Benelux Trade Mark Act entered into force on 1 January 1996.

The Benelux is an economic union in existence prior to the European Economic Community as it was called before, having a similar object: to create one internal market. One of the consequences of this aim was that the Benelux countries did away with their old national trade mark laws and on 1 January 1971, a uniform Trade Mark Act came into force. This Act is considered to contain one of the most modern trade mark laws in Europe. This Act had a lot of influence on the final text of the Harmonization Directive. Comparable to the Court of Justice in Luxembourg the Benelux countries instituted a Benelux Court of Justice being a supranational court established to avoid differences in interpretation of uniform Benelux laws, such as the Benelux Trade Mark Act.

[1] OJEC No. L 40/1, 11.2.1989.
[2] OJEC No. L 11/1, 14.1.1994.

The second instrument of trade mark law in Europe is the afore-mentioned Council Regulation. It creates the possibility to apply for a uniform trade mark right valid for the whole of the European Union. This system will exist next to the continuing existence of national trade mark rights and it became operative on 1 April 1996, although filing started on 1 January 1996, at the Office for the Harmonization of the Internal Market in Alicante – Spain.

Both instruments contain similar provisions with respect to conflicts between earlier trade mark rights and marks or other signs. One can find these in Article 4 (1)(b) and Article 5 (1)(b) of the Harmonization Directive as criterion for the refusal or invalidity and infringement respectively. As far as the Community trade mark is concerned, it can be found in Article 8 (1)(b), Article 52 (1)(a) and Article 9 (1)(b) as a relative ground for refusal, for invalidity and as an infringement criterion respectively. The criterion is that in case of identity with or similarity to the earlier trade mark and the identity or similarity of the goods or services covered by the trade mark, there must be a likelihood of confusion on the part of the public. This criterion then says "the likelihood of confusion includes the likelihood of association with the earlier trade mark".

2. What does "likelihood of confusion including likelihood of association" mean?

The origin of the words "likelihood of association" is to be found in Benelux trade mark law. Under this law the criterion risk of confusion is not applied. Risk of association is the relevant infringement criterion as explained hereunder.

In former texts of proposals for both the Directive and the Regulation the conflict criterion was much more restrictive. Words like "serious risk of confusion" were used and one could also find the principle that the only function of a trade mark is to guarantee the trade mark as an indication of origin.

The Benelux countries feared that if risk of confusion as to origin would be the standard for infringement, protection in the Benelux countries would become less than it has been since 1971. That is the reason why one finds the words risk of association included in the Directive and Regulation. Unfortunately there is no explanatory memorandum or other explaining document accompanying the Directive or the Regulation. There are, however, some considerations at the beginning of the texts of both instruments. First of all it is said that the function of a trade mark is in *particular* (emphasis added, Gielen) to guarantee the trade mark as an indication of origin. Apparently the origin function is not the only function. In fact both the Directive and Regulation protect functions other than the origin function since they provide that the trade mark owner can also oppose the use of his mark or a similar sign for non-similar goods or services. In order to enjoy the benefit of this criterion, the trade mark owner has to prove that his mark has a reputation and that the use of his mark or similar sign takes unfair advantage of, or is detrimental to, the distinctive character or the repute of the mark. This therefore is an anti-dilution protection meaning that functions such as the communication, publicity or goodwill function are recognized under European trade mark law.

Can one find anything about risk of association in the considerations? The - answer is yes but it does not help us much further in explaining the notion of likelihood of association. In the considerations it is said:

"Whereas the likelihood of confusion, the appreciation of which depends on numerous elements and, in particular, on the recognition of the trade mark on the market, the association which can be made with the used or registered sign, the degree of similarity between the trade mark and the sign and between the goods or services identified constitutes the specific conditions for such protection". Since this does not help us further and since the words "likelihood of association" originate from Benelux law, it is useful to consider how this notion was developed under Benelux law and what it means there. According to the Benelux Trade Mark Act of 1971 the trade mark owner can oppose the use of his mark or a similar sign for identical or similar products. These are the words of the infringement criterion in the case of identical or similar products. The concept of risk of association was born in a famous judgment by the Benelux Court of Justice, explaining the words "similar sign".[3] The Benelux Court of Justice decided that there is similarity:".... when taking into account the particular circumstances of the case such as the distinctive power of the mark, the mark and the sign each looked at as a whole and in correlation, show such a resemblance phonetically, visually or conceptually, that by this resemblance alone *associations* between the sign and the mark are evoked (emphasis added)".

This covers a wide variety of situations. First of all it covers the classical notion of *direct* confusion: confusion between the mark and the sign themselves. In other words: the risk that one takes one sign for the other. It also covers what I call *indirect* confusion, meaning the likelihood that notwithstanding the fact that the mark and the sign as such will not be confused, it would be assumed on the basis of the resemblance of the mark and the sign, that there is some kind of relationship between the proprietor or user of the mark and the user of the sign, for example, relations such as a licence, a merchandising or franchising agreement or a relation of sponsorship.

Finally, it covers the likelihood that (subconscious) connections or associations are made by virtue of the fact that through the perception of a sign, recollection of the mark might be stirred up. In other words: The likelihood that the mark is called to mind by the perception of a sign. It therefore also covers the likelihood of *dilution* in case of similar goods or services. It is clear that this offers a broad infringement criterion based on a modern approach of the functioning of trade marks. For example it takes into account the protection of trade marks against look-alike in day to day supermarket reality.

It can very well be argued that under European trade mark law the possibility to use the concept of likelihood of association as developed under Benelux law

[3] Decision of 20.5.1983, Nederlandse Jurisprudentie 1984, 72, Re UNION/UNION SOLEURE.

is offered. The reason first of all is that neither the Directive nor the Community trade mark Regulation do consider the origin function as the only valid function worthy of protection; the texts clearly provide for anti-dilution protection. The reason is also that the words "likelihood of association" are part of the infringement criterion in the words "likelihood of confusion includes the likelihood of association". This, however, sounds somewhat strange. It seems as if the wide criterion is mentioned as a genus of the species likelihood of confusion. In my opinion this wording means that likelihood of confusion should be understood in a very broad sense. In particular to include "likelihood of association" as applied under Benelux law.

Support for this opinion can be found in two documents which are called Statements for entry in the Minutes of the Council Meeting at which the Directive and (in 1994) the Community trade mark Regulation were adopted. These statements were partly meant to clarify certain clauses in the Directive and the Regulation and as such they could have an interpretative value. One of these statements reads: "The Council and the Commission note that "likelihood of association" is a concept which in particular has been developed by Benelux case-law". It could not be said clearer. However, life is not always that easy. In this context reference is made to a case opposing the marks WAGAMAMA and RAJAMAMA, both for restaurant services. The plaintiff in that case started an action in the High Court of London on the basis of the new English Trade Marks Act of 1994 and decided to use Benelux law as a means of interpretation of the words "likelihood of association" which occur in Article 10 of the new Act as adapted on the basis of the Harmonization Directive.[4] The High Court of London in a decision of 31 July 1995,[5] was not prepared to accept the aforementioned statements as a means of interpretation of the Directive. The Court said: "In my view it would be wrong for the court to draw any conclusions as to the meaning of a directive on the basis of suggestions as to what is said in the minutes when the minutes themselves are closed to inspection". Indeed, it is true that there has never been an official publication of the minutes of the Council meeting. Such minutes contain sometimes hundreds of pages and annexes and it simply is not possible to publish them all. There is case law from the Court of Justice in Luxembourg, however, in which minutes were considered in the context of interpretation of a certain European legislative text.[6]

Official publication of the statements in the Official Journal should be promoted not only because of the statement by the Council and the Commission that likelihood of association is a concept which in particular has been devel-

[4] In this case I acted as expert witness on the side of the plaintiff.

[5] [1996] ETMR 23.

[6] *Conseil National de l'Ordre des Architectes* v. *Egle* (1992) 2 CMLR 113. See, however, also EC Commission v. *Belgium* (1988) 2 CMLR 865, *R* v. *Immigration Appeal Tribunal ex parte Antonissen* (1991) 2 CMLR 373 and *EC Commission* v. *Greece* (1994) 1 CMLR 803. See also Ch. Gielen, European Trade Mark Legislation: The Statements (1996) 2 EIPR, p. 83.

oped by Benelux case law. There is for example a statement in the minutes of the Council Meeting during which the Community trade mark Regulation was adopted on genuine use which will certainly play a very important role. That statement reads "the Council and the Commission consider that use which is genuine within the meaning of Article 15 in one country constitutes genuine use in the Community". This has always been considered as one of the main selling points of the Community trade mark system. However, it is not mentioned in the Community trade mark Regulation itself.[7]

The conclusion of the High Court of London was: "there are two possible constructions which may be placed on Article 5 of the 1988 Directive and s. 10(2) of the 1994 Act. The rights of the proprietor against alleged infringers may be limited to classic infringement which includes association as to origin or, following the Benelux route, it could cover not only classic infringement but also non-origin association. In my view the former construction is to be preferred. If the broader scope were to be adopted, the directive and our Act would be creating a new type of monopoly not related to the proprietor's trade but to the trade mark itself. Such a monopoly could be likened to a quasi-copyright in the mark". Happily the plaintiff won the case under the classic doctrine of confusion as to origin and was not faced with an unfavourable outcome as a consequence of the afore-mentioned old fashioned attitude towards trade marks.

To summarize, the concept of likelihood of association as developed under Benelux trade mark law would be a very good standard to be applied under European trade mark law. The description of the function as well as the text of both the Directive and the Community trade mark Regulation, read in connection with the statements in the Council Minutes, offer this possibility. It would seem logic in view of the non-origin functions of a mark protection of trade marks against dilution is not only given in the case of non similar products (such as Article 5 (2) Directive and 8 (5) and 9 (1) (c) Community trade mark Regulation) but also (and *a fortiori*) of similar products. In the meantime some courts in other countries do apply the association criterion.[8] The real advantage of applying the principle of likelihood of association is that it fulfils the needs of trade marks as they function in modern day to day market reality.[9]

[7] See for the text: Official Journal OHIM 5/96, p. 607; Ch. Gielen, European Trade Mark Legislation: The Statements, (1996) 2 EIPR 1996, p. 83.

[8] See for example Court of Naples 10.5.1996, ETMR 43 *BARILLA* v. *DANIS*.

[9] The question of the meaning of "likclihood of association" was referred to the Court of Justice in a decision of 29.6.1995 by the German Bundesgerichtshof in a case in which PUMA opposed an application for registration of a mark by SABEL. See Gewerbliche Rechtschutz und Urheberrecht 1996, p. 60.

The Registration Procedure

This chapter is a study of the procedure for registration of Community trade marks from the filing of the application up to the decision thereon, pursuant to the provisions of Regulation 40/94, and basically Articles 25 to 45. The chapter further includes some notes on general aspects associated with the registration procedure (including matters relating to representation, languages and costs) and others on appeal proceedings from decisions of the Office for Harmonization in the Internal Market (hereinafter OHIM).

1. Filing of the application

Taking into account that a Community trade mark is obtained by registration, pursuant to Article 6 of Regulation 40/94, dated 20 December, 1993, it is only logical that the first aspects of the registration procedure to be considered should be precisely the filing of the application, the place of filing, the content of the application and the examination it undergoes.

1.1. Place of filing

Pursuant to Article 25 (1) of the Community trade mark Regulation, an application for a Community trade mark may be filed, at the choice of the applicant:

- At the OHIM directly, or
- At the national Trade mark Offices
  (or at the Benelux Office).

The national Offices (or the Benelux Office, where appropriate) will forward the application to the OHIM within two weeks *from* filing and may charge the applicant a fee not to exceed the administrative costs of receiving and forwarding the application (Article 25 (2) Community trade mark Regulation).

1.2. Conditions or content of the application

Article 26 of the Community trade mark Regulation provides that an application for a Community trade mark must contain:

a) a request or application as such;
b) identification of the applicant, including his name, nationality, address, etc.

c) a list of goods or services in respect of which the registration is requested;

d) a representation of the trade mark;

e) the application fee (payment of which may be delayed up to one month, pursuant to Article 27, *in fine*, Community trade mark Regulation) and, where appropriate, fees for the classes of goods or services, exceeding three, covered by the application (Article 26 (2) Community trade mark Regulation and Rule 4 6 of Commission Regulation 2868/95, of 13 December, 1995, implementing Community trade mark Regulation, hereinafter IR).

Where appropriate, the application may also include a declaration claiming the priority or seniority of one or more earlier rights, as we shall see later.

1.3. Examination of the application

Pursuant to Article 36 of the Community trade mark Regulation, the Office will have to examine the following aspects:

a) whether the application satisfies the requirements for the accordance of a filing date pursuant to Article 27 (in which event it will be equivalent, in accordance with Article 32, to a regular national filing in each of the Member States of the European Union).

The above-mentioned Article 27 establishes that the filing date of a Community trade mark application will be:

- the date on which the application was filed at the Office, or
- the date on which it was filed at a national Office (or at the Benelux Office).

In the latter case, however, it is a necessary condition that the application filed at the national Office, or at the Benelux Office, reaches the OHIM within one month from its filing date. Otherwise, the application *must* deemed withdrawn (Article 25 (3)). It is therefore important that anyone opting for non-direct filing at the OHIM check on the effective status of his applications before the end of that one-month period. Furthermore, although it is not specified either in Article 36 or Article 27 of the Community trade mark Regulation, it is naturally obvious that the OHIM will have to check or examine whether the *above*-mentioned condition is satisfied.

The Office will also have to examine:

b) whether the applicant satisfies the conditions required in Article 5 of the Community trade mark Regulation *in order* to be the proprietor of a Community trade mark.

If the conditions established in that Article are not satisfied, the Community trade mark application will be refused (although the applicant must first be given the opportunity to withdraw his application or submit his observations): Article 37 (2) Community trade mark Regulation.

The office will likewise examine:

c) whether the application, pursuant to Article 36 (1) (b) Community trade mark Regulation, complies with the requirements of a formal nature laid down in the IR.

d) whether the class fees, where appropriate, have been paid within the prescribed period (Article 36 (1) (c)).

If the Community trade mark application does not satisfy the minimal requirements for the accordance of a filing date, the applicant will be given the opportunity to remedy the deficiencies of which he is notified (Article 36 (2)).

If the deficiencies are remedied, the filing date accorded to the application will be that on which the deficiencies are remedied (Article 36 (3), last sentence).

If the deficiencies are not remedied, the application may not be dealt with as a Community trade mark application (Article 36 (3), first sentence) and will ultimately have to be deemed dismissed or refused. Likewise, if any deficiencies observed in relation to compliance with the formal requirements set forth in the IR are not remedied, the Office will also have to refuse the application (Article 36 (4)).

Finally, if default on payment of the class fees is not remedied, the application will be deemed withdrawn, unless it is clear which categories of goods or services the amount paid is intended to cover, in which event the application will be deemed to be confined to those classes (Article 36 (5)).

Naturally, if the deficiencies concern a claim to a priority right, or a claim to the territorially limited rights of an earlier trade mark, these being issues which we shall address below, failure to remedy such deficiencies will only result in loss of the priority or seniority rights claimed (Article 36, paragraphs 6 and 7). In the latter event, the application would be taken in all respects as an ordinary application without any priority or seniority claim.

2. *Priority*

2.1. A Community trade mark application may benefit from the priority of the following prior rights:

2.1.1. Those derived from a first regular application filed up to six months earlier in any of the States party to the Paris Convention for the Protection of Industrial Property (hereinafter PUC) or to the Agreement establishing the World Trade Organization (hereinafter WTOA), provided that the Community trade mark is for the same trade mark as the regular application and seeks to covers the same goods or services as the earlier trade mark or a narrower list of those goods or services. All this follows from Article 29 (1) of the Community trade mark Regulation, as worded in Council Regulation (EC) 3288/94, of 22 December, 1994, amending the Community trade mark Regulation for the implementation of the agreements concluded in the framework of the Uruguay Round.

The determination of whether a national application may be considered equivalent to a regular national filing capable of giving rise to a right of priority is left to the national legislation of the State where it was filed (Article 29 (2)), although it is specified (Article 29 (3)) that regular national filing *means* any filing that is sufficient to establish the date on which the application was filed (independently from the ultimate fate of that application, of course).

As in subparagraph (4) of paragraph C of Article 4 of the PUC, in the Stockholm version of 14 July, 1967, the Community trade mark Regulation considers as a first filing capable of giving rise to a right of priority an application which, while not being the first in time, is filed in the same State as a previous application, for the same trade mark and for the same goods or services, provided that, at the date of filing of the subsequent application, the previous application has been withdrawn, abandoned or refused without being open to public inspection, without leaving any outstanding rights and without having served as a basis for claiming a right of priority (Article 29 (4)).

Aside from this, if the priority claim is made in relation to an application filed in a State which is not party to the PUC or to the WTOA, the provisions of Article 29 of the Community trade mark Regulation (on which we have just commented) may only be applied if that State grants a first filing made at the Community Office a right of priority having effects equivalent to those established in the Community trade mark Regulation itself (Article 29 (5)).

2.1.2 Priority may also be claimed from the display of goods or services under the mark applied for at an international exhibition of an official nature within the terms of the Paris Convention on International Exhibitions dated 22 November, 1928 and revised on 30 November, 1972 (Article 33 (1)).

In this case the priority period is also 6 months, from the date of the first display at the exhibition of the goods or services under the mark applied for.

Naturally, in no event will this priority serve to extend any period for priority derived from the PUC or the WTOA, which was examined in the preceding point (Article 33 (3)).

2.1.3 Although it is not regulated in the same way in the Community trade mark Regulation and does not have the same effects in practice as the typical priority right we have just studied, another type of priority is recognized in the case of identity of the Community trade mark with national rights obtained in Member States of the European Union (thus being territorially limited rights) in the same trade mark for which the Community trade mark application is filed. This is regulated under the heading "Claiming the seniority of a national trade mark" in Article 34 of the Community trade mark Regulation.

With this mechanism the proprietor of a registered trade mark right in one Member State (or in the three covered by registrations at the Benelux Office) can benefit, for the Community trade mark, from the seniority of the earlier territorial right, for the protection it enjoys in the Member State where it is already registered (both if the right is derived from a national registration or from an international registration having effect in the State concerned). For the seniority claim to have effect, it is necessary not only that the trade marks belong to the same party, but also that they be identical and that the goods or services covered by the Community trade mark application be identical with those of the earlier registered right, or more limited than the coverage of that earlier right (on the understanding that even if the Community trade mark covers a broader list of goods or services, the effects of seniority will only extend to those which are common).

2.2. Proof of the priority right

In all cases, to enforce the priority right it is naturally necessary to claim it, to petition its recognition and, additionally, to prove it.

For the latter purpose, Article 30 of the Community trade mark Regulation provides that a claim to the priority of a previous application must be proven, as is usual in national systems, by filing a copy of the previous application giving rise to the priority right (with the additional requirement that the copy be certified and translated into one of the five languages of the Office if the application was filed in a different language).

In the case of priority derived from an exhibition, Article 33 (2) of the Community trade mark Regulation simply indicates that the applicant must file "evidence" of the display at the exhibition of goods or services under the mark applied for and refers one to the conditions laid down in the IR (which naturally require the filing of a certificate issued by the authority organizing the exhibition).

Finally, when seniority based on earlier national territorial rights is claimed, the IR provides that the applicant must submit to the OHIM the certified copy proving the national rights claimed.

It is to be observed, however, that a decision of the President of the OHIM (No. Ex-96-3, of 5 March, 1996) has relaxed the requirement that priority and seniority claims be proved by submitting originals of certified copies, which may be replaced by photocopies duly authenticated by the applicant or by his representative before the OHIM).

2.3. The effects of the priority right

The effects of the priority right will differ according to the nature of the rights claimed.

Those rights are established, on a general basis, in Article 31 of the Community trade mark Regulation, within the Section dealing with the priority right arising from an earlier application, when it provides that for the purposes of establishing which rights take precedence it will be considered that the filing of the Community trade mark application took place on the date of priority.

Obviously, this rule is likewise applicable to the case of priority arising from an exhibition.

However, the effects will be different when the claim relates to the seniority of earlier national rights. Here, the rights are more extensive, as it follows from the provisions of Article 34 (2) of the Community trade mark Regulation that when the proprietor of earlier national rights obtains registration of the Community trade mark, with recognition of the seniority of such rights, he will continue to enjoy the same rights as he would have had if the earlier trade mark had continued to be registered and in force. This is so even if the proprietor of the earlier trade mark surrenders it or allows it to lapse. However, those effects will evidently be limited to the territory of the State where the national rights existed prior to the Community trade mark application.

Aside from the foregoing, for a claim to the seniority of earlier national rights to have such effects, the surrender or lapse of the rights derived from the earlier territorially-limited registration must not occur before registration of the Community trade mark. Otherwise, the effects derived from the seniority of the national rights will not occur. The same negative effect will be produced if, prior to registration of the Community trade mark, the national registration is declared invalid (Article 34 (3) Community trade mark Regulation).

2.4. To end with the issue of priority, it may be added that the time at which the priority right must be claimed is as follows:

- Together with the Community trade mark application (or up to two months after the filing date of the application, in accordance with the IR) if priority is claimed from a previous application or from the display at an exhibition of goods or services under the mark;
- If the seniority of earlier national rights is claimed, the effects are not subject to the claim being made at the time of filing the Community trade mark application or immediately thereafter. Indeed, the claim to that type of priority may be accepted and have effect even if registration of the Community trade mark has already been obtained, as this is specifically established in Article 35 (1) of the Community trade mark Regulation.

3. Examination as to absolute grounds for refusal

Given that another chapter of this book is more appropriate for an adequate study of the content of Article 7 of the Community trade mark Regulation, which is the provision defining absolute grounds for refusal, or the reasons for refusing a Community trade mark application that comes under any of the prohibitions contained in that provision, we are going to concentrate here on the issues raised by the actual examination of an application to see whether it comes under any of the grounds for refusal set forth in the mentioned article.

This examination will be carried out by the Office after the application has passed the check for the formal and documentary aspects to which we referred earlier in this chapter. Obviously, the result of this examination may be the acceptance of the application and the continuation of the prosecution thereof (a favourable alternative which does not present further problems) or its refusal (a situation which may lead to a certain variety of possibilities, as set forth below), as provided in Article 38 of the Community trade mark Regulation, from which it follows that the applicant must be notified of the outcome of the examination regulated there.

The applicant will thus have the opportunity to withdraw or to amend the application and, obviously, to submit his observations on the objections made. In a nutshell, the applicant will always be able to defend his aspiration, his trade mark.

The Community trade mark Regulation does not establish a time limit, either for the examination by the OHIM or for the submittal thereto of a defence by the proprietor of the application. Moreover, on the latter issue the IR likewise does not establish a strict time limit, but provides that the Office will specify the period granted to the applicant (which must not be less than one month and not more than six months, saving an additional extension granted at the request of the applicant himself).

There may be cases where the applicant's defence is based on accepting that his trade mark contains an element which is not distinctive, but which may nevertheless not affect the eligibility of the mark for registration on an overall basis. In such cases (and to avoid any doubts that might arise in the future as to the scope of protection of the Community trade mark) Article 38 (2) of the Community trade mark Regulation authorizes the OHIM to request that the applicant make a statement whereby he will not be able to claim in the future any exclusive right to the element which is non-distinctive. In short, here the Community trade mark Regulation adopts a system which is well known in the practice of numerous national legislations, following the experience emanating from U.S. Trade Mark Law, and makes provision for the possibility of entering disclaimers in relation to certain elements forming part of a composite trade mark.

Aside from this, there may also be cases where the OHIM considers (notifying the applicant accordingly upon completion of its examination as to absolute grounds for refusal) that the mark examined does not, as a whole, come under one of the prohibitions regulated in Article 7 of the Community trade mark Regulation, but is only partially affected thereby (for only part of the goods or services covered by the application, for example).

Evidently, the final decision on the outcome of the examination by the OHIM as to absolute grounds can be none other than the acceptance of the defence submitted by the applicant and the forwarding of the application to the next procedural stage (with any limitations derived from the disclaimer entered, if appropriate, in relation to some element of the mark, the elimination therefrom of the element causing the objection or the partial waiver of protection for a particular category of goods or services) or the refusal of the application.

Therefore, if the OHIM continues to consider, notwithstanding the defence submitted and any amendments to the application, that the mark comes under some of the prohibitions regulated in Article 7 of the Community trade mark Regulation, the Community mark "shall not be registered" (in the terms set forth in the opening sentence of Article 7 itself), although the refusal may be partial, referring only to the goods or services affected by the prohibitions established in the mentioned Article 7 of the Community trade mark Regulation (see Article 38 (1) thereof). Naturally, the applicant will always be entitled to appeal, in accordance with Title VII of the Community trade mark Regulation, in the manner and with the scope and other details which we shall examine later.

4. Search: Examination for earlier trade marks

In addition to the examination of the Community trade mark application in relation to formalities and documents, as to whether the applicant satisfies the conditions required in order to be the proprietor of a Community trade mark, and the examination of the mark applied for as to whether it comes under any of the absolute grounds for refusal established in Article 7, the Community trade mark application also has to be examined for earlier trade marks.

That examination or search will be twofold:

- the one conducted by the OHIM, and
- the one that may be carried out by the central industrial property offices of the Member States of the European Union.

4.1. The OHIM search

This relates to earlier Community trade mark only.

Article 39 (1) provides that once the OHIM has accorded a date of filing to a Community trade mark application and has established that the applicant satisfies the conditions laid down in Article 5 to be the proprietor of a registration of that nature (and although the provision does not say so, it should be understood that this is after the application has passed the examination as to absolute grounds for refusal to which we referred above), it will draw up a Community search report citing any Community trade mark registration or application which, being of earlier *date* than the mark under examination, may be invoked against the registration of the Community trade mark applied for on coming under some of the situations regulated in Article 8 of the Community trade mark Regulation (the details of which are studied in another more appropriate chapter of this work, as here we are only referring to the procedural aspects of the search and examination).

4.2. The decentralized examination for earlier trade marks

This is optional for the Member States and relates to national rights only.

In accordance with Article 39 (2) of the Community trade mark Regulation, as soon as the corresponding application has been accorded a date of filing the Alicante Office will transmit a copy of the Community trade mark to the central industrial property offices of the Member States of the European Union which have informed the OHIM of their decision to operate a search in their own registers of trade marks to discover any earlier rights which may be invoked against the Community trade mark applied for.

The central industrial property offices which have opted for the mentioned possibility will conduct the corresponding examination for earlier marks and transmit to the OHIM, within a maximum period of 3 months from the date on which they received a copy of the Community trade mark application, a report which, in accordance with Article 39 (3) of the Community trade mark Regulation, will state:

- either that the search has not disclosed any prior rights which may be invoked under Article 8 against the Community trade mark application examined;
- or the list of earlier national registrations or applications (or international registrations enjoying protection in the Member State) that may be invoked against the Community trade mark *application*.

4.3. The overall search report and its effects

The Office will transmit to the applicant both the report on the search conducted in its own registers and those corresponding to the national searches received within the established time limit (Article 39 (5) Community trade mark Regulation).

Upon receipt of those reports, the applicant may naturally withdraw the application or amend it, limiting the application in some way, in order to avoid conflict with all or some of the earlier marks cited therein.

Upon expiry of at least one month from the transmission of the search reports to the applicant, the Office will publish the Community trade mark application and give notice of the publication to the proprietors of the earlier Community trade marks (registrations or applications) cited in the Community search report (Article 39 (6) Community trade mark Regulation).

This formula designed by the Regulation suggests some reflections. Undoubtedly, the basic principle used as a starting point is that the Administration itself should defend the interests of those who hold prior rights in distinctive signs with which the trade mark applied for at the OHIM may conflict. And it was probably as a result of an interventionist reflection that it was considered pertinent that the Office should not simply conduct an official examination or search for earlier marks, but *was also* entrusted with the additional task of reporting the existence of the Community trade mark application to those parties who might be interested in opposing it. However, this "paternalism" cannot leave anyone satisfied, for the following reasons:

a) because the notification will only be transmitted to the proprietors of earlier Community trade marks (registrations or applications);

b) because that notification will only be received by parties owning an earlier Community trade mark with which the new mark may be in conflict in the opinion of the examination services of the Office, whose reports may be the result of overzealous or of deficient work;

c) because the notification will not be transmitted to those parties who merely hold national rights, regardless of their importance and the extension they may enjoy in various Member States.

Thus, there is a clear and evident difference between the scope given to the effects of the search report of the OHIM and of those issued by the Member States. This is, without doubt, designed to promote the filing of Community trade mark applications, given that the proprietors will receive this "bonus" of knowing (theoretically, at least) that their trade marks will enjoy more examination and information privileges.

Aside from the foregoing, neither the Community trade mark Regulation nor the IR contains provisions as to what the national offices may do in relation to possible informative notifications (concerning a Community trade mark application referred to them for examination in their own registers) addressed to the proprietors of the prior rights cited in the search report they subsequently send the OHIM for transmittal by the latter to the proprietor of the Community trade mark application. Evidently, the Member States will be left free to adopt, or not to adopt, for their own search reports formulas similar to that under consideration in the Community trade mark Regulation. However, it seems obvious that in this area, as in many others, trade mark attorneys will have to operate their professional watching services with particular care.

In any event, for these and other reasons, the issue of searches was one of the last to be settled during the preliminary work on the drafting of the Community trade mark Regulation. It is naturally the result of a consensus reached after confrontation of varying positions of the different States. However, the best proof that the solution was not entirely satisfactory is the reference made in paragraph 7 of Article 39 of the Community trade mark Regulation to the fact that 5 years after the opening of the OHIM for the filing of applications there, the Commission will submit a report to the Council on the operation of the system of searching established in the current Regulation and, if it is deemed necessary, appropriate proposals for amending it.

5. Publication of the application

Publication will take place once all the requirements to be met by the Community trade mark application have been satisfied and after the expiry of the period of one month from the date on which the Alicante Office transmits the search reports to the applicant (Article 40 (1)).

6. The intervention of third parties in the procedure

These issues are addressed in Section 4 of Title IV of the Community trade mark Regulation, where a distinction is made between what are referred to in Article 41 as "Observations by third parties" and the procedure referred to as "Opposition" in Article 42.

6.1. Observations

This is the name given to the comments that may be submitted to the OHIM to justify that registration of the Community trade mark applied for should be refused "ex officio", particularly because it comes under any of the absolute grounds for refusal laid down in Article 7 of the Community trade mark Regulation.

The observations have to be submitted in writing and the persons who file them will not acquire the status of parties to the proceedings before the Office (meaning they could therefore be defined as assistants to the examination activities of the Office). The observations may be submitted:

- by any natural or legal person (given that the Community trade mark Regulation does not subject this possibility to proof of any legitimate interest to raise an objection); and
- by groups or bodies representing manufacturers, producers, suppliers of services, traders or consumers (who may be presumed to have some legitimate interest considering that their associates will always be directly involved in the marketplace).

The observations submitted will be communicated to the applicant, who, in accordance with the literal tenor of Article 41 (2), "may comment on them".

However, the Community trade mark Regulation does not contain any provisions concerning the action the OHIM may take as a consequence of the observations submitted. Serious doubts have been expressed about this, on the one hand because it would seem logical that the OHIM be able to decide on the applicability or otherwise of the grounds for refusal cited by a third party, but on the other hand the Community trade mark Regulation does not empower it to do so, among other reasons because the decision would imply a review of a question already decided upon the favourable conclusion of the examination prior to publication of the application. Along these lines, it may be held as more appropriate that the OHIM should not make a decision on the observations and that these should simply be added to the file for possible consideration in the event of an invalidity action (if the registration is granted) within the framework of Article 51 of the Community trade mark Regulation (or even in a revocation action based on Article 50 (1) (d)). This would ultimately be somewhat similar to what the European Patent Office does in relation to the observations a third party may submit regarding the patentability of a European patent application under Article 115 of the Munich Convention of 5 October, 1973 on the Grant of European Patents.

6.2. The opposition procedure

6.2.1. Entitlement

The following parties may oppose the registration of a Community trade mark(Article 42 (1)):

a) The proprietors of earlier trade marks, within the meaning defined in paragraph 2 of Article 8. In short, the holders of earlier registered rights in Community trade marks or in national trade marks and international trade marks having effects in a Member State, as well as those to which the protection afforded to well known trade marks under Article 6 *bis* of the Paris Convention may be invoked in a Member State.

b) The holders of a licence under any of the previously mentioned registered rights who are authorized by the proprietors thereof to file oppositions.

c) The legitimate proprietors of trade marks in *respect of* registration which has been applied for, without their consent, by an agent or representative.

d) The proprietors of non-registered earlier trade marks or signs used in the course of trade of more than mere local significance who have acquired the right to use the sign and to prohibit the use of a subsequent confusingly similar mark.

e) Any person authorized under the relevant national law to exercise the right to challenge the use of a subsequent confusingly similar mark.

6.2.2. Opposition period

The period to give notice of opposition is 3 months from the publication of a Community trade mark application (Article 42 (1)).

6.2.3. Form of the opposition

The opposition must be expressed in writing and specify the grounds on which it is made, paying the corresponding fees. It will also be necessary to submit (together with the opposition or within a period fixed by the Office) the documentation and evidence the opponent may deem pertinent (such as documents proving the registered rights in a Member State invoked as the basis of the opposition): Article 42 (3).

6.2.4. Examination of the Opposition

Once the opposition has been filed and entered, the Office will forward it to the applicant and invite the parties (the opponent and the proprietor of the opposed application) to submit observations concerning the arguments and communications of the other parties or of the Office itself (Article 43 (1)). Additionally, the Office may invite the parties to make a friendly settlement (Article 43 (4)).

It thus follows from the text of the Community trade mark Regulation that the opposition procedure established is a genuine adversary procedure (with replies and rejoinders) under the direction of the OHIM.

Aside from the foregoing, perhaps the most outstanding aspect of the opposition examination procedure is that relating to proof of use of the mark or marks on which the opposition is based. The principle is established in one of the clauses of the Preamble to the Regulation. Indeed, it is indicated there that:

> "... there is no justification for protecting Community trade marks or, as against them, any trade mark which has been registered before them, except where the trade marks are actually used."

And in harmony with this principle, paragraphs 2 and 3 of Article 43 of the Community trade mark Regulation establish rules whereby a trade mark which has not been used under certain conditions may cease to have effects in the opposition procedure.

Indeed, the applicant may request that the proprietor of an earlier trade mark who has given notice of opposition (and the same applies to the proprietor of an earlier national trade mark invoked as the basis of an opposition) prove that his mark, or the earlier marks invoked, has been put to genuine use, during the period of 5 years preceding the date of publication of the Community trade mark application, in connection with the goods or the services for which it was registered, or to prove, where appropriate, that there are proper reasons for non-use.

If proof of use is not submitted, the opposition will be rejected. If the mark on which the opposition is based had been used in relation to part only of the goods or services for which it is registered, for the purposes of the examination of the opposition it will be deemed to be registered in respect only of the goods or services on which it is used.

In order to be effective, use will evidently have to have been made in the Member State where the earlier mark is registered, when a national registered right is invoked, and in the Community, when a Community trade mark is invoked (although it should be recalled that there is a practically unanimous view to the effect that use of a mark in one Member State constitutes use in the Community and that this is the opinion which was reflected in the declaration on Article 15 contained in the minutes of the Council meeting at which the Community trade mark Regulation was adopted).

It is impossible to consider here all the problems which may arise with the use of trade marks and the nuances of that particular issue. There are many questions that will have to be resolved in practice, although this is not the proper place of this work to deal with them. We shall therefore simply put forward the suggestion that it is highly probable that the established formula will reduce the number of oppositions which would otherwise be filed at the Alicante Office, above all if it is taken into account that the cost factor may also have a bearing on the opposition procedure, as we shall see later, in Section 9.4.

6.2.5. Decision

At the end of the opposition procedure, the decision should obviously be none other than the acceptance of the opposition and the refusal of the Community trade mark application or the rejection of the opposition and the grant of the Community trade mark application (although the refusal of the application may be partial, if an opposition is accepted in part only, in which case the Community trade mark registration will be granted with a restriction of the goods it covers, in accordance with Article 43 (5) Community trade mark Regulation).

However, an opposition may also be "disposed of", pursuant to Rule 21 of the IR. This will also occur if several oppositions are entered against the same application and only one of them is accepted and the refusal of the application becomes definitive. The solution given in the mentioned event of several oppositions may not be very fair in some instance, however, because an opposition filed by a party interested in obtaining an express decision on the conflict between the rights invoked by him and the opposed application may actually be disposed of without examination and discussion of its grounds.

7. Amendment of the application

Article 44 of the Community trade mark Regulation makes provision for the possibility whereby the applicant for a Community trade mark may withdraw it or restrict the list of the goods or services to be covered. Such amendments may be made at any time, but if the application has already been published as initially filed, the withdrawal or restriction will also be published.

It is established that a Community trade mark may only be amended at the request of the applicant and solely to correct his name and address, errors of wording or of copying, or obvious mistakes, provided that the correction does not substantially change the trade mark or extend the list of goods or services to be covered. In any event, if the amendments were to affect the representation of the trade mark or the list of goods or services and were made after publication of the application, the latter would be published again as amended.

8. Registration

If the Community trade mark application meets the requirements established in the Community trade mark Regulation, and has not encountered any oppositions (or if any oppositions filed have been rejected by a definitive decision), the trade mark will be registered as a Community trade mark. Needless to say, however, that registration is effective subject to payment of the registration fee and if that fee is not paid within the period of 2 months prescribed in the IR (or within the additional period allowed by the IR itself) the application will be deemed withdrawn.

Once again, with the registration of the Community trade mark we are faced with what we have already seen in many other national or supranational regulations concerning industrial property: one can almost definitely state that any error may have a solution unless the error is not having paid fees on time.

Aside from the foregoing, it is easy to realize that the procedure for registration of a Community trade mark will probably take a long time, much longer than would be desirable for companies wishing to avail of immediate protection for signs intended to be used in the extensive marketplace of the European Union. Nevertheless, it is evident that the tool placed in the hands of those companies themselves is very important and responds to a long awaited desire which will presumably enjoy at least the same degree of success as the European Patent, thereby additionally giving the noble Spanish city of Alicante the opportunity to become a bastion of clearly supranational and harmonizing rights.

9. Relations with the OHIM during the registration procedure

Up to *this point* we have *examined* the procedure for registration of a Community trade mark and the different phases an application has to undergo until the mark becomes a registration. However, the presentation would not be complete if we were not to make some references to important aspects of the relations between interested parties and the OHIM. For this purpose, we set forth below some ideas concerning proceedings before the Office and the corresponding representation of interested parties, the languages that may be used, the regulations concerning fees and costs, and certain general provisions concerning procedure and information to the public.

9.1. Representation

When dealing with such an important matter as an attempt to register a trade mark, it will no doubt be unanimously agreed that in general it is highly advisable to do so through a qualified professional (as is customary practice), but this is even clearer in such a complex system as that of the Community trade mark, valid at the same time for 15 European States.

In actual fact, that professional representation is mandatory, pursuant to the Community trade mark Regulation itself (Article 88 (2)), for natural and legal persons not having either their domicile or their principal place of business or a real and effective industrial or commercial establishment in the Community. There is only one exception for the mere filing of an application for registration of a Community trade mark by the interested party, who may do so directly. This is no doubt designed to allow a party to obtain a filing date when there is literally no time for him to establish contact with a professional representative.

In principle, therefore, natural and legal persons located in non-Community States will have to act through a professional representative. However, in some cases, legal persons may act through an employee of another legal entity which has economic connections with the applicant, provided that legal entity has its domicile or its principal place of business or a real and effective industrial or commercial establishment in the Community.

In a work like this it may not be of major interest to undertake an analysis of who may become accredited professional representatives before the OHIM. We shall therefore simply indicate, with the necessary precision, that the status of professional representative is only open to those referred to in Article 89 (1) (b) of the Community trade mark Regulation as "professional representatives whose names appear on a list maintained for this purpose by the Office", and to legal practitioners having their place of business within the Community who are entitled to act on the territory of a Member State as a representative in trade mark matters.

As necessary requirements to be entered on the list of professional representatives before the OHIM, Article 89 (2) of the Community trade mark Regulation establishes that the candidate must:

a) be a natural person,

b) be a national of one of the Member States of the Community,

c) have his place of business in the Community,

d) be entitled to act as a representative in trade mark matters before the central industrial property office of the Member State where he has his place of business, either on being qualified to act as such or on having habitually so acted for at least 5 years.

9.2. Languages

One of the peculiarities of the European continent is that, notwithstanding its reduced territorial extension, it is divided into numerous States whose inhabitants speak a wide variety of languages. As of 1 January, 1995 the European Union consists of 15 sovereign States, as the 6 founder countries that signed the Treaty of Rome on 25 March, 1957 (Belgium, France, Germany, Italy, Luxembourg and The Netherlands) were later joined by another 6 countries (Denmark, Ireland and the United Kingdom, in January 1972, Greece, in May 1979, and Spain and Portugal, in June 1985) and most recently by Austria, Finland and Sweden (whose accession took effect on 1 January, 1995).

The result is, in accordance with the provisions of one of the Annexes to the Treaty regulating the most recent accessions (signed in Corfu on 24 June, 1994), that the official languages of the institutions of the European Union are 11: Danish, Dutch, English, Finnish, French, German, Greek, Italian, Portuguese, Spanish and Swedish.

Although the preparatory work on the Community trade mark Regulation was concluded before the latest accessions, the official languages of the European

Community were nonetheless 9 when the mentioned Regulation was approved. All the interested sectors agreed on the difficulties that would be involved in recognizing 9 official working languages at the Community Trade Mark Office, but in practice no State wanted to allow its own official language to be left out of the Community trade mark Regulation or to consent to the political conquest that would have resulted if one language, from among the 9 possible tongues, had been designated as the single official language of the Office in question.

Finally, as always occurs in these cases, a compromise was reached and it is set forth in Arts. 115 and 116 of the Community trade mark Regulation. These are complex texts, but the most outstanding aspects thereof can be summarized as follows:

a) Applications for Community trade marks may be filed in any one of the official languages of the European Union.

b) Notwithstanding the foregoing, the official languages of the Office will only be 5: English, French, German, Italian and Spanish.

c) At the time of filing the application, a second language, different from the language of the application, will be indicated. This language must be one of the 5 official languages of the Office, the use of which is accepted as a possible language of proceedings in all cases of actions where third parties intervene (opposition, revocation and invalidity).

d) If no third party intervenes in the procedure for registration of the Community trade mark, the language of the proceedings will be the language in which the application was filed (although the Office may communicate with the applicant in the second language indicated in the application if the language of the application is not one of the 5 languages of the Office).

e) Notices of objection filed by third parties (oppositions, applications for revocation and for invalidity) must always be in one of the 5 languages of the Office. If this language is the same as the one in which the application was filed or as the alternative language indicated by the applicant, the common language will be the language of the proceedings.

f) If the notices of objection filed by a third party are in a language which is neither the language of the application nor the alternative language indicated there, the opponent or the party seeking the revocation or invalidity of a Community trade mark registration will produce a translation of his notice into the language of the application or into the alternative language indicated by the applicant. In that case, the language of the proceedings will be the language of the translation produced.

g) In all cases, the parties to an adversary procedure, whether opposition, revocation or invalidity, or an appeal, will be free to agree that the language of the proceedings be an official language of the European Union, even if it is not one of the languages of the Office.

h) Aside from the foregoing, applications for Community trade marks and any relevant information which must be published concerning the applications or decisions of the Office, will have to be published in all the official languages of the European Union. The same will have to be done with entries in the Register.

i) In the case of doubt, the authentic text will be that of the language in which the Community trade mark Regulation application was filed or registered, if it is one of the 5 official languages of the Office, or the text of the alternative language indicated by the applicant, if the application was filed in a language other than one of the 5 official languages of the OHIM.

Upon reviewing all these rules, it is reasonable to ask which languages will, in practice, be the most used. Although it cannot yet be predicted as a certainty, everything appears to indicate that the number one language will be English and the second language will probably be Spanish. The reason is that in addition to the large number of applications filed already and that will no doubt continue to be filed by natural or legal persons located in States having English as their official language, or accustomed to using that language in their international commercial relations, many of the applications filed in English have indicated, and will continue to indicate, Spanish as the alternative language, considering the location of the OHIM, the level of perfect knowledge of this language by all the officials at that Office and the fact that in many cases the professionals acting for the parties will be established or have an office in Spain.

9.3. General provisions on procedure

As has readily been gathered from the comments made so far, proceedings before the OHIM are rather complex. They are already explained to a great extent in the Community trade mark Regulation and set forth in further detail in the IR. Moreover, aside from the specific provisions relating to each procedure or to each procedural stage, Title IX of the Community trade mark Regulation contains a series of procedural provisions, from among which we consider it of interest to highlight the following general declarations or principles:

a. The decisions of the Office will always state the reasons on which they are based and may not be based on reasons on which the parties have not had the opportunity to submit their comments.

b. In examination proceedings as to relative grounds for refusal (that is, in proceedings for the examination of oppositions), the Office may only take into consideration the facts provided and proven by the parties and the decision will be restricted to the petitions *presented* by them.

c. If the Office considers that oral proceedings would be expedient, they will be held either at the instance of the Office or at the request of any party to the proceedings.

d. In any proceedings before the OHIM, all types of evidence may be taken, including the following:

- hearing the parties,
- requests for information,
- the production of documents and items of evidence,
- hearing witnesses,
- opinions by experts,
- statements in writing, sworn or having a similar effect.

e. In cases where the applicant for or proprietor of a Community trade mark, or any other party to proceedings before the OHIM, was unable to observe a time limit, he may request that his rights be restablished (what Article 78 of the Community trade mark Regulation refers to as "Restitutio in integrum") if he can prove that he acted with the care required by the circumstances, but was nevertheless unable to avoid the loss of a right or any means of redress.

The application for restablishment of the rights (which will only be admissible within the year immediately following the expiry of the unobserved time limit) must be filed in writing within two months from the removal of the cause of non-compliance with the time limit and the omitted act must be completed within the same two-month period. Naturally, the application must state the grounds on which it is based and the facts giving rise to the inaction must be proven (and a special fee paid).

Aside from the foregoing, it is clear that when the rights of the applicant for or proprietor of a Community trade mark are restablished, those rights may not be invoked against a third party who, in good faith, has put goods on the market or supplied services under a sign which is identical or similar to the Community trade mark in the course of the period between the loss of rights in the application or in the Community trade mark and publication of the mention of reestablishment of those rights.

It is readily understood that these provisions will be applied in exceptional cases and will have to be interpreted carefully to determine the conditions under which they may be applied. In any event, the provision (Article 78 (5)) makes it clear that the institution of "Restitutio in integrum" may not be applied to the actual time limits established for requesting it (to which we referred above), to the period for claiming Paris Union priority or to the period established for the filing of oppositions (the latter because it is evident that a party who has missed the time limit for filing an opposition may always subsequently bring an action for invalidity of the registration, in the event the application is granted, in accordance with article 52 of the Community trade mark Regulation).

9.4. Fees and costs

Although the minimum cost of registering a Community trade mark is clearly higher than the normal cost of registering a national trade mark, it is also evident that the cost will be much lower than that of protecting a mark at the Benelux Office and at the Offices of the remaining 12 Member States of the European Union (and even lower than the costs of protecting a mark at more than 4 or 5 of those Offices).

Now then, apart from the objective costs that all interested parties will necessarily have to face, it will have to be taken into consideration that Article 81 provides that the losing party in adversary proceedings, that is to say, in opposition, revocation or invalidity proceedings (or the appeal following a decision made in one of those proceedings) will have to pay the winning party the fees incurred by the latter, as well as all the indispensable costs the winning party might have expended in the proceedings, including those corresponding to the remuneration of a professional (although the latter category of costs will have the maximum limit established in Rule 94 of the IR).

Aside from the foregoing, to avoid rash actions or those solely aimed at inconveniencing the adversary, the losing party, who will therefore have to bear the other party's costs, will be deemed to be the party who terminates the adversary proceedings by withdrawing the Community trade mark application, or the opposition, or the applications for revocation or invalidity, or the appeal, or by surrendering the Community trade mark registration. However, to ensure that costs are kept to a minimum in cases where there is little room for doubt as to the decision that will be issued (for example, in cases where an application faces oppositions that appear to be sufficiently founded), Rule 19 of the IR provides that the applicant will be granted a period of two months, from the notification served on him of the oppositions filed against his application (and entered by the OHIM), so that he may decide whether to withdraw the application or restrict the list of products or services to be covered by the application. If the application is withdrawn or amended in such a way that the opposition filed is no longer an obstacle, the fee paid by opponents will be refunded. Moreover, on thus avoiding the opening of the adversary proceedings to which an opposition gives rise, numerous costs (including the fees of professionals) are saved and this ultimately guarantees a better and more efficient system.

9.5. Publications and information to the public

The OHIM will keep a register of Community trade marks, which will contain all pertinent entries and which will be public. Provision is also made for the possibility of public inspection of the files relating to Community trade mark applications as from the time of publication thereof, although certain documents may be reserved, particularly those considered in Rule 88 of the IR to be of a confidential nature. These are: documents relating to the exclusion of or objection to OHIM officials pursuant to Article 132 of the Community trade mark Regulation, draft decisions and opinions, and all other internal documents, as well as parts of the file which the party concerned has shown a special interest in keeping confidential before the application for inspection was made (unless the party applying for inspection can justify overriding legitimate interests for access to the information).

A party may even be authorized to inspect a file before publication of the application if the party requesting such inspection proves that the proprietor will bring an action against him based on the Community trade mark as soon as it is granted registration. The threatened party may thus determine the grounds or lack of grounds of the threatened action.

Additionally, for more general dissemination, the OHIM will publish:

a. a Community Trade Marks Bulletin containing the applications and the various entries made in the Register of Community trade marks, as well as the particulars or notifications the publication of which is prescribed by the Community trade mark Regulation itself or by the IR; and

b. an Official Journal (which, at the time of preparing this work, has commenced being published) containing notices and information of a general character issued by the President of the Office, and any relevant information for the application and implementation of the Community trade mark Regulation.

10. Appeals from decisions of the OHIM

10.1. Jurisdictional powers of the OHIM

One of the obstacles that had to be overcome in designating Spain as the seat of the OHIM by Decision of the representatives of the Governments of the Member States, meeting in Brussels at Head of State and Government level on 29 October, 1993 (which Decision was published in the Official Journal of the European Communities – hereinafter OJ –, No. 323, of 30 November, 1993, pages 1 et seq.) was precisely an objection repeatedly raised by the Government of the Grand Duchy of Luxembourg. According to the Government of Luxembourg, the seat of the Community Trade Mark Office would have to be located precisely in that country, based on the application of another Decision of the representatives of the Governments of the Member States, also made in Brussels, but on 8 April, 1965 (when the Member States only consisted of the six founders of the European Communities). According to article 3 of that Decision, the jurisdictional and quasi-jurisdictional bodies existing at the time or that might be created subsequently under the Treaties establishing the European Communities would be located in Luxembourg. The decision of 8 April, 1965 was published in the "Journal officiel des Communautés européennes", No. 152, of 13 July, 1967, p. 18, and was recalled at the end of the Preamble to the previously mentioned Decision of 29 October, 1993.

The Government of Luxembourg understood that the body entrusted with the application of the Community trade mark Regulation, which would have to be created for the implementation thereof, would be a jurisdictional or quasi-jurisdictional body and would therefore have to have its seat in Luxembourg. It stated this claim repeatedly, at least after a Note submitted by its Delegation on 17 February, 1988 to the third session of the Intergovernmental Conference for the Establishment of the Seat for the Community Trade Mark Office, where it took a clear position (based on the theses put forward by Professors Boulouis and Jacobs) to the effect that a major part of the activities that Office would be called upon to carry out would be jurisdictional or quasi-jurisdictional activities. To support this assertion, reference was made to the powers that would be attributed to the Boards of Appeal of the Office in what finally became Article 62 of the Community trade mark Regulation because that provision actually establishes that the decision of the Boards of Appeal will be binding for the department which issued the appealed decision.

Luxembourg remained very firm in its position until the last moment. At an Internal Market Council meeting held in Athens in July 1988, it rejected a compromise formula, proposed by the Greek Presidency, whereby the seat of the Office would be in Madrid and the Boards of Appeal in Luxembourg. Its government made a unilateral declaration, which appears at the end of the Decision of the representatives of the Governments of the Member States, made in Edinburgh on 12 December, 1992, concerning the selection of a definite seat for the institutions of the European Communities (including the Court of Justice and the Court of First Instance), to the effect that Luxembourg accepted the formula set forth in the Decision in a spirit of compromise, but that this did not mean that it could be interpreted as a waiver of the provisions and of the potentialities of the Decision of 8 April, 1965, as can be read in OJ C 341, of 23 December, 1992, p. 4). Without a doubt, it was because of this statement that subparagraph h) of article 1 of the aforementioned Decision of 29 October, 1993 included a reference to the fact that a city to be designated by the Government of Spain would be the seat of the OHIM, including its Board of Appeal.

Having *stated* all the foregoing, a valid question to ask is whether or not the activity of what are referred to as Boards of Appeal in Article 130 of the Community trade mark Regulation, governed in Arts. 57 to 62, is jurisdictional.

"Iuris-dictio" is the Latin root of the term and is therefore equivalent to diction, declaration or affirmation of law. Spanish doctrine has thus understood that the concept corresponds to what is considered, in Article 117-3 of its 1978 Constitution, as the exclusive attribution of the Courts and Tribunals determined by the laws: to judge and to enforce what is judged.

Jurisdiction would ultimately be the activity proper to one of the three powers of the State, the Judiciary, although in line with modern doctrine other strictly non-judicial bodies also participate in that function, being genuine jurisdictional bodies integrated in the structure of the Administration, separated from the judiciary and independent from the active Administration. This has led to the graphic statement that while administrative courts do not form part of the judiciary, their members are genuine judges. Hence the position defended by the Government of Luxembourg, supported by the opinions of Professors Boulouis and Jacobs, paying attention above all to the nature and functions of the Boards of Appeal and to the independence of their members.

10.2. Actions challenging decisions of the OHIM

The Community trade mark Regulation regulates a variety of actions and appeals, which can be divided into actions challenging decisions of the Office (actual appeals), actions challenging registrations (for invalidity and revocation), actions concerning the infringement and validity of Community trade mark Regulations, defined in Article 92 of the Community trade mark Regulation, and other actions relating to Community trade marks not included in Article 92 of the Community trade mark Regulation.

Leaving aside the last three groups, which are dealt with in other chapters of this work, here we shall consider the first one, basically consisting of two types of appeals, namely, appeals to the Boards of Appeal of the OHIM and the appeals that may be taken with the *European Court of Justice* (hereinafter *ECJ*).

10.2.1. Appeals to the Boards of Appeal of the OHIM

All decisions issued by authorities and divisions of the OHIM are subject to appeal, which will have suspensive effect.

Pursuant to Article 57 (1) of the Community trade mark Regulation, appeals will lie from "decisions of the examiners, Opposition Divisions, Administration of Trade Marks and Legal Division and Cancellation Divisions", but not from decisions which do not terminate proceedings as regards one of the parties, which may only be appealed together with the final decision, unless the decision itself allows separate appeal.

Jurisdiction to hear these appeals corresponds to the Boards of Appeal of the OHIM, pursuant to Article 130 (1) of the Community trade mark Regulation, although provision is made for the possibility of the appealed decision not being remitted to them in cases referred to in Article 60 as "interlocutory revision". Indeed, that provision establishes that "if the department whose decision is contested considers the appeal to be admissible and well founded, it shall rectify its decision", although this will not apply in any case "where the appellant is opposed by another party to the proceedings". The latter will naturally occur where there is an appeal from a decision terminating a registration procedure with a third party opposition or from decisions issued in actions brought before the OHIM for revocation and invalidity of a Community trade mark registration.

Pursuant to Article 58 of the Community trade mark Regulation, the persons entitled to appeal to the Boards of Appeal are any party to proceedings adversely affected by a decision, and any other parties to those proceedings will be considered as parties to the appeal proceedings as of right. This means that the parties entitled to appeal will always be those whose claims were dismissed in the initial proceedings: a) the applicant for a Community trade mark which was not admitted or was refused, regardless of the cause therefor; b) the party who opposed an application which was granted and whose opposition was rejected; c) the proprietor of a Community registration declared revoked or invalid in an action for revocation or invalidity brought by a third party; d) the applicant for revocation or invalidity of a registration whose claim was dismissed.

The basis of the appeal (the "grounds", in the terminology of Article 59 of the Community trade mark Regulation) may obviously be the violation of any provision that should have been applied when issuing the challenged decision. The time limit to appeal will be "two months after the date of notification of the decision", pursuant to Article 59 of the Community trade mark Regulation, which also allows a longer period, of up to "four months after the date of notification of the decision" to file "a written statement setting out the grounds of appeal".

The stages of the proceedings will be as follows:

a) A notice of appeal must be filed in writing at the OHIM itself within the previously mentioned period, although the notice will not be deemed to have been filed if the appellant does not pay the corresponding fee, as is categorically stated in the second sentence of Article 59 of the Community trade mark Regulation.

b) Once the appeal has been filed and the grounds stated, it will be examined by the same department, division or authority that issued the challenged decision, which will have to determine its admissibility and, within one month after receipt of the statement of grounds, it will either (as stated above) accept the appeal, if it considers that it is well founded and there are no third parties that may oppose such acceptance, or remit it to the Board of Appeal without comment as to its merit.

c) Once the appeal is received by the Board of Appeal, the latter will examine it and determine again whether it is admissible and, of course, whether it is allowable. In any event, it will naturally give the parties the opportunity to file observations on the notifications issued to them or on communications from the other parties, in the framework of an adversary procedure, before the OHIM itself, of course, which will also evidently come under the general provisions on procedure contained in Title IX (Article 73 et seq.) of the Community trade mark Regulation, as summarized above.

d) Following the examination procedure, the Board of Appeal will issue the corresponding decision, where it may exercise the competencies of the department responsible for the appealed decision (that is, decide on the grant or the refusal of the Community trade mark application, the acceptance or rejection of an opposition, the revocation or invalidity of a registration, etc.) or remit the case to that department so that it may comply with the decision and prosecute the case further. In the latter event, the department will be bound both by the decision and by the ratio decidendi or grounds therefor of the Board, although "in so far as the facts are the same". All this is as provided for in Article 62, paragraphs 1 and 2, of the Community trade mark Regulation. The effects of the decision of the Board of Appeal are not immediate, however, as they are delayed until the date of expiration of the period allowed by the Community trade mark Regulation to appeal to the ECJ (2 months from the date of notification of the decision of the Board of Appeal of the OHIM, pursuant to Article 63 (5) of the Community trade mark Regulation) or until the dismissal of the appeal filed with the ECJ and the consequent confirmation by the latter of the decision of the Board of Appeal of the OHIM.

10.2.2. Actions before the Court of Justice of the European Union

After the comments concerning appeals before the Boards of Appeal of the OHIM, it remains to consider, within what we have called actions challenging decisions of the OHIM, appeals to the ECJ. They are admissible on a general basis from decisions of the Boards of Appeal of the OHIM, pursuant to Article 63 (1) of the Community trade mark Regulation and, as is explained in the Preamble to the Regulation, jurisdiction to hear them in first instance proceedings is attributed to the Court of First Instance of the European Communities (hereinafter CFI), created by Council Decision 88/591, of 24 October, 1988, Article 3 (1) of which provides that "the Court of First Instance shall exercise at first instance the jurisdiction conferred on the Court of Justice by the Treaties establishing the Communities and by the acts adopted in implementation thereof: ... c) in actions brought against an institution of the Communities by natural or legal persons pursuant to the second paragraph of Article 173 ... of the EEC Treaty...".

As is logical, the persons entitled to file an appeal to the CFI are "any party to proceedings before the Board of Appeal adversely affected by its decision", as is literally stated in Article 63 (4) of the Community trade mark Regulation.

Additionally, this is inexcusable given the wording of the second paragraph of Article 173 of the EECT: "Any natural or legal person may ... institute proceedings against a decision addressed to that person".

Until the amendments adopted on 6 July, 1995, to which we shall refer below, to the Rules of Procedure of the CFI (hereinafter CFIRP), the standing of the possible respondent in adversary proceedings before the OHIM was less clear. Although it seemed logical, in line with the provisions of Article 58 of the Community trade mark Regulation concerning appeal proceedings before the OHIM, that the parties to proceedings before the latter could be parties to proceedings before the CFI, naturally petitioning the Court to uphold the appealed decision in so far as it was favourable to them, there were technical difficulties that could only be resolved by the amendments mentioned above. Indeed, Article 37 of the Statute of the ECJ, signed in Brussels on 17 April, 1957, provides that the parties who may intervene in litigation submitted to the Court, in addition to the Member States and the institutions of the Community, include any other person showing an interest in the outcome of the litigation, but that the conclusions of the petition for intervention may only be intended to support the conclusions of one of the parties. Considering that an appeal from a decision of the Board of Appeal of the OHIM takes the form of an appeal for the annulment of an act subjected to Community Law, as an appeal intended to control the legality of an act of a Community institution, it is clear that the OHIM will be a party thereto and that, strictly speaking, the party favoured by the decision of the OHIM, appealed to the CFI, could not have any standing other than that allowing him to intervene in the manner indicated in the previously mentioned Article 37 of the Statute of the ECJ, that is to say, to support the conclusions of the defendant party (the OHIM).

No one was in doubt about the limitations the situation could imply. For example, it would affect the ability of the proprietor of a registration granted notwithstanding the claims of an opponent to defend himself appropriately, or the defence of priority rights held against a trade mark whose refusal by the OHIM is subject to an appeal by the applicant. For this reason, immediate ground was gained by a tide of opinion that led to the following two successive amendments:

a) A Decision of the Council of the European Union dated 6 June, 1995 (published in OJ No. L 131, of 15 June) amended Article 46 of the Protocol on the Statute of the ECJ. The amendment was necessary, in the words of the Preamble, "in order for the Rules of Procedure of the Court of First Instance to be adjusted to take account, by special rules of procedure, of the specific features of the proceedings relating to intellectual property rights which the Court of First Instance is called upon to hear".

b) Making use of the powers granted by the new article 46 of the Statute of the ECJ, the CFI approved, also on 6 July, 1995, the amendments to its Rules of Procedure, which were published in OJ No. L 172, of 22 July. Following that decision, the CFIRP were given a new Title 4 concerning "proceedings relating to intellectual property rights", where Article 133 provides that "the Registrar shall inform the Office and all the parties to the proceedings before the Board of Appeal of the lodging of the application" (of the appeal). Additionally, Article 134 further provides that the parties to the proceedings before the Board of Appeal, other than the appellant "may participate, as interveners, in the proceedings before the CFI" and that they "shall have the same procedural rights as the main parties" and may "support the form of order sought by a main party and they may apply for a form of order and put forward pleas in law independently of those applied for and put forward by the main parties".

The issue of the standing of respondents having thus been resolved, it is pertinent to say now that in accordance with article 63 (2) of the Community trade mark Regulation (coinciding with Article 173 of the Treaty of Rome establishing the European Economic Community or EECTR), an appeal from a decision of the Board of Appeal of the OHIM may be based on lack of competence, on infringement of an essential procedural requirement, infringement of the Treaty, of the Community trade mark Regulation itself or of any rule of law relating to their application or misuse of power. Naturally, each one of those grounds poses various questions concerning its nature and scope, and it will obviously be necessary to resort to the interpretation received thereby in doctrine and in jurisprudence (no doubt very extensive) arising from the study of Article 173 of the EECTR.

We cannot undertake a detailed study of each of those grounds here, as this would exceed by far the framework of this work. It will suffice to say that their origin lies in the contentious-administrative system of French Law and that:

a) it appears in principle that lack of competence, understood by the ECJ as a defect of public order which must be considered even if the parties do not lay any claim thereto, may only be raised in our case "ratione materiae", as there will obviously be no ground to consider that it may arise "ratione loci", in view of the unitary nature of the body issuing the challenged decision (the OHIM, through a Board of Appeal);

b) infringement of an essential procedural requirement (equally referred to as such in Article 173 of the EECTR) may arise whenever a decision is handed down in the application or appeal proceedings due to forgetfulness, or failure to apply or incorrect application of the provisions by which the proceedings are governed, as in the case of giving a decision without stating the grounds therefor;

c) appeals based on infringement of the Treaty, of the Regulation or any rule of law relating to their application will no doubt be the most frequent, given that it will have to be understood that the list of provisions that may be infringed includes all those constituting what has been called the block of Community legality, that is, any provision of substantive Community Law, regardless of its rank, and therefore including the general principles of Law, an expression which has to be considered as comprising the general principles arising from the very nature of the Treaties (such as that of equality and of solidarity), the general principles of International Law and what are referred to in the second paragraph of Article 215 of the EECTR as "general principles common to the laws of the Member States".

d) the perfect example of the misuse of power is found in cases of decisions taken for a purpose other than that which should prevail over the action of the authority or body issuing the decision.

The action must be brought within two months from the date of notification of the decision of the Board of Appeal, pursuant to Article 63 (5) of the Community trade mark Regulation, and it will be prosecuted in accordance with the provisions established in the previously mentioned CFIRP of 2 May, 1991 (with the amendments introduced by the decisions of the Court dated 15 September, 1994 and 6 July, 1995), which makes provision for a written stage and an oral stage. In the first stage, the parties will have the opportunity to file their allegations, in the form of a claim or application and a response or counterstatement (which may be followed by a reply and a rejoinder), with the respective statements of facts and legal grounds, definition of petitions and proposals of evidence. During the taking of evidence the Court may order the implementation of procedural steps consisting of the personal appearance of the parties, requests for information and production of documents, examination of witnesses or oral testimony, expert opinions and inspection of the place or thing by the Court (Article 65 of the CFIRP). The proceedings will end with the corresponding judgment, where the Court may annul or alter the challenged decision, pursuant to Article 63 (3) of the Community trade mark Regulation. In accordance with Article 83 of the CFIRP, the judgment will have binding force from the day it is issued.

10.2.3. Appeal for annulment

The judgment rendered by the CFI may be the subject of an appeal for annulment before the ECJ. That appeal is regulated in Article 49 et seq. of the Protocol on the Statute of the Court of Justice of the European Economic Community, in accordance with the text added to the Protocol by Article 7 of the previously mentioned Decision of the Council dated 24 October, 1988, establishing the CFI.

The appeal, which must be filed within two months from notification of the CFI's decision, may be brought by any party whose submissions were totally or partially dismissed by the CFI. In this connection, and although the second paragraph of Article 49 of the Statute of the Court of Justice states that "interveners other than the Member States and the Community institutions may bring such an appeal only where the decision of the CFI directly affects them" (which could raise doubts as to whether or not an appeal to the ECJ is admissible when it is filed by a party who, as was said above, is an intervener in an appeal for annulment before the CFI), it has to be affirmed categorically that in the same way as a party before the Board of Appeal of the OHIM favoured by a decision of that Board may be party to the appeal before the CFI filed by the party adversely affected by that decision, he will equally be entitled to file an appeal to the ECJ from the decision of the CFI revoking the decision that was favourable to him on accepting in full or in part the appellant's claims, thereby making him become an adversely affected party. No other conclusion may be drawn from the second paragraph of the new Article 134 of the CFIRP, where, as we saw, it is established that interveners "shall have the same procedural rights as the main parties".

Aside from the foregoing, an appeal for annulment, as is proper to any appeal of that nature, will be confined to points of law and, pursuant to Article 51 of the Statute of the ECJ, it must be based on grounds derived from lack of competence of the CFI, from procedural irregularities that have adversely affected the interests of the appellant and from infringement by the CFI of the applicable Community Law (which has to be considered to include all the specific provisions on the Community trade mark, whether the basic Regulation or the Implementing Rules thereto).

An appeal for annulment will be filed in writing either at the CFI or directly at the ECJ and the procedure will be that regulated in Article 110 et seq. of the Rules of Procedure of the Court of Justice dated 19 June, 1991. The petitions made may be addressed to the total or partial annulment of the decision of the CFI or to the total or partial acceptance of the claims submitted in first instance proceedings. No new claims are allowed.

10.2.4. Languages in proceedings before the CFI and the ECJ

To end with the question of appeals before the ECJ, we shall make some brief comments on the issue of languages. As is known, Article 115 of the Community trade mark Regulation establishes that English, French, German, Italian and Spanish are the languages of the OHIM and that adversary proceedings before the Office (as is the case of oppositions and appeals involving the applicant and one or more third parties) will be prosecuted in one of those languages. However, once a conflict between parties goes beyond the scope of the OHIM, as a result of an appeal filed with the CFI, Article 115 of the Community trade mark Regulation is no longer applicable because it only refers to proceedings that take place precisely before the Office, not to all proceedings concerning Community trade mark Regulations. The applicable provisions in proceedings before the CFI will be those contained in the new Article 131 of the CFIRP, that is, the following rules:

a) The appeal shall be drafted, at the choice of the appellant, in one of the languages mentioned in paragraph 1 of Article 35 (Danish, Dutch, English, Finnish, French, German, Greek, Irish, Italian, Portuguese, Spanish and Swedish).

b) The language of the proceedings will be that in which the appeal is drafted, if the appellant had been the only party to the proceedings before the Board of Appeal of the OHIM, or if no other party to the proceedings objects, or if the parties to the proceedings agree on the choice of that language.

c) If the parties to the proceedings before the Board of Appeal of the OHIM do not agree that the language of the appeal before the Court of First Instance be the language in which the appeal was drafted, the language of the proceedings will be that in which the Community trade mark application was filed.

d) Notwithstanding the foregoing, if, at the request of one of the parties and after hearing the others, the President of the CFI were to conclude that the use of that language would not enable all the parties to follow the proceedings and guarantee their defence, he may designate as the language of the proceedings another from among those indicated in the previously mentioned Article 35.

e) In all cases, however, the appellant may use the language chosen by him, and all the other parties may use the language they choose from among those listed in the mentioned Article 35, in all written communications addressed to the Court, although they will have to produce authentic translations thereof into the language of the proceedings.

f) All statements made during the oral stage of the proceedings in a language other than the language of the case will have to be translated into that language and, at the request of any of the parties, into another language used by it in accordance with the powers of election set forth in the preceding paragraph.

Jurisdiction and Procedure in Legal Actions relating to Community Trade Marks

A. Introduction

1. Title X of Council Regulation (EC) No. 40/94[1] deals with the litigation system relating to Community trade marks. In general terms, it sets out the rules on jurisdiction and procedure governing any legal action involving a Community trade mark.

The Community trade mark is a new industrial property right created by Regulation 40/94 within the framework of the Community legal order. Community law has therefore to offer judicial protection against breach by third persons of the rights conferred by the trade mark. It must, on the other hand, open to third persons the means to challenge the validity of the Community trade mark once it has been registered by the OHIM. Finally it must provide as to how to proceed with legal disputes which may concern the Community trade mark under other aspects, e.g. as an object of property, as to the entitlement to the right or as to the performance of contractual obligations based on its use.

It is a typical feature of Community law that Regulations are directly applicable in the EC States.[2] The rights conferred as well as the obligations or prohibitions imposed by Regulations may be directly invoked before the national courts of the EC States. These courts are obliged to enforce such Regulations and not to apply national provisions which would be in conflict with the Community rule, thus ensuring the primacy of the latter.[3] The Court of Justice has the constitutional task of "ensuring that in the interpretation and application of the [EC]

[1] Council Regulation (EC) No. 40/94 on the Community trade mark (OJ EC L 11 of 14.1.1994), amended by Council Regulation (EC) No. 3288/94 of 22.12.1994 (OJ EC L 349 of 31.12.1994). A consolidated text of the Regulation in the five languages of the OHIM has been published in the Official Journal of the OHIM No. 1/95.

[2] Article 189 (2) EC Treaty.

[3] Decision of the Court of Justice of 15.7.1964 in the case 6/64 "Costa/ENEL" Rep. 1964 p. 585.

Treaty the law is observed".[4] Keystone of the co-ordination between the national courts and the Court of Justices tasks is the mechanism of preliminary rulings instituted by Article 177 EC Treaty.

The trade mark law contained in Regulation 40/94 does not derogate from these general rules. The original features of the Community Trade mark require, however, a set of rules concerning the settlement of legal disputes more explicit and complex than in the usual cases of Community rules of direct application. The reasons can be easily understood if one considers the nature of a unitary Community-wide trade mark and its difference from a bundle of parallel national trade marks.

National trade marks – including "international trade marks" registered under the Madrid Agreement – are subject to the principles of national territoriality and autonomy. The rights each of such marks confers on its holder are limited to the territory of the State in which the trade mark is registered or has effect. It is a consequence of the principle of autonomy that, even if various trade marks are identical – i.e. contain the same distinctive sign and apply to the same products or services – their judicial protection is governed, in each of the States concerned, by the domestic national law. This law does not only establish the extent and limitations of the rights conferred, but also the rules applicable to matters of jurisdiction and procedure. For the national trade marks of the EC States the First Council Directive 89/104/EC[5] has, broadly speaking, unified the substantive trade mark laws, but not the national provisions on jurisdiction and procedure, with the consequence that the existing, differing national rules remain applicable. Retaining these differences is justified from a Community point of view under the principle of subsidiarity[6] and in any event it is not felt that these differences affect, at the present stage of integration the functioning of the internal market to an extent that would require an approximation of the laws.

The Community trade mark is subject to a principle of Community territoriality and its unitary nature prevents any autonomous treatment of the trade mark in different parts of the European Union.[7] The same distinctive sign is protected by one single trade mark for the same products or services in all the 15 EC States. Community law was needed in order to regulate all aspects of this new instrument, including the settlement of legal disputes relating to it. There were two possible approaches for the legislator:

a) a substantive approach, based on the adoption of unitary Community rules directly regulating the matter,

[4] Article 164 EC Treaty.

[5] First Council Directive 89/104/EC of 21.12.1988 to approximate the laws of the Member States relating to trade marks (OJ EC L 40 of 11.2.1989).

[6] Article B second paragraph of the Maastricht Treaty on the European Union and Article 3b EC Treaty.

[7] Regulation No. 40/94 Article 1.

b) an international private law approach, based on the adoption of Community rules of conflict which, according to the circumstances of each case, would identify and declare applicable one of the 15 national legislations of the EC States.

Regulation No. 40/94 has made use of both approaches, but in different proportions according to the sector concerned. For substantive law, unitary Community rules prevail and referral to national legislation takes place only in case of lacunae. For jurisdiction and procedural rules, rules of conflict are mostly provided, but there are also many interesting points of unification which will be duly stressed in the present commentary.

2. The implementation of the law instituted by Regulation 40/94, and in particular the implementation of the rights conferred by a Community trade mark, are entrusted to courts of the EC States which also control the validity of Community trade marks, but only to the extent that such control is not carried out by the OHIM which shares this jurisdiction with them.[8] As we are dealing with a unitary Community-wide right, the system has to provide rules enabling the identification in each case of which court, in which EC State, has jurisdiction to hear the case and which substantive and procedural law it has to apply. It is also necessary to have rules ensuring that any decision adopted by a court of an EC State in implementation of the Regulation is recognised and, if necessary, enforced in the other EC States. This is achieved by Title X of Regulation 40/94.

Title X has two basic sources of inspiration: the 1968 Brussels Convention on Jurisdiction and the Enforcement of Judgments in Civil and Commercial Matters – hereinafter referred to as the "Brussels Convention"[9] – and the Protocol on Litigation annexed to the 1989 Luxembourg Agreement relating to Community Patents – hereinafter referred to as the "Protocol on Litigation".[10] They are both international instruments concluded among EC States and belonging to the so-called "body of tertiary Community law", existing alongside the European Treaties and the secondary Community legislation adopted on their basis.

The starting point of Title X is the consideration that common rules in matters of jurisdiction, recognition and enforcement of judgments in civil and commercial matters have already been agreed by EC States in the Brussels Convention. Section 1 of Title X therefore establishes the basic principle that, unless otherwise provided by the Regulation, the provisions of that Convention apply to litigation involving a Community trade mark.

Derogating from this principle, Section 2 of Title X contains an original set of rules specifically governing disputes concerning infringement and validity of Community trade marks. This is the central and most innovative part of the

[8] Regulation, Article 55 and 92 d).

[9] The most recent consolidated text of the Brussels Convention is to be found in OJ EC C 189 of 28.7.1990. For more details concerning this Convention see Part B. Chapter II. below.

[10] The text of the Agreement relating to Community Patents is to be found in OJ EC L 401 of 30.12.1989. The Protocol on Litigation is on p. 34 and followings.

system, pushing as far as possible the unification of infringement law within the European Union. Section 2 also establishes the necessary co-ordination with the jurisdiction conferred upon the OHIM by other provisions of Regulation 40/94 on matters of validity. This Section is largely inspired by the rules of the Protocol on Litigation, even though a fundamental difference has to be indicated in the absence in this Section of a central judicial body corresponding to the Common Court of Appeal for Community Patents, or COPAC,[11] whose tasks are shared, for Community trade marks, between national courts and Community authorities (Boards of Appeal of the OHIM, Court of First Instance and Court of Justice).

Section 3 of Title X contains a few rules supplementing the general rules of the Brussels Convention. They apply to legal actions other than actions concerning infringement or validity.

Section 4 of Title X deals with a transitional provision concerning the application of the Brussels Convention.

3. The present commentary analyses Title X according to the two following aspects:
- jurisdiction, recognition and enforcement (Part B),
- the law applicable (Part C).

The three other following aspects would probably deserve greater attention, but are simply outlined below.

a) *Criminal prosecution of infringement of the Community trade mark*

Regulation 40/94 does not mention this aspect.[12] The question arises in each EC State as to whether the penal provisions repressing the breach of the rights conferred by a national trade mark can be applied in case of breach of those conferred by the Community trade mark. An answer to this question must be given by each EC State according to its own legal order on the basis of the constitutional principles governing criminal actions and of the wording of the criminal provisions involved.

b) *The direct actions of revocation or invalidity before the OHIM.*

In practice actions for revocation or invalidity of industrial property rights are closely related to actions for infringement. They correspond to one of the most natural and frequent defences of the alleged infringer. Their treatment under Regulation 40/94 is based on a sharing of the jurisdiction between OHIM

[11] See in particular Article 2, 22, 23, 28 and 30 of the Protocol on Litigation.

[12] Contrary to the Community Patent Convention which provides, in Article 74, that in case of infringement of a Community Patent "the national penal provisions in the matter of infringement shall be applicable, ... , to the extent that like acts of infringement would be punishable if they had similarly affected a national patent" (see OJ EC L 401 of 30.12.1989 p.25). Such an extension of the criminal law can be realised by a rule contained in a convention to be duly approved in each contracting State according to the national constitutional requirements. The jurisdiction of the Community to legislate on criminal matters by way of Regulation would be, on the contrary, highly questionable.

and Community jurisdictions, on the one hand, and national courts, on the other hand.[13] The commentary will deal only with the actions raised before national courts. The detailed rules concerning the actions brought directly before the OHIM are contained in a different Part of Regulation 40/94.

c) *Arbitration in disputes concerning Community trade marks.*

This is an aspect which is going through interesting and rash developments, thanks in particular, to the activity of specialised bodies such as the International Chamber of Commerce of Paris or the Arbitration Centre of WIPO in Geneva. Regulation 40/94 does not contain provisions regulating this aspect.

B. Jurisdiction, Recognition and Enforcement

I. Introduction

1. According to Article 90 of Regulation 40/94 the issues of jurisdiction and recognition and enforcement of judgments in legal proceedings relating to Community trade marks are governed by the Brussels Convention.

This principle suffers a derogation: jurisdiction in legal proceedings concerning infringement and validity of Community trade marks is governed by a specific unitary set of rules contained in Section 2 of Title X. No derogations are provided as to recognition and enforcement of judgments.

II. The Brussels Convention

2. The origin and Community nature of the Brussels Convention

The conclusion in Brussels, on 27 September 1968, of the Convention on Jurisdiction and the Enforcement of Judgments in Civil and Commercial Matters[14] was the answer by the "6" original EC States to a real need for the proper functioning of the common market. There could have been no satisfactory way of implementing the free movement of goods, persons, services and capital without ensuring "the free movement" of judicial decisions in civil and commercial matters between the EC States. This need had been recognised in the original text of the EC Treaty, in which Article 220 requires that the EC States enter into negotiations "with a view to securing for the benefit of their nationals ... the simplification of formalities governing the reciprocal recognition and enforcement of judgments of courts and tribunals and of arbitration awards". The Brussels Convention is the main result of the implementation of this provision.

[13] Regulation, Article 50 to 52, 55 and 56, 92 d), 95 and 96.

[14] The text of the 1968 Convention is to be found in OJ EC L 304 of 30.10.1978 p.36 in the English language, in OJ EC L 299 of 31.12.1972 p.32 in the four original languages.

The Brussels Convention has gone, however, far beyond the wording of Article 220 EC Treaty, which only mentions recognition and enforcement. It has unified to a very large extent the national rules on jurisdiction, thus establishing one of the fundamental pre-conditions for a future "European judicial space" in the civil sector. In other words, it has created a body of Community rules of international private law which replaces, in each State party to the Brussels Convention, the national rules if the defendant in a civil action is domiciled in such a State, and, independently from this condition of domicile, for those legal actions for which rules of exclusive jurisdiction are dictated.[15]

Although contained in a separate Convention, the Community nature of these rules is confirmed by the following considerations:

a) the legal basis on which the Convention is concluded, i.e. Article 220 EC Treaty,

b) the fact that the Court of Justice has been given exclusive jurisdiction to interpret this Convention by a Protocol which contains a mechanism inspired by the preliminary rulings mechanism of Article 177 EC Treaty,[16]

c) the existence in secondary Community legislation – and Regulation 40/94 is only one important example among others – of Community rules supplementing the rules contained in the Brussels Convention.

The Brussels Convention contains in its Title II rules permitting to identify, for almost every sector of civil and commercial law[17] the contracting EC State – and within that EC State the court – which has jurisdiction to hear a case. But the feature which makes this Convention so different from traditional conventions on jurisdiction and enforcement is that it entrusts fully to the judge who is seized of the merits of the case the task of applying the rules on jurisdiction. If the judge ascertains that he has jurisdiction and proceeds with hearing the case, his decision cannot in principle be re-examined by the judge of recognition or enforcement of another contracting EC State. Such a rule is only conceivable between countries which have reciprocal and full trust in the capacity and objectiveness of their respective judicial bodies.

[15] See Article 16 of the Brussels Convention.

[16] Protocol signed at Luxembourg on 3.6.1971 on the interpretation by the Court of Justice of the Convention of 27.9.1968 on jurisdiction and the enforcement of judgments in civil and commercial matters. The text of the 1971 Protocol is to be found in OJ EC L 304 of 30.10.1978 p. 50 in the English language, in OJ EC L 204 of 2.8.1975 p. 28 in the four original languages.

[17] Article 1 of the Brussels Convention mentions a few exceptions which are expected to be filled by further conventions: status and legal capacity of natural persons, rights in property arising out of matrimonial relationship, wills and successions, bankruptcy, social security and arbitration. Such exceptions, a part from bankruptcy and arbitration, have normally little bearing on matters dealt with in this commentary.

3. The Conventions of Accession to the Brussels Convention

The Brussels Convention has been supplemented and amended to date (February 1997) by four accession conventions, following the four successive enlargements of the Community:

- the Convention of Accession of Denmark, Ireland and United Kingdom, signed at Luxembourg on 9 October 1978,[18]
- the Convention of Accession of Greece, signed at Luxembourg on 25 October 1982,[19]
- the Convention of Accession of Spain and Portugal, signed at San Sebastian on 26 May 1989,[20]
- the Convention of Accession of Austria, Finland and Sweden, signed in Brussels on 29 November 1996.[21]

Due to the recent day of conclusion the fourth Convention of Accession has not yet entered into force.

The Brussels Convention, as supplemented and amended by the three first Conventions of Accession mentioned above, has been ratified, at the date hereof, by 11 out of the "12" EC States concerned.

Only Belgium still has to ratify the San Sebastian Convention of Accession.

At the present date (February 1997) the overall situation concerning the implementation of the Brussels Convention may be summed up as follows:

a) the Brussels Convention, as amended and supplemented by the three first Conventions of Accession, governs the following relations:
i) the relations between the 9 following EC States: Denmark, France, Germany, Greece, Ireland, Italy, Luxembourg, the Netherlands and the United Kingdom,
ii) the relations between each of these 9 EC States and Spain or Portugal,
iii) the relations between Spain and Portugal;

b) the Brussels Convention, as amended and supplemented by the two first Conventions of Accession, governs relations between each of the 9 EC States mentioned under a) i) and Belgium,

c) the Brussels Convention does not yet govern:
i) the relations between Belgium, on the one hand, and Spain or Portugal, on the other hand,
ii) the relations between each of the "12" EC States which were parties to the Community before the last enlargement, on the one hand, and Austria, Finland or Sweden, on the other hand,
iii) the relations between Austria, Finland and Sweden.

[18] OJ EC L 304 of 30.10.1978 p. 1.
[19] OJ EC L 388 of 31.12.1982 p. 1.
[20] OJ EC L 285 of 3.10.1989 p. 1.
[21] OJ EC C 15 of 15.1.1997 p. 1.

4. The application of the different texts in which the Brussels Convention is in force and the problem of the relations between EC States which are not yet bound by it

The situation resulting from the existence of different texts of the Brussels Convention which can be simultaneously in force in the same EC State is the reason for Article 104 of Regulation 40/94. This article contains a transitional provision according to which "the provisions of the Convention on Jurisdiction and Enforcement which are rendered applicable by the preceding Articles shall have effect in respect of any member State solely in the text which is in force in respect of that State at any given time".

This provision caters for situations such as the following: at present time (February 1997) a country like the United-Kingdom or France, in its relations with Belgium, is bound by the Brussels Convention as supplemented by the two first Conventions of Accession, whilst, in its relation with Germany, Spain or Italy, is bound by the Brussels Convention as further supplemented by the San Sebastian Convention. Even if the expected swift conclusion of the ratification procedures of the San Sebastian Convention by Belgium should shortly eliminate such situations as far as the "12" EC States are concerned, similar situations will arise as soon as the Convention of Accession of Austria, Finland and Sweden comes into force, bearing in mind that Article 14 paragraph 1 of this Convention provides for entry into force as soon as two EC States, one of which at least must be one of the three acceding countries, have deposited their instruments of ratification. It should also not be overlooked that, notwithstanding its affirmed "transitional" nature, Article 104 will remain applicable for quite a long period due to the prospects of enlargement of the European Union to other European countries.

Article 104 does not, however, cater for the fact that already at present – and no doubt also in future – the relation between some EC States is not covered at all by the Brussels Convention. As we have seen, this is the case at present, e.g., in the relation between Belgium and Spain, or in the relation between each of the "12" and Austria, Finland or Sweden. It is therefore to be expected that, pending ratification of the new Conventions of Accession to the Brussels Convention in accordance with the constitutional requirements of each EC State, the issues of jurisdiction, recognition and enforcement will remain governed, in the relations which are not yet covered by the Brussels Convention, by the bilateral or multilateral agreements in force between the EC States concerned or, if no such agreement exists, by the internal rules of private international law of each of these States. It is regrettable that such a clarification has not been introduced in the Regulation, contrary to Article 38 of the Protocol on Litigation.[22]

[22] "The provisions of the Convention on Jurisdiction and Enforcement rendered applicable by the preceding Articles shall not have effect in respect of any Contracting State for which that Convention has not yet entered into force until such entry into force".

It is suggested that considering the absence of a provision to this effect as a lacuna to be filled as suggested is a much more acceptable interpretation than considering that Regulation 40/94 obliges EC States to apply in such relations the rules of the Brussels Convention in advance, before they have been duly ratified in accordance with the appropriate constitutional requirements.

The perspective that for a certain time the relations between some EC States will not be covered by the Brussels Convention might well affect to a certain extent the efficiency of the litigation system instituted by the Regulation. However, at least with respect to Austria, Finland and Sweden, the practical consequences of this situation on the operation of the Regulation would probably be minimal. These States are all signatories of the Lugano Convention on Jurisdiction and the Enforcement of Judgments in Civil and Commercial Matters.[23] The contents of this Convention corresponds so closely to that of the Brussels Convention that the Lugano Convention has become known in legal circles as the "Parallel Convention". Finland and Sweden have already ratified the Lugano Convention which at present (February 1997) is in force in the relations between these two States and in the relations of each of them with the following other EC States which have also ratified that Convention: France, Italy, Luxembourg, the Netherlands, Portugal and the United-Kingdom.[24]

5. The declaratory nature of Article 90 (1)

According to its Article l, the Brussels Convention applies "in civil and commercial matters". For such matters it determines the issue of the jurisdiction of the courts of the contracting States and it provides for an expeditious procedure for recognition and enforcement of judgments issued by such courts. Litigation concerning Community Trade marks belongs to litigation in civil and commercial matters.[25] The Community origin of these trade marks, as opposed to national trade marks, does not affect the civil or commercial nature of the legal proceedings based on them. The general principle enacted by Article 90 (1) does therefore appear to be of a declaratory rather than a constitutive nature. Even in the absence of this provision the Brussels Convention would have found application in such cases, at least in the relations between EC States which are contracting parties to the Brussels Convention. It has been set out under point 4. why it would be difficult to assume that Article 90 has a constitutive value for those relations between EC States which are not yet covered by the Brussels Convention.

[23] Convention on Jurisdiction and the Enforcement of Judgments in Civil and Commercial Matters, concluded at Lugano on 16.9.1988 by the EC- and the EFTA-States – OJ EC L 319 of 25.11.1988.

[24] Switzerland and Norway have also ratified the Lugano Convention, which applies to their internal relations and in the relations with each of the 10 EC-States mentioned above.

[25] Regulation 40/94 does not deal with criminal prosecution of infringement of Community trade marks, but a civil decision adopted by a court as a consequence of a penal judgment would be covered by the Brussels Convention.

This statement of principle, useful for the clarity of the text, serves mainly as a legal linkage to Article 90 (2), which contains the derogations and qualifications to the application of the Brussels Convention required by the specific regulation of the issue of jurisdiction for proceedings concerning infringement and validity of Community Trade marks, set out in Section 2 of Title X.

6. The legal proceedings to which the general rules on jurisdiction of the Brussels Convention apply

The principle that jurisdiction is governed by the Brussels Convention applies to any legal action concerning Community Trade marks, with the sole, albeit important, exception concerning infringement of the rights conferred (including declarations on non-infringement) and the control of the validity of such trade marks.

The following, merely illustrative list, gives an idea of the main types of legal proceedings covered by the Brussels Convention: actions concerning the entitlement to the right, actions concerning the Community trade mark as an object of property, actions for contractual obligations relating to the Community trade mark, including assignment, licences, franchising, merchandising or sponsoring agreements.

The jurisdiction for these types of actions will be determined according to the Brussels Convention. This means basically the following:

a) if the defendant is domiciled within an EC State for which the Brussels Convention is in force, the rules of Title II of that Convention will apply,

b) if the defendant is domiciled in a country which is not party to the Brussels Convention (normally a third country, but provisionally, as we have seen under point 4., it could also be an EC State), the lex fori will apply, i.e. the national rules of international private law of the EC State where the court seized is situated.

In the case under a) the defendant can always be sued before the court of the place of his domicile. The defendant may also be sued before a court in another contracting party to the Brussels Convention under one of the headings of special jurisdiction opened by Article 5 of this Convention. Article 5 No. 1) is particularly relevant, as it points to the court of the place of performance of a contractual obligation: this could play an important role in actions concerning breach of licences or of other contractual agreements based on the Community trade mark. The defendant may also be sued before a different court under the conditions provided for by Article 17 or 18 of the Brussels Convention on prorogation of jurisdiction.

Once the international jurisdiction has been determined in accordance with the Brussels Convention, the national court territorially competent will be determined by applying the rules of procedural law of the EC State concerned which would be applicable if the legal action concerned a national registered trade mark of that State. This results from Article 102 (1).

7. The derogation from the general rules on jurisdiction

Article 90 (2) contains an important derogation from the Brussels Convention, with the effect of replacing or qualifying the rules on jurisdiction of that

Convention by the set of rules contained in Section 2, applicable to legal proceedings concerning infringement and validity.

Before exposing the contents of this set of rules, two questions arise:

a) was it admissible for the Community legislator to derogate by way of Regulation from the Brussels Convention?

b) why did the Community legislator feel a need to derogate from the Brussels Convention?

There is a clear positive answer to the first question. Article 57 (3) of the Brussels Convention states as follows: "This Convention shall not affect the application of provisions which, in relation to particular matters, govern jurisdiction or the recognition or enforcement of judgments and which are or will be contained in acts of the institutions of the European Communities ...". Trade mark law is such a "particular matter" and the Regulation on the Community trade mark indeed such an act.

As to the second question, there is a sound justification for the attitude of the Community legislator. Article 2 (1) of the Brussels Convention contains the fundamental rule on jurisdiction: "...persons domiciled[26] in a contracting State shall, whatever their nationality, be sued in the courts of that State". According to Article 3 exceptions to this rule are only possible in the cases provided for by the Brussels Convention itself under the headings of special or exclusive jurisdiction. According to Article 4, finally, "if the defendant is not domiciled in a contracting State, the jurisdiction of the courts of each State shall ... be determined by the law of that State". It results from the above that if the Regulation had relied exclusively on the Brussels Convention, unitary rules of jurisdiction in the fundamental field of infringement would not have been warranted if the defendant was domiciled in a third country.[27] In such a case the non-harmonized national rules of international private law of each contracting State would have been applicable, with a risk of positive or negative conflicts of jurisdiction between judges of different EC States, with a risk of irreconcilable judgments in the same dispute between the same parties and, finally, with a risk of "forum shopping" to an extent incompatible with the proper functioning of an integrated market.

These inconveniences obviously are also present with respect to other types of legal actions concerning the Community trade mark, but their effect would have been much stronger in the field of infringement. The attractiveness of the Community trade mark for undertakings would have been lowered to an unacceptable level if the enforcement of the rights conferred by it could have become uncertain in the sensitive case where the rights holder has to deal with an alleged infringer having his domicile in a country outside the European Union. These

[26] By virtue of Article 53 of the Brussels Convention the seat of a company or other legal person is treated as its domicile.

[27] This would be also true, of course, of persons domiciled in an EC State which is not yet bound by the Brussels Convention, but this can be considered as a provisional situation (S. point 4.).

same arguments had previously convinced the "12" EC States to develop, in the Protocol on Litigation, special rules on jurisdiction for actions concerning infringement or validity of a Community patent and derogating from or qualifying the Brussels Convention.[28] It was therefore natural for the Community legislator to take those rules as a source for the corresponding rules for the Community trade mark.

The legal technique of "derogating" from the Brussels Convention used in Article 90 (2) does not, however, give a fair picture of the real purport of the specific set of rules instituted by Section 2 of Title X. As we shall see, this set of rules does not in any way go against the spirit of the Brussels Convention, but improves the unifying effect of the latter by covering cases which would not otherwise have been dealt with in a unitary manner.

8. Recognition and enforcement

A swift and undisputed procedure for recognition and enforcement of judicial decisions is needed for the attractiveness of the Community trade mark. The system provided by the Regulation is of great simplicity: it simply declares applicable the provisions of the Brussels Convention, in particular those of Title III which deal explicitly with these matters. These provisions apply to:

a) decisions adopted by applying the rules on jurisdiction of the Brussels Convention;

b) decisions adopted with respect to defendants domiciled in third countries by applying the rules on jurisdiction of the State of origin of the decision, including the rules of exorbitant jurisdiction mentioned in Article 3 of the Brussels Convention;

c) decisions adopted by applying the special set of rules of Section 2 of the Regulation, as it results from Article 57 (2) b) and (3) of the Brussels Convention.

Article 25 of the Brussels Convention prescribes that the rules on recognition and enforcement apply to "judgments" given in a contracting State, where "judgment means any judgment given by a court or a tribunal of a contracting State, whatever the judgment may be called ...". According to Article 26, decisions adopted by a court of a contracting party to the Brussels Convention are recognised in the other contracting parties without any special procedure being required. According to Article 31, they can be enforced in another contracting party if they have been declared enforceable in the contracting party of origin. Enforcement takes place on request by any interested party addressed to one of the civil courts listed in Article 32. The recognition or the enforcement may be refused only for a short list of grounds mentioned in Article 27 and 28. The jurisdiction of the court of the State of origin may not be reviewed, not even to apply a test of public policy (Article 28 third paragraph). It is only if the decision has been issued in clear violation of the rules on jurisdiction of the Brussels

[28] See in particular Part II, Article 13 and 14 of the Protocol of Litigation.

Convention, that this ground may be evoked before the court of recognition or enforcement, but the latter is bound by the findings of fact on which the court of origin has based its jurisdiction (Article 28 first and second paragraphs).

As to the relations between EC States which are not yet covered by the Brussels Convention, recognition and enforcement will be governed provisionally by any bilateral or multilateral agreement in force between the countries concerned or, failing this, by the national rules of the EC State where recognition or enforcement is sought. As in the case of jurisdiction, the 1988 Lugano Convention might easy very much the inconveniences arising out of this situation as far as the relations with Austria, Finland and Sweden are concerned.

III. The rules on jurisdiction in legal proceedings concerning infringement and validity

9. The legal proceedings governed by Section 2 of Title X

Article 92 of Regulation 40/94 contains the list of legal actions governed by the set of rules on jurisdiction established by Section 2 of Title X. The list is as follows:

- actions for infringement of a Community trade mark,
- actions in respect of threatened infringement of a Community trade mark (provided they are permitted under the national law of the court having power),
- actions for a declaration of non-infringement of a Community trade mark (provided they are permitted under the national law of the court having power),
- actions for reasonable compensation in respect of matters arising between the date of publication of the Community trade mark application and the date of publication of the registration of the said trade mark,
- counterclaims for revocation or for declaration of invalidity of a Community trade mark raised in infringement actions or actions for threatened infringement.

According to Article 92, actions for threatened infringement and actions for declaration of non-infringement can be brought only if the competent court is situated in an EC State whose national law permits such actions. While understanding the reluctance of the Community legislator to interfere with national rules of procedural civil law, it must be stressed how unfortunate such limitations are. Their effect is one of discrimination against the person concerned, whose rights will differ according to the EC State where the competent court is situated. It is going to be particularly disappointing that in some EC States a person should be prevented from requiring a declaration of non-infringement to clarify his position and should be compelled to wait to be summoned in an action for infringement. Tactical considerations could also persuade the rights holder of the Community trade mark to exploit the flexibility of the system of choice of jurisdiction by addressing courts situated in EC States where the adversary party cannot anticipate his action by a request for a declaration of non-infringement, and this also does not seem to be fair.

Bearing in mind the various other measures interfering with national procedural civil law introduced by Regulation 40/94,[29] it is regrettable that the Community legislator did not show more courage by obliging the EC States which do not know this type of actions to introduce them in their legal systems at least as far as the Community trade mark is concerned.

As to revocation or declaration of invalidity, a direct action is open before the OHIM under Articles 55 and following of Regulation 40/94. In order to favour this centralised action, no direct action requiring a revocation or a declaration of invalidity of a Community trade mark is allowed before a national court. The defendant in an infringement action is, however, permitted to raise such a question before the court, provided this is achieved by way of a counterclaim. A limited exception to this rule is contained in Article 95 (3), according to which in some cases it is also possible to invoke before a court revocation or invalidity of the Community trade mark "otherwise than by way of counterclaim", in other words by way of a defence on the merits.

What are the reasons for this obligation to raise the issue by way of a counterclaim, hardly tempered by the exception mentioned above? The idea behind this requirement is that it would not be excessive to expect from a person who is accused for infringement to react by a counterclaim, thus putting the judge in a position to decide with effect erga omnes and throughout the territory of the European Union on the validity of the Community trade mark. If the defendant could simply raise the issue of revocation or invalidity as a defence on the merits, the results of the findings by the judge would only have effect inter partes. The advantage of keeping the Community trade mark Register "clean" of any rights which have been found invalid by a competent jurisdiction prevails over the limited procedural extra-onus which is put on the defendant by requiring from him that a counterclaim be formulated.

10. The instruments: a list of "specialised" courts and a unitary mechanism of choice of jurisdiction

To govern jurisdiction for the legal actions listed in the previous point, Regulation 40/94 makes use of two main instruments:

a) the designation by each EC State of a number as limited as possible of so-called "Community trade mark Courts",

b) a set of rules of choice of jurisdiction to the effect that in each case, irrespective of whether the parties have their domicile within or beyond the European Union, a competent court can always be univocally identified.

[29] See, for example, Article 91 on the specialisation of the national courts, Article 95 on the presumption of validity, Article 96 on counterclaims or Article 98 on the Community remedy of injunction.

11. The Community trade mark Courts

Under Article 91 (1) EC States are required to designate a number as limited as possible, of national courts of first and second instance to act as "Community trade mark Courts" with exclusive jurisdiction for infringement and invalidity proceedings relating to Community trade marks.

The nomenclature used in the Regulation should not deceive us: these courts are not "Community Courts". They remain part of the legal system of the EC State in which they are situated and, when implementing the Community trade mark Regulation, they act as any other national court called upon to implement Community law.

Article 91 must be seen in the light of the unitary set of rules on international jurisdiction contained in Article 93, according to which it can be established in each case in which EC State a court has jurisdiction for dealing with infringement and invalidity proceedings. Once the relevant EC State has been determined and if there is more than one single court which is competent, the choice of the court territorially competent will result from the measures adopted by the EC State in question in implementation of Article 91.

Clearly Article 91 partially interferes with the rules organising the judiciary system of each EC State, in particular those establishing the territorial jurisdiction of the national courts. The philosophy behind Article 91 is the institution of "specialised" courts. The interference is justified by the need to ensure that a right representing such a valuable asset as a Community trade mark be dealt with in court by skilled and experienced judges. This argument is strengthened by the consideration that these courts will also have jurisdiction, if so requested by the defendant in infringement proceedings by way of a counterclaim, to revoke or to declare invalid the Community trade mark with effect erga omnes and for the whole territory of the European Union. In the absence of a rule like Article 91, given the variety of rules governing territorial and substantive jurisdiction of the civil courts of the EC States, there would be such a multiplicity of possible fora in each of them, that the risk that in some cases the actions in question would be heard by courts lacking the indispensable experience could not be excluded.

The reasoning behind the institution of "Community trade mark Courts" is the same as that on which the "Community Patent Courts"[30] are based and, hopefully in a near future, the "Community Design Courts"[31] will be based. The Annex to the Protocol on Litigation (subject to the necessary completion for Spain, Portugal, the new Länder of the Federal Republic of Germany, Austria, Finland and Sweden) already contains a list of the Community Patent Courts and their territorial jurisdiction. The legal technique followed by Regulation 40/94 is different. The list of the Community trade mark Courts is not contained

[30] See Protocol on Litigation, Article 1 and Annex to the Protocol.

[31] See Article 84 of the Proposal for a European Parliament and Council Regulation on Community Design, submitted by the Commission on 3.12.1993 – OJ EC C 29 of 31.1.1994.

in the Regulation itself, but, according to Article 91 (2), has to be established following the communication that each EC State undertakes to forward to the Commission before 16 March 1997.[32] Article 91 (4) provides for notification of this information by the Commission to the other EC States and its publication in the Official Journal of the European Communities. By virtue of Article 91(3) and (4) any subsequent modification to the list decided by an EC State will be subject to the same procedure.

There is clearly no obligation on the EC States to adopt the same list of courts as for the Community Patent or the Community Design, but it would no doubt facilitate the access to the litigation system of Community industrial property rights and further its unity if the lists of Community trade mark, Patent and Design Courts were identical.

Article 91 (5) ensures that, if an EC State delays the designation of its own Community trade mark Courts and the need arises to bring an action for infringement of a Community trade mark in that State, the national courts which would have jurisdiction under national legislation if the Community trade mark were a national trade mark will be competent. This implies that the case might be heard by a court which is not "specialised", but this would be a minor evil with respect to a lack of jurisdiction which could result in a denial of justice, bearing in mind the rigid rules on international jurisdiction set out in Article 93.

12. The rules of international jurisdiction for infringement actions

Article 93 sets out unitary rules concerning international jurisdiction for the list of actions mentioned in Article 92. For infringement actions it basically gives the plaintiff in each case the choice between two alternative jurisdictions:

- a court situated in the EC State where the defendant (the alleged infringer) has his domicile or, if this criterion fails, in an EC State determined by applying some subsidiary criteria,
- a court situated in the EC State where the act of infringement was committed (place of the harmful event).

Article 93 only deals with "international" jurisdiction, i.e. it enables the identification of the EC State in which the competent Community trade mark Court is situated. The definition of which of the possibly several Community trade mark Courts existing in that State is territorially competent is left to the national measures taken in implementation of Article 91, supplemented by the rules of procedural law of the State in question.

13. The extent of the jurisdiction of the Community trade mark Courts

The choice between the two alternative fora created by Article 93 is not without consequences as, by virtue of Article 94, the extent of the jurisdiction of the

[32] This date, corresponding to three years from the day of entry into force of Regulation 40/94, results from Article 143 (2). At the present date (February 1997) no EC State had communicated such a list to the Commission.

court having power will vary according to it. A court of the first category will have jurisdiction in respect of any act of infringement committed within the European Union, a court of the second category only in respect of acts of infringement committed within the territory of the EC State where it is situated. This system presents a very high level of flexibility so as to meet the procedural and tactical needs of the right- holder.

The system points in each case to at least[33] one court which can, with a single action, decide on acts of infringement committed anywhere in the European Union. This Community-wide jurisdiction presents an enormous advantage with respect to the present situation, where separate actions are needed in each EC State where a protected right is infringed.

It could, however, occur that, notwithstanding its more restricted jurisdiction, the rights holder prefers to address the court of the place of the harmful event. It might be more convenient for the purpose of bringing the necessary evidence, or the judicial system of the EC State in question might operate more rapidly or be less costly or simply inspire more confidence in the plaintiff. These considerations could play such an important role that they would offset the advantage of a Community-wide action.[34]

The system based on two alternative fora with a different extent of jurisdiction looks quite straightforward. Its application could, however, give rise to a number of questions to which it is not easy to give an answer before the system has been tested in practice.

It will, for example, often occur that the place where the acts of infringement have been committed coincides with the place of domicile of the defendant. Should in such a case the court having power systematically consider that it acts as the judge of the domicile, given the favour for concentration of proceedings with a unique forum clearly emerging from Regulation 40/94, or should the qualification of the head of jurisdiction be left to the plaintiffs choice? The question is not purely theoretical. Apart from the different extent of jurisdiction, there are other important differences resulting from the qualification of the head of jurisdiction. If the court acts on the basis of Article 93 (1) to (3) a prorogation of jurisdiction to another Community trade mark Court is possible, if it acts on the basis of Article 93 (5) the situation in this respect, as we shall see, is far from being clear.

[33] The assimilation of the "establishment" of the defendant to his "domicile" amplifies in some cases the choice of the right holder, by giving him the possibility of choosing between two or more Community trade mark Courts situated in different EC States (see Article 90 (2) c)). If the adversary party agrees, a Community trade mark Court with such extensive jurisdiction can also be chosen by an agreement of prorogation of jurisdiction (see Article 90 (2) b) and 93(4)).

[34] The broadening of the number of courts with nationally limited jurisdiction due to the interpretation of the notion of "harmful event" given by the Court of Justice may increase the flexibility of the system (s. point 15. below).

The qualification of the head of jurisdiction may also have consequences on the application of the rules on lis pendens and related actions. Supposing that the court of the place of the harmful event has been seized first, obviously only for the acts committed within its jurisdiction, and the court of the place of domicile, whose jurisdiction extends to the acts submitted to the first Court, has been seized later, how should the rules on lis pendens or on related actions operate? There is no clear answer in the Regulation.

14. The criteria for determining the court with Community-wide jurisdiction
According to Article 93 (1) to (3) the EC State where the Community trade mark Court with Community-wide jurisdiction is situated is identified by applying, successively and in the order in which they are reproduced below, the following criteria:

- the EC State in which the defendant has his domicile (its registered office in case of a legal person),
- the EC State where the defendant has an establishment,
- the EC State where the plaintiff has his domicile (its registered office in case of a legal person),
- the EC State where the plaintiff has an establishment,
- the EC State where the OHIM has its seat, i.e. Spain.

The criterion of the defendant's domicile corresponds to the basic criterion of Article 2 of the Brussels Convention. The subsequent criteria (defendant's establishment, plaintiff's domicile or establishment, seat of the OHIM) are "exorbitant" rules. Article 3 of the Brussels Convention prohibits contracting States from applying this type of rules to persons domiciled within their territories. Contracting States are, on the other hand, by virtue of Article 4 of the Brussels Convention, free to apply this type of rules to persons domiciled in third countries, if their national law so provides. The introduction of such criteria in the Regulation is therefore by no means in conflict with the spirit of the Brussels Convention.

It is important to stress that the rules on jurisdiction of Section 2 of Regulation 40/94 are in force also in those EC States which are not yet bound by the Brussels Convention. While in such EC States for other types of actions national legislation may provisionally continue to govern jurisdiction (See point 4. above), for infringement and validity actions the rules of Section 2, instituted by a Community instrument, prevail over any different national rule and must be applied irrespective of the legal situation of the EC State concerned with regard to the Brussels Convention.

15. The jurisdiction based on the place where the act of infringement has been committed
According to Article 93 (5) the EC State where the Community trade mark Court with jurisdiction limited to its own territory is situated is "the member State where the act of infringement has been committed or threatened".

If the acts of infringement have taken place in several EC States, there will be a corresponding number of EC States whose Community trade mark Courts have separate jurisdiction. If the acts of infringement have been committed in places falling under different territorial jurisdictions of Community trade mark Courts situated within the same EC State, the procedural rules of that State will determine whether and how the actions can be joined before a single Community trade mark Court or whether they have to be conducted separately. This results from Article 93 which only deals with the issue of "international" jurisdiction.

Notwithstanding the difference in wording,[35] it seems legitimate to take into account the interpretation given by the Court of Justice to the notion of "place of harmful event" contained in Article 5 No. 3 of the Brussels Convention. On this notion is based the special jurisdiction, alternative to the jurisdiction based on domicile, in matters of tort, delict or quasi-delict, to which infringement by nature belongs. According to the Court of Justice such place can be "the place where the damage arose as well as the place where the act having caused the damage occurred".[36] If this interpretation is extended to Article 93 (5), it could occur, under certain circumstances, that the plaintiff would have a further possibility of choosing among different EC States the Community trade mark Court competent under this head of jurisdiction.

The Court of Justice has, however, indicated in its more recent case-law[37] that the choice of jurisdiction opened by this interpretation does not extend "to the place where the prejudice has been suffered", meaning by this the financial consequences of the harmful event. If this interpretation were admitted, it would be tantamount to recognizing an exorbitant forum of the plaintiffs domicile, as normally it is at that place that such consequences are felt. It can therefore be considered that, if the trade mark has been applied to the infringing products in EC State A and the sale of such products has taken place in EC State B, provided this can be construed as the expression of a unique infringing activity, there will be two alternative courts competent under Article 93 (5).The court of the place where the financial consequences of the infringement are felt – which is likely to coincide with the place of the rights holder's domicile or registered office – would on the contrary not be competent under this heading.

16. The prorogation of jurisdiction

Infringement is a tortuous action which affects the private interests of the trade mark holder. Contrary to the issue of invalidity of such rights, where the Brussels

[35] "The member State in which the act of infringement has been committed or threatened" in Article 93 (5) and "the place where the harmful event occurred" in Article 5 No. 3 of the Brussels Convention.

[36] See Decision of 30.10.1976 in the Case 21/76 "Bier/Mines de potasse d'Alsace" – Rep. 1976, p. 1735-1758.

[37] See Decision of 11.1.1990 in the Case C-220-88 "Dumez France and Tracoba" – Rep. 1990 p. I-49 – and Decision of 7.3.1995 in the Case C-68/93 "Fiona Shevill"/Presse Alliance SA".

Convention provides for the exclusive jurisdiction of certain courts which cannot be derogated by the parties, in matters relating to tort, like in most other area of civil law, the parties are free to "defer" the jurisdiction resulting from the rules of the Brussels Convention to a different court. This is in line with the principle that in civil matters the will of the parties prevails, provided some conditions, mainly aiming at protecting the weaker party, are fulfilled. These conditions are set out in Article 17 of the Brussels Convention. Similarly, if a party enters an appearance before a court which is not competent under the rules of the Brussels Convention, and this party does not contest its jurisdiction, that court will acquire exclusive jurisdiction by virtue of Article 18 of the Brussels Convention.

Article 93 (4) establishes that the prorogation of jurisdiction (with this double meaning, as resulting from Article 17 or 18 of the Brussels Convention) remains possible in case of actions for infringement of a Community trade mark. The parties might find it more convenient to address a court other than the one with Community-wide jurisdiction resulting from the application of the criteria set out in Article 93 (1) to (3). To do this the parties have to comply with the requirements of Article 17 of the Brussels Convention (or the defendant has to comply with the requirement of Article 18 of the Brussels Convention). Article 93 (4), however, adds a further requirement: the court to which the jurisdiction is deferred has to be a Community trade mark Court. If all these conditions are fulfilled, the deferred court has exclusive jurisdiction an to hear the case. Prorogation to a different court, even if legitimate under Article 17 or 18 of the Brussels Convention, is not admitted. This limitation, confirmed by Article 90 (2) b), is intended to warrant that litigation relating to Community trade marks will be in any case heard by experienced and skilled judges.

Article 93 (4) raises a number of difficult questions which will probably require future clarification by the Court of Justice.

The first difficulty results from the fact that Article 93 (4) does not mention prorogation agreements of the jurisdiction of a Community trade mark Court competent under Article 93 (5). As Article 90(2) b) makes the application of Articles 17 and 18 of the Brussels Convention subject to the qualification that the deferred court is a Community trade mark Court only in the cases mentioned in Article 93 (4), it can be argued that Article 17 and 18 of the Brussels Convention remain applicable without any qualification if the prorogation agreement concerns the jurisdiction of a Community trade mark Court competent under Article 93 (5). This means that in that case prorogation to a court which is not a Community trade mark Court would also be lawful. If we accept this reasoning, which is based on the letter of the Regulation, the exclusive character of the Community trade mark Courts is jeopardised, as we could have other courts, possibly manned by less experienced judges, hearing infringement cases, admittedly with a jurisdiction limited to a single EC State. It is not clear, from the text of the Regulation, whether such a court could also decide, if so requested by way of a counterclaim by the alleged infringer, over the validity of the Community trade mark, with effect erga omnes and for the whole European Union in case of revocation or declaration of invalidity. The wording of Article 103[38] could lead to the conclusion that this is possible, thus opening an important inroad into the mechanism of specialisation.

It could also be suggested that, contrary to the interpretation set out above, the legislator intended to exclude any prorogation of jurisdiction in the case of Article 93 (5). Article 93 deals exclusively with "international" jurisdiction. In the case of Article 93 (5) the Community trade mark Court has jurisdiction only for acts committed on the territory of the EC State where it is situated and the legislator might have considered that under these circumstances the prorogation to a Community trade mark Court of another EC State should be avoided. The favour of the forum loci delicti commissi should in this case prevail over the autonomy of the will of the parties. The need of qualifying Article 17 and 18 of the Brussels Convention in Article 93 would therefore arise only in respect of the heads of jurisdiction under Article 93 (1) to (3), where Community trade mark Courts with Community-wide jurisdiction are designated and where assessment by a court situated in a given country of acts committed in another country is admitted.

It is difficult to accept this reasoning. First of all the principle that the place of the harmful event should prevail over the autonomy of the parties will in civil disputes is a new one, unprecedented in international private law experience. Secondly, if this were the case, the text would show a lack of logic. Article 17 and 18 of the Brussels Convention apply not only to international, but also to "internal" prorogation of jurisdiction from one court to another of the same contracting State.[39] In the case of Article 93 (5) the text would therefore only exclude the prorogation of jurisdiction to the court of another EC State, but not to a different, specialised or non-specialised, court of the same EC State. This breach of the favour of the forum loci delicti commissi would be hardly compatible with the alleged existence of such a principle in the Regulation.

A second difficulty arises from the fact that Article 17 of the Brussels Convention makes its application dependent upon the condition that at least one of the parties to the dispute is domiciled within a contracting State. The wording of Article 93 (4) does not affect this condition. It results that prorogation of jurisdiction to another Community trade mark Court can never be agreed upon in those cases where both parties, the rights holder and the alleged infringer, are domiciled outside the European Union. This can only further even beyond the natural propensity of persons not having a strong territorial link with the European Union the conclusion of agreements of prorogation of jurisdiction to

[38] Article 103: "A national court which is dealing with an action relating to a Community trade mark, *other than the action referred to in Article 92*, shall treat the trade mark as valid" (emphasis added).

[39] This results clearly from the wording of Article 17 of the Brussels Convention: "If the parties ... have agreed that *a court or the courts of a contracting State* are to have jurisdiction ..., *that court or those courts* shall have exclusive jurisdiction. ..."(emphasis added).

courts of third countries. It is objectionable that in such circumstances the Community should deny any value to an autonomous expression of will of the parties, by refusing them the possibility of addressing a Community trade mark Court different from the one to which point the criteria of Article 93 (1) to (3), with the result that the dispute would be settled outside the legal framework established by the Regulation.

A third difficulty arises in connection with the situation of those EC States which are not yet bound by the Brussels Convention. How should they apply Article 93 (4) which uses the legal technique of qualifying Article 17 and 18? Would this be sufficient to justify their anticipated incorporation in their national legal systems?

Such a conclusion can hardly be accepted without abandoning the line of thought set out under point 4. above. The legislator probably overlooked this problem. The "effet utile" of the provision can be equally reached by considering that such EC States are provisionally obliged, in applying their national rules, to accept the result of agreements of prorogation only if they lead to the designation of a Community trade mark Court.

17. Actions for infringement before a court of a third country

Neither Regulation 40/94 nor the Brussels Convention can prevent rights holders and alleged infringers from prorogating the jurisdiction to hear their dispute to a court situated in a third country, if this court, under its own legislation, can entertain such an action. There are also cases where the jurisdiction of a third country court would exist independently of any agreement of prorogation by the parties. If one of the parties is domiciled in a third country it could well be that, under the rules on international jurisdiction in force in that country, a domestic court would have jurisdiction to hear a case of infringement of a Community trade mark. If the party in question is the plaintiff, this could be held to be an exorbitant head of jurisdiction by an EC State, but it would not be less legitimate in the country in question.

Decisions rendered under these circumstances could encounter difficulties in recognition or enforcement in an EC State. This would, however, depend exclusively on the bilateral, multilateral or national rules applied to judgments of the third country in question by the EC State where recognition or enforcement is sought. Decisions based on exorbitant jurisdiction heads could be particularly difficult to enforce.

18. The conflict of Article 93 with the Lugano Convention

In some cases the rules instituted by Article 93 (1) to (3), particularly those based on the defendant's establishment or the plaintiffs domicile or establishment, could be in conflict with international commitments undertaken by EC States with respect to third countries. The provision of Article 234 EC Treaty would apply to such cases.

There is a specific case of conflict which has been identified and which concerns the 1988 Lugano Convention on Jurisdiction and Enforcement.[40] This Convention, which has been signed by the "12" EC States and which is rapidly entering into force in their relations with third countries which are contracting parties,[41] contains rules which oblige EC-contracting States, in an infringement action concerning the Community trade mark, if the defendant is domiciled in such a third country, to accept the jurisdiction of the court of the country of domicile. This is in clear conflict with the provisions of Regulation 40/94 which provide in such cases for the jurisdiction of the court of the place of the defendant's establishment or of the plaintiffs domicile or establishment. This also applies to the jurisdiction of the court in the EC State of the seat of the OHIM.

Obviously, following the accession to the European Union and to the Brussels Convention of Austria, Finland and Sweden, the problem of the conflict with the Lugano Convention may have lost its importance with respect to those three countries, but it remains to be solved as far as the relationship to Iceland, Norway, Switzerland and Liechtenstein is concerned.[42] According to the doctrine of "implied powers" of the Community expressed in the "AETR" case, the Community itself is competent to negotiate an agreement with the relevant third countries in order to dispose of the conflict, at least as far as the application of the Lugano Convention to disputes relating to Community trade marks is concerned. The European Commission should take an initiative in this sense, as legal disputes could give this matter some urgency in a very near future.

It is worth mentioning the odd solution given by the Community legislator to this problem in the Council Regulation on Community rights on plant varieties.[43] Article 101 of that Regulation provides that civil disputes concerning such rights are governed, as a matter of general principle, by the Lugano Convention (and not by the Brussels Convention, as it would have been expected). This undoubtedly solves the conflict, but it is surprising to see the Community declaring applicable to relations between EC States a Convention which explicitly excludes such relations from its scope of application, leaving this function to the Brussels Convention.[44]

[40] See footnote (23).

[41] See point 4 and footnote (24) above. It should be noted that, according to Article 61 (1) b) of the Lugano Convention, third countries other than EC- or EFTA-States could be invited to accede to this Convention. Proposals to this effect concerning Poland, the Czech Republic and Hungary have been recently submitted respectively by the Netherlands, Austria and Finland.

[42] For a detailed exposition of the similar conflict arising out of the provisions of the Protocol on Litigation applicable to disputes concerning Community Patents, s. V. Scordamaglia: "Die Gerichtsstandsregelung im Gemeinschaftspatentübereinkommen und das Vollstreckungsübereinkommen von Lugano" in "Festschrift für H. Doktor Kurt Haertel" – GRUR-International 1990, p.777.

[43] Council Regulation (EC) No. 2100/94 of 27.7.1994 on Community rights on plant varieties (OJ EC L 227 of 1.9.1994), amended by Council Regulation (EC) No. 2506/95 of 25 October 1995 (OJ EC L 258 of 28.10.1995).

[44] See Article 54b of the Lugano Convention.

19. The rules of international jurisdiction in counterclaims for revocation or invalidity

The revocation or the declaration of invalidity of a Community trade mark can be requested before a Community trade mark Court by way of counterclaim during an infringement action, irrespective of the head of jurisdiction under which the court is seized.

The jurisdiction of the Community trade mark Court competent to hear such a counterclaim is therefore fully determined by the rules set out above concerning the jurisdiction in matters of infringement, including the Community trade mark Courts to which the competence is deferred in accordance with Article 93 (4).

In accordance with Article 50 to 52 of Regulation 40/94 the departments of the OHIM have exclusive jurisdiction for the direct action for revocation or declaration of invalidity.

It might be questioned whether this set of rules sharing the jurisdiction between national courts and departments of the OHIM complies with the rule of Article 16 No. 4 of the Brussels Convention for actions relating to the validity of industrial property rights. This provision establishes an exclusive head of jurisdiction, regardless of the domicile of the defendant, "in proceedings concerned with the registration or the validity of patents, trade marks, designs, or other similar rights required to be deposited or registered, [of] the courts of the contracting State in which the deposit or registration has been applied for, has taken place or is, under the terms of an international convention, deemed to have taken place".

The wording of this provision, established having in view national industrial property rights or those resulting from an international registration, as under the 1891 Madrid Agreement or the 1989 Madrid Protocol, is not adapted to a Community unitary right. The EC State where the registration has taken place cannot be simply identified with the EC State where the OHIM has its seat. It corresponds to the logic of a system where the national territoriality principle is replaced by a Community territoriality principle, that the courts of any EC State should be able to decide over the validity of the Community right. Determining which of such courts should be competent in any given case is a matter which, in a unitary system, should be settled by a Community rule allocating the territorial jurisdiction among the courts concerned.

This result has been achieved in Regulation 40/94 by a twofold mechanism: the jurisdiction has been basically entrusted to a Community central authority, the OHIM, under the judicial control of the Court of First Instance and the Court of Justice, but this jurisdiction is shared with the Community trade mark Courts when they are seized by way of counterclaim in an infringement action. In the latter case the rules on choice of jurisdiction established for the infringement action, integrated by the national procedural rules on territorial jurisdiction, operate as Community rules determining the territorial jurisdiction of each of those courts within the European Union.

Under these circumstances it might have been useful to clarify in the Regulation that the rule allocating the jurisdiction to the Community trade mark Courts to hear revocation or invalidity proceedings implements Article 16 No. 4

of the Brussels Convention. This would have also clarified that it is not permitted to challenge the validity of a Community trade mark before a court of a third country. Such a rule under the present wording of the Regulation must be deduced from the general principle that, as an industrial property right is the expression of a sovereign act of the entity which has granted it (normally a State, in our case the Community), its validity can only be challenged before a body deriving its power from that sovereign entity. If the question of validity of a Community trade mark should be raised in infringement proceedings brought before a court of a third country, that court could only decide to stay the proceedings and invite the parties to clarify the question of validity before the OHIM within the European Union.

20. The derogations and qualifications of the Brussels Convention

Article 90 (2) a) of the Regulation mentions a few provisions of the Brussels Convention which are declared inapplicable, to the extent that they are replaced by the rules contained in Article 93.

Article 2 of the Brussels Convention is declared inapplicable. This is a declaratory provision and the result of a formal concern. As we have seen, the main criterion of Article 93 (1) for identifying the court with Community-wide jurisdiction is the domicile of the defendant, which is identical to the criterion contained in Article 2 of the Brussels Convention.

Article 4 of the Brussels Convention has been also declared inapplicable. This mention aims at avoiding a possible conflict of rules when the defendant is not domiciled within an EC State party to the Brussels Convention. Under that Convention those States would be called in this case to apply their national law on jurisdiction, whilst Article 93 (1) to (3) obliges them to apply the unitary criteria provided by these provisions. But the statement concerning Article 4 in Article 90 (2) a) is also of declaratory nature, as the same result would have been achieved independently by applying the principle of the primacy of the Community provisions of the Regulation over the provisions of a Convention, even if the latter belongs to the body of tertiary Community law.

Article 5 No. 3 of the Brussels Convention has also been declared inapplicable. There is no substantive difference between this provision and Article 93 (5), both opening a forum loci delicti commissi. Article 93 (5) only has a broader scope, as it also applies when the defendant is domiciled outside an EC State party to the Brussels Convention. It is regrettable that, in this specific case, the legislator has followed the legal technique of declaring inapplicable the corresponding provision of the Brussels Convention: the differences in wording of Article 5 No. 3 and Article 93(5) could give rise to discussions concerning the impact on the second provision of the case-law of the Court of Justice interpreting the first one.[45]

[45] See point 15. above and footnotes (36) and (37).

Article 5 No. 1 of the Brussels Convention has been also declared inapplicable. The legislator has feared that the plaintiff could disguise his infringement suit as proceedings to obtain the performance of a contract and thus circumvent the exclusive jurisdiction of the Community trade mark Courts. This provision raises, however, some difficulties. The place where a contractual obligation has to be performed is one of the most commonly used heads of jurisdiction in civil and commercial matters. It can be used in particular for breach of licensing agreements on intellectual property rights as a handy alternative forum to that of the defendant's domicile. According to Article 22 (2) of the Regulation the action for infringement is also available to the right holder for the violation of some important contractual obligations contained in licensing agreements of a Community trade mark.[46] The aim of this provision is to give the right holder a second and efficient legal weapon, next to contract law. The provision declaring Article 5 No. 1 of the Brussels Convention inapplicable seems to imply that, wherever both grounds – infringement and violation of contract law are invoked, the choice of jurisdiction is governed by the infringement action. Difficulties could arise if the action for breach of contract is the main action and the infringement is invoked only as subsidiary action, or if the findings of the court concern a breach of contractual obligation which is not assimilated to infringement (for instance, failure to pay the royalty by the licensee): should in these cases the Community trade mark Court decline its jurisdiction and require the parties to bring their action before the court competent under Article 5 No. 1 of the Brussels Convention? Would it be possible, on the other hand, for the right holder, by limiting his action to breach of contract and by bringing it before the ordinary competent court, to avoid any risk that the licensee can counterclaim the revocation or the invalidity of the Community trade mark, but would be obliged, if he so wishes, to start direct proceedings before the OHIM?

Article 5 No. 4 and No. 5 of the Brussels Convention are also declared inapplicable for similar reasons. The legislator has feared that, if the infringement is prosecuted in criminal proceedings and the court seized has jurisdiction under its own law to entertain civil proceedings, or if the civil action is presented as an action arising out of the operation of a branch, agency or other establishment, the rules concerning the exclusive jurisdiction of the Community trade mark Courts could be circumvented.

The provision of Article 90 (2) b) has already been dealt with under point 16. on prorogation of jurisdiction.

[46] "The proprietor of a Community trade mark may invoke the rights conferred by that trade mark against a licensee who contravenes any provision in his licensing contract with regard to its duration, the form covered by the registration in which the trade mark may be used, the scope of the goods or services for which the licence is granted, the territory in which the trade mark may be affixed, or the quality of the goods manufactured or of the services provided by the licensee".

An interesting provision which deserves attention is Article 90 (2) c) which specifies that the rules of the Brussels Convention applicable to persons domiciled within an EC State, when applied to proceedings relating to infringement of a Community trade mark, are also applicable to persons who, although not having a domicile, have an "establishment" in an EC State. The effect of this provision is to amplify the scope of application of several rules of the Brussels Convention. Article 17 on prorogation of jurisdiction will, for example, also apply if at least one of the parties has an establishment within an EC State. Similarly by virtue of Article 20 concerning judgment by default the rights of the persons domiciled in an EC State will be extended to the persons having an establishment therein. However the main field of application of this provision is probably going to be Article 6 No. 1 of the Brussels Convention, by making it possible, in case of plurality of defendants, to choose the court by using indifferently the criterion of the domicile or that of the establishment of anyone of them.

This provision increases the flexibility of the system, but possibly to an excessive extent. Persons domiciled outside EC States could oblige the right holder to sue them in the EC State of their preference by simply opening an establishment there. This flexibility may also be used – and possibly abused – by the right holder, who can obtain an amplified range of choices of jurisdiction when he has to deal with a plurality of defendants. A problem may arise if the establishment is in an EC State which is not yet bound by the Brussels Convention, where the provisions of Title II of that Convention may not simply be applied by anticipation. Difficulties will also probably arise from the absence of any definition of the notion of "establishment" in the Regulation, as it could be argued that the interpretation given to this notion by the Court of Justice in the framework of the application of the EC Treaty is not necessarily valid in this case.[47] Finally, on a more theoretical level, it is questionable whether, for the purpose of choice of jurisdiction, the link created by an "establishment" with a given legal system is sufficiently strong to be assimilated to the "domicile".

21. Lis pendens and related actions

The Brussels Convention contains rules of general application on lis pendens (Article 21) and related actions (Article 22). These provisions also apply to infringement actions brought before Community trade mark Courts.

For lis pendens (proceedings involving the same cause of action and between the same parties successively brought before two different courts) the governing principle is that such proceedings have to be stayed in the second court having power, which has to decline jurisdiction once the jurisdiction of the first court seized has been established. The Regulation does not provide for any derogation or qualification of such a rule. In the relations with EC States not yet bound by the Brussels Convention the provisions on lis pendens of the lex fori will apply.

[47] See the leading case 33/1978 "Somafer/Saar Ferngas" – Decision of 22.11.1978 Rep. 1978 p. 2183.

It must be stressed that the rule on lis pendens does not apply where several actions of infringement have been brought in different EC States on the basis of the head of jurisdiction of the place of the harmful event. The Community trade mark involved and the parties may be the same, but the cause of action differs as it concerns necessarily different acts having taken place in different States. This kind of situation remains, however, subject to the rule on related actions.

Related actions ("connexité") (actions that are so closely connected that it is expedient to hear and determine them together to avoid the risk of irreconcilable judgments resulting from separate proceedings) are governed by Article 22 of the Brussels Convention. According to that provision the court second seized may stay the proceedings. To avoid any denial of justice, declining the jurisdiction by this court is subject to the condition that the two actions can be joined before the court first seized. Finally the provision only applies if the actions are both pending at first instance.

Article 22 of the Brussels Convention has seemed too flexible for actions of infringement of Community trade marks. Without clarifying its relationship to Article 22, which remains applicable, Article 100 of the Regulation has supplemented it by a much more rigid system.

According to Article 100 (1), if the issue of the validity of a Community trade mark is already pending before another Community trade mark Court or before the OHIM, the court seized of the issue in the second place has to stay the proceedings. The decision is taken at the request of one of the parties, the other parties having been heard, or by the court of its own motion, after hearing the parties. The court second seized may, if it is expedient, continue the hearing (e.g. in order to gather evidence which would be more difficult or more costly to obtain at a later stage), but it may not deliver the judgment until the court first seized or the OHIM has ruled on the issue of validity or concluded the proceedings in some other way. It must be stressed that this rule applies even if the persons which have raised the issue of the validity of the Community trade mark and the facts invoked have no relation whatsoever with the parties and the facts invoked in the first action.

According to Article 100 (2) the same rule applies where the OHIM is seized of an application for revocation or for a declaration of invalidity while the validity of the same Community trade mark is already being contested in an action pending before a Community trade mark Court. The Regulation tends, however, to favour that decisions on the validity of Community trade marks are taken by the OHIM. This has led to provide that the Community trade mark Court first seized may, in such a case, at the request of one of the parties and having heard the other parties, decide to stay the proceedings and let the OHIM rule first on the question of validity. The OHIM, although seized in the second place, is obliged to revoke its decision of staying the proceedings and to continue the application before it.

Article 100 does not contain the limitation to the first instance contained in Article 22 of the Brussels Convention. It could therefore also apply if the infringement action before the Community trade mark Court first seized is already in the second or third instance. Similarly it could apply if the proceedings for a revocation or for a declaration of invalidity are pending before the OHIM at the Board of Appeal stage. Although this is not expressly covered by the text, it would be in the logic of the system to apply the same provision if the issue of validity as decided by the OHIM is being considered at the further appeal level by the Court of First Instance or the Court of Justice.

It is difficult to say whether Article 100 represents an improvement or a worsening of the general system on related actions under the Brussels Convention. It certainly favours legal certainty, by avoiding contradictory decisions and superfluous procedural activities. It could on the other hand excessively slow down procedures and facilitate dilatory measures, to an extent which could eventually jeopardise the attractiveness of the Community trade mark. Any third party, by simply starting at an early stage proceedings for revocation or for declaration of invalidity of a Community trade mark before the OHIM, would be in a position to prevent any judge appointed after this date from issuing a decision on an action for infringement of the same Community trade mark as long as the OHIM, and possibly the Court of First Instance and the Court of Justice, have taken a final decision on the revocation or invalidity proceedings. If one considers the time that this procedure could require, there is a clear risk for the holder of the Community trade mark. Obviously, if the request for revocation or for a declaration of invalidity is eventually rejected, the right holder will be in a position to enforce his rights, but in commercial matters the time needed to reach a decision is often just as important as the quality or the objectiveness of the decision.

Article 100 (1) does not apply to actions for a declaration of non-infringement. It would simply be unfair to oblige a person, entitled under the lex fori of the court seized to obtain clarification of his position with respect to a Community trade mark without being able to raise the issue of validity, to wait until such issue has been finally determined in the other instance.

Article 100 (3) provides that, when a decision to stay proceedings is taken under the conditions set out in this Article, the Community trade mark Court staying the proceedings may order provisional measures for the duration of the stay in order to safeguard the interests of the various parties.

22. Jurisdiction for provisional, including protective, measures

The Brussels Convention regulates in Article 24 the jurisdiction of the courts competent to issue provisional, including protective, measures. In order to ensure a swift and efficient procedure this provision permits application for such a measure at a court of any contracting party, provided this court has jurisdiction, under the lex fori, to issue such an order. It is irrelevant whether the jurisdiction as to the substance of the case belongs to the courts of another contracting party.

Article 24 of the Brussels Convention has been declared inapplicable by Article 90 (2) a) and replaced by Article 99 (1). The latter provision does not, however, as far as the issue of jurisdiction is concerned, differ substantially from Article 24 of the Brussels Convention. The holder of the Community trade mark may therefore request a provisional measure to a court competent to deliver it under the lex fori in whatever EC State, even if the jurisdiction as to the substance of the case belongs to a Community trade mark Court situated in another EC State.

Article 99 (2) contains a qualification which could explain the statement, superfluous given the primacy of Community law, that Article 24 of the Brussels Convention does not apply. According to this provision Community trade mark Courts having jurisdiction under Article 93 (1) to (4) are entitled to issue provisional measures extending to the territory of other EC States.

At first sight this provision simply draws the logical consequences from the Community-wide substantive jurisdiction of those courts. The last sentence of Article 99 (2) establishes, however, that "no other court shall have such jurisdiction". This raises a serious question about the appropriateness of the provision. The sentence seems to imply that courts without a Community-wide jurisdiction can never grant provisional measures having effect in the territory of other EC States. There is no such limitation in the Brussels Convention, according to which provisional measures issued by a judge competent under the lex fori are to be recognized and enforced in the other contracting parties like any other judicial decision falling under the scope of the Brussels Convention. These measures may have extra-territorial effects, if the lex fori so allows. As Article 90 (2) c) declares inapplicable Article 24 of the Brussels Convention, the last sentence of Article 99 (2) represents a regrettable step backward with respect to the Brussels Convention. Dealing with Community trade marks, European judges, unless they have a Community-wide jurisdiction on the main case, could not follow the interesting practice developed in the recent years by Dutch courts of adopting provisional measures in "kort geding" proceedings with extra-territorial effects and to obtain their enforcement in other EC States under the Brussels Convention.[48]

Article 99 applies in all EC States, irrespective of their participation in the Brussels Convention, for measures linked to infringement or invalidity actions. It must be stressed that Article 24 of the Brussels Convention fully applies for provisional measures linked to actions relating to Community trade marks other than infringement or invalidity actions, whilst in EC States not yet bound by the Brussels Convention the national rules on jurisdiction will apply in those circumstances.

[48] In order to avoid any unjustified concern it should also be recalled in this context that the case-law of the Court of Justice has clearly indicated that recognition and enforcement of provisional measures under the Brussels Convention cannot be carried out if the measure has been taken without the presence of the party against whom it has been granted and without prior notification to such a party (Case 125/79 "Danilauer/SNC Couchet Frères", Decision of 21.5.1980, Rep. 1980 p. 1553).

C. The Applicable Law

I. Introduction

1. Having examined the rules on jurisdiction, we can turn now to the question of the law to be applied by the court in the framework of legal disputes concerning Community trade marks. We shall distinguish four aspects:
- substantial law,
- procedural law,
- civil remedies,
- provisional, including protective, measures.

II. Substantive law

2. Article 97 (1) and (2);
The starting point is the principle of autonomy of the trade mark law contained in the Regulation with respect to the national trade mark laws of the member States. This legal situation is not affected by the fact that the First Council Directive 89/104/EEC to approximate the laws of the member States relating to trade marks[49] and the Regulation have been developed as two elements of a unitary Community system so that the national laws contain, as a result of the implementation of the Directive, substantive rules fundamentally identical to those of the Regulation. Courts dealing with legal actions concerning a Community trade mark are to apply first and foremost the substantive law resulting from the provisions of the Regulation.

Article 97 (1) establishes that this principle applies to disputes concerning infringement or validity of a Community trade mark. The provision reads as follows: "The Community trade mark Courts shall apply the provisions of the Regulation". The wording of Article 97 (3)concerning procedural law shows a contrario that (1) deals with substantive law.

The Regulation contains a fully developed trade mark legislation covering in particular all the main issues which can normally be raised in infringement, revocation or invalidity actions. A substantive issue may, however, arise for which no appropriate rule can be found in the Regulation, so that the judge would be confronted with a lacuna. This possibility is foreseen in Article 97(2) which stipulates as follows: "On all matters not covered by the Regulation a Community trade mark Court shall apply its national law, including its private international law". This last provision establishes the principle of the complementary applica-

[49] See footnote (5).

tion of the lex fori. The mention of the international private law aims at introducing more flexibility in this rule. This is justified by the fact that, as a result of the application of the rules on choice of jurisdiction, it may occur that the link between the lex fori and the facts brought before the court is rather thin. If the features connecting the case with the legal order of another State are sufficiently important to lead, under the application of the rules on choice of law of the lex fori, to the application of the substantive law of the other State, the court is called to apply the latter. It has to be stressed that Article 97 (2)does not contain a limitation to the laws of the EC States, so that the law applicable could be, for a specific issue, the law of a third country.

3. The relation of Article 97 (1) and (2) to Article 14 (1)

Article 97, which belongs to Section 2 of Title X, applies only to legal proceedings concerning infringement and validity. Article 14(1), contained in Section 2 (Effects of the Community trade mark) of Title II (the Law relating to the Community trade mark), provides as follows: "The effects of the Community trade mark shall be governed solely by the provisions of this Regulation. In other respects, infringement of a Community trade mark shall be governed by the national law relating to infringement of a national trade mark in accordance with the provisions of Title X".

Article 14 (1) first sentence is an horizontal provision which can also be invoked in actions other than those concerning infringement or validity. To this extent it fills a gap in Title X by establishing that in principle it is the substantive trade mark law of the Regulation, and not the substantive lex fori, which has to be applied. On the other hand it makes Article 97 (1) redundant. As to Article 14 (1) second sentence, it is difficult to read into it something different from what is covered by the wording of Article 97 (2). The only doubt is whether the terms "in other respects" mean the same as "all matters not covered by the Regulation" contained in the latter provision. If the answer is positive, Article 97 (2) would also be redundant. Article 97 (2) contains, however, an important feature which is not expressed in Article 14 (1) second sentence: the mention of the international private law of the EC State where the court is situated.

To give an "effet utile" to Article 97 (2) it could be argued that, on matters of infringement, Article 14 (1) second sentence operates as lex specialis with respect to Article 97 (2), which would deal exclusively with lacunae in other fields of law. On matters of infringement, in the presence of a lacuna in the Regulation, the application of a law other than the lex fori, even if justified by the specific features of the case, would not be possible. Quite apart from the fact that it would be difficult to justify the policy behind it, such an interpretation cannot be accepted as the reference to the provisions of Title X, contained in Article 14 (1) second sentence, includes Article 97 (2) and therefore, the reference to the international private law. It seems more likely that the legislator, inspired by the precedent of the 1989 Agreement relating to the Community Patent, has overlooked the fact that Article 14 (1) and Article 97 (1) and (2) are largely redundant and, from a systematic point of view, should have been merged in a single provision to be applied across the board to all legal actions relating to Community trade marks.[50]

III. Procedural Law

4. The applicable law: the lex fori

The basic rule on matters of procedure is that the law applicable is the lex fori. Article 97 (3) provides, for disputes concerning infringement or validity, that each Community trade mark Court has to apply the rules of procedure governing, under its national law, the same type of actions relating to a national trade mark. Other provisions of Title X contain, however, unified rules of procedural nature which are binding on each Community trade mark Court and prevail over the lex fori. Article 96, 98 and 99 contain examples of such unified rules.

Article 14 (3), which deals only with infringement, contains a reference to the provisions of Title X. Once more we are confronted with redundant provisions.

The Regulation is silent as to the legal actions other than those governed by Section 2 of Title X. Contrary to Article 71 of the Community Patent Convention which expressly provides that actions other than those on infringement or validity are subject to the rules of procedure governing the same type of actions relating to a national patent, there is no similar provision in the Regulation, nor does Article 14 (3) help, as it is only concerned with matters of infringement. The procedural law applicable will in such cases be the lex fori by virtue of the rule commonly accepted in international private law according to which, unless there is a specific provision to the contrary, this is the law that a court applies on procedural matters.

5. The procedure for infringement, revocation or invalidity actions

It follows from the above that an action for infringement of a Community trade mark will be dealt with by the competent Community trade mark Court, from the procedural point of view, as if it were an infringement action of a nation trade mark of the member State where the Court is situated. This rule applie each of the three possible instances which are usually opened to the pa under national procedural law. The Regulation contains, however, a num rules which could interfere with the national procedural law and which of conflict, would prevail.

We have already met one such rule in Article 91, where the EC compelled to adapt their rules on territorial jurisdiction of their co

[50] The existence of two different provisions in that Agreement Community Patent Convention and Article 32 (2) of the Protocol or explained by the fact that they are contained in two separate acts, albe framework of the same Agreement.

the need for specialisation. Uniform rules, which streamline the procedure in the various instances are also contained in Article 101.

According to Article 101 (1) there is a right to appeal against a decision reached by a Community trade mark Court of first instance before the competent Community trade mark Court of second instance. According to Article 91 the latter Court has to be situated in the same EC State as the former and, at least if the pattern of the Protocol on Litigation is followed,[51] it has the same territorial jurisdiction. It cannot, however, be excluded that large member States might prefer to concentrate the territorial jurisdiction more at the appeal level and provide an even more limited number of Community trade mark Courts of second instance – possibly even one single court – thus covering several judicial jurisdictions of courts of first instance. The inconvenient of such a measure would be, particularly for parties not domiciled in the EC State in question, that they would have to entertain the action in different places in the first and in the second instance.

Article 101 (2) establishes that the conditions under which an appeal may be lodged shall be determined by the lex fori. As there are no uniform rules on this topic in the European Union, this may entail some difference of treatment according to the EC State where the case is being heard. This seems to be, however, an inconvenient that must be accepted at the present stage of development of European integration, bearing in mind in particular the principle of subsidiarity.

According to Article 101 (3) a further appeal against a decision by a Community trade mark Court of second instance can be lodged before the higher national judicial level, if such a remedy is admitted by the lex fori. This covers in particular the "recours en cassation" before the "Cour de Cassation" in France and the parallel further appeals in the other civil law countries, and the further appeal to the House of Lords in the United Kingdom. The conditions under which such a further appeal may be lodged are also determined by the lex fori.

It is recalled that, at each of the three instances where infringement, revocation or invalidity actions may be heard, the national court may address to the Court of Justice, in accordance with Article 177 EC Treaty, preliminary questions concerning Community law, in particular the interpretation or the validity of provisions of the Regulation or of provisions of secondary law adopted on this basis (Implementing Regulation, Fees Regulation, Rules of Procedure of the Board of Appeal). The presentation of such questions is facultative in the first and second instance, but becomes mandatory in the final instance.

Such questions could also concern the provisions on jurisdiction or on recgnition and enforcement, including those rules of the Brussels Convention ich the Regulation declares applicable. A question arises in this context, due he fact that the Protocol on the interpretation by the Court of Justice of the sels Convention[52] only authorises the referral of preliminary questions by

Annex to the Protocol on Litigation.
footnote (16).

the national courts of second instance and by the Supreme Courts. As the questions raised by provisions of the Regulation are governed by Article 177 EC Treaty and not by the said Protocol, national courts of first instance should, however, also be able to raise this type of question.

6. The counterclaim for revocation or invalidity and the burden of proof
Article 95 (1) sets out the principle that the issue of revocation or of invalidity, to be considered by the court if raised as a defence in an infringement action, has to be raised by way of a counterclaim. According to Article 96 (1), the grounds on which such a counterclaim can be based are exclusively those mentioned in Articles 50, 51 and 52. The limitation in consequence of acquiescence contained in Article 53 is also applicable.

The entitlement to bring a counterclaim for revocation or for invalidity belongs, by its very nature, to the defendant in the infringement action. If the grounds invoked are grounds for revocation or absolute grounds for invalidity, there is no further personal limitation to the entitlement. If the grounds for invalidity invoked are relative grounds there is the further limitation that the party bringing the counterclaim must be the owner of the earlier right invoked.

Article 95 (3) authorises two exceptions to the obligation of operating by way of counterclaim: the case where the defence is based on the ground for revocation of lack of use within the meaning of Article 50 (1) a), and the case where the defence is based on the ground for invalidity of the existence of an "earlier right" within the meaning of Article 52. In the second case the entitlement to raise the defence is restricted to the holder of the "earlier right" in accordance with Article 95 (3). Instead of sticking to the rule of revocation or declaration of invalidity with erga omnes effect so as to maintain a "clean" Register, Article 95 (3) considers that in the two circumstances referred to above the alleged infringer should be offered the alternative route of requiring rejection of the infringement action with an assessment of the validity of the Community trade mark with inter partes effect only.

Apart from these two exceptions, if the alleged infringer files a plea for revocation or invalidity as a means of defence, restricting his plea to rejection of the infringement action without requesting a ruling on the validity of the Community trade mark with erga omnes effect, the court is obliged to reject the plea and to treat the trade mark as valid, without being able to enter into the merits of the arguments advanced. The requirement that in principle the issue of revocation or of invalidity can only be raised by way of counterclaim is intended to strengthen the value of the Community trade mark by obliging the alleged infringer to occupy the procedural position and the responsibility in terms of costs of a person launching a full-scale action against the Community trade mark. The burden of proving that the Community trade mark is invalid lies on the author of the counterclaim, who becomes, technically speaking, the plaintiff in the counterclaim action. The right holder will find himself in the position of a defendant: he has to react to the evidence and arguments presented in order to convince the judge that the grounds invoked do not prejudice the maintenance of his Community trade mark. In doing so he will be able to limit himself to combating the evidence and arguments brought forward by the adversary.

Article 95 (2) rules out that revocation or invalidity of the Community trade mark be placed in issue in an action for declaration of non-infringement. Accepting the contrary would be tantamount to transforming the action for declaration of non-infringement into a direct action for revocation or for a declaration of invalidity, which the Regulation reserves to the exclusive jurisdiction of the departments of the OHIM.

7. Counterclaim brought by a licensee

According to Article 96 (3), if the counterclaim is brought in an infringement action lodged by a licensee or the holder of a right *in rem* in respect of the Community trade mark,[53] the proprietor of the trade mark has to be informed and may be joined to the proceedings in accordance with the lex fori. This is justified by the fact that the court is going to consider an issue of vital importance to the proprietor, i.e. whether his trade mark should be revoked or declared invalid with effect for the whole Community.

8. The information of the OHIM about counterclaims

According to Article 96 (4) the Community trade mark Court seized of a counterclaim has to inform the OHIM so that the public at large may be informed of this fact by an entry in the Register. This information enables in particular other Community trade mark Courts to establish whether proceedings for revocation or invalidation are pending, a consideration of importance for the application of Article 100 on related actions.

According to Article 96 (6), when the judgment with respect to the counterclaim becomes final, the court has to communicate of its own motion the decision to the OHIM, which will enter a mention of the contents of the decision in the Register. If the decision pronounces the revocation or the invalidity of the Community trade mark, the latter will be deleted from the Register. In the case of maintenance of the Community trade mark the entry will inform the public at large, and the other Community trade mark Courts in particular, of the termination of the revocation or invalidity proceedings. To avoid any risk of delay or omission, any interested party is entitled to approach the court to make sure that the decision has been forwarded to the OHIM.

9. The judgment on the issue of revocation or invalidity

Article 96 (5) indicates, by reference to Article 56 (3) to (6), the two possible conclusions that a Community trade mark Court may reach on the issue of revocation or invalidity of a Community trade mark raised by a counterclaim:

[53] See Regulation Article 22 (3) and 19.

- revocation with ex-nunc effect[54] or declaration of invalidity with ex-tunc effect,[55]
- rejection of the counterclaim and maintenance of the Community trade mark.

The revocation or the declaration of invalidity need not be total, but it may be limited to some of the goods or services for which the trade mark is registered.

10. Possibility of staying the proceedings and letting the issue of revocation or invalidity be decided by the OHIM

Article 96 (7) tends to favour the concentration of revocation and invalidity disputes before the OHIM. It gives the possibility to any Community trade mark Court before which the issue of the revocation or invalidity has been raised to stay the infringement proceedings and to invite the alleged infringer having lodged the counterclaim, to submit an application for a revocation or a declaration of invalidity before the OHIM in accordance with Article 55. Such a decision, for which the court has full discretion, can only be taken on request by the proprietor of the Community trade mark and after hearing the other parties. It is expected that a court will normally stay proceedings if the grounds for revocation or invalidity invoked require difficult technical expertise which could be more easily gathered at the OHIM. The fact that the request must originate with the person who claims to be the victim of infringement warrants against any use of this possibility in order to delay the decision on the issue of infringement. The court may, in any event, order provisional and protective measures.

If the court decides to stay the proceedings and to invite the alleged infringer to sue before the OHIM and said infringer does not follow the invitation within the time limit prescribed by the court, the counterclaim will be deemed withdrawn and the proceedings concerning the issue of infringement will be resumed.

11. The principle "ne bis in idem"

Article 96 (2) provides that if the OHIM has taken a final decision in proceedings for revocation or invalidity of a Community trade mark, the same issues cannot be raised again before a Community trade mark Court by way of counterclaim for the same subject-matter and cause of action and between the same parties. It is a case of application of the principle "ne bis in idem", which the Regulation considers useful to express possibly in view of the ambiguous nature of the OHIM, administrative and quasi-judicial authority. In this case the judicial nature of the decisions of the OHIM is recognized.

It goes without saying that the same rule applies if a final decision has been taken by a Community trade mark Court and, by making use of the alternative fora opened by Article 93, the same issue should be brought again between the same parties before a second Community trade mark Court. In this case, how-

[54] See Regulation Article 54 (1).
[55] See Regulation Article 54 (2).

ever, the rejection of the counterclaim would directly result from the principle of procedural law "ne bis in idem" generally recognized in the EC States.

In specific cases the final decision on the revocation or the invalidity of a Community trade mark might be taken by the Court of First Instance or the Court of Justice by way of amending a decision of the OHIM which is appealed.[56] In this case too, obviously, the principle "ne bis in idem" would prevent a Community trade mark Court from taking a new decision on the same issue.

XIV. Civil Remedies

12. Civil remedies in infringement actions

Article 98 deals with the issue of civil remedies in actions for infringement. This is a particularly sensitive question. Interested circles have repeatedly indicated that an efficient enforcement of the rights conferred by the Community trade marks and a greater uniformity in the way national courts react against infringement would be fundamental for the success of the Community trade mark project.

It has to be recognized that, at the present stage of European integration, it is difficult to interfere to a large extent on matters where the traditions and the substantive and procedural rules of civil law applied by the courts of the EC States differ profoundly. It is on the other hand difficult to develop common rules in the limited specific field of trade mark protection. The smooth functioning of the common market will require sooner or later a "unitary civil judicial space" and in particular a uniform judicial treatment of non-contractual liability, including civil sanctions. This is, however, a task which cannot be undertaken under the coverage of regulating the implementation of some industrial property rights.

The issue of the civil remedies in infringement actions is regulated in Article 98 (2) by a rule of conflict which declares applicable the law of the EC State where the acts of infringement have been committed or threatened. This rule contains:

a) an exception in Article 98 (1), which institutes the injunction prohibiting continuation of the acts of infringement as a Community civil remedy,

b) a mitigation in Article 98 (2), which includes a reference to the international private law of the EC State whose law is applicable.

13. A Community civil remedy: The injunction

Article 98 (1) has achieved a first shy step in the direction of instituting Community civil remedies against infringement. It requires from the judge who finds that the defendant has infringed or threatened to infringe a Community trade mark, that he issues, unless there are special reasons for not doing so, an

[56] See Regulation Article 63 (3), which contains the possibility for the Community jurisdiction to "alter" the decision of the OHIM appealed against.

order prohibiting the infringer from proceeding with the infringing acts. This is a final injunction, pronounced at the conclusion of the infringement proceedings, not to be mistaken for the interlocutory injunction which is a provisional measure.

The prohibition against continuing with the infringing acts had already been accepted by the "12" EC States as a uniform civil remedy for infringement of a Community Patent.[57] It is important to stress the Community nature of the remedy instituted by the Regulation, notwithstanding its identity with similar measures in most of the legal systems of the EC States. This nature warrants in particular the autonomy of the interpretation to be given to this notion with respect to the corresponding national notions.

The legal means to ensure that the injunction is complied with will be determined by the lex fori. The injunction will have to be contained in, or accompanied by, a legal act taken by the court in accordance with its national law and enforceable in the country in question, like a decree, an order, a decision, a writ of execution. Such an act will also be enforceable in the other contracting parties to the Brussels Convention, should the remedy be executed abroad.

As has been stated, the Regulation has been particularly shy in providing uniform Community remedies. The pending proposal for a Regulation on the Community Design suggests the creation of two further Community civil remedies, the order of seizure of the infringing products and the order imposing upon the alleged infringer the obligation to give information concerning the manufacturer and the commercial routes of the infringing products.[58] It is to be hoped that, as soon as these measures will be adopted in that Regulation, the Commission will present a proposal in order to aline the Regulation on the Community trade mark on these new developments.

14. Other civil remedies

National civil remedies other than the injunction can also be imposed upon the infringer. The most common of these are the award of damages, the seizure of the infringing goods, their transfer to the proprietor of the Community trade mark, their destruction and the publication of the judgment in the press.

According to Article 98 (2) for imposing civil remedies other than injunction, the court has to apply the law of the EC State where the acts of infringement have been committed or threatened. If the jurisdiction of the Community trade mark Court is based on Article 93(5), this is tantamount to affirming that the further remedies which can be imposed upon the infringer are those provided by the lex fori.

[57] See Article 35 (1) Protocol of Litigation.

[58] See Article 93 (2) of the Commission Proposal of 3.12.1993 for a Regulation of the European Parliament and Council on the Community Design (OJ EC C 29 of 31.1.1994). See also footnote (31).

This provision raises a difficult problem when the Community trade mark Court has jurisdiction to hear cases of infringement committed throughout the whole territory of the Community. According to this provisions the judge has then to apply the law of the EC State in which the acts of infringement have taken place. As these States may be several, the judge has then to apply different laws to the various sets of acts of infringement, according to the country where they have been committed. This corresponds, however, to a rather unusual approach for a judge, who quite naturally tends to give a unitary assessment of the consequences his findings require. It also seems rather unlikely that a judge would impose a remedy provided in a foreign legal system, if it would be considered objectionable in his own legal system (e.g. in some EC States the destruction of infringing products).

Even in respect of remedies where such objections could not be raised, as for the award of damages which is common to the legal systems of all the EC States, the application of this provision is not going to be easy. The judge could be obliged to award damages for each set of acts of infringement committed in a given EC State in accordance with the practice and the amounts generally recognized in that State. This would be, no doubt, a guarantee against forum shopping, since a plaintiff would no longer be inclined to take his case to a particular court merely because the practice of the law in that State awards generous damages. It is, however, legitimate to express doubts as to the practical possibility for the judge of applying this rule as soon as the number of countries involved in the infringement exceeds two or three.

The mention in Article 98 (2) of the international private law could, to a certain extent, mitigate this inconvenient. Thanks to this the judge will be in a position to reduce the number of different remedies called by a decision if the international private law of the law applicable (the law of the EC State where the acts of infringement have been committed or threatened) returns back to the lex fori.

V. Provisional and Protective Measures

15. Provisional and protective measures

Provisional and protective measures play a role even more important than civil remedies in the protection of industrial property rights. Waiting for a judgment to be given, or pending the judgment, such measures can forestall the development of a market situation which, in the short term, might irreparably jeopardise the right holder's economic position.

As we have seen, the jurisdiction for such measures is spread throughout the EC States, irrespective of where the court competent as to the substance of the case is situated. The measures which can be requested are all those provided by the national law of the court seized. The most common are the seizure of the allegedly infringing products or of machines and factories for manufacturing such products, the description of such products, machines and factories, the interim order prohibiting the alleged infringer from continuing with the acts which might constitute infringement (interlocutory injunction).

Contrary to the provision on civil remedies, Article 99 does not contain any Community measure equally applicable in each EC State. An effort to introduce Community provisional measures has been undertaken in the Proposal for a Regulation on the Community Design, where the interlocutory injunction, the provisional seizure and the order to furnish information concerning the manufacturer and the commercial routes of the allegedly infringing products are indicated as instruments available to each court, alongside to the other national provisional measures.[59] In this case too, it is expected that the solutions which will be retained for the Community Design will be extended in future to the Community trade mark.

16. The issue of invalidity in Proceedings for provisional measures

The question can be raised as to whether it should be possible for the alleged infringer to invoke, in proceedings relating to provisional measures, the revocation or the invalidity of the Community trade mark on whose basis the measures are requested. The prohibition of invoking the revocation or the invalidity of a Community trade mark as a defence otherwise that by way of counterclaim[60] applies in the course of the main action for infringement. Actions for infringement may, however, be preceded or accompanied by requests for provisional measures which play an important role in procedural tactics. Obliging a defendant to raise the defence of revocation or invalidity by counterclaim within the framework of a procedure for a provisional measure is often not possible: many legal systems do not allow a counterclaim during such a procedure which by definition must be speedy and based on prima facie considerations. It would on the other hand be unjustified to prohibit the defendant from raising the revocation or the invalidity of the Community trade mark as a defence, as the arguments he could develop could be extremely useful for the judge in taking his decision.

For these reasons it is suggested that the absence of any provision regarding this topic in Article 99 should be interpreted as meaning that the defendant has the right, in proceedings for preliminary measures, of raising the defence of the revocation or invalidity of the Community trade mark otherwise than by way of counterclaim. Obviously his arguments, if they are accepted by the judge, will have effect only inter partes and will have no impact on the formal validity of the Community trade mark at issue.

It should be noted that sometimes, particularly in case of urgency, the provisional measure is granted in proceedings which are conducted "inaudita et altera parte". In such cases the objection of the revocation or invalidity of the Community trade mark can be raised only at a later stage of the proceedings or

[59] See Proposal for a Regulation on the Community Design, Article 94 (1).
[60] See Regulation Article 95, including the exception under Article 95 (3).

in the context of an appeal against the measure or in the main proceedings. The judge will, however, in such cases only decide if he has a strong prima facie case or if the proprietor is prepared to furnish financial security if the measure should eventually appear to be unjustified.

Community Trade Marks and Domestic Laws

Foreword

This paper intends to cover the problem of the possible interference between Community trade mark substantive law and domestic law, on the premise that rights given by a Community trade mark co-exist with the national trade mark rights. We are going to identify limits and aims of the Community trade mark law in connection with the purposes pursued by the European legislator. We are also going to analyse the impact of the Community trade mark on the national trade mark system and to deal with some crucial issues of the possible conflicts between the two systems.

The survey concludes with some remarks as to the forthcoming development of the Community and national trade mark law.

The article is not exhaustive of the subject matter. All the opinions expressed by the author reflect his personal views, and they neither reflect the views of the Office for Harmonization in the Internal Market nor its Chambers of Appeal.

1. Background

It has been known for some time, that the *"Community Law relating to trade marks does not replace the laws of the Member States on trade marks"* (Fifth "Considerando" to the Council Regulation on the Community trade mark, No. 40/94). However this statement deserves an additional explanation and has to be linked with the Council Directive No. 89/104 to approximate laws of the Member States relating to trade marks.

The point of departure of this very long story was the "Preliminary Draft Treaty" (1964) published in 1973, which was then followed by the famous "Memorandum on an EEC Trade Mark" of the Commission (1976). The story covers about 30 years, but since the beginning the main concern of the European Community towards national trade mark laws has been to avoid disparities in the Member States which might preclude the free movement of goods and services so as to distort competition within the Common Market.

In a broad sense, competition, business development and consumers standard of living were considered as depending *"on commerce and industry in producing and trading in marked goods"* (EC Commission Working Paper, I, 1980).

To this end the approximation of domestic trade mark laws was considered sufficient, in particular with reference *"to those national provisions of law which most directly affect the functioning of the Internal Market"* (Third "Considerando" of the Council Directive, No. 89/104). Therefore the Directive proposed the basic principles governing the minimum standards for the protection of trade marks and in the course of the years these standards have been adopted by the majority of the Member States. Some of the substantive principles of the Directive are the same as the those included in the Community trade mark.

The Regulation has re-stated the need to eliminate barriers and distortions, but, in addition, it has set up the legal conditions *"which enable undertakings to adapt their activities to the scale of the Community"* (First "Considerando").

The idea is to create a trade mark designed for the entire territory of the Community. Indeed the Community trade mark is neither conceived as a simple pure territorial over-extension of the national trade mark protection nor as a sort of *medium* between the different national laws. The *new* law introduces, by means of the *new* instrument (the Regulation), a *new* kind of trade mark, the Community trade mark, which is quite independent from the previous national legal rules (Report of Commission on Regulation, Draft Proposal, 1980). Through the use of the Community trade mark, undertakings can obtain, by means of a procedural system, a uniform protection for the whole territory of the Community. Indeed, the *unitary* character of the Community trade mark is fully consistent with this approach (Muhlendahl, 1976). For these reasons the option to use the Community trade mark system goes beyond the mere idea of harmonising laws on trade marks of the Member States.

It follows that a Community trade mark is to be interpreted according to the new perspectives and challenges of a unified single market and to be related to the dimension of investments, the impact of media, the huge consumer target, the international competition, the market relevance, as it already stressed several years ago: "European trade mark law should be oriented more closely, both in registration and in infringement proceedings, to the *actual market conditions, the actual need of protection and the realities of trade mark use*" (Beier, 1977).

2. Construction

Clearly, the Community trade mark system does not replace laws of the Member States on trade marks and we do not expect a different approach in the future, national registrations, being, among other things, subject to possible renewal. This means that, by the Regulation, the European Union has established a *new* legal system that is completely separated and independent from home legislation, with its own substantive and procedural rules, administration, organisation, institutions and jurisdiction.

In the light of this binding interpretation, it is of material importance to assess the Regulation and its implementation (*Commission Regulation (EC) No.*

2868/95 of Dec. 13, 1995 implementing Council Regulation (EC) No. 40/94 on the Community trade mark, in OJ L. 303 of 15 December, 1995) as well as its interpretation and application, shall provide for the Office, the Chambers of Appeal and the practitioners the *prior* legal basis of reference.

The principles of *unitary* character (Article 1.2 of the Regulation) and that of national jurisdiction on infringement matters (Article 14.1) confirm that, unless otherwise provided for, the effects of the Community trade mark are governed solely by the Community Law.

3. Nature and function of Community trade mark

As above mentioned, the key of access to a Community trade mark is given by the identification of the nature, function and scope of the trade mark that the new law intends to protect. This is not an easy question to answer as novelty, invalidity, forfeiture, confusing similarity, likelihood of association, counterfeiting, consolidation, extension of use and many other problems may be rightly approached only when there is general consensus about what the actual interests at stake are.

To begin with, it has to be remembered that no protection can be granted to those situations which are without worth. In the Regulation the *use requirements*, in particular for an actual or *serious* use of the trade mark, clearly meet this need.

As far as the main question, the EC Commission and the ECJ, even today, retain that the minimum requirement for the protection of a *national* trade mark is to guarantee the identity of source, in the sense of *indication of origin*.

However the Directive, dated 1989, states that the "function (of the registered trade mark) is *in particular* to guarantee the trade mark as an indication of origin" (Tenth "Considerando"), and *"in particular"* means that other functions have to be considered. At the same time under Article 2, legal protection is given to trade marks, provided that they are *"capable of distinguishing the goods or services of one undertaking from those of other undertakings"*.

Thus the minimum of the pre-requisite for registering a trade mark sounds somehow different from the concept of *indication of origin*. However, this traditional and well-established definition seems, in my view, not to be fully appreciated by the EU legislator, in so far as the consequences to be drawn therefrom.

As it has been noted recently by authoritative doctrine (Beier, 1995; Lehmann, 1995; Sena, 1989), during the course of the years the trade mark has surprisingly changed in its role and developed in its value. Indeed, in the recent years the trade mark has acquired, more and more in all western countries, a *plus* value becoming a business, an asset sometimes worthy of huge investments, so to be *"per se"* exploited, advertised, conferred, licensed or assigned.

Member States, giving application to the Directive, somehow recorded in their home laws this alteration of course in the economy and market. Some scholars, accordingly, did not fail to raise the problem of the inadequacy of the traditional theory, by stressing the character of an *intangible asset* of the enterprise (Schriker, 1980) or talking about *symbolic value* (Sena, 1989) and *marketing issue* (Beier, 1995).

Overall, in the Directive, and *per relationem* in the Regulation, there are rules which, in my view, seriously challenge the traditional conception of a trade mark conceived as an indication of origin. I would recall, for instance, those rules concerning the absolute protection in the case of identity between the mark and goods, the free circulation of the sign disregarding the goodwill, the entrepreneurial capacity as no longer necessary for the application, the enlarged protection, in certain cases, over the category of the affinity of goods and services, the protection of the interest of the owner of a trade mark having reputation to the integrity of its distinctiveness and goodwill, the conception of the trade mark as an object of property: all these rules indeed apparently cut all links between trade marks and undertakings. Moreover the *quality standard control clause* in licensing agreement would be hardly acceptable without granting the trade mark the function of guaranteeing the *quality* of products and/or services.

Although it is true that the wording in the Directive, as well as in the Regulation, is almost the same as that proposed in the '70s by the *Memorandum* and other additional drafts, it has to be noted that the very same Memorandum, (see No. 68), in 1976 mentioned the function of quality guarantee and advertising. However, these functions were considered as strictly dependent from and related to the principal function of trade marks, i.e., *"to certify the origin of the product"*.

In the '80s the Commission again recognized the identification function for products and services as *"coming from companies"* (cited Report of Commission to Regulation Proposal, 1980).

Looking at the recent Regulation, we see that the function of trade marks is, once again, related to *the guarantee of the indication of origin* (Seventh "Considerando"). However, it is also acknowledged that trade marks are *"enabling the products and services of undertakings to be distinguished by identical means trough the entire Community"* (First "Considerando") and that they have *"to be regarded as an object of property which exists separately from the undertakings whose goods or services are designated"* (Tenth "Considerando").

It is not the case to examine closely in this paper the issue of where the trade mark is going, although, in my view, this is at the moment the key question to be confronted. However, I would try to explain better the meaning of the statement that, under the Regulation, the function of the Community trade mark is mainly to identify the origin of goods and services (GATT TRIPs, Article 15.1, Section 2, Part II, governs by way of similar wording when a sign may be eligible for registration as trade mark).

Indeed, there is not in the statement a special consideration of the undertaking as *such as source of origin*. The core of the system lays rather on the economic and legal interest: a) to avoid confusion among consumers; b) to guarantee the quality standard of products expected by consumers (N.B. and not to guarantee that quality must be always the same); c) to set up a *clean market* and to safeguard fair competition; d) to protect the investments and their return by advertising, marketing and communication.

If we look at the example of the recent German trade mark law (the *"Lex Mulendhal"*) and we construe this in the context of the *Property Rights* by a positive approach, i.e., not on the mere basis of a right of interdiction against third parties (Lehmann, 1995), it seems that the legal protection is primarily directed to the interest of the owner of the trade mark. Trade mark is therefore an essential element of the market strategy of companies which has to be consistent with the new dimension and characteristics of the unified market. The trade mark is, in this *scenario*, a basic instrument of communication which is able not only to gather and unify the mere transmission of information (Lehamann, 1986 and 1995), including that of quality, but also to promote the image, to activate advertising (that, in my view, must not be related only to well-known trade marks) and to meet the needs of competition policy.

Therefore, it follows that the scope of protection of trade marks as retained in a Member State that shares a traditional approach, i.e., to refer the sign to the source of the products or services, can lead to possible divergent interpretations with the Regulation and the Community law.

Now it is time to give an answer to the basic question which was raised 20 years ago: *"in the European proceeding, does the national mark apply with its substantive scope of protection as it is recognized under the national law or with the scope of protection granted to European marks?"* (Muhlendahl, 1976). In the event of conflict with domestic law, *interpretation and application of a Community trade mark, as it is defined as to its function and scope for the time being, takes precedent.*

4. Community trade mark as an option

National trade marks will continue to be necessary for those undertakings which do not need protection of their trade marks at a Community level. A Community trade mark may be attractive only for those undertakings which are positioning their strategy in the new technological and marketing environment and which want to match the new business with the enlarged and unified single market of the Community. In this way it is up to the undertakings whether or not to exercise this option.

However, it is difficult to imagine that the two systems can go on in a divided, even if parallel, way.

Looking more closely at the Regulation and the Directive, it is possible to identify and select some issues which highlight the discrepancy between national trade marks discipline and the Community discipline.

5. Actual use, genuine use

"There is no justification for protecting Community trade marks or, as against them, any trade mark which has been registered before them, except where the trade marks are actually used" (Ninth "Considerando").

It goes without saying that the *actual use* of a trade mark is of fundamental importance for protection of a Community trade mark. The expression may be regarded in a double sense:

firstly, it means that a Community trade mark, as provided under Article 50 (*Grounds for Revocation*) cannot enjoy legal protection whenever the registration is forfeited for non-use (N.B.: the English wording *"declared to be revoked"* sounds incorrect for what never comes into existence cannot be revoked).

Secondly, neither prior registration can be opposed to a pending application of a Community trade mark, nor even a registered Community trade mark be invalidated, if the concerned party does not produce proof that, during the five years preceding the date of publication of the Community trade mark application or the declaration of its invalidity, the earlier Community trade mark has been put to *genuine use* in the Community, as provided by Article 43.2 (*Examination of Opposition*), and by Article 56.2, (*Examination of the Application*).

Genuine use has to be referred to the territory of the Community wherein the earlier trade mark is actually used, and even the territory of one single Member State could be considered as sufficient to meet this requirement.

However the *concept* of genuine use has to be understood according the Community trade mark Regulation, rather than to the domestic law. The Regulation is silent on this and Article 15 (*Use of Community trade marks*) just says that the use shall also be satisfied if used *"in a form differing in elements which do not alter the distinctive character of the mark in the form in which it was registered"* (Article 15.2 (a)) and in *"affixing to goods or to the packaging thereof in the Community solely for export purposes"* (Article 15. 2 (b)).

Article 50, that rules the forfeiture of a non-use trade mark after a period five years and that sanctions the revocation of the Community trade mark registration, does not help much in the construction of what *"use"*, or *"genuine use"* means, so as to avoid the forfeiture and to safeguard the validity of a Community trade mark registration.

In this paper I understand that *genuine* and *actual* use are equivalent in the wording of the Regulation (see the five languages, Italian in particular: *"uso effettivo"*). At any rate *genuine use* is something which goes beyond the simple use. We assume that the use of a trade mark is *genuine/actual* if it is effective, and not a mere *fictio juris*. It has to meet the essential function which is eligible for legal protection, e.g., to be apt to affect the concerned competition and economic environment (competitors, consumers, market) (Mayr, 1991).

An advertising campaign, planned in due time and supported by substantial investments, can be considered a sign of serious preparation for the introduction into the market of a new product the trade mark for which has not been used yet. *Vice versa*, a promotion carried out only by a sponsorship activity, a mere market test or a sampling distribution in a negligible quantity, without any existing industry in the concerned field, might be considered just a simple expedient to by-pass the law requirements for the actual use of the sign.

Further, in my view the concept of *genuine/actual use*, means a use that is also qualified to justify the protection of a trade mark *as a Community trade mark* and we all agree that Community trade mark is dimensioned for a single unified market of some hundred million consumers and for a territory which tends to a dramatic expansion.

Under Article 8.4 (*Relative Grounds for Refusal*) the proprietor of a non-registered trade mark or of another trade sign can file opposition against a Community trade mark application, provided that the sign was acquired *"pursuant to the law of the Member State governing that sign"*. The same provision also confers on the proprietor the right to prohibit the use of a subsequent trade mark.

However the extension, intensity, duration and effectiveness of the use of a local trade mark (which shall be *"of more than local significance"*) and of all trade prior symbol rights cannot be evaluated by the examiners of OHIM only on the basis of the national law concerned. What may be considered reliable and productive according to principles elaborated by domestic law cases and doctrine (as to judge whether a non-registered trade mark is eligible for protection through use or a registered trade mark has to be invalidated for lack of use in a Member State), might not be compatible with the *genuine/actual* use requirement provided for by Community law. Therefore these principles may not be considered sufficient to remove the full validity of a Community trade mark, because of the different function and scenario in which the Community trade mark must be placed.

It therefore means that the reference in the Article 8.4 to the *"Law of the Member State"* shall be applied only insofar as to the assessment of the two conditions required under a) and b) for prior symbol rights (and not, in my view, for non-registered trade marks).

With regard to this conclusion it is not without significance that Article 108.2 (a) (*Conversion*) clearly makes a distinction between a "use which would be considered to be *genuine use under the laws of that Member State*" and a use which cannot prevent" the revocation of a *Community trade mark* on the grounds of non-use" (Ubertazzi, 1995).

6. Local use, non use

The evidence of our argument can be extrapolated from Article 8.4 of the Regulation, according to which a non-registered trade mark or another sign can be opposed by the proprietor to a Community trade mark application, *provided* that such sign has been used *"in the course of trade of more than mere local significance"*. The appreciation of the extension in the use of an earlier trade mark and of all prior trade symbol signs shall be carried out within the latitude of the national territorial extension, but, however, along the line of the Community trade mark criteria (Muhlendahl, 1976), in particular as far as the genuine/actual character of the use. Consequently it is clear that *local significance* should be interpreted in a qualitative way, i.e., the consistency with the real function to be given today to the trade mark, rather than in the meaning of a mere geographical extension. On the other hand it is self-evident that the appreciation of the *de minimis* local situation without the support of a uniform and stable guideline risks becoming incompatible with certainty of the law.

Even the enforcement of Article 53.2 (*Limitation in consequences of acquiescence*) seems to be problematic. According to this provision, the proprietor of an earlier trade symbol right (as referred to in Article 8.4), is no longer entitled to apply for a declaration of invalidity of a later Community trade mark when he has acquiesced, for a period of five successive years, in the use of the latter sign in his Member State, unless the registration of the Community trade mark has been applied for in *bad faith*. Nevertheless it can be seriously questioned, as a matter of fact, how the owner of a registered Community trade mark could be aware, so as to be in bad faith, of a sign (for instance a sign board, a trade name or a packaging) used only at local level, provided of no mere local significance (e.g., a region or even a single town). In any case this assessment is subject to dispute.

On the contrary, the same problem should not occur in the case that the earlier right is represented by a prior Community trade mark, as provided for by Article 53.1. Since the Community trade mark can be created only through the registration, it reasonably follows that the proprietor of a later Community trade mark should be aware of use of a trade mark which is expected to mark products or services in all the territory of the Community or in a large part of it.

Acquiescence, on the other hand, does not apply to invalidation proceedings as ruled by Article 53.2 in case of prior copyright, right to a name, right of personal portrayal or other industrial property right. In many European countries these intellectual rights are not subject to any publicity requirements. Therefore, it is hard to say how Community trade mark applicants might be aware of these prior rights and prevent proceedings for invalidity of their Community trade mark.

To complete the picture, something should be said about the non-use, which represents the same way of approaching the problem but from the negative side.

Article 15.1 and Article 50.1 (a) deny the revocation of the registration (rectius: forfeiture) whenever *"there are proper reasons for non use"*. Once again nothing is said about the real meaning of this statement. However we may assume that the concept of *proper reasons* should not be so far from that of *force majeur*.

Indeed, *force majeur* is familiar to the laws of the Member States n such a way as to avoid the elaboration or the construction of a specific concept of *proper reasons* at the Community level.

7. Well-known and reputed trade mark : What about famous trade mark?

It is commonly acknowledged, by following the example of Benelux law, that *"famous"* trade marks enjoy a broader protection *"against unfair exploitation of their reputation and against dilution of their distinctiveness"* (Kur, 1992; Beier, 1995). It is also admitted that the protection over the similarity or affinity of products or services *"constitutes a derogation from the principle of "speciality" of the trade mark"* (Vanzetti, 1993; Sena, 1995). In this paper I am going to use on purpose for sake of clarity the term *famous* trade mark (*"celebre"*, *"beruhmter"*, *"de haute rennommée"*), since the term *well-known* is somehow ambiguous and misleading (Schricker, 1980; Kur, 1992; Vanzetti, 1989).

Article 8.2 (c) of the Regulation (and Article 4.2, (d) of the Directive) indeed, includes in the concept of earlier trade marks those which are *"well-known"* (*"notoriamente conosciuti, notoirement connues"*, *"notoriamente conocidas"*, *"notorish bekannt"*) *in a Member State"*. The EU legislator removes all the incertitude adding that the sense in which the words *"well-known are used is the same as in Article 6 bis of the Paris Convention"*.

Such rule engages the Members of the Union to grant protection to a trade mark *"notoirement connue comme étant déj la marque d'une personne admise bénéficier de la présente Convention et utilisé pour des produits identiques ou similaires"*. This protection, therefore, has nothing to do with that given to famous trade marks as far as to products or services not identical or similar to those covered by the statement of protection (Kur, 1992). On the other hand Article 6 *bis* of the Paris Convention supposes that the subject sign is *not* already registered as such in the State concerned (AIPPI, Question 100,1990).

As a matter of fact the Regulation, as well as the Directive, does not explicitly refer to famous trade marks, dealing only with a trade mark which has *reputation* and providing relevant protection *"where use of that sign without due cause takes unfair advantage of, or is detrimental to, the distinctive character or the repute of the Community trade mark"* (Article 9.1 (c) (*Rights Conferred by European Community trade mark*).

However, it is not clear whether the term *reputed trade mark*, for which the are no definitions at all both in the Regulation and in the other Community sources, has to be retained in a sense such as *famous/de haute rennommée/berhumte/celebre trade mark* or not. On one hand, the presence, in the Regulation, of Article 9.1 (c), above (fully corresponding to Article 5.2 of the Directive), extends the scope of Community trade mark protection, in this case, to goods or services which are *not similar* to those for which a Community trade mark is registered, e.g., the typical case of a famous trade mark (according to the cited Report of Commission, 1980, the *ratio* of the extended protection would stay on the *"fame"* of the mark). On the other, the wording of Article 9.1 (c) in the Italian, German and Spanish languages (*"gode di notorieta"*, *"in der Gemeinschaft bekannt"*, *"notoriamente conocidas"*) goes in the opposite direction, i.e., the meaning of Article 8.2 of the Regulation.

I feel that the term *reputed* means something more than *notoirement connue* and something less than *beruhmter*, even though the former term may in fact be interpretated and applied in such a way as to include the latter one (De Benedetti, 1996). It will be up to the jurisprudence of OHIM to solve this problem. In this connection the attitude of law cases and doctrine of the Member States of the Community shows an extremely varied landscape. In Italy, for example, there is incertitude as to the interpretation to give to Article 1 (b), of the Trade Mark Law No. 480/92, which reproduces Article 5.2 of the Directive. It has been maintained, in fact, that one has to refer to past case law so as to judge whether a *marchio celebre* is protectable or not, and so to criteria (e.g., economic link between companies or material differences in the characteristics of the compared goods) which are different from dilution of distinctiveness and undue exploitation.

Lately Article 6 *bis* of the Paris Convention has caught the attention of the WIPO. WIPO indeed, putting aside more ambitious projects (WIPO-TLT, 1990), has set up a special committee of experts purposely to examine the criteria that should be followed to identify the scope of a well-known sign and to grant it a more effective protection. WIPO, in particular, has pointed out the difference between the content of Article 6 *bis*, which covers trade marks *notoirement connue* and a real and famous trade mark (WIPO, 1995).

It follows therefrom that the way you address the issue of the nature and function of a trade mark and assess the latitude of the interest related to it in the Community law rather in the Member State law, may lead to different conclusions as to the protection of a trade mark *which has reputation*.

8. Some TRIPs implications

An additional matter of incertitude, if not confusion, is due to the coming into force of GATT-TRIPs because the Community law is expected to be consistent with them.

Article 16.3 of those Agreements extends the application of Article 6 *bis* of the Paris Convention, *mutatis mutandis*, to those cases whereby the goods and services which have to be protected against counterfeiting are *not similar* to those covered by the registration concerned. This article adds that: *"in determining whether a trade mark is well-known, account shall be taken of the knowledge of the trade mark in the relevant sector of the public including knowledge in that Member obtained as a result of the promotion of the trade mark"*. It follows therefrom that the GATT-TRIPs Agreement propose their own parameters (De Benedetti, 1996) as to interpret when a trade mark should be considered well-known (even when its protection is extended beyond the principle of speciality) *in the Member States*, without any special evaluation of the Community or international market. Moreover these parameters do not support the idea of a positive appreciation and a better quality which the word reputation/réputation/reputazione seems to imply.

By the application of the TRIPs rules alone, we should say that all brands of beers, simply because they are promoted at a distribution level in all supermarkets of a Member State, might be acknowledged by relevant consumers as well-known trade marks in such a way as to enjoy protection also against their reproduction on perfumes or swimming costumes.

9. Likelihood of confusion

Under Article 8 of the Regulation (*Relative Grounds for Refusal*), a Community trade mark application shall not mature into a registration if, upon opposition by the proprietor of an earlier trade mark because of the similarity between the mark or the sign, on one hand, and the goods or services on the other, there might exist a *likelihood of confusion among* the public in the territory in which the earlier trade mark is already protected. In this case the likelihood of confusion will be ascertained by taking into account the territory in question and the criteria in force in that territory.

However the definition of likelihood of confusion has to be drawn from the Regulation system, for it is up to the Office to judge whether the sign is eligible for application. Moreover, as we know, both the Regulation and the Directive have introduced the concept that likelihood of confusion includes the *likelihood of association* with an earlier trade mark. At the same time both the Community sources have given an identical interpretation as far as what they mean by *likelihood of association*, providing some guidelines thereabouts.

It must be noted that the likelihood of association concerns the direct comparison between signs, and not between products or services.

Accordingly, Article 9.1 (b), in dealing with the rights conferred by the Community trade mark, expressly limits the likelihood of association *"between the sign (the earlier right) and the trade mark"*. This statement is therefore consistent with the interpretation we have given above on the nature and function of a Community trade mark, which, under Community law, is that of a communication tool apt to identify and to distinguish products and services from identical or similar ones, rather than a sign to indicate the origin of products and services from one undertaking rather than another (i.e., a sort of information which is in fact without interest for the consumers).

The Regulation (Seventh "Considerando"), and the Directive, have proposed their own criteria to appreciate the likelihood of confusion, as the followings:

a) the recognition of the trade mark on the market;

b) the association which can be made with the used or registered sign;

c) the degree of similarity between the trade mark and the sign and between the goods or services identified.

These parameters, even if not mandatory, are not necessarily coincident with those put into practice by the Member States law, especially when case law privilege the trade mark function of indication of origin over the others. It follows that the Office examiners will be called to the not easy task of applying the likelihood of confusion, as construed under the Regulation for the Community, to a public and a territory which belong to the social, historical and commercial environment of the single Member State.

On the contrary, it is an easy forecast that opposition against refusal of registration will be filed with the Office on the basis of legal and traditional concepts that the proprietor of the earlier right and his counsel are familiar with at home. This attitude, in my view, should be firmly resisted by the Office, adopting the stand that the Community trade mark law, when applied, prevails over all domestic laws.

10. In the Dictionaries

According to Article 7.1 (d) (*Absolute Grounds for Refusal*) *"trade marks which consist exclusively of signs or indications which have become customary in the current language or in the bona fide and established practices of the trade"* shall not be registered. The same principle is applied also when this happens after the registration.

As provided for by Article 50.1 (b) as well as by the identical Article 12.2 (a) of the Directive, the registration shall be declared to have been revoked *"if, in consequences of acts or inactivity of the proprietor, the trade mark has become the common name in the trade for a product or services in respect of which it is registered"*.

In some domestic case law this consequence directly derives from the insertion of the trade mark in a dictionary or in a similar reference work. This presumption has been now rectified by the Regulation which denies that the mere reproduction of a Community trade mark in dictionaries and alike implies *per sé* the lack of distinctiveness of the sign. The reproduction should just give *"the impression that it constitutes the generic name of the goods or services for which the trade mark is registered"* (Article 10- *Reproduction of Community trade marks in Dictionaries*). The proprietor could request the publisher to accompany it, at the latest in the following edition of the publication, by an indication that this name is a registered trade mark.

Although this rule concerns only a Community trade mark, it is reasonable to think that in the near future the same approach will also be followed by domestic law in connection with national registered trade marks.

11. Less protection of a reputed trade mark against a Community trade mark ?
There could exist another problem of diverting protection between a Community trade mark and national registration for a trade mark when it has a reputation in the Community.

On the basis of Article 5.2 of the Directive, referred to above, Member States have introduced (or are going to introduce, in their own domestic legislation) the protection of a trade mark in respect of goods or services that are not similar to those for which the trade mark is registered, when the latter has a reputation in its territory, provided that the other conditions envisaged by such a rule are met. In other words, if a proprietor has registered for classes A and B a reputed trade mark in one country, he is entitled to prosecute for infringement a competitor who has used the identical trade mark in class C, enjoying a broader legal protection which is beyond the registered class. If a third competitor applies for a Community trade mark in class C, it seems that the proprietor of the earlier right for the classes A and B could be impeded from filing opposition against the Community trade mark application according to Article 43.5.

Indeed this provision states that the application shall be refused only in respect to those goods or services which have not been used by the proprietor of the earlier right. Furthermore, if the national registration would have been used in relation only to a part of the goods or services for which it had been registered, e.g., only for class A in our example, the earlier right *"shall, for the purposes of the examination of the opposition, be deemed to be registered in respect only of that part of the goods or services"* (Article 43.2, last sentence), i.e., class A.

In this case the proprietor of the prior registration for classes A and B can benefit from full protection in another country (against class C), provided that his registration has reputation there and could suffer a material limitation in protecting his right against a subsequent Community trade mark.

In one way or another, the proprietor of a trade mark having a reputation in his country could benefit from a broader protection there against a counterfeit than that which he could obtain against a competitor who can apply the same trade mark at Community level (Community trade mark).

Clearly this conclusion is not satisfactory, is perhaps not acceptable, and would therefore deserve careful attention.

12. Some perspectives

National registrations are subject to renewal: then, presumably, they will remain for a long time in the registers of the home trade mark office. On the other hand, as we have already underlined, the Community trade mark does not supersede the domestic system and it cannot force the undertakings, associations and other legal entities qualified for trade marks, to apply for a Community trade mark when they are not concerned or interested in so doing.

However many considerations induce us to think that the two systems are drawing closer. The Directive has already exercised some influence in the Member States by harmonising their existing laws which have been or are going to be amended. The fundamental principles are governed in the same terms by both the Directive and the Regulation.

The Regulation itself, furthermore, is directly enforceable in the Member States and it constitutes a part of their substantive legislation in the trade marks area. The EC Commission, in supporting the new European trade mark system through the instrument of Regulation instead of Convention, has noted that the Regulation ensures *uniformity*, having *"the same binding force everywhere"* (EC Commission Working Paper, II, 1980).

My analysis has given some examples in which domestic trade mark law is materially affected by Community law on the Community trade mark. Some emerging problems of interference, if not conflict, between the two systems should be addressed and solved through the interpretation and application of the Regulation which is expected to follow its own rules and to prevail, in case of diversion, over the domestic laws.

The Courts will also play an important role in this perspective. The Courts of Appeal, at first instance, and the Court of Justice, at the second level, are expected to produce in the near future general indications as far as to the key problems.

At the level of every Member State the *"Community trade mark Courts"* (Article 91) are envisaged by the Regulation as performing the function assigned to them by it, as they have exclusive jurisdiction over infringement and validity (Article 92), when counterclaimed. The Community Courts, unless otherwise provided in the Regulation, will apply the rules of procedure governing the same type of action relating to a national trade mark in the Member State where they are based (Article 97 – *Applicable Law*), although their material laws on assessing in the future counterfeiting might diverge (Desantes Real, 1996). However, the Courts will apply the substantive law laid down by the Regulation and their decisions, due to the principle of the unity of a Community trade mark, will be effective throughout the territory of the Community. Notwithstanding the limits of the Courts jurisdiction, their decisions will certainly concur to approximate both the national and the Community law, in order to face the challenge of a real and unified single market in Europe.

The Impact of the Community Trade Mark on Applicants in Non-Member Countries

The countries comprising the European Union are a significant market for United States companies. Thus, obtaining, maintaining and enforcing trade marks in these countries is important to United States trade mark owners. With the recent passage of European Community Council Regulation No. 40/94, trade mark owners in all countries belonging to the Paris Convention, including the United States, will soon be able to file applications to obtain a single "Community trade mark", conferring rights in all European Union countries. Although many details of the implementation of Community trade mark are still to be determined, trade mark owners in the United States and other non-European Community ("EC") countries should familiarize themselves with this new option. This article will assess possible advantages and disadvantages of registration under the Community trade mark and discuss the Madrid Agreement and the Madrid Protocol international trade mark systems.

I. Procedural and economic ramifications

Business growth depends on maximization of value for each good and service purchased. In determining value, both costs and benefits must be considered. The cost of registering a trade mark is fairly predictable, but the benefit to be achieved through the registration is difficult to foresee. However, scholars agree that the value of the right to exclude others from using one's intellectual property, such as trade marks, is proportional to the size and importance of the market covered by the exclusive right.[1] Prior to the implementation of the Community trade mark, the benefits of registering a trade mark in one European country may not have outweighed the costs. The Community trade mark, which covers

[1] Bendnarek and Lisso, "Global Trade mark Strategy," *Managing Intellectual Property*, Issue 49 (May 1995)

15 countries, will significantly increase the value of registration through cost savings, simplified handling, and uniformity of regulation.

Though it was feared that the European Union would impose a high price tag on filing and maintaining a mark which would be enforceable in so many countries, the fees proposed by the European Union are reasonable, considering the geographic coverage and the population. The proposed application fee is ECU 700 (approximately $888 US) and the proposed registration fee is ECU 1100 (approximately $1395 US). Thus, for just less than $2300 US, a mark may be afforded protection in 15 countries having a population of over 300 million consumers. In addition, the proposed additional class fee of ECU 200 (approximately $254 US) and renewal fees of ECU 2500 (approximately $3172 US) seem equally appropriate. Therefore, from a purely economic standpoint, if a company wants to apply for more than three national marks in Europe, it would be beneficial to go the Community trade mark route.

1. Filing and Examination

Applications for a Community trade mark may be submitted up to three months prior to the official 1 April 1996 opening date of the Community trade mark office, under Article 143, Par. 4 of Regulation 40/94. Thus, applications may be submitted 1 January 1996, but will receive a filing date of 1 April 1996. Under Regulation Article 25, Par. 1, a Community trade mark application can be made at the Office of Harmonization in the Internal Market (OHIM) (Trade Marks and Designs) in Alicante, Spain, or at the central trade mark office of each Member State (including the Benelux Trade mark Office). National offices will send the application to Alicante within two weeks from filing and may charge an administrative fee for doing so. It should be noted that applications filed at national trade mark offices which do not reach the OHIM office in Alicante within one month will be deemed withdrawn.

After a Community trade mark application is filed, a compulsory search, similar to the one which exists today in Benelux, will be made by the OHIM office (Article 39). The search in Alicante will be restricted to prior existing Community trade mark applications and registrations. In addition, as provided for in Article 39, Par. 3, any member country wishing to do so may also make a search among its own national trade marks, the results of which must be transmitted to OHIM "within three months from the date on which it received the Community trade mark application." OHIM in turn will send the Community and national search results to the applicant "without delay." OHIM will then notify the owners of previous Community trade mark applications or registrations uncovered by the search of the existence of the new Community trade mark application. Under the system of OHIM and national office searches, it is thought that search criteria will differ somewhat among the Member States. For this reason, applicants might do their own individual searches in the relevant countries prior to application for a Community trade mark.

OHIM will analyze applications for conflicts with Community trade mark registrations and ensure that there is technical conformity with the regulations and refuse registration if the mark is ineligible under Article 38. Applicants who attempt to register similar marks will be afforded an opportunity to alter registrations or even withdraw their registrations. After searches and initial examination at the OHIM, the application will be published.

2. Rejection/Cancellation/Appeal

If a Community trade mark application is refused or cancelled in one EU Member State, the Community trade mark will not be registered. It is anticipated that Community trade marks will be subject to attack in Member States and will, in many circumstances, be refused registration or cancelled. Due to this, under Articles 108, 109 and 110, refused, cancelled or withdrawn Community trade mark applications or registrations can be converted into national trade marks which retain the date of the Community trade mark application. There are two exceptions to the possibility of conversion: if the Community trade mark has been revoked for non-use, or if the grounds for refusal of the Community trade mark apply to the national mark.

Appeals may be taken from decisions of the examiners, decisions of opposition divisions of OHIM, decisions of the Administration of Trade Marks and Legal Division, and decisions of cancellation divisions. Instigation of an appeal suspends the Community trade mark or application (Article 57).

3. Oppositions

The prior rights upon which opposition may be based are: 1) Community trade mark registrations and applications; 2) national registrations and applications in EU Member States or at the Benelux Trade Mark Office; 3) trade marks registered under international arrangements which have effect in an EU Member State; 4) trade marks which are "well known" as that term is defined in the Paris Convention (Article 8, Par. 2).

Applicants should be aware that an opposition to a Community trade mark application has the potential of creating several serious and costly problems. If an opposition to the OHIM is not successful, the contending party is liable for the competitor's fees, including the applicant attorneys' costs. This possibility is an indicator that a Community trade mark may be more advantageous for coined marks and famous marks where there is a high likelihood that the Community trade mark registration would be unopposed. Obviously, the costs of an opposition proceeding in the Community trade mark forum could be great, outweighing the savings in fees and procedure occasioned by filing a centralized application.

4. Seniority and National Trade marks

Another aspect of Community trade marks that could be critical is the ability to claim seniority through national marks. Under Articles 34 and 35, an applicant for a Community trade mark can claim the seniority of a national mark in a Member State. The EU predicts that owners of existing national trade marks will be the first to file Community trade mark applications. If the Community trade mark is registered, then the owner will have both a Community trade mark and an identical national trade mark. The Regulation provides that, under certain circumstances, trade mark owners are not required to renew national trade marks but nevertheless may retain the rights deriving therefrom. This ensures that national trade marks retain status. The above non-lapse provision is of particular interest when a Community trade mark is converted into a national mark under Article 108. The applicant will be given the benefit of the earlier filed national application. Proponents envision that claiming seniority will be simple and inexpensive, ensuring that EU applicants and registrants who choose to make such a claim will stand on equal footing with Member State applicants.

Notification of seniority during the application procedure (Article 34) or after registration (Article 35) does not appear to require payment of additional fees. Articles 34 and 35 provide that the proprietor of the Community trade mark may claim seniority based on an earlier national trade mark at the time of application, during the application procedure, or after registration. Each trade mark owner should examine its trade mark portfolio to determine whether any national trade mark should be registered as a Community trade mark.

A Community trade mark application can be utilized to consolidate trade mark registrations. For example, an owner of a trade mark that is registered in various European Union countries must track renewal dates and other requirements for each country; an agent must be paid in each country to handle renewal filings; separate paperwork must be prepared and signed and separate cheques issued. By consolidating registrations through Community trade mark, the trade mark registrant could contact one agent instead of 15.

5. Assignments/Licensing

The Regulations provide for filing one assignment document when Community trade marks are assigned. This could be advantageous to non-member applicants because the complexities of, and wide variation in requirements for, assignments in different countries can lead to high agents fees and considerable accumulated expenses. The fees for filing assignments of a Community trade mark may not be less than filing assignments in individual countries, but the savings in burdensome procedures is almost certain to be great. Centralized filing of assignments is also facilitated by the provision that assignments can be for some of the goods or all of the goods and with or without goodwill (although the designation of goods and services and goodwill must be the same for all European Union countries) (Article 17).

The Regulations governing a Community trade mark registration also allow for licensing in the Community as a whole or in specific countries. As with assignments, licensing can be limited as to certain goods and services but must be the same for all the European Union countries (Article 22).

In sum, each owner will be looking at each registration critically – not all trade marks are good Community trade mark candidates. The fee structure is low enough for an initial application that it would be possible to use the Community trade mark application as a means of testing what can be expected in Europe and what obstacles will need to be overcome. The applicant can then decide on the appropriate registration strategy (at a lower cost than searches and applications in individual countries). Whether to file a registration for a Community trade mark or in individual countries will depend upon the applicant's goals for the future, such as market expansion, contemplated divisions of the business, or company mergers.

II. Uniformity of law

The Community trade mark will be governed by a new body of law. As a result, uncertainty and unpredictability are likely, particularly at the outset. How provisions which include language never before applied will be interpreted is unknown and as such should cause concern. Because United States trade mark owners and practitioners will be unfamiliar with both the application process and the scope of protection, applicants in non-member countries should proceed cautiously. There are several provisions in Regulation 40/94 that differ somewhat from United States practice.

Under the Community trade mark Regulation, the trade mark owner must put the trade mark to "genuine use" within five years in respect of the goods and services for which it has been registered, or otherwise face sanctions. (Article 15). In addition, suspension of "genuine use" for a period exceeding 5 years will cause similar consequences unless the period of non-use is "proper". The Regulation specifies that genuine use is satisfied by 1) the use of the Community trade mark in a form which only differs in part from the registered mark without influencing the distinctiveness thereof; and 2) affixing the Community trade mark to goods which are destined only for export to non-member states. Although the Regulation permits genuine use to be found when it exists in only one member country, the level of proof required by each country to find "use" may vary. For example, what may be considered "token" use by one country may be interpreted as "genuine" by another.

Another provision which may prove confusing is the "acquiescence" provision. The policy behind this provision is similar to that of the "incontestability" aspect in United States law. Under United States trade mark law, the owner of an earlier registered trade mark cannot, in most cases, request cancellation of an identical or similar later filed mark, if the owner of the earlier mark does not make such a request within a specified time period. Therefore, after a period of time, in the United States, under incontestability, the earlier owner is estopped from challenging the use of the mark. The EU "acquiescence" provision takes a somewhat different tact. It provides that "[w]here the proprietor of an earlier trade mark has acquiesced...in the use of a later Community trade mark registered in that Member State while being aware of such use, he shall no longer be entitled [to challenge the later mark]." (Regulation 40/94, Article 53). Such a provision, which is different from any provision familiar to United States owners and practitioners, may prove troublesome.

Because the Community trade mark would be governed by a single body of law, consistency in application and enforcement of the mark generally would be an attractive aspect to the European Union mark. Moreover, with the Member countries all committed to the "Directive" for trade mark law harmonization, it seems fairly certain that the national laws of the Member countries are slowly but surely becoming more uniform. However, there may be instances where the law of an individual EU Member is more beneficial to a trade mark applicant.

Likewise, infringement actions involving Community trade marks can be brought against an infringer as one action in a Community trade mark Court and decisions of the Court will apply throughout the EU. However, the advantages of simplicity and uniformity should be weighed against the potential problems of litigating one's trade mark rights under the European Community Regulation. The Community trade mark Court system is set forth in Article 91 of the Regulation, which requires each Member State to nominate Community trade mark Courts – Courts of first instance (trial) and Courts of second instance (appeal). Article 92 of the Regulation gives the Community trade mark Courts jurisdiction over infringement actions relating to Community trade marks and counterclaims challenging validity of Community trade marks. The forum for a particular action is determined as follows: The action is brought in the Courts of the Member State where the defendant is domiciled or has a commercial establishment. If the defendant has no domicile or commercial establishment within the EU, the action is brought in the Courts of the Member State where the plaintiff is domiciled or has a commercial establishment. If neither of the above applies, the Spanish Courts are to have jurisdiction unless the parties agree to a Court that would otherwise not have jurisdiction or a defendant enters an appearance before a Court that would not otherwise have jurisdiction. The Courts of a Member State where acts of infringement are committed or threatened may also assume a limited jurisdiction (Article 93).

The law to be applied by the Community trade mark Court is set out in the Regulation. However, matters not covered by the Regulation and the rules of procedure are taken from the national law of the forum country. At present, there is no legal precedent interpreting and applying the Regulation. The gaps in the Regulation to be filled by the law of the forum country have yet to be determined. For now, one can only look to the legal precedent of the Member State in which the Community trade mark Court sits for guidance as to how that Court might rule.

Moreover, it would not be unreasonable to assume that Community trade mark Courts in different Member States, with differing national laws and interests, might arrive at differing results when faced with the same legal questions. However, there is no appellate Court of last resort to resolve these discrepancies in interpretation of the Regulation. Once a Community trade mark Court has been chosen in a particular Member State, there is no appeal to a Court outside that Member State. Needless to say, care should be exercised in choosing a forum or submitting to jurisdiction of a Community trade mark Court. Consideration might also be given, even before filing a Community trade mark application, to the possibility of litigation before a Community trade mark Court.

III. The Madrid Agreement and the Madrid Protocol

The United States is not a member of The Madrid Agreement Concerning the International Registration of Marks ("Agreement"). This Agreement was adopted in 1891 and has 43 member states. The related Madrid Protocol ("Protocol"), drafted in 1989 and expected to go into effect April 1, 1996, has not been ratified by the United States thus far. Both the Agreement and the Protocol have the same purpose: to allow a resident of a member country to make a single trade mark *application*, equivalent to a national application, for any member country of the Agreement. There is a single procedure, a single basic fee (for up to three classes), and one fee to be paid for each claimed country.

1. The Madrid Agreement

Under the Madrid Agreement, an applicant must reside in one of the member countries and must first obtain a registration in his home country. This home country registration can then be *extended* to the Madrid Agreement by making a second application in Geneva through the country where the basic registration has taken place. The Madrid Agreement application will be reviewed by the World Intellectual Property Organization ("WIPO") and published in "Les Marques Internationales" in French, the official language of the Agreement. At the time of application, or at any time thereafter, the applicant of the international registration can indicate the countries where he seeks protection and pay a fixed (relatively low) official fee per claimed country. The entire process provided for by the Agreement serves to expedite multiple trade mark applications in multiple countries. The advantage of this system is that in some countries there is a waiting period of three to five years before a first response from the Trade mark Office is received.

One major problem with the Agreement is "central attack." If for any reason the home registration is cancelled (partially or totally) within five years of the filing of the corresponding international trade mark, then the international trade mark will also be cancelled. In contrast, the Community trade mark system provides that in the event of cancellation, a Community trade mark application can be converted to a national application.

Since the Agreement depends on membership of the Madrid Union, applicants residing in countries that are not members, such as the United States or Japan, cannot take advantage of the Agreement. If, however, a United States or a Japanese company has an affiliated or subsidiary company vested in a member state, then this company can apply. However, the trade mark can never be assigned back to the parent company in the non-Madrid Agreement country; it can only be assigned to another company vested in a member country.

2. The Madrid Protocol

The Madrid Protocol, though similar in many respects to the Madrid Agreement, contains some improvements from the standpoint of a United States applicant. The Protocol, for example, accepts both English and French as official languages and requires only an application as opposed to a registration in a home country. With the Protocol the international mark can often be converted into a national mark retaining the date of application of the international Protocol mark. (This provision is parallel to Community trade mark Regulation, Article 108.) One of the criticisms of the Agreement by the United States was that the examination period was limited to 12 months. The examination period is 18 months under the Protocol. In addition, the fees under the Protocol have been brought into line with fees for national trade mark offices.

The primary obstacle, at this point, to United States ratification of the Protocol is State Department opposition to voting rights given in the Protocol to intra-governmental organizations, such as the European Union, as well as its member countries. In 1995, a bill ratifying the Protocol passed the House before the State Department raised problems with the fairness and precedent that would be set by European Union "double" voting. The House Subcommittee on Courts and Intellectual Property recently completed hearings on a new bill that contains the major provisions of the Madrid Protocol. The testimony at the hearings was strongly in favour of the Protocol and of an international trade mark system. Testimony centred around the advantages of filing one application, the use of one local agent, and the benefits to the American business community which should outweigh problems with the voting rights.

A Community trade mark application by an EU resident can be the basis of a Protocol mark. However, due to the complicated nature of the Community trade mark application and registration processes and the likelihood of it being subjected to cancellation, this is not a likely sequence of events. In addition, an applicant for a national trade mark, not a member of the European Union, but a member of the Protocol, who files a Protocol mark can obtain a Community trade mark through an application made according to the Protocol with WIPO. That is, a non-EU member applicant having no subsidiary or affiliate in the European Union could still obtain Community trade mark protection through the provisions of the Protocol.

The Community trade mark requires only a single application, a single renewal, and a single assignment; it will be administered by one set of rules with respect to registration and enforcement. The Protocol, on the other hand, is merely a vehicle for filing multiple applications, not a single mark enforceable in multiple countries.

IV. Conclusion

With all the unknown aspects of the Community trade mark, applicants from non-Member States should proceed with caution. Many owners may choose to obtain national rights in one or more countries first and then obtain a Community trade mark, claiming seniority based on the national trade mark. By taking this route, an owner could achieve bona fide national protection while at the same time maintaining the option for Community trade mark registration at a future time. At this juncture, owners and practitioners in non-Member States should begin to assess each existing and potential mark individually as to whether a Community trade mark is viable from a procedural and economic standpoint.

Index